Interpreting Sports at Museums and Historic Sites

AMERICAN ASSOCIATION *for* STATE *and* LOCAL HISTORY

Interpreting History

About the Organization
The American Association for State and Local History (AASLH) is a national history membership association headquartered in Nashville, Tennessee, which provides leadership and support for its members who preserve and interpret state and local history in order to make the past more meaningful to all people. AASLH members are leaders in preserving, researching, and interpreting traces of the American past to connect the people, thoughts, and events of yesterday with the creative memories and abiding concerns of people, communities, and our nation today. In addition to sponsorship of this book series, AASLH publishes *History News* magazine, a newsletter, technical leaflets and reports, and other materials; confers prizes and awards in recognition of outstanding achievement in the field; supports a broad education program and other activities designed to help members work more effectively; and advocates on behalf of the discipline of history. To join AASLH, go to www.aaslh.org or contact Membership Services, AASLH, 2021 21st Ave. South, Suite 320, Nashville, TN 37212.

About the Series

The American Association for State and Local History publishes the *Interpreting History* series in order to provide expert, in-depth guidance in interpretation for history professionals at museums and historic sites. The books are intended to help practitioners expand their interpretation to be more inclusive of the range of American history.

Books in this series help readers:

- quickly learn about the questions surrounding a specific topic,
- introduce them to the challenges of interpreting this part of history, and
- highlight best practice examples of how interpretation has been done by different organizations.

They enable institutions to place their interpretative efforts into a larger context, despite each having a specific and often localized mission. These books serve as quick references to practical considerations, further research, and historical information.

Titles in the Series

Interpreting Sports at Museums and Historic Sites

Edited by Kathryn Leann Harris
with Douglas Stark

ROWMAN & LITTLEFIELD
Lanham • Boulder • New York • London

Published by Rowman & Littlefield
An imprint of The Rowman & Littlefield Publishing Group, Inc.
4501 Forbes Boulevard, Suite 200, Lanham, Maryland 20706
www.rowman.com

86-90 Paul Street, London, EC2A 4NE

British Library Cataloguing in Publication Information Available

Library of Congress Cataloging-in-Publication Data

Names: Harris, Kathryn Leann, editor. | Stark, Douglas (Douglas Andrew),
    1972- other. | American Association for State and Local History,
    sponsoring agency.
Title: Interpreting sports at museums and historic sites / edited by
    Kathryn Leann Harris, with Douglas Stark.
Description: Lanham, Maryland : Rowman & Littlefield, [2023] | Series:
    Interpreting history | Includes bibliographical references and index. |
    Summary: "Interpreting Sports at Museums and Historic Sites provides a
    step-by-step guide for museums and historic sites developing an
    interpretive plan inclusive of sports"-- Provided by publisher.
Identifiers: LCCN 2022038524 (print) | LCCN 2022038525 (ebook) |
    ISBN 9781538103166 (Cloth : acid-free paper) | ISBN 9781538103180 (eBook)
Subjects: LCSH: Sports--Exhibitions--Methodology. |
    Recreation--Exhibitions--Methodology.
Classification: LCC GN454 .I68 2023 (print) | LCC GN454 (ebook) |
    DDC 306.4/83--dc23/eng/20221202
LC record available at https://lccn.loc.gov/2022038524
LC ebook record available at https://lccn.loc.gov/2022038525

♾™ The paper used in this publication meets the minimum requirements of
American National Standard for Information Sciences—Permanence of Paper
for Printed Library Materials, ANSI/NISO Z39.48-1992.

Contents

Acknowledgments

As sports fans and professionals in the sporting heritage industry, we realize that teamwork is essential to accomplishing any significant task. That is no different with this project. We are grateful to a large and varied group of individuals who caught our vision and ensured this project was a success.

We send enduring gratitude to our contributing authors for their willingness to join us on the journey of discussing sports history interpretation and ways to improve current practice. We thank each of you for your patience with our requests, commitment to doing "good sports history," ability to critically examine your own organizations, and willingness to provide recommendations to better the field.

Editorial research included an immeasurable number of conversations with sports professionals, sports historians, sports museum professionals, and public historians, which added great depth and insight to this project. To Murray Phillips, thank you for your early scholarship on this topic and for intersecting with and validating our work at various points of this process. We are grateful to all our colleagues across these various fields who gave their time and energy to progress this conversation for the common benefit.

From the beginning, Bob Beatty championed this project and made the first significant assist by connecting the two of us who had individually expressed interest in writing a book about interpreting sports history. He was instrumental as a sounding board for the book's conceptual framework and provided extensive editorial comments throughout the project.

Our fellow *Interpreting* series authors/editors guided and inspired our work. Kristin L. Gallas, Raney Bench, Julia Rose, Susan Ferentinos, and Michelle Moon contributed scholarship that carved brave space for this conversation and workshopped aspects of our book at various stages. Michelle Moon contributed invaluable perspective as an outside reader and content editor. Her editorial insight shepherded us through the final stages of compiling and completing the manuscript.

We offer special thanks to our publisher Charles Harmon for his guidance, persistence, and patience during an enduring writing process. We also extend our gratitude to Aja Bain at the American Association for State and Local History for seeing and believing in the heart of this work and granting support to make it complete.

To everyone involved—thank you for playing this sports interpretation game with us!

From Kathryn Leann: Colleagues throughout the sports museum and public history fields provided ongoing professional guidance and invaluable partnerships. I offer this work in return for all you have given me and in hopes of what we can continue to do together. An intricate network of family and friends surrounded me with enduring love, in support of my commitment to an early career vision that took a winding path. To my parents, thank you for infusing me with a love of sports and history combined with an appreciation for a socially just and kind world.

From Douglas: For the past twenty-plus years, the sports museum field has provided me with immeasurable experiences and friendships. The opportunity to give back to the field in some small way continues to be a goal of mine. I wish to thank my wife Melanie, who afforded me time to work on this even as our children Ben and Tessa were born during this project.

Foreword

Murray G. Phillips

In many ways, sports museums and halls of fame represent a paradox. They are prominent institutions, particularly in the Western world, which places an incredibly high cultural status on sport, but few public historians or museum professionals have written on the subject. Any literature that does exist is the product of scholars, specifically academics in sport history, sport sociology, and heritage studies. These accounts certainly offer something meaningful to our understanding of sports in museums, but it is important to remember they provide a one-dimensional perspective: a view from scholars with specific disciplinary interests, many of whom, including me, have very little experience in the business and practice of museums and public history institutions.

Consequently, *Interpreting Sports History at Museums and Historic Sites* is an important addition to the literature on sports museums and halls of fame because it fills this gap. In twenty-six essays covered over six chapters, professionals throughout the industry explore a wide range of sports exhibits and topics, combining critical museum scholarship and practical interpretative experiences. The book serves an eloquent mix of theoretical, conceptual issues in museum practice and case studies presented by curators and museum professionals whose involvement extends to a range of sport exhibitions across North America and elsewhere.

One question underpins this book: How can museums, historic sites, and similar institutions better incorporate sports as part of their exhibitions and programming? The authors offer models for implementing sports history as public education, conversation about the various ways sports history can impact communities, the best methods for public engagement through sports history, common mistakes to avoid, and valuable lessons any museum professional can glean by analyzing this wide range of case studies.

These issues are addressed through a very appealing and effective structure. The book is introduced by the section "Brushing Sports History Against the Grain," which effectively sets the scene through a critical and reflective analysis of the relationship between museums and sport. This critical reflection continues through a series of themed essays about sporting participants, community connections, authenticity and voice, sports and globalization, sports and identity, and museum education and sport.

Each of these themed essays is supported by a series of case studies written by museum professionals in a multiplicity of locations. These illustrations include prominent displays in Washington, D.C., at the National Museum of African American History and Culture, National Women's History Museum, National Museum of the American Indian, and Lemelson Center for the Study of Invention and Innovation, and in Boston at the Boston Public Library and Sports Museum. Represented institutions throughout the United States include a cross section of sports museums and historical societies such as the NASCAR Hall of Fame in North Carolina, Concord Museum in Massachusetts, Henry Sheldon Museum in Vermont, Packers Hall of Fame in Wisconsin, International Tennis Hall of Fame in Rhode Island, LBJ Presidential Library in Texas, and the Sports Legends Museum at Camden Yards in Maryland. International case studies draw on the Bata Shoe Museum and Canadian Museum of History (both in Canada), the Amsterdam Museum in Denmark, and the District Six Museum in South Africa.

Interpreting Sports History at Museums and Historic Sites is a comprehensive book composed of critical understandings from museum studies, sports history, and sports heritage, combined with a terrific array of practical experiences from museum professionals. This is the book that those interested in sports museums have been waiting for. Finally, we have something that balances out the contributions of scholars with the practical experiences and the intellectual insights of museum professionals. I commend editors Kathryn Leann Harris and Douglas Stark for providing this addition to the field and look forward to seeing where this conversation goes from here.

Preface

Kathryn Leann Harris and Douglas Stark

Gear up, tee up, start your engines! Starting lines of sports matches evoke excitement—for the thrill of the game and the limitless possible outcomes unfolding in real time. Virtually everyone knows this feeling. Sports, competition, and play are inherent in the human experience. Sporting dynamics intersect with nearly all facets of life, infiltrating social, cultural, and political realms. Yet, sports and its interpretation occupy a small segment of the museum field, often relegated to surface-level content on the periphery of public history practice. Sports museums tend to be large and thrilling, while traditional history museums shy away from sports altogether or offer an interpretation that rarely matches the potential historical depth. Often, museums interpret sports through the realm of nostalgia and victory celebration, opting for grand displays of trophies, jerseys, victory photos, and vintage equipment used by famous and accomplished figures. Sports museums and exhibits can exist as more than a repository of great objects and moments. Instead, they can reflect the work of thought leaders in their specific domains—work that amplifies the immense positive aspects of sports, lends insight and support to the often-ignored challenges of the sporting world, and attracts a large sector of the population. In presenting this volume, our goal is to elevate sports interpretation out of the realm of nostalgia and hype and integrate it into a more inclusive and impactful conversation, offering avenues for the public to celebrate, mourn, *and* reflect together, and to navigate and implement lasting societal change.

Interpreting Sports: A Vast Playing Field

Sports *are*, in fact, central to the human experience. Play begins in early childhood and continues to the end of life—showing up in youth and recreational leagues, independent pursuits, and group activities. Sports provide an opportunity to view the world through the lens of competition, social interaction, and community building. They identify who we are and what we aspire to be. Those aspirations include being part of a team or community and dedication to being responsible, determined, celebratory, hardworking, fun, fair, and empathetic.

From the games of early civilizations to the televised competitive extrava-ganzas of today, sports have made indelible marks on the fabric of American culture. Presently, sports are a multibillion-dollar industry. Radio shows, television stations, and live streaming services devoted to teams and college conferences create a smorgasbord of sports consumption. Social media provides an unending forum for discussion and celebration.

Culturally, sports are intricately intertwined with the highs and lows of the human experience, yet sports commemorative practices tend to occupy a tepid middle space that does little to reflect the full impact of the sporting world. Typically, sports interpretation is celebratory in a way that distances visitors from, rather than connects them to, their idolized sports heroes. Museums too often focus sports interpretation on anecdotal content, statistics, and images of victory. Sports historian Murray G. Phillips notes that museums "have been caught up in the popularity of sport heritage tourism that promotes physical structures such as historical stadia and facilities, heritage experiences through goods and services, as well as rituals, traditions, chants, and memories."[1] Professional and college sports museums create branded experiences that predominantly speak to and benefit from fan emotions. Many American halls of fame serve as tools to recruit athletes to teams or universities, and are attached to campus, stadium, or historic site tours. Large-scale sports museums serve as economic engines, anchors for cities seeking to become a tourist destination, and a resource for community connection. Often, visitor expectations line up with these museum agendas, leaving opportunities for additional interpretive depth unexplored.

Cultural museums and historic sites capitalize on the public's sporting interest when they develop sports-related exhibits that appeal to both sports fans and casual visitors alike. Sports museums, halls of fame, exhibitions, historic sites, and educational pro-grams have significantly expanded over the past several decades, in tandem with an ever-growing global sports interest. Sports figures and sports coverage have moved beyond the game itself and into the realm of current events and societal concerns. Public interest in the business of sports, labor disputes, physical risks such as concus-sions, controversies over performance-enhancing drugs and cheating, protests such as kneeling during the national anthem, and mental health have often surpassed attention to achievements on the playing fields. This confluence of factors opens a significant opportunity for sports museums to offer fans a chance to celebrate their favorite sports figures and moments while also engaging the wider public with in-depth conversa-tions regarding culturally significant topics.

Because athletics intersect with points of fundamental human connection—cultural value structures, identity politics, the sense of belonging—sports provide an unparal-leled opportunity for museum practitioners. Children learn to play sports as early as they can move, an instinct that eventually grows into a societal value structure of sport-related concepts, such as winning and losing, team spirit, personal achieve-ment, and loyalty. Further, fan connections to athletic organizations generate local or global community relationships that become intertwined with identity politics. People entertain and expand this identity through cultural activities, family connections, and ritualistic behaviors that foster a deep connection to a personal sense of belonging.

Museum professionals are increasingly using the public interpretive space to foster that same deep connection. As public historians, we do not simply report the historical record; rather, we navigate an environment in which history is used to define identity and fulfill personal and/or political agendas. A mere understanding of historical facts does not adequately equip a museum professional to interpret history in public spaces. Good interpretive work also demands empathy with the visitor. "*Now* is the time to spark a paradigm shift toward an empathy-driven unifying worldview, and museums have a unique position and responsibility on this important journey,"[2] appeals Elif Gokcigdem, founder of the *Empathy-Building Through Museums Initiative* and *ONE (Organization of Networks for Empathy)*. Museum professionals can transfer this empathy to an interested sporting public, as well as connect to wider audiences through shared interest and sense of humanity.[3]

Sports museums, exhibits, and educational programming can *and should* create dialogue among disparate groups. Viewing society through the lens of sports can help people better understand issues of race, gender, class, business, globalization, and national identity. "Nostalgia is fine in modest doses and certainly sells tickets and memorabilia, but the wholesome past presented to sports consumers often sits at odds with our tumultuous realities," notes Josh Howard, a scholar of sports in public history.[4] Sports do have a unique power to bring people together, and at the same time, museums function as a trusted source of education and information. That position offers a platform to create deeply relevant material that illuminates the intersection of the sporting past with the present and can help to inspire a better future—a hefty and worthwhile task that is central to the content of this edited compilation.

This volume is among the first comprehensive treatments combining academic and practitioner perspectives into a framework for sports interpretation, following the recent publication of Kevin Moore, John Hughston, and Christian Wacker's edited compilation, *Sports in Museums* (2022). Phillips's work on sports history in museology lays the theoretical foundation upon which this book builds. To date, there has been little other comprehensive and practical study of best practices for sports interpretation. *Interpreting Sports History at Museums and Historic Sites* explores the interpretive opportunities and challenges that museums, historic sites, and cultural institutions encounter when they seek to include sports in their exhibit space or tour, embark on a sports history educational program, or approach an advocacy project. Our public, collective understanding of sports is changing to something more nuanced, complicated, thought-provoking, and unsettling. This compilation of voices from the field provides a guide for navigating this change. They explore attempts (successful and unsuccessful) at attracting the public and communicating both the uplifting and difficult issues surrounding sports history.

A Brief History of Sports Museums

The modern history of sports museums and halls of fame in the United States began after the 1932 Summer Olympics in Los Angeles, California, inspired in part by the development of many new sports museums in 1920s Europe. The year 1935 saw the founding of the Helms Athletic Foundation, and a year later its sports hall of fame museum was created. Soon after, 1936 also witnessed the founding of two of America's most prominent sports museums: Golf House (now known as the United States Golf Association [USGA] Museum) in Far Hills, New Jersey, and the National Baseball Hall of Fame and Museum in Cooperstown, New York, which opened its doors in 1939 with a star-studded class of inductees.

The number of sports museums expanded throughout the second half of the twentieth century. The post–World War II years were a boom for this industry. Growth in the 1950s included the International Tennis Hall of Fame, Naismith Memorial Basketball Hall of Fame, Indianapolis Motor Speedway Hall of Fame, and the U.S. National Ski Hall of Fame. The boom continued into the 1960s with the Pro Football Hall of Fame in 1963. Coinciding with the American Bicentennial, the 1970s saw the birth of new institutions such as the International Motorsports Hall of Fame, Pro Rodeo Hall of Fame and Museum, and Babe Ruth Birthplace and Museum. The 1990s, with its strong economy and an increase in the financial success of the sports industry, was another decade marked by growth. Colleges and universities opened athletic halls of fame as a recruiting enhancement and a means of staying connected to boosters and alums. Professional sports teams launched their own halls of fame to enhance their brand and attract visitors year-round. Today, there are thousands of sports-related institutions in America that chronicle the achievements of teams, leagues, and individuals.

Consistent with national museum trends, as sports museums evolve, so do the ways in which they interpret their subject matter. In the earliest years of existence, sports museums tended to focus on building collections, displaying objects, and commemorating achievement. This aligned with the then-current academic and cultural theme of memorialization. Interpretation in these institutions provided only basic information about the object and the associated event. The story focused on the glory of the athlete and the moment. In recent decades, sports museums have kept pace with the evolution of the entire museum field, reflecting trends in exhibition development, interpretation and programming, collections stewardship, inclusion of technology, and participatory experiences.

Today's focus on audience development, community engagement, and multifaceted learning has led sports halls of fame and museums to feature vibrant multimedia presentations steeped in research and scholarship. Often positioning their subject matter in the broader context of American history and world events, these approaches have generated more modern, engaging, and fan-friendly experiences. In some cases, non-sports museums have developed sports-themed exhibitions that usually relate to a recently acquired collection, a national social issue, an anniversary, or an international event such as the Olympics or the World Cup. In these instances, sports are less a referendum on a milestone and more a vehicle to initiate a dialogue around a larger issue.

Building the Interpretive Playbook

This volume explores the practical and interpretive problems museums, historic sites, and cultural institutions encounter when they include sports in their interpretation. When we talk about doing "good" sports history, we are referring to the idea of applying accepted public history practices to the sporting past. This includes more than relaying a mythical, and often culturally appealing, sense of lore or nostalgic longing for the glory days. Instead, practitioners can thoroughly research, cross-reference multiple viewpoints, explore the breadth and depth of the human experience, relay difficult narratives, uncover hidden perspectives, give voice to silenced figures, and create safe spaces for hard conversations. We believe the issues addressed in this book provide a framework for better understanding by all museum, public history, and history professionals, and for creating more meaningful, engaging, and thought-provoking experiences.

There are three primary frameworks for interpreting sports history: a simplistic celebratory frame, a commemorative frame, and a wider socially relevant frame. Each frame can, and does, function independently of the others. We propose a hybrid method—one that takes a balanced and holistic view of humanity into consideration. After all, as sports historian Wray Vamplew contests, "Celebrations need not be without critique."[5] Sports can be, and are, fun, light, and simple while at the same time complex, in-depth, and controversial—just like the humanity reflected in them. Sports endeavors in museums should consider all dimensions of a person or entity to remain accurate and relevant.

At the most basic level of sports, interpretation is a sense of celebration combined with a simplification of facts. In this frame, sports are fun, playful, exciting, and evoke human emotions. They produce a record of wins and losses connected to specific people, groups, and teams. The combination of these two factors can easily and simply produce an exhibit that is enjoyable, straightforwardly factual, and interesting for the general viewing public.

The commemorative frame is perhaps the most common in sports museums. Commemoration is a social practice in codifying—an idea, person, moment, or collective. Sports communities, and museums, use this method to revere a cherished memory and affix it to a collective identity for current and future generations to absorb. While this practice is common, it stands to be examined. Commemoration as an isolated framework lends itself to imbalance at best and obtuseness or isolationism at worst. As historian John Gillis explains, commemorations have served to solidify a national victory identity, casting a nation's ideals in bronze and stone, and, later, in the interpretive text at museums and historic sites. But after nearly 250 years, the American "victory culture" narrative is yielding to a more subjective, comprehensive, and nuanced understanding of the nation's identity, and commemoration practices are going with it.[6] Toward the end of the twentieth century, an anti-monuments movement emerged. In its place is an open and inclusive space that runs counter to the absolutism of commemoration.

We advocate here for a third, socially relevant frame. Reflecting current best practices in public history, this third frame incorporates the emotional qualities and historical accuracy of the celebratory approach and the acknowledgment of sports' importance to identity highlighted by the commemorative approach, but sees sports and sports history through a broad, all-encompassing lens that incorporates critical thought and wider social context. An effective sports exhibit begins with a holistic awareness of the impact and reach of your topic. Invite your constituents into conversations that lie beyond typical commemorative discussions. Engage in social impact topics by connecting historically relevant societal patterns to present-day political actions on the field. Challenge single-stance thinking by presenting many sides of a complex issue. Explore the positive ways athletic engagement has and does affect your community, as well as any ills that harm individuals or communities, local and global. This book will introduce you to various directions this awareness may lead. Consider the themes and theories explored here as a guide for stretching the edges of traditional sports thought and discussion.

Sports history is an ideal vessel from which to pull the past into the present, connecting universal themes of identity, community, cultural bonds, and the inter-connected human experience.[7] The historiography of sports history is a rigorous academic discipline. Understanding how sports historians and practitioners can shed light on issues such as immigration, identity, race, equity, urbanization, and global-ization (to name a select few) *and* present those topics in public-facing spaces is a foremost objective of this work.

Look also to public history conduits and sources found outside of the formalized professional or institutional walls, namely the media, television documentaries, film, and print journalism. As Kevin Moore asserts, "sport history is *in* popular culture."[8] Much of the sporting conversation happens in a very active and engaged public dia-logue, leaving a trail of valuable historical sourcing and analysis. ESPN's ground-breaking *30 for 30* documentary series from the early 2000s went beyond television journalism and into the realm of public history. In more than one hundred episodes (to date), the sports channel explored intriguing and challenging sports stories that muse-ums often deem too uncomfortable for display. In many ways, ESPN showed where sports history can and should go.[9] Still, the media is not typically where we engage in the most balanced discourse. Museums are.

Public historians approach the interpretation of sports history through a variety of methodologies and agendas. A state athletic hall of fame is likely to interpret its subject matter differently than a team-based hall of fame or a theme-based sports museum. Some function as tributes to a specific sport or university athletics depart-ment, others as corporate or manufacturing museums. Furthermore, sports encompass a broad range of activities—from professionally organized leagues to children's play to leisure activities and pastimes. The agenda or methods of these sports-focused institutions may differ from those of a more traditional cultural institution who choose to produce a sports exhibit. In *Representing the Sporting Past in Museums and Halls of Fame*, Murray Phillips outlines a typology of sports museums as a guide for understanding the trends and patterns associated with each type.[10] For an exploration of that framework, look to Moore's field study essay in the introductory section.[11] Throughout this book, essay authors aimed to present ideas accessible for any type of institution, whether primarily sports related or not. With that being said, identifying which type of museum or public space best applies to your situation can support you in uncovering best practices and common pitfalls associated with each one and inform your interpretive strategy.

In seeking effective ways for varying types of museums to incorporate sports topics in their exhibitions and programming, we explored these questions:

- What are the different models for using sports history as education in a public space?
- What types and depths of conversations can museums convene around sports history?
- What are the common mistakes museums and historic sites make when attempting to present sports history?
- What can we learn from analyzing case studies along with additional research and examples in the field?
- What opportunities do sports offer to increase relevance and connect with audience interests?

Laying Out Your Game Plan

In response to the exploratory questions, this book is organized into five sections addressing different aspects of understanding and implementing best practices in sports interpretation. There is no set way to utilize this book. We have intentionally arranged it to be used both as a reference work and as a book to read from cover to cover. If you are at the start of a project, this can serve as a five-part road map for creating a well-balanced sports history exhibit or program, as outlined below.

The opening section provides a comprehensive overview of the field along with practical methods for approaching and implementing well-rounded sports interpretation. The next four sections comprise the body of the book, featuring six themed chapters. Each begins with a topic-specific essay offering key interpretive concepts to frame and guide discussion, and ends with a short list of replicable practices—ready-made methodological takeaways to help you get started. Following the lead essays, you will find a collection of twenty case studies, drawn from American and international sites, sports museums, professional teams, and non-sports-centric institutions, which expand upon the chapter's theme. The concluding section invites you to create your interpretive sports game plan. It revisits the simple road map provided here and ends with a timely reflection for developing relevant sports public history projects.

These five sections of the book are:

- Warm Up—Examine the Field & Develop Themes: Comprehensive Research and Focus
- Part I—Expand the Scope: Inclusive Narratives and Global Reach
- Part II—Consider Your Constituents: Invested Identities and Branded Interests
- Part III—Engage Your Audience: Community Involvement and Educational Programming
- Forward Motion—Advancing Sports History Interpretation

Below is an expanded outline to support you in determining how to best tackle the material for planning your own sports-related projects and building a solid sports history interpretation game plan.

Warm Up—Examine the Field & Develop Themes:
Comprehensive Research and Focus

Start your plan by identifying possible themes, key storylines, and objects/media available to use or acquire. Consider which types of sources you will need to consult and whether they are accessible. Think about how you can present a complete and balanced view of your subjects' humanity. For a well-rounded exhibit, include stories of celebration and defeat as well as those that challenge visitors to think beyond a win/loss paradigm. Julia Rose and Jason Rose offer a guide for rethinking what is possible with complex, contextualized sports interpretation. They provide a template for addressing difficult sports-related discussions; a call to "brush sports history against the grain" and "end the silence" that permeates the field.[12] We recommend this as part of a balanced interpretive plan.

When crafting a thematic outline, consider these questions:

- From which reputable sources can you construct the narrative?
- Can you verify facts and include a myriad of perspectives and voices?
- How can all source material be used to convey your intuition's message creatively and effectively?
- What research and collecting work will you need to do?

Building on this awareness, expand and reinforce your themes with a solid base of researched content. Begin with a thorough source examination plan to verify the facts and identify various approaches to the subject matter. Comprehensive research includes examining documents and objects as well as immersion in the topic and its scholarship. Go to relevant museums, archives, and repositories. Conduct interviews or host roundtable discussions with involved parties. Examine primary sources to trace an accurate timeline or historic figure's perspective. Consult academic research, taking into account the various perspectives of writers who have viewed similar primary sources.

In the included Field Survey, Moore presents "Sport History, Public History, and Popular Culture: A Growing Engagement," an analysis of the relationship between academic sports historians, public historians, and the public's intersection with sports. He articulates the importance of increased collaboration between sports historians and the museum field—opportunities to reposition traditional practices in the field as well as challenges that have eluded academics and practitioners in the past. Moore's essay also outlines the vastly expansive material culture of sports and practical perspectives on object utilization. Use this as a guideline for understanding, considering, and engaging the breadth of options in the sports history and public history professions and to gain clarity on how your institution might contribute to this growing field.[13]

Do not take anything for granted. Double-check sources and cross-reference footnotes. Even simple facts such as statistics are often misprinted or difficult to locate. Beyond accurate facts and figures, explore the life and impact of the team, sports figure, community, or sport you are interpreting. This will allow your institution to follow a full range of engaging topics, from simple and celebratory narratives to more complicated and contextualized subject matter.

Remain equitable, even when taking a stand. Be thorough and fair. Explore the subject matter's full range of humanity with empathy and inclusion. When covering contested histories, consider how you might present the discussion without drawing conclusions for your visitors. Bring in disparate voices, exhibit all sides, display the content as you find it, and leave them with reflection questions. Give them room to participate in the examining of long-held ideologies and uncovering of their own new perspectives. When challenging inaccurate historical records or including omitted narratives, stay centered on your institutional values and speak with candor, factual clarity, a sense of justice, and kindness for those involved or affected.

We have provided a list of sports-related sources and locations, located in the back pages, to help you start researching. This list includes a comprehensive, although not exhaustive, assembly of sports history, sports public history, and broader public history resources—articles, books, journals, national organizations, and some international bodies. Use this as a place to start, to get ideas of ways to connect with the field and engage in broader conversations, locally and globally. With more than six hundred sports museums and archives in the United States alone, the list of potential repositories is too long to list here; for a fuller list, you may wish to consult Victor J. Danilov's *Sports Museums and Halls of Fame Worldwide*.[14]

Be creative when considering which institutions may hold special collections, primary sources, objects, or papers that would inform the various layers of your project. Many of your options will be large and obvious, while others, such as local historical societies or libraries, may be harder to pinpoint. You may find yourself surprised at where the greatest enthusiasts or richest content for your sports topic lie hidden out of plain sight!

Developing a robust material culture and object management approach can add depth to the story. Great sports-related exhibits need to use evidence but might not require building an extensive sports collection, which may be onerous, especially for a community museum that has a great story but not a lot of objects. A good show can rely on photographs, records, oral histories, documentary items, exhibitory, audio, and video—and the institution may not need to own the material. Consult other museums, repositories, or the athletes themselves for object loan opportunities. If your institution is holding an overabundance of objects, pare down.[15] Strategically select the most relevant objects that speak to the mission of your project or exhibit, so as to not visually overwhelm the visitor. You can also consider the experience-based options at your disposal.

Go beyond fixed objects or interpretive text by getting into the physicality of the sport. If possible, *play* the game or games that sit at the center of your exhibit's subject matter. Playing the game provides a new perspective on the experiences of athletes, fans, coaches, and the community. Give visitors a chance to play with historical rules, equipment, and even team chants or songs. Keep it fun, accurate, engaging, and inclusive!

Part I—Expand the Scope: Inclusive Narrative and Global Reach

Next, consider the potential reach and depth of your topics. Widen the lens beyond the most immediate, obvious visitors. Include complex, nuanced, underrepresented, and even difficult narratives. Think of using the internet, the media, or sporting events to draw global interest. Widen your topic to include related cultures and themes from other parts of the world. Remember we are all connected, and work to establish unexpected connections—to the history, sport, culture, identities, and your institution.

Connections between sports, individual rights, and social justice movements are central to athletic endeavors at every level and worthy of discussion. In chapter 1, "Stepping Up to the Plate: Interpreting Sports with Well-Rounded Exhibits," Kristin L. Gallas addresses issues of race, class, gender, religion, sexuality, and ethnicity. Sports has played a key role in the construction of identity for countless groups and is currently a highly contested space for LGBTQ+ and Native American communities, among many others. This chapter discusses the intimate connections between sports and their social and geographical contexts, the need to represent athletes' full humanity and identities, and the individual agency of athletes both on and off the field, court, or rink. Gallas presents examples of sports interpretation as a vehicle for exploring sensitive topics, and shows how these types of exhibits can draw in more diverse audiences.[16] Case studies in this chapter delve into often-underrepresented sports stories, from the development of sports exhibitions at the National Museum of African American History and Culture and the National Women's History Museum, to chronicling the "fight for equality" at the LBJ Presidential Library, to the need for more public history projects that address the intersection of sports and LGBTQ+ athletes and communities.

Remember that playing sports is inherent to the human experience and stretches to every part of the planet. While some sports origins are specific to certain countries, information about athletes, teams, and fans circulates worldwide. In chapter 2, "From Local to Global: Interpreting Sports and Globalization," Dr. Bruce Kidd and Jenny Ellison explore the global growth and appeal of sports. Kidd and Ellison analyze how communication and social media affect the public consumption of sports history and consider what happens in the globalization of sports. They encourage us to address institutional silences and argue for the necessity and impact of sharing authority and decolonizing sports narratives.[17] Case studies in this chapter explore the paradoxes, tensions, and creative possibilities of linking local to global through exhibition projects on the worlds of tennis, European football, and hockey.

Part II—Consider Your Constituents: Invested Identities and Branded Interests

With a solid thematic interpretive outline and draft exhibit layout in hand, next consider your constituents. There are many possible relationships between individual visitors and sports history. This section's chapters view the core sports exhibit audience through two lenses of invested interests: participation and branding.

Sports exhibits are often written for an audience already actively engaged as a fan or participant in a present-day sport. In chapter 3, "Fans, Athletes, Coaches and Participants: Interpreting Sports and Identity," Kathryn Leann Harris analyzes the impact participants have on the content of a sports history exhibit or program. Fans, coaches, athletes, and participants play a particularly active role in sporting culture. They rally around the public display of their team's history, even claiming a stake in the way their collective identity is discussed and how memory plays a role in interpretation. This chapter explores themes related to the personal identification associated with sports, the relationships between firsthand experience with sports and history, and the need for balanced commemoration about athletes who are real humans, neither gods nor villains.[18] Case studies in this chapter look deeply at aspects of participation in sporting culture, including sports' relationship to mental health, the sense of belonging and meaning-making explored through the community of NASCAR fans, and sports' role in public memory, memorialization, and healing after the tragic Boston Marathon bombing.

The professionalization of sports, along with its abundance of financial stakeholders, brings with it additional considerations. Chapter 4, "Finding Authenticity with the Voice of Influence: Interpreting Sports and Branding," examines the business of sports and the ways in which sports exhibits are often driven or influenced by a sponsorship or promotional agenda. Erin Narloch explores how professional teams, universities, and corporate brands incorporate sports history into their brand experience. For colleges, universities, and professional teams, these experiences often serve as tools for recruiting prospective athletes, raising funds from alumni or past participants, and building emotional buy-in with a widespread fan base. Sports-branded corporations use history to appeal to collectors, craft historically themed marketing campaigns, and design new apparel and merchandise based on popular past styles. Narloch offers insight into ways to work with a brand's agenda, while also critically analyzing the historical narrative to fully inform the public—or decide when to choose to *not* work with a brand. This chapter offers thought on the strategic positioning of sports history content, the benefits and risks of brand relationships, and maintaining curatorial and interpretive independence.[19] Case studies in this chapter model thoughtful and responsible approaches to this work: an exhibit of sneaker fashion and history through a sociocultural lens, unique team–community relationships in a football hall of fame, and the direct engagement of one museum to challenge harmful Indigenous stereotypes in sports branding.

Allegiance need not be ignored, as it can subtly and blatantly impact sports interpretation. Also among your constituencies are your board, internal colleagues, and (in some cases) oversight agencies. Define the audiences you are targeting and determine if they are loyal to a certain team, athlete, or sporting community. If so, from where does this loyalty stem, and how does it affect your interpretive plan? An internal exploration of biases or prejudices that hinder values-aligned discourse may result in hard discussions or repositioning. Overall, we recommend aiming to appeal to your base while maintaining historical accuracy and public history integrity. How can you appeal to your audience's interests to draw attendance? Can you do this and remain fair and equitable? If needed, can you challenge traditional narratives that are doing harm to the sport or its participants, and, in doing so, demonstrate the intrinsic value, for the sustainability of the sport or health of the community, of disrupting the status quo? Celebrate the sporting past and present in a balanced way that considers the breadth and depth of the human experience as well as your audience's authentic engagement with the material in their lives outside of your museum.

xxvi *Kathryn Leann Harris and Douglas Stark*

*Part III—Engage Your Audience: Community Involvement
and Educational Programming*

Use your plan to determine the best methods for enrolling and teaching various groups within your reach. With so many options for play, welcoming a sporting community into the museum space can be a lot of fun! Moreover, sports can attract new audiences and opportunities to expand your visitorship. There are literally endless ways to engage museum audiences with sports content. Our essayists have provided a litany of options and best practices for creating authentic, informative, and enthralling experiences.

Sports can uniquely connect communities, uniting different people and generations for a shared experience, whether they are fans of the game or not. Sporting communities form bonds that at times are almost familial. In chapter 5, "Connecting to Your Community: Interpreting Sports and Place," Terence Healy and Kathryn Leann Harris take this discussion further, asking age-old questions about why and how sports bring people together. This chapter explores unique ways to use sports exhibits in both traditional museum settings and nontraditional venues to bring community members together. Utilizing sports in interpretation offers a museum the opportunity to address larger societal issues confronted by their various communities. Thus, this chapter also addresses deeper questions about community relevance, connections to place and space, and collective participation.[20] Case studies in this chapter consider a range of community relationships, from fan-friendly engagement with social histories of bicycling and baseball to profound connections between sports, identity, and belonging in exhibits on the power of sports in Indigenous communities and in addressing the legacies of apartheid.

Innovative sports history programs allow opportunities for students and teachers to explore collections, personal stories, and primary sources while connecting to historical themes and development. Museums and historic sites can present exhibitions, live interpretation, game playing, facilitated programs, tours, talks and discussions, workshops, and classes, game-focused or other special events, and offer resources accessible to the public, such as databases and research centers. In chapter 6, "Empowering with Knowledge: Interpreting Sports through Education," Amanda McAllen explores these and other ways of using sports to educate the public. This chapter offers approaches to creating accessible programming for diverse learners, incorporating interdisciplinary content, and applying best practices from museum education. Both the theme essay and case studies address specific ways to connect curriculum standards to games, participants, technology, and competition.[21] Case studies in this chapter highlight how powerful and unexpected learning experiences can be conveyed through sports content and reveal how deeper audience understanding through research can make those experiences more compelling.

Consider these additional questions while defining your key design outcomes:

- How can sports inspire a wide range of visitors?
- How can visitors see themselves in the content?
- How might you challenge visitors to both embrace and think beyond victory moments?

- How can the exhibit connect community members outside of the immediate sporting world?
- Which objects are most revered by fans and/or the public? Which are contested? Which offer powerful storytelling opportunities? Which will help foster connection?
- With (or possibly against which) entities will you need to work in order to communicate your message?
- How can the exhibit expand the visitors' perception of the sport, their community, or the world?

Forward Motion—Advancing Sports History Interpretation

Now it's your turn to insert your voice and chart your own path forward! The book's conclusion will guide you back through the ideas laid out here and help you craft a fresh and relevant sports interpretation plan. Use the *Game Plan* in the conclusion to creatively write or update a playbook that leads your institution to an expanded and engaged sports-related visitorship.

As a punctuation to this grand discussion, Kenneth Cohen offers closing thoughts in the Afterword, *Embracing the Inseparability of Sports and Politics*. Cohen positions discussions of sports and politics in its historically relevant place. He reminds us that social constructions are just that: constructions. Current efforts to keep sports and politics in separate corners are, in fact, a fairly recent phenomenon, one that is serving a specific societal purpose, and one that can be reversed, repositioned, or at the least, reinterpreted.

We hope this book will serve as a way for readers and practitioners to start or enhance sports-related interpretation. It is our goal that you gain a greater understanding of the historical narrative of sports and how sports can provide a lens that helps illuminate our history, heritage, and customs. This volume offers an overview of the field, selected bibliographical works, themed topics, and case studies—a framework for incorporating sports history into your museum's interpretive plan. By no means are ours the only ideas and questions that will emerge, but they are ones that will help you begin your journey. Our intent is for these collected ideas to help you generate your own questions and show us all what you will create in response. With these recommendations in hand, your institution can generate and foster an environment where the totality of sports is presented, discussed, and debated.

As authors and editors of this volume, sports have had a profound impact on our own personal and professional lives. We present this collection to help the field learn to employ the tool of sports history more effectively, holistically, and inclusively. We sought to learn what worked well, what did not, and how to improve sports interpretation. We hope this series of thematic essays and case studies illuminates the innovative and forward-thinking nature of great sports exhibitions and programming and shows us what is possible.

NOTES

1. Murray G. Phillips, *Representing the Sporting Past in Museums and Halls of Fame* (New York: Routledge, 2012), 3.

2. Elif M. Gokcigdem, ed., *Fostering Empathy Through Museums* (Lanham, MD: Rowman & Littlefield, 2016), xx.

3. The work of historians such as John Budnar and David Glassberg emphasizes the social construction of memory and identity in the practice of history. For more, see John Bodnar, *Remaking America: Public Memory, Commemoration, and Patriotism in the Twentieth Century* (Princeton: Princeton University Press, 1992) and David Glassberg, "Public History and the Study of Memory," *The Public Historian* 18, no. 2 (Spring 1996).

4. Josh Howard, "On Sports, Public History, and Public Sports History," *Journal of Sport History* 45, no. 1 (2018), 24.

5. Wray Vamplew, "Facts and Artefacts: Sports Historians and Sports Museums," *Journal of Sport History* 25, no. 2 (1998), 278.

6. John Gillis, ed., *Commemorations: The Politics of National Identity* (Princeton: Princeton University Press, 1994).

7. This chapter includes a selected bibliography, professional organizations, and sport- and public history-related journals that might prove useful.

8. Kevin Moore, "Sport History, Public History, and Popular Culture: A Growing Engagement," *Journal of Sport History* 40, no. 1 (Spring 2013), 42.

9. Aaron Tallent, "Ranking Every ESPN 30 for 30 Film," *Athlon Sports*, May 6, 2022, accessed July 17, 2022, https://athlonsports.com/girls/ranking-every-espn-30-for-30-film.

10. Murray G. Phillips, ed., "Introduction: Historians in Sports Museums," in *Representing the Sporting Past in Museums and Halls of Fame* (Abingdon: Routledge, 2012), 1–21.

11. Kevin Moore, "Sport History, Public History, and Popular Culture: A Growing Engagement," in *Interpreting Sports at Museums and Historic Sites*, Kathryn Leann Harris and Douglas Start, eds. (Lanham, MD: Rowman & Littlefield, 2023), 11. Originally published in *Journal of Sport History* 40, no. 1 (Spring 2013), 39–55, 44.

12. Julia Rose and Jason Rose, "Introduction," in *Interpreting Sports at Museums and Historic Sites*, Harris and Start, eds., 1.

13. Moore, "Sport History," 11.

14. Victor J. Danilov, *Sports Museums and Halls of Fame Worldwide* (Jefferson, North Carolina and London: McFarland and Company, Inc., 2005).

15. For in-depth discussion and guidance on why and how to weed collections, see Elizabeth Wood, Rainey Tisdale, and Trevor Jones, eds., *Active Collections* (New York: Routledge, 2018).

16. Kristen L. Gallas, "Stepping Up to the Plate: Interpreting Sports with Well Rounded Exhibits," in *Interpreting Sports at Museums and Historic Sites*, Harris and Stark, eds., 29.

17. Bruce Kidd and Jenny Ellison, "From Local to Global: Interpreting Sports and Globalization," in *Interpreting Sports at Museums and Historic Sites*, Harris and Stark, eds., 55.

18. Kathryn Leann Harris, "Fans, Athletes, Coaches and Participants: Interpreting Sports and Identity," in *Interpreting Sports at Museums and Historic Sites*, Harris and Stark, eds., 83.

19. Erin Narloch, "Finding Authenticity with the Voice of Influence: Interpreting Sports and Branding," in *Interpreting Sports at Museums and Historic Sites*, Harris and Stark, eds., 115.

20. "Connecting to Your Community: Interpreting Sports and Place," in *Interpreting Sports at Museums and Historic Sites*, Harris and Stark, eds., 149.

21. Amanda McAllen, "Empowering with Knowledge: Interpreting Sports through Education," in *Interpreting Sports at Museums and Historic Sites*, Harris and Startk, eds., 183.

Introduction

Julia Rose and Jason Rose

The sports arena provides fans opportunities to witness excellence and consider the value of success and failure. Athletics, professional or amateur, are avenues through which strength, perseverance, and moral character are highlighted. Witnessing games at any level, in person or on television, enables people of all backgrounds to participate in and belong to valued communities. Groups and communities often bond around a shared identity while playing and watching sports. Children and adults alike collect memories of games won, finish lines crossed, and world records set. "I was there!" says the fan at an Olympic competition after witnessing a part of history. Sports fans revel in revering athletic success and viewing athletes as heroes and role models. The cover story—of winners and losers—is often what fans care about most. However, when historians write about sports, the narratives tend to include more than the "end game" of winners and losers. Sports historical narratives also examine the human-interest stories: explanations of how athletes or teams trained, intersections with family life, and the subject's social, economic, and psychological journey. These narratives can reveal difficult moments or characteristics of beloved sports figures or teams. Some fans may find it difficult to learn the backstory behind an athlete's success or downfall. Yet, granting fans the liberty to imagine how a favorite athlete came to experience a moment of incredible achievement or defeat creates an opportunity to share in the emotional waves of the undulating joy and disappointment of competition. When, as museum workers, we allow space for exploring difficult sports narratives alongside victorious moments we can foster discussions from which audiences glean valuable insight from sports figures' very exposed human experiences.

Interpreting difficult sports histories at museums and historic sites can also illuminate the many and varied people who have been harmed by the insidious behavior of power brokers and silenced by economic, political, racist, and sexist social structures inside sports organizations. Americans are becoming ever more aware of the sports stories that have been ignored or suppressed for reasons more surreptitious than merely an athlete's lack of notoriety. In the first quarter of the twenty-first century, the nation watched an emerging barrage of news reports about lesser-known and unknown athletes, students, and participants who were victims of abuse, harassment, or inequitable and oppressive treatment. These revelations are not only a recent phenomenon. Major

League Baseball and the National Baseball Hall of Fame and Museum, for example, have historically blacklisted players for abhorrent behavior, including superstar Pete Rose's gambling and players accused of using illegal performance-enhancing drugs. However, many challenging stories rarely emerge on museum walls. While museum audiences historically tend to tolerate or overlook sports heroes' vulnerabilities and capacities for immoral behavior, many Americans can no longer ignore them. Today's museum audiences are demanding to know more. Stories of LGBTQ athletes being excluded and harassed, college and university coaches engaging in sexual misconduct and abuse, and situations of religious intolerance such as Muslim women being confronted with barriers to sports and exercise are just a few recent examples that help illustrate the sensitive and difficult histories with which athletes, fans, families, and communities must grapple and from which we can all learn. Moreover, the rise of the hashtag era and the maturing millennial generation have emboldened fans and audiences to challenge the status quo of sports histories and cover more complex stories behind victories and defeats.

When museums and historic sites do cover some of the more challenging sports narratives, the selected stories often reflect commonly known commentary about discrimination and intolerance. Due to the ways in which they disrupted social barriers, iconic sports figures Jackie Robinson and Billie Jean King are often discussed to explore the intersection of sports with race, class, and gender. Jackie Robinson broke the color line in professional baseball in 1947. Billie Jean King started the Women's Tennis Association against great resistance and challenged gender inequality in professional tennis in 1973. Their accomplishments provide examples of difficult sports histories that raise potentially uncomfortable discussions about racism and sexism. And yet, Robinson's and King's historic civil rights accomplishments have become so familiar that the retelling of these histories raises the risk of complacency and perpetuating a misguided belief that racial and gender inequities in sports may have been resolved.

Fortunately, today's public is listening more closely to the stories of athletes whose names have not traditionally been included in newspaper headlines. "I was there!" can mean much more than witnessing athletes win or lose competitions. It can also refer to disclosures about deplorable moments from within the sports world. Momentum from the #MeToo movement, which was initiated in 2017 from an influx of awareness around sexual harassment scandals in the entertainment industry, encouraged more people to step forward to reveal the injustices they endured and foster a social environment of support for their struggle. Today, witnesses and victims are more widely reporting long unnoticed or hidden traumatic events and unfair or immoral activities. Complainants aim to expose and disrupt systematized power structures in their pursuit for justice. In 2018, the *Washington Post* sports section reported that Miami Dolphins cheerleader Kristan Ann Ware filed a complaint against the Dolphins and the National Football League (NFL). Her complaint alleged that she faced sexual harassment and hostility from Dolphins cheerleading coaches and that she faced discrimination based on gender and religion. She contended that the NFL could have done more to protect cheerleaders but instead ignored the cheerleaders' grievances. "The silence needs to end," Ware said. "The intimidation needs to end."[1] This type of silence had an even more sinister effect when it protected serial pedophile Jerry Sandusky, a former assistant football coach from Pennsylvania

State University, and sexual predator Larry Nassar, former USA Gymnastics team physician, as they engaged in years of sexual abuse of those entrusted to their care. As Rachael Denhollander, one of Nasser's victims, explained in the *Washington Post* on January 24, 2018, "The reason that everyone who heard about Larry's abuse didn't believe it is because they did not listen."[2] The exposure of these scandals has increased public awareness.

Revelations of abuses and injustices within the sporting world play a productive role in the lives of our institutions. These sports histories expose many of the institutional forces that present obstacles to social justice in the world of sports and society at large. Sports-related museums and historic sites can be powerful instruments for social change. These organizations can serve as advocating voices for victims through research, exhibitions, documentaries, and other interpretation strategies that elevate, validate, and inform the public about the histories of social injustice and immoral behavior in the sports world. While difficult sports histories can make audiences uncomfortable, they are the stories with the power to incite active empathy, advocacy, and demands for change. Museums can interrogate persistent social barriers, give voice to the abused and oppressed, help communities and our nation retool education and public policy, and leverage powerful investments in sports for social good (e.g., investments in local economies and job growth, and preserve historic structures). In this chapter, we will consider some of the roles history institutions can play in advocating for social justice through sports interpretation.

Brushing Sports History against the Grain

Sports history is enmeshed in America's social fabric. From rural areas to urban centers, the people, places, and events of sports history reflect the social structures and political climates from where those histories unfolded. Thus, sports can provide museums and historic sites with a lens through which to examine the Jim Crow era and present-day racism. Institutions and visitors can explore the ways in which World War II impacted athletics and how participation in sports aided veterans' reintegration into civilian life. The history of women and social equity is evident in the ways Title IX impacted female participation in sports. We can begin to more ardently explore how the #MeToo movement is impacting the sports field.

Humanist Walter Benjamin's expression "brushing history against the grain" describes a critical method useful for reflection on historical content in museum interpretations.[3] Collecting insights and recollections from a wide and diverse breadth of witnesses has the potential to reveal previously hidden belief systems and influences that shaped historical events, thus relating unexplored aspects of sports history to present-day societal trends. Sports history includes multiple layers of memories from inside the field of play to beyond the bleachers and into communities. No matter their age, memories of an event are stored in the minds of many, many people: spectators, players, coaches, instructors, suppliers, groundskeepers, reporters, stakeholders, and supporting communities. And yet, it is important to probe further by asking, "Who have we not asked about that moment in history?" and "What happened behind the scenes?" and "Whose voices are not being heard?" Brushing history against the grain is about approaching the current narrative in a more critical way. In doing so, we can include both the prevailing narrative perspectives and those in the margins, consider counterpoints, provide audiences with time and resources for thoughtful critical review, question old stories, more deeply interpret new ones, and reorient well-known narratives.

When brushing sports history against the grain, we are more likely to hear the voices from a wider variety of denizens in sports communities. The American philosopher and gender theorist Judith Butler argues that ideas are more closely allied with the pursuit of truth when institutions foster contested intellectual views because, through open and engaged conversation, thinking becomes more nuanced, more grounded, and more persuasive.[4] Multiple perspectives and diverse investigations lead to robust historical research and interpretations, which accomplishes far more than merely increasing the historical canon. Museum workers can impact opinions, shape values, and encourage advocates with critical history investigations. Thus, we might hear voices from heretofore-unknown participants on playing fields, in boardrooms, in classrooms, in press boxes, from behind closed locker room doors, or in doctors' offices. We stand to discover the stories of immoral, illegal, and wicked behavior—real-life stories that were ignored or silenced and that reveal histories of physical abuse, homophobia, misogyny, racism, sexism, fraud, and violence. Such revelations can do more than acknowledge these injustices. They can also hold perpetrators accountable, enable reconciliations, and inform wholesale changes in teams, sports, and public policy.

Throughout the centuries, global society has long constructed a concept of the "sports hero," a role model who achieved success through virtue and talent both on and off the field. Over the past fifty years, American society has begun to more aggressively hold heroes (sports or otherwise) accountable for their wrongdoings as part of a growing sense of social change that came with the rise and impact of the civil rights movement. While much of American society previously concealed or simply ignored injustice, a light of objectivity is now being shone on our collective past, even if doing so reveals the failures of our heroes, including athletes. In the past two decades, Americans have watched quarterback Michael Vick, cyclist Lance Armstrong, golfer Tiger Woods, baseball players Roger Clemens and Barry Bonds, Olympic track and field champion Marion Jones, and football coach Joe Paterno fall from grace in dramatic fashion. These examples demonstrate a genuine, understandable fear that turning such scrutiny on the past might destroy the beautiful idea of the sports hero altogether and that society at large stands to lose something genuinely valuable in the process. Thus, reexamined sports history quickly becomes difficult history.

Difficult history arises because sports' supposed purity provides an excellent vantage point from which society can view the highest human aspirations and draw inspiration. We love sports because they ostensibly represent something good, true, and just. Most games are deontological; they are judged based on absolute rules rather than on circumstances outside the actions of the game. This makes them fair in a way the real world is all too often not. Participation in a sport requires one to accept and adhere to certain rules to facilitate play (this is why a cheater will always attempt to hide the fact he or she is cheating). If only the real world were so clear-cut. People desire justice in the universe; it is easy to see how the ideal of sportsmanship is a perfect vessel for that noble emotion.

Playing well has become an accepted and treasured form of heroism. After all, to succeed at sports, one must overcome challenges, while holding true to an absolute code—in this case, the rules of the game. Thus, playing well and winning are viewed as virtuous, heroic behaviors that are highly valued by society and hold incredible economic value. There is much money to be made in selling the appeal of sports heroes. If the oppressive, immoral, and wicked behaviors from within the sports world are hidden or ignored, the optics of a valuable and consumable sports economy remains viable. This results in sacrifices to the willful ignorance of myth; for the less we know about an athlete, the easier it becomes to invest them with the heroic ideals of virtue. In the same way, those who know more about a treasured hero, beloved sport, or the institutions surrounding them run the real risk of dashing that illusion.

Brushing history against the grain is a crucial step in researching and interpreting sports history because history is fluid and notions of authenticity and neutrality are organic. Some museum workers and visitors commonly and inaccurately believe that all history is factual. However, many aspects of history are subject to debate and interpretation. Counterpoints lay behind nearly every interpretation. For nearly everything that is said and seen in historical representations, there is the unsaid and the unseen. While some interpret Jackie Robinson's role in breaking the Major League Baseball color barrier as a purely positive narrative, the alternative perspective is of equal interest and importance, though more painful to learn. Robinson's feat documents the appalling nature of racial and ethnic segregation. He took great risk to pursue a career in a sport that was, at that point, exclusively populated by whites. The intricacies of his story represent a larger picture of the harsh realities of racial segregation and social oppression in the United States that were supported by systems of racially segregated transportation, public facilities, housing, and schools. To give voice to the diversity of people from numerous levels of involvement in history, museum workers should help audiences brush history against the grain and ask, "What do you think of the story?" With each divergent perspective of a historical event, new information, connections, and understandings about the meanings of a difficult history will surface for both museum workers and audiences.

To critically interpret sports history from multiple perspectives, museum workers should look for networks and relationships of power, talent, subjugation, resistance, and agency. In this way, institutions have interpretive frameworks to recall the stories of achievement and affliction. Each major sport has its own social hierarchies, political structures, economies, and cultural traditions. By vigorously interpreting these historically complex relationships, museum workers have an opportunity to critically analyze power dynamics and highlight instances when those relationships have either historically or presently jeopardized the safety or civil rights of athletic participants. Brushing history against the grain means looking for and questioning the ideology and institutional social dynamics that empowered authorities and offenders. This method also includes validating, identifying, and locating events that cause exclusion and victimization. The stories uncovered in this process can be shameful, upsetting, uncomfortable, and even shocking. However, exhibits and programs that expose abusive or otherwise destructive behavior could create real and lasting social change; if left undetected and uncorrected, destructive power dynamic patterns will likely perpetuate into the future.

Sports history matters. Sometimes we need to be inconvenienced and feel un-comfortable to empathize with historical individuals and groups and to pursue justice for the benefit of society at large. Difficult histories are the tough stuff with which museum workers and audiences must grapple to acknowledge and respond to misdeeds, affronts, inequities, and systems of injustice.

Difficult History Is Difficult Knowledge in Sports

Difficult knowledge, which educational theorist Deborah P. Britzman defines as the knowledge that is upsetting, stressful, or too hard to bear, has the capacity to disrupt the learner's internal world and disrupt how a visitor understands the external world.[5] In the context of a history organization or museum, difficult history is a kind of dif-ficult knowledge.[6] Britzman writes that difficult knowledge asks people to recognize the discontinuities between the new information and their existing base of understand-ing. Learning from this place asks something intimate of learners. It requires them to recognize how they might be implicated in the new knowledge and to recognize attachments that organize their own self-identity.

Resisting difficult knowledge is, in large part, a learner's effort toward psychic self-preservation. The museum visitor's discomfort or psychological pain is contained in his or her memory. This can cause the visitor anxiety and stress. When museum visitors are confronted with difficult knowledge that asks them to consider immoral and shocking events, visitors are then pressed to make sense of the new information. When the knowledge is too difficult, emotional disruption can be extreme and can shake the visitor. Britzman argues that this is painful in the way it jeopardizes the learner's psychic balance and thereby creates felt scenarios of loss. This feeling of loss requires the visitor-as-learner to work through the difficult knowledge to make sense of the history.[7]

The painful personal stories of struggle and injustice within sports history are dif-ficult histories that, if sensitively interpreted, have the potential to take us beyond the more familiar narratives. Maureen Costello, Director of the Southern Poverty Law Center's *Teaching Tolerance* project, suggests we keep in mind that "schools often just teach the 'highlight reel' of civil rights victories—the Rev. Martin Luther King Jr.'s *I Have A Dream* speech, Rosa Parks' bus stand—without in-depth stories of in-dividual struggle and resistance."[8] Visitors can feel uncomfortable when approached with the shameful and implicating behaviors that lesser-known, more challenging histories often evoke. This experience might incite angst when visitors feel pain for historical subjects or recognize attachments that organize their own self-identity. Sports history museums and historic sites can and should push the boundaries of the well-known sports stories of difficult histories—such as Jackie Robinson and Billie Jean King's successes. In doing so, we can expand the highlight reel and shed light on stories of inequity that have not yet been represented.

Museum workers are sometimes hesitant to take on the risky project of interpret-ing a difficult sports history. Difficult history can be both personal *and* political. It can make frontline staff uncomfortable, embarrassed, or concerned about upsetting or offending visitors. When organizations present controversial exhibitions or programs, they might risk losing funding or support. Interpretations of these challenging topics can upset the political status quo in a community and sway public opinion on current issues. Ambivalent attitudes to take on the project of learning and interpreting difficult sports histories help staff avoid feeling uncomfortable. Conversely, such avoidance keeps visitors (and eventually society) from learning about the injustice. Resistance puts the history at risk of social forgetting, or worse, puts the history at risk of annihilation.[9] Butler describes the frightening political impact that power brokers exert through controlling knowledge. She refers to this as the "criminalization of knowledge"—a move to advocate for ignorance, which includes silencing history and debating through deliberate censorship.[10] Once forgotten or trivialized, the difficult history no longer holds the necessary effects to counter injustice and advocate for change.

How then do public historians equitably represent difficult histories? How can we simultaneously represent the histories of massive, diverse populations? We do so by constructing representations of historical topics comprised of both individual biographies and an empirical persuasion that informs museum audiences about oppressive events. The "aggregate of anonymous victims" is a useful concept from American writer, filmmaker and philosopher Susan Sontag that speaks to the power that numbers (e.g., thousands of people) have in communicating the scope and impact of an injustice.[11] Institutions can construct descriptions of oppressed masses by unpacking the sports-specific social architecture of a team, players, and stakeholders and then exploring the multiple sociohistorical contextual layers among these relationships. Each layer of empirical information helps learners imagine and reflect on the variability of incidents experienced by the oppressed peoples. Public history organizations can also effectively use biographic cameos of historical individuals and groups (whether they are sports heroes or not) to further bring personal experiences into focus. With so many stories to tell, we are pressed to research and select stories to highlight. Some cameos represent the path many sufferers endured from a historical injustice, while others represent unique or unusual experiences. Public historians should ask, "Does this story enable learners to get more intimately connected to the difficult history?"

Passion for Ignorance: Risk and Benefits

Are the histories about misdeeds, criminal behavior, or biased and oppressive systems necessary information? Visitors or sports fans might ask, "Can't I just enjoy the game without all of this?" American literary critic Shoshana Felman explains that ignorance is a form of resistance. When museum visitors choose not to pursue reading label copy about a traumatic history because it is too hard to bear, the visitors are choosing not to know the information at that moment. If the visitor chooses to ignore the challenging aspects of the past, then they can believe the history did not happen or that it does not matter. The visitor can avoid discomfort and instead feel relieved of taking responsibility for knowing about the problematic events. Sometimes, it is just easier to be indifferent, complacent, or even deaf to difficult history. But as Haitian American anthropologist Michel-Rolph Trouillot contends, when history is simply ignored, "this ignorance produces a silence of trivialization."[12]

The resistant visitor will argue that not knowing the pain and anguish of the sufferer keeps him or her from feeling pain and from needing to respond.[13] Felman asserts that ignorance is not simply an opposition to knowledge; it is instead an integral part of the structure of knowledge. "Ignorance," she writes, "is not a passive state of absence, a simple lack of information: it is an active dynamic of negation, an active refusal of information."[14]

Risks of Silence and Benefits of Taking Risks

When we risk not learning a difficult history or silencing the past, we increase the likelihood of the loss of collective memory and the knowledge of the conditions upon which social structures rest. These social structures include the traditions, rules, and laws that govern and control how sports are played, how players are trained, and how the sports economy is run. Widespread social forgetting and sub-jugation puts historical, sociological, and political information, and the respective material culture at risk of being lost or trivialized. Understandably, uncomfortable and controversial historical content can be the difficult knowledge with which sports museum visitors must grapple and for sports communities to share. How-ever, controversies are an integral part of the collective production of knowledge. Disagreements and intellectual tensions productively motivate further investigation and dialogue that expand the search for the meaning of historical events. Interpreta-tions of difficult histories can ignite community outrage that can lead to the exposure of injustices and reveal ways to make rules, public policy, and safety more equitable. Debates may become heated, thereby putting the host institution at increased risk of offending audiences, jeopardizing financial and community support, and putting the museum workers under public scrutiny in ways that can challenge the institution's au-thority. Yet, when visitors can work through feelings of resistance, they can more fully engage in learning the difficult histories. Visitors are then more likely to ask questions and demand to know more about the history. Empathy can emerge when we attempt to move visitors to respond to injustice. Empathetic visitors are more likely to have compassionate visions for a more just world.

Such empathetic responses to difficult histories are demonstrations of hopefulness. Active empathy can stimulate visitors to influence policies such as how athletes are selected for team membership or steps to enhance inclusive team cultures. Ongoing national debates regarding team mascots and iconography reflect this type of influ-ence. Some previous and current professional team mascots, such as the Cleveland In-dians, Atlanta Braves, and the Washington R*dskins, are examples of hotly contested cultural debates that represent to critics a lack of empathy toward Native Americans.[15]

Interpreting difficult history through sports can also offer deep personal benefits for visitors. Those affected by injustice will find museum exhibits valuable places for recon-ciling, validating, grieving, and empowering communities to action. Such memory work can happen when the silences are disrupted and multiple voices from outside and within the sports community can be heard. Exhibitions and programs in museums provide space for expanding conversations and encouraging the work of sharing memories. If a museum chooses to engage in a discussion from an empathetic stance, then visitors may choose to respond to sports controversies in personal ways—by evolving their attitude about equity, switching team allegiances, signing a petition, donating to a social cause, refusing to consume particular products, and pursuing changes in laws, rules, and sports' customs.

Exhibits and public history programs help visitors determine how they are connected to the historical evidence. "Do I believe this?" "Is this relevant to me?" "Does this make sense to me?" The interaction between visitors and an interpretation is an opportunity to validate or change what he or she believes. Young visitors have the chance to learn about the personal experiences of athletes by gathering examples of good and immoral behavior from the interpretations of difficult histories. Young visitors benefit from accumulating an understanding of historical rights and wrongs. This becomes a source of knowledge that helps them build personal matrices for moral living. Thus, while a difficult history in sports may have made negative headlines when it was first reported, museum interpretations of the difficult history can play a positive, educational role for audiences today.

End the Silence

People across the globe felt empathy, pain, and anger when they learned about the Team USA gymnasts who suffered sexual abuse, and they felt rage when they learned that the powers in charge kept the reports of abuse silent for decades. Does this rage stemming from our new awareness of the young American gymnasts' stories of abuse discolor our support or interest in gymnastics? Does our knowledge about the history of racism in baseball change our relationship to that sport? Perhaps these are some of the changes that are needed to better both the sport and society at large?

Exhibitions and programs about difficult sports histories should change how fans and museum visitors view their athletic heroes, the sport itself, and participants. However, they are productive and purposeful changes. Public historians and museum workers should critically and sensitively curate collections and carefully select accounts to represent horrific histories through exhibitions and programs. Unlike at a sporting event, museum audiences are not merely spectators; they are learners. Museum exhibitions and programs are not meant to be spectacles. Rather, museums and history organizations share historical accounts and perspectives from witnesses who experienced authentic moments tied to sports history. Those who exclaim "I was there!" give a voice to penetrate silences that otherwise would conceal histories of impropriety, illegality, injustice, and immoral behavior in the sports world.

Interpreting difficult history is a hopeful enterprise. As Bryan Stevenson, lawyer, social justice activist, and founder of the Equal Justice Initiative, told the 2018 graduating class of Johns Hopkins University, "Hope is your superpower."[16] Stevenson went on to demand that present generations be willing to be uncomfortable and inconvenienced to be moved to respond. We need to care enough to change the narratives—to seek out and challenge the politics of fear and abusive power in the sports industry. Difficult history interpretation in sports can embolden us to care enough to change the status quo.

NOTES

1. Adam Kilgore, "Dolphins Cheerleader Alleges Discrimination," *Washington Post*, April 13, 2018.

2. Will Hobson, "Larry Nassar, Former USA Gymnastics Doctor, Sentenced to 40–175 Years for Sex Crimes," *Washington Post*, January 24, 2018.

3. Walter Benjamin, *Walter Benjamin Illuminations: Essays and Reflections*, ed. Hannah Arendt (New York: Schocken Books, 1968), 60.

4. Judith Butler, "The Criminalization of Knowledge: Why the Struggle for Academic Freedom is the Struggle for Democracy," *The Chronicle of Higher Education* 64, no. 35 (2018), B14–B16.

5. Deborah P. Britzman, *Lost Subjects, Contested Objects: Toward a Psychoanalytic Inquiry of Learning* (Albany: State University of New York, 1998), 19.

6. Julia Rose, *Interpreting Difficult Histories at Historic Sites and Museums* (Lanham, MD: Rowman & Littlefield, 2016), 28–29.

7. Rose, *Interpreting*, 72–78.

8. Erin Shaw Street, "Helping Kids Absorb a Stark Story: A Mother's Take on Visiting a New Alabama Museum and Memorial to Lynching Victims," *Washington Post*, June 3, 2018.

9. Iwona Irwin-Zarecka, *Frames of Remembrance: The Dynamics of Collective Memory* (New Brunswick, NJ: Transaction Publishers, 1994), 118–20; Jennifer L. Eichstedt and Stephen Small, *Representations of Slavery: Race and Ideology in Southern Plantation Museums* (Washington, D.C.: Smithsonian Institution, 2002), 105.

10. Butler, "The Criminalization of Knowledge."

11. Susan Sontag, *Regarding the Pain of Others* (New York: Picador/Farr, Straus and Giroux, 2003), 61.

12. Michel-Rolph Touillot, *Silencing the Past: Power and Production of History* (Boston: Beacon Press, 1995), 147–148.

13. Shoshanna Felman, *Jacques Lacan and the Adventure of Insight: Psychoanalysis in Contemporary Culture* (Cambridge: Harvard University Press, 1987), 147–48.

14. Felman, *Jacques Lacan and the Adventure of Insight*, 78–79.

15. Cleveland's MLB team changed the Indians mascot to the Guardians in 2021. Washington's NFL team eliminated the Redskins mascot in 2020 and introduced the Commanders mascot in 2022.

16. Bryan Stevenson, "Commencement Address," May 24, 2918, Johns Hopkins University, *YouTube* video 24-50, https://www.youtube.com/watch?v=HRJIEjU7vO8.

Field Study

Sport History, Public History, And Popular Culture: A Growing Engagement

Kevin Moore[1]
National Football Museum

Academic sport history has come a long way in a relatively short period of time, using a growing range of theoretical approaches, drawing on an expanding range of disciplines, tackling an increasingly wider range of subjects. This includes exploring sport as a popular cultural practice. Yet we must also recognize that public sport history has been around for much longer and has grown even more significantly in recent decades. The relationship between academic and public sport history has been relatively weak and at times problematic. The wider public, even those with an interest in sport history, has little knowledge of the work of academics. This paper argues for a much greater academic engagement with public sport history, embracing and exploring new ways of communicating the subject, in new collaborations, to new and much more diverse audiences.

Sport history has come a long way in a relatively short period of time. There is an increasingly rich and diverse sport history, using a growing range of theoretical approaches, drawing on a growing range of disciplines, tackling an increasingly wider range of subjects. The subject, it appears, has never been in better shape. This does not just mean academic sport history, hugely significant though its development over the past thirty years or so has been. The development of other forms of the public history has been equally significant. As the main theme of the conference from which this paper was generated stated, "The sporting past is everywhere."

However, some do not see the position of sport history as quite so positive. A symposium at the University of Huddersfield, UK, in June 2011, "What Is the Future of Sport History in Academia?" posed that

> There is a large and excellent body of work produced within the sport and leisure sub-discipline. However, with the exception of a few classic texts, a good deal of significant and ground-breaking work has been, and continues to be, overlooked despite the increasing recognition of sport's political, cultural and economic importance by government and media.[2]

It also referred to "the problems of past and present relationships between the mainstream historical community, and the sub-branches of sports and leisure research."[3] There is a danger that as a new subject trying to break into the mainstream, feeling initially marginalized, sport historians have perhaps inevitably grouped together, including in organizations such as the Australian Society for Sports History (ASSH), the British Society of Sports History (BSSH), and the North American Society for Sport History (NASSH), but this might perversely have contributed to this isolation.

So perhaps now is a good opportunity to pause for thought and to consider some of the fundamental questions about sport history that have been raised by several writers, particularly by Douglas Booth.[4] In this paper, this will be particularly in terms of the relationship between academic sport history and the wider public history of sport. In this paper I will pose, in terms of academic and public sport history and the relationship between these two, a number of key questions, as follows: What has been achieved? What has not been achieved? What is it that we are collectively trying to achieve? Where are we going next? Is there indeed a "we," and if so, what does that mean?" This paper is structured in terms of the three key themes of the conference from which it is drawn, namely: first, general trends in sport history and the incorporation of popular culture; second, specific intersections between sport history and popular culture; and third, sport history, popular culture, and public intellectuals.

General Trends in Sport History and the Incorporation of Popular Culture

This paper begins by exploring the link between sport history and popular culture. The first question is, is there an "and?" Is not sport part of popular culture? Therefore, is not sport history already part of popular culture? Of course, popular culture is notoriously difficult to define, as I have explored elsewhere.[5] But as Germaine Greer has argued, commenting on the U.K. Government's Department for Culture, Media and Sport, "Football counts as culture just as much as opera does. To list media and sport as co-equal with culture is like referring to food, eggs, and chips as separate categories."[6]

Reflecting the wider developments in social history, academic sport history has increasingly embraced popular culture, has widened its gaze from elite athletes and governing bodies to the study of the every day. It has broadened its lens through class, gender, ethnicity, and disability. It has been recognized that studying sporting governing elites is essential to understanding issues of class, gender, ethnicity, and disability in sport. It has moved from what might be termed formal sports to the informal, looking at, for example, the history of children's football in the street. Sport history has increasingly explored the popular culture of the game, in the sense of, for example, fandom, and here it has begun to move away from an undue emphasis on the topical but atypical, such as football hooligans, to look at the more mainstream aspects of fandom. It has explored links between sport and literature, and the beginnings of the study of sport and music, as in, for example, the work of John Bale, Anthony Bateman, and Davie Russell.[7] Further, sports historians are increasingly engaging with the new approaches to their subject that cultural studies can offer, so that sport history has increasingly had a "cultural turn."[8] Of course, there are widely varying and differing approaches to this, including the development of a postmodern approach to sport history. As part of all this, particularly welcome in my view have been anti-sport studies, whether by academics, such as John Bale, or journalists, such as Andy Miller.[9]

At the same time, academic sport history has increasingly engaged with the popular culture of sport in another sense. It has begun to explore the popular *material* culture of sport. First, there has been a "turn to the visual," exploring both "high" art and popular imagery, loosely defined as a two-dimensional material, including photography. Groundbreaking work by Peter Kuhnst and Pierre Chazaud has led to a wide range of studies.[10] Studies have ranged from, for example, John Hughson's studies of Olympic posters, a single football painting, and a single Olympic poster to Joyce Woolridge's study of the covers of football magazines.[11] A recent major acquisition for the National Football Museum has been "The Homes of Football" photographic collection of Stuart Clarke, over 100,000 images of football fandom, mainly in Britain, since 1989. The Hillsborough disaster in which ninety-six Liverpool fans tragically died led Stuart to turn his back on the pitch and to explore instead the culture of the terraces. How are we to read this collection? Tara Brabazon has begun the process.[12] Booth has explored the ways in which historians have moved away from a reliance on written sources, to engage with oral testimony, and visual materials, including film and photography, but has also considered the way in which such sources can be highly problematic.[13] With this proviso, the burgeoning work on the visual culture of sport, including sport film, is leading to valuable, fresh insights.

Beyond this, more tentatively, because it is much more out of the comfort zone of historians, there has been a "turn to the material," to explore three-dimensional artifacts as evidence. Inspired by developing material culture studies, particularly the work of Susan Pearce, I have outlined how historians can explore and understand the meanings in all, including the most seemingly ordinary, pieces of material culture. As Pearce quotes from a label in a museum, "When you are looking at an object, you are looking at a person's thoughts."[14] In many ways, we are still only beginning to explore artifacts as evidence and what their histories reveal. I have explored in detail the history of the ball from the 1966 FIFA World Cup Final, which is hugely revealing of postwar relations between England and Germany. Just before the EUFA Euro 96 tournament, the ball was at the center of a "war" between two British tabloid newspapers, the *Sun* and the *Daily Mirror*, to bring it back to England—from Germany—in an act of "cultural restitution." I argued that "[f]ootball as a game has become symbolic of the popular perception of the decline of England, the relative failure of the national football team inextricably linked with our decline as a country, and the end of empire. The ball represents a supposedly more positive and hopeful past."[15]

The 1966 FIFA World Cup Final ball is just one object from over 140,000 items in the collections of the National Football Museum, the national museum of English football, which is just one of many hundreds of sport museums worldwide. The analysis of the ball demonstrated what is possible, and historians are increasingly engaging with the material culture of sport, but the potential remains enormous. Alexander Jackson has successfully completed a major PhD study of the consumer culture of English football fandom, c.1880 to c.1960, which is leading to publications.[16] There has been a study of the Jules Rimet trophy, of Diego Maradona's shirt from the quarterfinal of the FIFA World Cup in 1986, and a special issue of the journal *Soccer and Society* on sounds and things.[17] There are a growing number of studies of the memorialization of great figures in sport, especially through statues.[18] There is also the analysis of the largest piece of material culture associated with sport, the stadium, through in particular Bale's pioneering and seminal work, and his use of topophilia—and topophobia.[19] The material culture of other sports has received even less attention than football. You cannot play cricket without a bat. Or a ball. But of the millions of words written on the cricket, precious little has been written about the two items most central to the sport.

Sport history is engaging with and incorporating popular culture in a number of senses. It appears to be flourishing, while still to a degree feeling somehow outside the mainstream of history. But this development of sport history carries a problem. It is increasingly difficult to keep up with the burgeoning academic literature, even if you are a full-time academic. Thirty years ago, you could conceivably read everything of relevance in the secondary literature, but this is becoming impossible to do. It is the equivalent of the museum bursting at the seams with so many objects that the staff do not know what to do with them all, and most remain unseen, not just by the public but also by the curators. Booth states that his key book *The Field* (2005) was not a review of the literature:

> I make no claim to have read every piece of academic literature in the field. Small as the history of sport may be, the volume of literature is vast and I doubt whether anyone today . . . actually pores over every scholarly article or book.[20]

This is not to say that any of this academic sport history should not have been written. But we must recognize that this explosion in publishing means that today we are in a very different position to historians just twenty or so years ago. Compare the secondary literature Richard Holt was able to draw upon for his book *Sport and the British* (1989) with that for Matthew Taylor for his *The Association Game: A History of British Football* (2008).[21] The burgeoning academic literature means that we simultaneously need more such works of synthesis, even though they are an increasingly greater challenge to write. This includes the need for syntheses across disciplines and reviews of the literature. The *Routledge Companion to Sports History* is particularly useful here, as will be the volume for football.[22]

There is another area of engagement to consider, which is that sport history is *in* popular culture. Academic sport history is only one form of sport history. While some of the burgeoning—increasingly overwhelming—publications on the history of sport may be dubious quality, there is much history of quality outside academia, from journalists, sports club historians, and others. There is also a substantially growing sport history in the form of radio, film, and television documentaries and sport museums in particular. The academic sport historian has a rapidly expanding wealth of literature to keep on top of. The museum sport historian is also expected to be fully aware of the published nonacademic sport history, television documentaries, websites, and blogs *and* keep up with sport history in museums. This is in the form of new sport museums, temporary displays in existing sport museums, and temporary displays and sport history in other museums. This cannot be done from the desk. There is a danger, in both museums and academia, in feeling overwhelmed rather than inspired by the rapidly growing interpretations of sport history.

If we struggle to keep up with it all, there is no chance for a wider, even highly educated, readership. But there is an even bigger problem here. Despite the work of such organizations as ASSH, BSSH, and NASSH in bringing historians together, there is a huge gulf between the academic and the public history of sport. Taking part in a "Public and Popular History" seminar at the University of Cambridge in May 2011 on football history, it was clear that the two respected sports journalists speaking with me, who have both written excellent books on aspects of football's history and popular culture, had no idea that there was *any* significant academic engagement by historians with sport. To them, thirty years of academic sport history may as well just not exist. This is not a result of journalistic arrogance. Whose responsibility is this? If these popular sports historians have not engaged with academics, have the academics engaged with them? There is not a tension in sport history between academic sport history and public sport history, because for there to be a tension, there has to be a connection. And in many senses, there is no connection.

Academic sport history has little impact on popular culture; it is largely unknown. Like it or not, the public perception of sport history is populist works by journalists, television documentaries, museums, and halls of fame. Is this a problem? For whom are academic sports historians writing? If this is just for each other then this is not a problem. But if there is a desire to have a greater impact then this is a problem. Does it matter that the average academic paper is read by only a handful of other scholars? If it is objected that the best academic history has a much greater readership, we are talking sales and readers of at best a few thousand.

Take one example from cultural history. Dave Russell's book *Looking North* (2004) is an excellent piece of scholarship exploring the history of cultural perceptions of the north of England and northern identity. It has sold a few hundred copies. Journalist and broadcaster Stuart Maconie has written *Pies and Prejudice* (2008), a nonacademic book that explores similar themes, which provides fascinating insights into the same subject in a different way, and that has sold over 250,000 copies.[23] There is room for both, but they need to inform and benefit each other. And the success of Maconie's book demonstrates that there is an audience for Russell's work, if only they were aware of it. Academics can also learn about how to communicate to a wider audience from more popular writers. This is equally true in sport history. The book that conveys more to me the essence of football and its history than any academic text is *Football in Sun and Shadow* (1997), by the Uruguayan writer, novelist, and journalist Eduardo Galeano. This is a literary approach to history, similar in style to his epic work on South American history through the retelling of tales, myths, and folklore, the *Memory of Fire* (1982–1986) trilogy.[24]

Academic sport history deserves a wider audience. It has transformed knowledge of the subject. But it has largely only transformed *academic* knowledge of it, not that of a wider audience. They are still largely unaware of it. It has had a little wider public impact. This wider audience deserves to understand this work; this work deserves this wider audience. Scholarly history should not be hidden away in an academic cul-de-sac. An objection may be that this is dumbing down; the subtlety of academic argument will inevitably be lost in more popular, public history. But this need not be the case. Popular history can and should have scholarly rigor. Simon Schama and Niall Ferguson's highly successful television histories do not lack academic rigor. They are a different form of history but still a scholarly one. And they connect a wider audience to scholarly history, leading them to their publications. Sport history deserves this wider audience, this wider engagement. And if the scholars do not get involved in this, then the public history of sport, and the public understanding of sport history, will not be enriched in a way that it could and should be.

Specific Intersections between Sport History and Popular Culture

This second section explores the relationship between academic sport history and sport history in the museum. Sports museums are a relatively recent but burgeoning phenomenon. As I have written elsewhere, there is a slightly uneasy relationship between sport museums and academic sport historians.[25] Here, I will explore what underpins this and consider how more effective relationships may be developed.

Many sport historians might agree that engaging with a wider audience through more popular publications is appropriate. The royalties are certainly much better. And being a television historian will appeal to at least some. But museums may seem like a step too far. A popular book is still written word. A television documentary is like an illustrated lecture. But a museum exhibition appears to be something very different. This was not an issue thirty years ago. While there were some sports museums, they were mainly in North America and were largely Halls of Fame rather than museums. But today sports museums are growing significantly in number, and sport is being reflected more in other history museums and also in science and technology museums and art galleries.

Murray Phillips has developed a very useful typology of sports museums,[26] which in simple terms is:

- Academic: the formal, usually publicly funded museums;
- Corporate: those run by sporting clubs and governing bodies, with some better-termed Halls of Fame;
- Community: the local, largely volunteer-run;
- Vernacular: sporting artifacts in other settings—including equivalents of the Hard Rock Café.

Historically there has been a relative absence of, in Phillips's terms, "academic" sports museums, as I have explored elsewhere. There were clearly issues of social class and cultural value at work here. Museums traditionally were temples of high culture; sport, as part of popular culture, was "other," though there are of course differences between sports. Clearly, there are also specific national cultural factors at play. The National Football Museum for England opened in 2001, the equivalent for the United States in 1979.[27]

Today, we have a growing number of museums that can be described as "academic" in Phillips's typology. Taking just England as an example, in July 2012, the Urbis building in the heart of Manchester's city center became the new public face of the National Football Museum in a £8.5 million development. This is highly symbolic. It is a major step forward in the recognition of the value of sports museums in the UK.

There is also a growing engagement with sport in local history museums. In the UK, this has been developing for a few years, but in 2012 this increased significantly. For the London 2012 Olympics and Paralympics, the Sports Heritage Network developed a project called "Our Sporting Life," to encourage and assist exhibitions of sport history in towns and cities across England. The take up has exceeded all expectations, with over one hundred local sport history exhibition festivals taking place. This will be the largest exhibition festival ever held across England on any subject and conservatively will reach an audience of at least one million people. There is clearly huge, latent public interest in sport history. It is also taking sport history to new audiences, with the exhibitions taking place not just in museums but also in other locations, such as sport and leisure centers, places where people are actively participating in sport.[28]

"Corporate" museums including Halls of Fame are also increasingly popular, but there is a danger that they pander to the nostalgic desires of their audience, or are largely public relations vehicles for sport governing bodies or clubs, and may be prone to bias in favor of the sponsor. They have been of interest to the historian and sociologist as a subject, exploring why sports fans appear to wish to wallow in nostalgia and myth, but otherwise they tend to be ignored, as not providing an "objective" history. However, many employ professionally qualified staff, and it is too simplistic to dismiss all as offering a partial, commercialized history. The concern remains, however, that many are delivering an ersatz sports history to their substantial audiences.[29] "Community" and "vernacular" sport museums have been less considered, but the academic analysis is beginning.[30] "Community" sports museums potentially embrace every sports club in the world, as all tend to display in some form the club's history and achievements.

Sport historians have rightly analyzed and criticized many "corporate" museums, especially Halls of Fame, for offering an overly nostalgic and often highly partial sport history. But many sport historians struggle even with the history in "academic" sport museums, they see the presentation of information as too simplistic and that it fails to demonstrate the subtleties of historical argument.[31] However, museum history is public history, not academic history, and should not be judged in academic terms. Museum history is a different kind of history, in a very different form, for a different audience, with almost no limits of age or educational attainment. Murray Phillips and Richard Tinning have put this very well: "Criticism of museums for lacking detailed historical arguments, for failing to provide complex arguments or for providing minimal contextual material are akin to criticizing written histories for being visually static, or not engaging the senses, or lacking kinesthetic appeal."[32] When some academics have been involved in creating exhibitions, their experiences have often been quite negative because they have not understood the differences. The historian wants to put a book on the wall, does not want to be limited to just two hundred words on a topic, and wishes to qualify each statement.[33] A visitor's experience of a museum is very different from a reader's experience of a book. As John Falk and Lynn Dierking's studies of visitors have found:

> Visitors are strongly influenced by the physical aspects of museums, including the architecture, ambience, smell, sounds, and the "feel" of the place. . . . Visitors encounter an array of experiences from which they select a small number.[34]

Visitors devote most of their time to looking, touching, smelling, and listening, not to reading. Visitors tend not to be very attentive to labels. Unlike a book that one hopes is read all the way through, visitors only sample museums. And at least for first-time and occasional visitors, museum fatigue tends to kick in after only thirty minutes, after which most people switch to a "grazing" mode.[35]

In their favor, museums have a greater range of sources to draw upon and a wider range of interpretive tools, including multimedia. Museums provide a multisensory context through the combination of material culture, sound, film, photography, oral testimonies, stories, interactive experiences, and active participation. Unlike a book, quoting Phillips and Tinning again, "objects are experienced visually as well as through touch, hearing and movement in ways that make the museum exhibition potentially a much more complex interaction with the past than that provided by the written word."[36] At the National Football Museum, you can, for example, handle material culture, take a penalty, dress up, and learn through play.

Scholarly history generally engages only one learning style, the "linguistic," whereas drawing on Howard Gardner's work, museums ideally at least attempt to engage with seven different styles of learning. In addition to the linguistic, they seek to engage with the logical-mathematical, musical, spatial-visual, bodily-kinesthetic, interpersonal, and intrapersonal.[37] Museum visitor studies have shown how powerful in particular smell and taste are in creating involuntary memories, akin to the way a madeleine cake dunked in a cup of tea summoned up for Marcel Proust the world of his childhood in his seven-volume novel series, *À la recherche de temps perdu* (1913–1927):

> And once I recognized the taste of the crumb of madeleine soaked in her decoction of lime-flowers which my aunt used to give me (although I did not yet know and must long postpone the discovery of why this memory made me so happy) immediately the old grey house upon the street, where her room was, rose up like the scenery of a theatre.[38]

It is not just the artifacts and the multisensory nature of the experience that is different about museums. Museum history is also distinctive in that it is a social, interpersonal experience. Most visitors come to the museum as part of a social group, and what visitors see, do, and remember is mediated by that group. To quote from an academic review of the National Football Museum's Preston site,

> [T]he real distinctiveness of museums is that they are physical, and crucially, communal spaces which people inhabit together during their visit. The social nature of museum visiting is important because it entails exchanges and interactions between visitors. . . . The interaction between museum visitors as they respond, not just to the displays but to each other's interpretation of those displays, results in an important exchange of memories and histories between individuals. . . . [M]useum visiting is as much about negotiating and cementing relationships between visitors as it is about seeing material culture.[39]

This can be quite profound. Research into visitor experiences at the National Football Museum found that, for example: "My son, Owen, came with granddad and it gave him a chance to tell Owen about different things and he was in his element and they managed to bond for the first time, and he had something to say that Owen was interested in listening to."[40]

Sport history is usually written by individuals working in solation. Visitors are effectively creating history *together* as they walk around the museum. Because no matter what museums try to convey, "All visitors personalize the museum's message to conform to their own understanding and experience. . . . Each visitor learns in a different way, and interprets through the lens of previous knowledge, experience and beliefs."[41]

Sport history museums therefore face a number of different challenges to written history. They need to engage seven learning styles, not one. They are physical, multisensory experiences. They are a personal experience but usually also a social one. Their primary form of evidence is not the written word but material culture. A further challenge is the nature and scale of the audience. The audience is of all ages and all levels of educational attainment. It is also a sizable audience. Consider writing a piece of text for the new National Football Museum. It is anticipated that the museum will attract 400,000 visitors each year. The minimum expected life span of the main new display is ten years. Potentially, each piece of text will be read by four million people. A label in a case read by only 1 percent of all visitors will still reach forty thousand people.

As Booth has explored the different kinds of academic sport history, so there are different kinds of history in museums, including therefore sport museums, as I have explored elsewhere.[42] However, there is still insufficient debate and analysis regarding the form these histories take. Museum history, including museum sport history, is insufficiently self-reflective nor is there an adequate climate of constructive criticism. Sport museums, being the "new kid on the block" in history museums, and still feeling like outsiders, are especially loath to self-reflect or critically evaluate the work of others. The growing number of informed academic critiques of sport museums and exhibitions is therefore very much to be welcomed.[43] A further challenge is that, unlike an academic text, a museum exhibition of any significant scale does not have a single author or creator. It is the product of the work of often scores of people, in a wide variety of roles. Rarely if ever is there a single script writer or "auteur" director. Museum history by its very nature is highly collaborative. It is more akin to a film than a book but is far more collaborative even than a film.

Museums have to select which histories to communicate to visitors. A museum is not akin to an academic text, even a work of synthesis, nor is it an encyclopedia. It is inevitably a very careful selection and distillation. When the first National Football Museum for England was created in Preston in 2001, it took the classic approach that the staff had researched the subject, distilled that knowledge, and could communicate, to the very best of their ability, the "truth." In the new National Football Museum that opened in Manchester in 2012, the authorial voice has been minimized. The museum's staff is not simply passing their expert knowledge to the visitor. The museum is offering "stories," in the form of quotations,

poems, films, series of images, arrangements of artifacts, and fragments of memories. The museum admits these stories are its selection and creation and that it could
have chosen many others. It is not claiming to be creating a postmodern museum. But
it is creating a museum that is more reflective and honest about how it has created and
selected the histories it is presenting.

So, museums offer a very distinctive form of public history; they require a
different and specific set of skills to write history. But they do need to engage
with scholarly history; they must be informed by the work of academics, to avoid
a cliched, outdated, hackneyed, fact-driven history, based on a limited scholarly
knowledge of the subject, and no appreciation of the subtleties of the argument.
Too many museum histories in the past, including in sport museums, have been
reconstructionist in Booth's sense.[44] Of course, all curators read into the subject but
not to the depth of academics, and they need to have other skills, such as collections
management, and communicating with a very different audience, through a variety
of forms of interpretation, including exhibitions.

Building stronger partnerships between sport museums and academia are therefore vital. The International Centre for Sports History and Culture at De Montfort
University, Leicester, and the Sports Heritage Network secured funding from the
Arts and Humanities Research Council (AHRC) to bring together academics with
an interest in sport history and museum practitioners in the UK, for a series of semi-
nars, and this has led to a publication.[45] But, equally importantly, it will lead to new
ways of working between academia and museums. The National Football Museum
has a research partnership with the University of Central Lancashire, the International Football Institute, headed by Professor John Hughson, and this has a number
of research projects, including one funded by the AHRC, exploring the cultural role
of sport museums. A further step is for academics to be actively engaged in exhibitions. For example, as part of an AHRC-funded PhD project, Alex Jackson led the
creation of an exhibition at the National Football Museum on his research. Marion
Leonard of the University of Liverpool cocurated a major exhibition on popular music for National Museums Liverpool and has written about the issues and challenges
of this form of collaboration, which has strong resonances with sport.[46]

But in coming to museum history, sport historians need to understand the particular
challenges of interpreting artifacts. They need to get away from an approach based on
written sources. Approaches to the study of material culture have come in large part
from archaeology, where there is very often no surviving written evidence, only material evidence. Material culture studies as a result have always tended to be open to a
more diverse range of theoretical perspectives, to try to decode the artifact. As I and
others have explored, history from things is a very different history.[47] We must also be
aware of the cultural differences toward material culture. To quote from the first panel
of an exhibition at Brisbane Museum on the culture of the Torres Strait Islanders in
2011: "Torres Strait Islanders believe their objects are imbued with the spirituality of
their creator and the wisdom of their ancestor."[48]

Sports museums are not just institutions for academics to analyze as a research topic,
valuable though this is for both academia and museums. Sport museums are an exciting location for potential collaboration in the exploration of sport history, in new ways.

Sport History, Popular Culture, and Public Intellectuals

What is the purpose of sport history and when might it come to an end? This is not in the "end of history" sense or of sport history transforming into sport studies, as ASSH discussed at its conference in 1999. I have posed the scenario that an individual museum may achieve its mission and that therefore it should dissolve itself. Indeed, that museums, as modernist institutions par excellence, may prove to be a peculiarly nineteenth- and twentieth-century institution and may have served their purpose. The end of the museum may be in sight. The interaction between people and material culture may continue but in a completely new form.[49] It is in this sense that I pose the end of sport history. For example, ASSH has a mission statement. Missions can be completed and so ASSH may one day decide to dissolve itself. Sport history could end in its current form or transform into something radically different. Of course, sport itself may come to an end, and we will have no further history to consider. In which case, sport historians may redouble their efforts to trawl back through history, to find earlier forms of activity that they may redefine as sport or proto-sport.

What is it that sport historians are collectively trying to achieve? Where is the subject going next? It might be objected that having a "mission" for sport historians as a collective is far too prescriptive. While we as individuals may be working collegiately within the field, are we actually working together to a specific agenda at all? And should we be? ASSH has a mission statement. But this is a broad statement of purpose. It does not formally give any particular direction; it is an umbrella to embrace all, as of equal value. We may be loosely affiliated to bodies such as ASSH, but the mission we are actually working toward, however loosely, is that of the organization that pays our wages, whether it is a university, a museum, or other.

But should sport historians collectively have an aspiration or aspirations for the future of the subject? Without this, is there a danger of fragmentation? One view may be that sport history needs to carve out its territory, have a clear purpose, and establish a niche. Conversely, a view may be that this risks marginalization from mainstream history. But might integration into mainstream history lead to the end of a specific sport history?

Sport history began, so there is no reason why sport history will not come to an end. It takes a particular kind of arrogance to argue for perpetual continuity. So how could sport history come to an end? When sport history began, it was hard to justify studying sport, particularly in academia, it was seen as somehow inappropriate, too frivolous, a hobby, not an appropriate academic pursuit. This perception has not entirely gone away. So, sport history (and sociology) was justified in part by what it could reveal about much more generally accepted issues as gender, social class, and ethnicity, rather than the study of sport per se. Studying football fans was not acceptable. Studying hooligans was acceptable because it was solving a social problem, and such research received substantial funding on this basis.

The danger of this is that: first, the social problem, such as hooliganism, passes, or is no longer of public or media interest even if it still exits; and second, that other areas of study may, or may be seen to, address issues such as gender, social class, and ethnicity, in a more productive way. If sport history is a lens, a prism to understand issues of social class, gender, ethnicity then what happens when another lens seems to provide a better focus for such issues? Social history has moved on in this way. Sports historians should not be defensive about studying sport per se. They should be studying sport in terms of issues of gender, class, ethnicity, and so on, drawing on the valuable theoretical perspectives of, for example, feminism. However, I do not believe such issues need to be used as a kind of "cover" for studying sport, which somehow otherwise might still be seen as too trivial. For example, studies such as Jonathan Wilson's book on the history of football tactics are to be greatly welcomed, for this is not considered in isolation, it explores how tactics have been shaped by economic, social, and cultural forces acting on the game.[50] History may simply move on from sport not because of any significant academic rationale, or an ideological reason, but simply because of fads and fashions, to which it cannot be denied that academic history is prone.

So, what is it that sport historians are currently trying to achieve, if only loosely collegiately? Is the goal simply to have more and more written sport history, with an increasing range of subjects and approaches, drawing upon and linking with an ever-increasing range of other disciplines, using an ever-growing range of theoretical approaches, embracing postmodernism, and continuing in this vein? This is just a mission of continuity. Within an academic environment, it may meet the needs of the institutions, in terms of a research assessment exercise and bringing in funding. There is a danger that from the outside looking in, this can look like an intellectual game. The public understands academics who are seeking to solve a social or economic problem. They perhaps do not understand academics studying sport history. There is a danger that the public elides sport history with the kind of cultural studies of sport that get pilloried in the popular press, "Beckham studies" as they have been termed. And so, sport history is tarred with the same brush. While academic sport history is increasingly accepted in universities, it still has some way to go even here. And it is not as yet accepted in the popular imagination.

Using Booth's typology, and simplifying greatly, reconstructionist sport history has no agenda but reconstruction, this is an end in itself. Constructionist sport history has an agenda, in that it is driven by a particular ideological position.[51] But potentially this could lead to an argument that to explore history from that ideological position, topics other than sport could be more valuably studied. For the reconstructionists and constructionists, postmodern sport history has been like opening Pandora's Box. They knew where they were and then postmodern sport history has led to the questioning of everything. To the postmodern sport historians, it is not opening Pandora's box but letting the genie out of the bottle and opening up a fabulous range or *mélange* of possibilities. Yet, what though, precisely, is the ultimate purpose of postmodern sport history?

I once lost my faith in history. And I used the word "faith" deliberately. It was after I read Milan Kundera's novel, *The Unbearable Lightness of Being* (1985):

[A] life which disappears once and for all, which does not return, is like a shadow, without weight, dead in advance, and whether it was horrible, beautiful, or sublime, its horror, sublimity, and beauty mean nothing. We need take no more note of it than of a war between two African kingdoms in the fourteenth century, a war that achieved nothing in the destiny of the world, even if a hundred thousand black people perished in excruciating torment.[52]

This was not a postmodern novel leading me to question whether it was possible to write history at all. It was a deeper question, as to whether, even if it was possible, history had any purpose at all. Unless, as Kundera posits, one ascribes to Nietzsche's philosophic provocation of eternal return, in which case history has weight because it recurs ad infinitum.

How did I come back from this? In many senses, I have not fully, because although I am engaged academically, I have largely worked subsequently in public history. Here, I see a more direct need and a more instrumental outcome. For example, the National Football Museum, through its learning projects, has improved the life chances of disadvantaged youngsters. Football is a powerful hook to engage their interest. But enabling the public to explore the history of football in the museum has an *intrinsic* and democratic value.

Why do we do what we do? How can we justify researching, writing, and interpreting sport history? In my view, sport history needs a clearer purpose. And sport historians need to have a much more public role, as public intellectuals. An analogy is the academic curators working within major national museums, such as the British Museum and the Natural History Museum in the UK. While there has always been a greater expectation for them to engage in public history than academics in universities, they previously had a great deal of freedom in what to choose to study. Now their work, even that which might be described as purely academic, and not for a wider audience, has to fit much more closely to the mission statement of their institutions. This is not seen as a constraint on academic freedom but an appropriate direction to their work based on public need and providing a clearer, more relevant social purpose for what they do.

This is not just about engaging with a wider audience, useful though this would be. It is also about having a social impact. In my view, sport historians should have an impact on society today; they should have an impact on sport today. Sport needs to learn lessons from its own past. Who else but sport historians can try to make this happen? Objections to this will be that being a "public" intellectual is very difficult, particularly in sport, as Alan Bairner has explored.[53] However, many of those in sports administration at the top level are deeply personally interested in sport history. And this is not about developing blueprints for the development of a sport; this public intellectual engagement is perhaps more along the lines of the "soft driver" "Postmodern boosterism" suggested by John Hughson and Geoffery Kohe.[54]

Sport history should have an impact, on sport, on society. This is not a Marxist call that the philosophers have only interpreted the world; the point is to change it because ideologically sport historians will not agree with each other as to the impact they wish to have. But there is a responsibility as a sport historian to try to engage with sport and to try to engage with a wider, nonacademic audience. Academic sport history projects should at least consider having a popular audience outcome, or contributing to one. Some academics naturally cross over; have this ability to communicate with a wider audience. If there is one book by an academic that educated football fans have read about the game, and enjoyed, it is *The Soccer Tribe* by Desmond Morris—and this was published in 1981. Matthew Taylor has followed his landmark academic study of British football with an excellent, short (sixty-four-page) popular publication.[55]

Murray Phillips has written that "postmodern history promotes the idea of historians writing in the first person, of playing with the voices of historical figures, of utilizing the language and imagery of fiction, comic strips, poetry and tarot cards, of representing the past through humour, mystery, parody and pastiche."[56] It is also time to look at moving away from relying purely on the written word as the form of communication for scholarly sport history. In 1997 I wrote, "I look forward to the possibility in the not too distant future of producing a version of this book in multimedia form."[57] Postmodern sport history will surely embrace such new forms of communication. Academic outputs do not always have to be written texts. Academic historians in other fields are leading the way in this. One example is the work of Scott Anthony of the University of Cambridge, working with the British Film Institute (BFI) on documentary film, which has taken the form of screenings, curatorial projects, book and DVD releases, and an interactive educational documentary.[58]

If Niall Ferguson can convince commissioners to make a major television series that is a partial defense of the British Empire[59] then sport would seem an easier pitch to make. Sport is potentially such an attractive subject matter to the media. Of course, all sport historians cannot or do not want to aspire to be Niall Ferguson or Simon Schama, but the impact of their television work cannot be denied. The explosion in new media means that there is no barrier of a television program budget to be able to communicate in this way. Radio is also a much cheaper option. The International Centre for Sports History and Culture at De Montfort University collaborated with BBC Radio 4 on a major thirty-part series on the history of British sport, *Sport and the British*, which was broadcast to great acclaim in the spring of 2012. This more collaborative type of project avoids the criticism that major television histories such as those by Ferguson and Schama are too much the cult of individuals, providing one viewpoint, and not enabling the public to understand wider debates. Academic sport historians can and should in my view engage with the public in different ways, through radio, television, DVDs, blogs, and social media.

This is still fairly reliant on the written word. Even a television film tends to be an illustrated lecture. Postmodern history is still *written* history, even if it may stray into drama, it still relies on language, with all its limitations, as Robert Rinehart has discussed.[60] Perhaps, a truly postmodern history would be multisensory. It could be an exhibition. There is a growing engagement between artists and history museums, artists offering a new perspective interpreting artifacts in new ways. Sport historians might consider curating an exhibition, in collaboration with a museum, based on the study of the visual and material culture of sport. This might be an interactive experience, using light, sound, touch, taste, and smell.

Such collaboration may also encourage sport museums to be braver than they have been to date. Sport museums have not broken away from an over reliance on communicating through the written word. This is not the end of the written history in academia or museums; far from it. But it is a call to embrace and explore new ways of communicating sport history, in new collaborations, to new and much more diverse audiences.

KEYWORDS: PUBLIC HISTORY, SPORT HISTORY, POPULAR CULTURE, HERITAGE, MUSEUMS

NOTES

1. Correspondence to kevin.moore@nationalfootballmuseum.com.Spring 2013.

2. http://www2.hud.ac.uk/mhm/history/research/conferences/future-sport-history-academia.php [July 17, 2011].

3. Ibid.

4. Douglas Booth, *The Field: Truth and Fiction in Sport History* (Abingdon: Routledge, 2005).

5. Kevin Moore, *Museums and Popular Culture* (Leicester: Leicester University Press, 1997), 1–4.

6. Germaine Greer, "Football Counts As Culture Just As Much As Opera Does," *Guardian* (Manchester), March 24, 2008, http://www.guardian.co.uk/music/musicblog/2008/mar/24/footballcountsasculturejus [March 3, 2013].

7. John Bale and Anthony Bateman, eds., *Sporting Sounds: Relationships between Sport and Music* (Abingdon: Routledge, 2010); Dave Russell, "Abiding Memories: The Community Singing Movement and English Social Life in the 1920s," *Popular Music* 27 (2008): 117–33.

8. See, in particular, Douglas Booth and Murray G. Phillips, eds., *Sporting Traditions*, special issue: "Sport History and the Cultural Turn" 27 (2010); John Hughson, *The Making of Sporting Cultures* (Abingdon: Routledge, 2009); and John Hughson, David Inglis, and Marcus Free, *The Uses of Sport: A Critical Study* (Abingdon: Routledge, 2005).

9. John Bale, *Anti-Sport Sentiments in Literature: Batting for the Opposition* (London: Psychology Press, 2008); Andy Miller, *Tilting at Windmills: How I Tried to Stop Worrying and Love Sport* (London: Penguin, 2003).

10. Pierre Chazaud, *Art et Football. Football and Art. 1860–1960* (Touland: Mandala Edition, 1998); Peter Kuhnst, *Sports: A Cultural History in the Mirror of Art* (London: Gordon & Breach Science Publishers Ltd., 1996); Mike Huggins, "The Sporting Gaze: Towards a Visual Turn in Sports History," in *L'Art et Le Sport: Actes du XII colloque International Du CESH*, ed. Laurent Daniel (2007): 115–32; idem, "The Sporting Gaze: Towards a Visual Turn in Sports History—Documenting Art and Sport," *Journal of Sport History* 35 (2008): 311–29; Mike O'Mahony, *Sport in the USSR: Physical Culture—Visual Culture* (London: Reaktion Books Ltd., 2006); idem, *Olympic Visions: Images of the Games through History* (London: Reaktion Books Ltd., 2012).

11. John Hughson, "The Cultural Legacy of Olympic Posters," *Sport in Society* 13 (2010): 749–59; idem, "Not Just Any Wintry Afternoon in England: The Curious Contribution of C.R.W. Nevinson to 'Football Art,'" *International Journal of the History of Sport* 28 (2011): 2670–87; idem, "An Invitation to 'Modern' Melbourne: The Historical Significance of Richard Beck's Olympic Poster Design," *Journal of Design History* 25 (2012): 268–84; Joyce Woolridge, "Cover Stories: English Football Magazine Cover Portrait Photographs 1950–1975," *Sport in History* 30 (2010): 523–46.

12. Tara Brabazon, *Playing on the Periphery: Sport, Identity and Memory* (Abingdon: Routledge, 2006), 7–40.

13. Booth, *The Field*, 289.

14. Moore, *Museums and Popular Culture*, 121–23; Susan M. Pearce, *Museums, Objects and Collections: A Cultural Study* (Leicester: Leicester University Press, 1992), 7.

15. Moore, *Museums and Popular Culture*, 121–23, 122 [quotation].

16. Alexander Jackson, "The Baines Card and Its Place in Boys' Popular Culture between 1887 and 1922," in *Recording Leisure Lives: Histories, Archives and Memories of Leisure in 20th Century Britain*, eds. Robert Snape and Helen Pussard (Brighton: Leisure Studies Association, 2009), 47–72; idem, "Sporting Cartoons and Cartoonists in Edwardian Manchester: Amos Ramsbottom and His Imps," *Manchester Region History Review* 20 (2009): 68–90; idem, "The Chelsea Chronicle, 1905–1913," *Soccer and Society* 11 (2010): 506–21.

17. Martin Atherton, *The Theft of the Jules Rimet Trophy: The Hidden History of the 1966 World Cup in England* (Aachen: Meyer and Meyer, 2008); John Hughson and Kevin Moore, "'Hand of God,' Shirt of the Man: The Materiality of Diego Maradona," *Costume: The Journal of the Costume Society* 46 (2012): 212–25; Kath Woodward and David Goldblatt, "Special Issue: Football, Sounds and Things," *Soccer Society* 12 (2011): 1–141.

18. Gary Osmond, Murray G. Phillips, and Mark E. O'Neill, "'Putting Up Your Dukes': Social Memory and Duke Paoa Kahanamoku," *International Journal of the History of Sport* 23 (2006): 82–103; Dave Russell, "'We All Agree, Name the Stand after Shankley': Cultures of Commemoration in Late Twentieth-century English Football Culture," *Sport in History* 26 (2006): 1–25; Maureen Margaret Smith, "Mapping America's Sporting Landscape: A Case Study of Three Statues," *International Journal of the History of Sport* 28 (2011): 1252–68.

19. See, for example, John Bale, *Sport, Space, and the City* (Abingdon: Routledge, 1993).

20. Booth, *The Field*, 20.

21. Richard Holt, *Sport and the British: A Modern History* (Oxford: Oxford University Press, 1989); Matthew Taylor, *The Association Game: A History of British Football* (London: Longman, 2008).

22. Steven Pope and John Nauright, eds., *Routledge Companion to Sports History* (Abingdon: Routledge, 2010); John Hughson et al., eds., *Routledge Companion to Football History* (Abingdon: Routledge, forthcoming).

23. Dave Russell, *Looking North: Northern England and the National Imagination* (Manchester: Manchester University Press, 2004); Stuart Maconie, *Pies and Prejudice: In Search of the North* (London: Ebury Press, 2008).

24. Eduardo Galeano, *Football in Sun and Shadow* (London: Fourth Estate, 1997).

25. Kevin Moore, "Foreword," in *Representing the Sporting Past in Museums and Halls of Fame*, ed. Murray G. Phillips (Abingdon: Routledge, 2012), xi–xv.

26. Murray G. Phillips, "Introduction: Historians in Sport Museums," in *Representing the Sporting Past*, ed. Phillips, 1–21.

27. Kevin Moore, "Sport in Museums and Museums of Sport," in *Sport, History and Heritage: An Investigation into the Public Representation of Sport*, eds. Jeffrey Hill, Kevin Moore, and Jason Wood (Woodbridge: Boydell and Brewer, 2012), 93–106.

28. Moore, "Sport in Museums," 95.

29. Victor Danilov, *Sports Museums and Halls of Fame Worldwide* (Jefferson, NC: McFarland and Co., 2005); Moore, "Sport in Museums," 93–106; E. E. Snyder, "Sociology of Nostalgia: Sports Halls of Fame and Museums in America," *Sociology of Sport Journal* 8 (1991): 228–38.

30. Phillips, *Representing the Sporting Past*.

31. See the discussions in Wray Vamplew, "Facts and Artefacts: Sports, Historians and Sports Museums," *Journal of Sport History* 25 (1998): 268–79; and idem, "Taking a Gamble or a Racing Certainty: Sports, Museums and Public History," *Journal of Sport History* 31 (2004): 177–92.

32. Murray G. Phillips and Richard Tinning, "'Not Just a Book on the Wall': Pedagogical Work, Museums and Representing the Sporting Past," *Sport Education and Society* 16 (2011): 63.

33. Vamplew, "Taking a Gamble," 183.

34. John H. Falk and Lynn D. Dierking, *The Museum Experience*, 2nd ed. (Walnut Creek, CA: Left Coast Press, 2011), 147–48.

35. Falk and Dierking, *The Museum Experience*, 67–81.

36. Phillips and Tinning, "'Not Just,'" 62.

37. Howard Gardner, *Frames of Mind: The Theory of Multiple Intelligence* (New York: Basic Books, 1993).

38. Marcel Proust, *Remembrance of Things Past* (London: Wordsworth Classics of World Literature, 2006), 1: 63.

39. Martin Johnes and Rhiannon Mason, "Soccer, Public History and the National Football Museum," *Sport in History* 23 (2003): 120–21.

40. *Visitor Research Report*, 2010, vol. 17, p. 12, Archives, National Football Museum, Manchester, U.K.

41. Falk and Dierking, *The Museum Experience*, 138–42, 136–38 [QUOTATION].

42. Moore, *Museums and Popular Culture*, 32–51.

43. See, for example, Daryl Adair, "When the Games Never Cease: The Olympic Museum in Lausanne, Switzerland," in *Sport Tourism: Interrelationships, Impacts and Issues*, eds. Brent W. Richie and Daryl Adair (Clevedon: Channel View Publications, 2004), 46–76; Tara Brabazon, *Playing on the Periphery: Sport, Identity and Memory* (Abingdon: Routledge, 2006); idem, "Museums and Popular Culture Revisited: Kevin Moore and the Politics of Pop," *Museum Management and Curatorship* 21 (2006): 283–301; Tara Brabazon and Stephen Mallinder, "Popping the Museum: The Cases of Sheffield and Preston," *Museum and Society* 4 (2006): 96–112; Warwick Frost, "The Sustainability of Sports Heritage Attractions: Lessons from the Australian Football League Hall of Fame," *Journal of Sport Tourism* 10 (2005): 295–305; Johnes and Mason, "Soccer, Public History and the National Football Museum"; Geoffery Z. Kohe, "Civic Representations of Sport History: The New Zealand Sports Hall of Fame," *Sport in Society* 13 (2010): 1498–515; Kevin Moore, "Sports Heritage and the Re-imaged City: The National Football Museum, Preston," *International Journal of Cultural Policy* 14 (2008): 445–61; Gary Osmond and Murray G. Phillips, "Enveloping the Past: Sport Stamps, Visuality and Museums," *International Journal of the History of Sport* 28 (2011): 1138–55; Phillips and Tinning, "'Not Just'"; Murray G. Phillips, "A Historian in the Museum: Story Spaces and Australia's Sporting Past," *Australian Historical Studies* 41 (2010): 396–408; idem, *Representing the Sporting Past*; and Gregory Ramshaw, "Living Heritage and the Sports Museum: Athletes, Legacy and the Olympic Hall of Fame and Museum, Canada Olympic Park," *Journal of Sport Tourism* 15 (2010): 45–70.

44. Booth, *The Field*, 25–42.

45. Hill, Moore, and Wood, eds., *Sport, History and Heritage*.

46. Marion Leonard, "Constructing Histories through Material Culture: Popular Music, Museums and Collecting," *Popular Music History* 2 (2007): 147–67.

47. Moore, *Museums and Popular Culture*; Steven Lubar and W. David Kingery, *History from Things: Essays on Material Culture* (Washington, D.C.: Smithsonian Institution Press, 1993).

48. Introductory panel, exhibition, "Torres Strait Islands: A Celebration," 2011, South Bank, South Brisbane, Queensland, Australia.

49. Moore, *Museums and Popular Culture*, 28–31.

50. Jonathan Wilson, *Inverting the Pyramid: The History of Football Tactics* (London: Orion, 2008).

51. Booth, *The Field*, 48–58.

52. Milan Kundera, *The Unbearable Lightness of Being* (London: Faber and Faber, 1985), 3.

53. Alan Bairner, "Sport, Intellectuals and Public Sociology: Obstacles and Opportunities," *International Review for the Sociology of Sport* 44 (2008): 115–30.

54. John Hughson and Geoffery Z. Kohe, "'Get into the Groove': Travelling Otago's Super-region," *Sport in Society* 13 (2010): 1552–66.

55. Desmond Morris, *The Soccer Tribe* (London: Cape, 1981); Taylor, *The Association Game*; idem, *Football: A Short History* (Oxford: Shire Library, 2011).

56. Murray G. Phillips, ed., *Deconstructing Sport History: A Postmodern Analysis* (Albany, NY: State University of New York Press, 2005), 250.

57. Moore, *Museums and Popular Culture*, ix.

58. See, for example, BFI, *Archive Interactive: Derek Jacobi on the GPO Film Unit* (London: BFI, 2008); and BFI, *The General Post Office Film Unit Collection Vol. 2—We Live In Two Worlds DVD* (London: BFI, 2009), further details at: http://www.hist.cam.ac.uk/directory/sma57@cam.ac.uk [20 December 2012].

59. *Empire*, Channel 4 (U.K.), 2003, linked to Niall Ferguson, *Empire: How Britain Made the Modern World* (London: Allen Lane, 2003).

60. Robert E. Rinehart, "Beyond Traditional Sports Historiography: Toward a Historical 'Holograph,'" in *Deconstructing Sport History*, ed. Phillips, 181–201.

Chapter One

Stepping Up to the Plate

Interpreting Sports with Well-Rounded Exhibits

Kristin L. Gallas

Clear away the cobwebs of nostalgia and mythology in sports. What do we see? We see real human beings engaged in physical feats: nothing more, nothing less. They are just like us, yet we want to be them. But, most of us don't want to be them when they fall outside the boundaries of our mythical hero worship, tightly drawn frame of what an athlete "should" be. This mythology says that if someone performs amazing physical feats, they must therefore be an amazing person. As New York Times sports columnist Ira Berkow writes, "There are those who believe that star athletes are endowed with lofty character by virtue of their athletic prowess."[1] When a society begins to elevate an athlete above others, his or her mystique of infallibility grows, and the athlete can do no wrong. One misstep by an athlete (such as engaging in protests, adultery, gambling, or excessive drinking), often results in public ridicule and shame, and sometimes a disappearance into oblivion altogether. What happens to the person when his or her human reality differs from the idyllic model of the hero athlete? What if they are gay, differently abled, Black, or a hijab-wearing woman? What if their actions precipitate a fall from grace? Can the society hold a "both/and" ideal for an athlete? Museums and historic sites can play a role by using sports as a lens through which society can explore the multidimensional lives of athletes and their identities, build a more inclusive narrative that includes context, humanity, and agency, and present a space where a sports figure's value lives beyond their on-field accomplishments.

Key Interpretive Concepts

1. *Context—Sports do not exist in a vacuum*: Putting athletes, teams, or sporting events, in historical and geographic context gives the story more meaning and definition.
2. *Humanity—Athletes are more than their scores*: Honor the athlete's identity to give visitors a robust understanding of the person.
3. *Agency—Athletic skills are not the only form of agency*: Athletes wield tremendous power on and off the court, field, or rink.

Sports figures generally either fall into the mythical categories of hero or failure—the popular narrative leaves little room for alternatives. Though these two traditional sports narratives—hero worship or the fall from grace—may appear contradictory, they are actually two sides of the same coin. These narratives reinforce an unrealistic, all-or-nothing ideal. The engaged public typically remembers sports figures for successes or failures, a construct that usually does not include the context of time, place, or history. This personal struggle is often lost or ignored, and if not, it fits into one of the tried-and-true heroic narratives: as an athlete's triumph over poverty, sacrificing a childhood to train for the Olympics, or the magnanimous team owner who supports many charities. These tropes, what I would refer to as the "glorified narrative," are so tied to a collective identity that we are often unable to separate what it means to be an American from what it means to be a success.

The glorified narrative and the inclusive narrative are not necessarily mutually exclusive. Heroic stories regale the highs of the human experience and demonstrate the infinite possibilities of mind, body, and spirit. It is important to remember that while the glorified narrative sometimes belies the truth, often it is not wrong. It is instead incomplete and needs to be balanced and nuanced with the athlete's humanity.

Museums can, and must, make public space for deeper and broader sports narratives and connections. They can best portray a 360° view of an athlete, sport, or team; to tell a richer, more nuanced story. Museums are creating multidimensional exhibits that shed light on exalted and complicated people. President Lincoln's Cottage in Washington, D.C., for example, does not shy away from discussing Lincoln's initial reluctance to abolition and his emotionally fraught personal life. In Pittsburgh, the Andy Warhol Museum portrays all sides of the artist—from his health issues to homosexuality—and contextualizes his artwork with the external influences in his life. So, why do so many sports museums insist on showing just one side of a story?

The Role of Identity in Interpretation

As a culture, we can, and should, pull back the curtain and explore more than just the heroic accomplishments of athletes and/or teams. One way to do this is by exploring identity. Individual identity is a construct of many (real and perceived) memberships in social groups and structures. We self-identify with groups; others put us into them. Using the following categories as a reference point, consider how you describe your identity:

- Race, ethnicity, nationality
- Religion
- Gender identity, sexual orientation
- Family
- Class
- Education
- Mental or physical health
- Immigration or citizenship status
- Community or region in which you were raised
- Generation or defining historical episodes (e.g., September 11, 2001; the Kennedy assassination; the fall of the Berlin Wall; etc.)

Each person views the world from a unique perspective, one that often does not reflect the complex totality of the world at large. Our identities—what we were born as, what we chose to be, or what others perceive us as—shape how we see the world. "It is through narrative," American sociologist Margaret R. Somers writes, "that we come to know, understand, and make sense of the social world, and it is through narratives and narrativity that we constitute our social identities [and] come to be who we are."[2] As a white, middle-class, well-educated, Episcopalian, cisgender woman raised in Vermont, my nascent worldview was shaped by the biases incumbent on these traits. I was exposed to certain narratives that led me to believe the world existed in a particular way. These identity narratives shaped who I was and what I understood about the world. When I started meeting other people with different identities and narratives, I began to understand that my way was not the only way to be in the world. I have spent my museum career trying to help others see the complexity of humanity and how individuals' stories feed the multifaceted narrative of the United States.

To grasp the complexity of our world, and the athletes who live in it, we should start by examining various paths to sports narratives. Sports history directly intersects with the crux of American history. It touches all of the bases of social and political history: race, gender, ethnicity, politics, and class. Examining the multiple dimensions of athletes' identities, including how they got to where they are and who and what shapes their world outlook, provides a rich tapestry from which to garner deeper meaning on the impact of their success or failures. A comprehensive outlook of the historical context of a sport, a team, or an athlete leads to a better understanding of a community's collective history and how it shaped (and shapes) culture. The bottom line is that a single individual's identity or worldview—the stories we tell ourselves and the ways we perceive others—is not the *only* truth. Everyone has his or her unique truth, one intertwined with personal identity. We must all be open to new identities for ourselves, and others, so that we can see the world in all its vivid colors. Sport provides a way to do just that.

Put the Athlete in Context

In order to fully glean the various meanings of a sport, an athlete, a coach, a team, or the outcome of a competition, museums must contextualize these topics within time, space, and culture, as well as in the frame of American and world history. Because an athlete's identity and actions are shaped by the world around him or her, museum audiences cannot best understand sports history in the absence of historical context. Museums are great third-party spaces in which to hold these conversations and the perfect venues for providing context. Although museums should not claim neutrality, they are full of material that provides a more robust portrayal of an athlete or sport.[3] Sports uniforms and equipment, letters and diaries, guidebooks and sports advice manuals, advertisements, artifacts, images, the built environment, and other material culture resources can give perspective on a life and times.[4] Setting sports in context is a way for visitors to understand how the world is interconnected, demonstrating how society influences sports, and vice versa.

An exploration of former National Football League (NFL) quarterback Colin Kaepernick's 2017 decision to kneel as the National Anthem was played before games offers one starting point for exploring the context in sport. Without explanation,

Kaepernick's choice ignited a countrywide debate regarding the bounds of American patriotism, nationalism, racism, and capitalism. As a biracial person, the son of an African American father and white mother, his rationale resonated with many. "I am not going to stand up to show pride in a flag for a country that oppresses Black people and people of color," he said. "To me, this is bigger than football and it would be selfish on my part to look the other way. There are bodies in the street and people getting paid leave and getting away with murder."[5] After sitting on the bench during the National Anthem for several games, Kaepernick and his teammate Eric Reid rethought their protest and started to kneel.

> After hours of careful consideration, and even a visit from Nate Boyer, a retired Green Beret and former NFL player, we came to the conclusion that we should kneel, rather than sit, the next day during the anthem as a peaceful protest. We chose to kneel because it's a respectful gesture. I remember thinking our posture was like a flag flown at half-mast to mark a tragedy.[6]

To many Americans embroiled in this debate, the athlete's decision to kneel was simply an act of disrespect that cast a dark and deep shadow on long-held American values. To Kaepernick and his teammates, kneeling during the national anthem served as a thoroughly considered act of protest that both upheld and challenged the nation's core ideals in hopes of igniting progress.

Museums and historic sites may be tempted to avoid exhibiting a controversial sports landmine such as the Kaepernick kneeling controversy; yet should consider the ways in which sites of public memory are responsible for engaging with meaningful topics. If an institution were to feature Kaepernick in an exhibit, his legacy would ring hollow without this culturally significant and career-defining moment. His actions did not make sense to many and highlighted an ongoing, deeply complex cultural conversation—escalating into a verbal dart-throwing contest that played out on television news outlets and social media. This backdrop further emboldened Kaepernick's beliefs and choices, as well as those of the people protesting his actions. Yet, none of this can be separated from an understanding of Kaepernick's place in the landscape of professional football without risking a whitewashing of the historical narrative. A blanket statement that Kaepernick disrespected the military by not standing for the anthem would ignore the nuance of the ways in which the military orchestrates the connection between the National Anthem, military support, and the NFL. Museums can contextualize public rejection of his protest as unpatriotic with the story of how the roots of the American ritual of playing the National Anthem before sporting events date to World War I.[7] They can also use the NFL's relationship with the United States military, noting how, between 2011 and 2014 the U.S. Department of Defense paid fourteen NFL teams $5.4 million to put on "elaborate, 'patriotic salutes' to the military . . . [essentially, the government was paying for] marketing and advertising contracts with professional sports teams."[8] While exhibiting controversially contested content might invite the types of emotional responses that surrounded the original debate, museums and historic sites carry a civic responsibility to engage and further discussions of cultural import.

As public historians, we can help visitors understand how sports fit into the broader picture of American and world history. In her essay, "Evening the Score: Interpreting the History of Women and Sports," Elizabeth L. Maurer contextualizes female athletes and their access to sports within the confines of the cultural, economic, social, and political barriers they overcame. "When contemporary women learn that most of American history was ridden with cultural ideals that portrayed competition as unfeminine, they more effectively confront the residual social stigma associated with being a competitive woman."[9] By putting women and their sporting achievements in context, visitors can better understand how the athletes fit within the larger American story. Museums and history organizations must apply this concept to any demographic, community identifier, or cultural representation.

Focus on the Athlete's Humanity

Our identity, and the identities of athletes or teams we follow, is comprised of many characteristics, all of which form our own unique brand of humanity. American culture, however, often demands perfection, which is the antithesis of allowing people to be "human" with flawed personalities and imperfect actions. In American culture, a hero is often seen as someone with a flawless countenance and extraordinary ability. The mystique that accompanies these exceptional skills also carries grand expectations. As writer Becky Lee states, "In exchange for athletic prowess, [Americans] create a different standard of humanness."[10] Are humans and heroes mutually exclusive or can our heroes be human too?

When museums consider including the stories of athletes in exhibits and programs, they should give thought to who, what, and how we interpret them. Society often expects athletes to fall into the "norm" (i.e., white, straight, able-bodied, and male), to perform beyond expectations, or act as a representative of their entire community. But we should realize nearly *all* people participate in sports and highlight the stories of humanity and integrity in every athlete. This reflects a more thorough portrayal of the United States (or local communities)—diverse in ethnicities, abilities, gender, sexuality, and so on. Thus, by using sport as a window to view a broader perspective, more visitors will be able to see themselves in an exhibit or program while building empathy with the athletes, and the institution becomes more relevant.

Revealing the humanity of sports figures allows people to connect with them on a more holistic level. The Museum of disABILITY History in Buffalo, New York, provides one example in that it strives to showcase the "participation of individuals with disabilities in sports and recreation as well as the development of adaptive sport."[11] By depicting people of all ability levels, the museum shows how an athlete represents more than just success athletically. For example, a visitor with a physical disability might not be able to make a deep personal connection with National Baseball Hall of Fame and Museum pitcher Sandy Koufax. However, when learning that pitcher Jim Abbott was born without a right hand and was still able to win eighty-seven Major League games (and even hit a home run), that same visitor can identify with universal themes found in stories of human struggle.

Seeing the whole of a sports figure's personhood means inviting comprehensive narratives that offer a deeper and expanded view of humanity. In her essay, "Striking Out: Museums Aren't Interpreting Queer Sports History . . . But They Should Be," Sarah E. Calise calls out the "glaringly obvious lack of queer representation" at sports museums nationwide. Calise expertly speaks to the vital importance of proactively exhibiting LGBT+ narratives, for the sake of inclusivity, and collective cultural accuracy.[12] The Kansas African American Museum's exhibit, *Undefeated: The Triumph of the Black Kansas Athlete*, provided visitors an opportunity to connect with a human story, not just the sports story. By depicting how Black athletes and their white coaches occupied the moral high ground when integrating sports in the Sunflower State, the exhibit highlighted universal themes of human struggle, race relations, and portraying humanity at its best. It also explored the legacies of the 1968 Kerner Commission report, which criticized federal and state governments for housing, education, and social-service policies that created and maintained separate and unequal communities. The museum used sport to demonstrate how a visible group within the Black community, its athletes, maintained their integrity and humanity throughout the adversity of segregation and discrimination. Exhibiting nuanced identity and purposeful struggle is an entrée to empathy for your visitors.

Recognize the Athlete's Agency

By breaking down the mythos of the athlete-as-hero and depicting sports figures as multidimensional people, museums can also underscore how athletes have a platform and a voice they can utilize to make a change in the world. This platform is commonly called agency, "the capacity, condition, or state of acting or of exerting power."[13] Historically, American society and the sports world have looked down upon (and even shunned) athletes who promoted certain social causes or political movements. The list of famed, and shamed, players is long and includes Kaepernick as well as iconic athletes like tennis player Billie Jean King and boxer Muhammad Ali. These athletes struggled against promoters, sports leagues, the news media, the government, and society to bring awareness to the causes important to them. Athletes and sports figures still capitalize on their hard-earned positions to bring awareness to issues that are important to them personally, and society as a whole. Museums can and should acknowledge that inherent agency by giving voice to sports figures' social platforms, past and present. Recognizing their positions as societal change makers is key to fostering a more comprehensive and conscientious sports narratives.

Giving present and historical voice to sports figures' personal agendas can and is happening in museums. The National Museum of African American History and Culture's exhibit *Sports: Leveling the Playing Field* chronicles how African American athletes used their positions in sports to fight for justice and equality.[14] *Breaking Barriers: Sports for Change*, a traveling exhibit from the National Center for Civil and Human Rights, features athletes, including Billie Jean King, Venus Williams, and Jesse Owens, who have used their platform for social change. "More than an exhibit," the exhibit's website notes, "it is an experience and a movement that will inspire attendees to find their voice and in big and small ways inspire healing and affect change."[15] The museum was able to use this exhibit as a means to amplify the athletes' voices and engage in a powerful conversation.

Athletes have been successful in using their platforms for societal change and need to be recognized for that. In their exhibit, *Get in the Game: The Fight for Equality in*

American Sports, the LBJ Presidential Library highlighted athletes as change agents during the turbulent times of Johnson's administration. They brought those activist-athletes to the forefront of contemporary discussion, recognizing that "legendary sports figures like Jackie Robinson, Muhammad Ali, and Billie Jean King proved that athletes are not only capable of changing the game, they can also change society."[16] In this way, the LBJ Presidential Library showed how sports heroes can use their platforms to advance important social causes.

By exploring an athlete's identity as a person rather than a hero on a pedestal or one who has fallen from grace, museums and history institutions demonstrate how sports represents more than just athletic accomplishments. Curators and educators can apply the concepts of context, humanity, and agency to create comprehensive and conscientious narratives of athletes and sports. Doing so will help foster a balanced sense of humanity on and beyond the playing field, for athletes and visitors alike.

The Ball's in Your Court: Replicable Practices

- **Determine your institution's values as they relate to the interpretation of sports history:** Is your goal to share a balanced narrative, one that combines a complex and compassionately humane narrative with a heroic, glorious, and triumphant one? If your institution traditionally speaks to only one of these sides of the sporting story, where can you find room to start expanding the narrative?
- **Decide the transformative changes you want your visitors to experience:** Will they see a sports figure in a new light? Will they be inspired to act on a community issue like an athlete did? A combination of the two?
- **Determine how you will facilitate that transformative experience through an exhibit, tour, or program:** Will your exhibits offer visitors a dual narrative about an athlete (e.g., their sports achievements and character flaws)? Can your programs engage visitors in a discussion about the societal influences on sports?
- **Ask your visitors for their opinion:** Post a question on an analog or digital feedback board and ask visitors to respond. This method asks visitors to reflect on the content and gives them a chance to add their voice to the interpretation. Possible questions include:
  - Against what moral yardstick do you measure your favorite athletes?
  - What non-sports actions might lead to an athlete's removal from a hall of fame?
  - Are professional athletes really worth what they are paid? Why or why not?
    - *Note: This technique takes a lot of care and feeding. You will need to weed through the visitor's responses to be sure none of them are inappropriate (i.e., vulgar or racist).*

- **Lean into the issues that arise in the sports zeitgeist:** Take the pay-to-play concept in college sports: invite an economist, a sociologist, and an administrator from a local college to speak to the issue during a public program. Avoid the expectation that they will solve the problem. The main benefit of this exercise is to provide your visitors with multiple perspectives on the issue.

- **Include the fullness of life:** Expand your interpretation to include a robust narrative about athletes and who they are off the field/court.
- **Tap into visitors' emotions, all of them:** Don't be afraid of challenging your visitors to feel something other than pride and happiness.

CASE STUDY

Evening the Score: Interpreting the History of Women and Sports

Elizabeth L. Maurer

Sports history is a microcosm of American culture, and women's participation in athletics has historically reflected their position in the national social construct. As a commentary on the import intersection of sport and American women, the National Women's History Museum includes sports programs and exhibits that contextualize this complex history. The museum explores the role of women in sports to meet two interpretive objectives. First, the exhibits support the institution's mission by integrating women's distinctive history into the history and culture of the United States (after all, as long as there have been organized sports, women have participated in them). Second, exploring women's participation in sports helps contemporary women better understand themselves and their place in modern society. Stories about historical female figures' involvement with sports challenge women to confront stereotypes about femininity, strength, and competition. Evaluating America's rich sports history narrative is an effective way to interpret the struggles of the ongoing movements for equal rights and empowerment.

Those who overcome cultural gender bias to become the first woman to accomplish a feat, particularly in the male-dominated field of sports, fascinate women's sports fans. Sports history is rife with examples. An article on the museum's website tells the story of Jackie Mitchell, a female teenage pitching phenom who struck out Babe Ruth in a 1931 exhibition game. The story exemplifies a popular narrative arc: a talented young woman seizes the opportunity to demonstrate her prowess in a predominantly male domain. By outperforming her male counterparts, she proves women are not only equal to men but also that society held misguided beliefs about women's roles and abilities. In Mitchell's case, her feat earned her a spot on a minor league baseball team. In 2018, *The New York Times* celebrated her achievement with a retrospective obituary. Notably, contemporary society recognizes her for challenging gender bias more than her actual sports achievements.

In sports parlance, Jackie Mitchell is the classic underdog. Her story demonstrates that women of the past, operating in more biased circumstances, overcame barriers to achievement through persistence. Audiences also embrace Mitchell as a role model for today's young women. Her accomplishments thus represent the American dream, the ideal that every U.S. citizen has an equal opportunity to achieve success and prosperity through talent, hard work, determination, and initiative. Sports stories like Jackie Mitchell's exemplify this ideal.

Other exhibits and programs at the National Women's History Museum challenge the notion that persistence is the essential ingredient to success. The museum instead argues that access to opportunity is paramount. After all, it is impossible to become a champion if one is not even allowed to participate. An examination of sports history reveals this point. When outdoor recreation and organized sports rose in popularity after the Civil War, both men and women embraced athletics as participants and spectators. But the public developed conflicting attitudes toward female athletes. While some embraced the image of a new, confident, athletic woman, the sight of women sweating, running, and competing disturbed many. America struggled to accept the idea of women in competition, the core element of the national sports obsession. The image of driven, female athletes did not fit the country's cultural vision of the ideal woman. While men were encouraged to vigorously pursue sports competition as a training ground for business success, socially elite women were discouraged and even blocked from the competition out of fear that it would make them less feminine. Thus, opportunities for female high-school and college athletes rapidly declined through most of the twentieth century. Museum programs that explore the cultural belief system that circumscribed women's sports participation offer contemporary audiences' insights into their own experiences.

Getting into the Games highlights the ways colleges, particularly predominantly white schools, systematically eliminated women's competitive sports programs from the 1920s to the 1960s. This resulted in fewer than thirty thousand women playing college-level competitive sports by 1970. In contrast, historically Black colleges more often encouraged women's sports competition than predominantly white institutions, thereby providing a contrast to the predominant ideal of womanhood. Three-time track and field Olympic gold medalist Wilma Rudolph is often interpreted as a story of persistence because she overcame polio to emerge as one of the world's most successful athletes. While Rudolph's persistent hard work was important, this interpretation ignores Rudolph's access to the expert coaching she received as a member of historically Black Tennessee State University's famed Tigerbelle track team. In fact, during his tenure from 1950 to 1994, head women's track coach Ed Temple produced forty Olympians that won a total of twenty-three medals. The exhibit demonstrates that supportive communities and access to resources influence women's success more than individual persistence.

The museum's digital and physical exhibits expose the inherent contradiction of celebrating high-level women's athletic achievements while at the same time stigmatizing female athletes as non-feminine. The early, widespread lack of professional women's sports training and coaching affected American female athletic success in international competition, particularly when facing the well-funded, expertly coached teams of the Eastern Bloc. This lack of access was antithetical to the American ideals of competitive success in the name of national honor. America lamented losing Olympic medals to the Eastern Bloc but not enough to overcome its prejudice toward competitive women. Rudolph was one of a line of successful female athletes who, though lauded for their athletic accomplishments, were often stigmatized as unfeminine. Sports writers in the 1930s likewise excoriated tennis champion Helen Wills Moody for being too competitive. Eighty years later, tennis champions Venus and Serena Williams face similar criticism. This contradiction was illuminated and explored in Penny Marshall's 1992 iconic sports movie *A League of Their Own*, in which Marshall perfectly (and accurately) illustrated the dichotomy between being athletic and feminine through the athletes' reactions to being issued skirts as baseball uniforms.

Two sets of medals held at the museum illustrate the arc of girls' sports competitions: those of a 1920s high-school track and field athlete, and medals from baton twirling competitions in the 1980s. Jean Steinhauser, a 1920s high-school student, won track and field medals in Philadelphia before the decline of girls' school sports. Her family saved the medals and an accompanying scrapbook before donating them to the museum in 2014. Steinhauser's accomplishments in an objectively competitive sport were noteworthy, and the medals reflect her accomplishments. The museum holds a second set of medals from 1980s baton twirling competitions. Baton twirling emerged as a sport in the 1950s, offering girls competitive opportunities in an activity that conformed to cultural ideals of womanhood. While athleticism, dexterity, and speed are important, judging is interpretive and includes points for nonobjective factors such as artistic expression. Contestants wear makeup and rhinestone-embellished costumes rather than more utilitarian athletic uniforms. Baton twirling is a companion to other sports closely associated with women including figure skating, synchronized swimming, and cheerleading, in which beauty is a competitive factor. The artifacts illustrate the emergence of feminized sports as the back door to athletic competition for women and girls through the mid-twentieth century.

The museum's digital exhibits *Game Changers* (2014) and *Getting into the Games: Women & the Olympics* (2016) also explore the cultural, economic, social, and political barriers women have overcome to play sports and the challenges that remain. *Game Changers* examines Title IX's impact on women in sport as well as the changing feminine ideal. Title IX was a watershed moment in American history that opened the front door to women's participation in school-sponsored, competitive sports. Women's athletic programs emerged in its wake, providing opportunities to join teams, travel, and compete, accompanied by the corresponding benefits. The law

Figure 1.1.   Track and Field Medals won by Jean Steinhauser, ca. 1923. *Source:* Collection of the National Women's History Museum.

ensured that girls and women would have uniforms and equipment, facilities, and skilled coaching. As a result, high-school girls' sports participation increased ten times and collegiate women's six-fold since the passage of Title IX in 1972.

Yet, access to organized sports for females has come slowly. Thirty years after Title IX, males occupied more than a million more spots on high-school teams than girls. Yet, high schools and colleges often cite Title IX compliance as the reason for cutting men's sports teams, illustrating the legacy belief that sports are more important for boys.[17] Through *Game Changers*, the museum revealed how Title IX and the subsequent increase in female athletic participation led to societal achievements. These included a 20 percent rise in female educational attainment for the generation that followed the new law, a 10 percent increase in the number of women working full-time, and a 12 percent spike in female participation in previously male-dominated occupations. The exhibit argued that the impact of women in sports is not more stories of individual achievement but rather that increased opportunities for *all* women leads to a more equitable society.

Sports history provides a lens through which the National Women's History Museum explores the evolving cultural ideal of American womanhood. When contemporary women learn that most of American history was ridden with cultural ideals that portrayed competition as unfeminine, they more effectively confront the residual social stigma associated with being a competitive woman. The subsequent barriers emerge throughout modern-day female life—on the playing field, in the boardroom, and on the shop floor. Encouraging the next generation of female athletes to play sports that are not traditionally considered feminine—such as lacrosse, soccer, or rugby—can lead to a further reformation in the social definition of ideal womanhood. Presenting these stories within a strong framework fulfills the museum's mission as an institution exhibiting women's history, to contextualize the past while inspiring the present. All museums with relevant collections can and should approach women's sports history topics. In doing so, they further our collective understanding of social barriers women faced as well as the important progress our society has made toward overcoming them.

CASE STUDY

Striking Out: Museums Aren't Interpreting Queer Sports History . . . But They Should Be

Sarah E. Calise

In the summer of 2015, I achieved a childhood dream. For ten weeks, I woke up every morning, put on my khaki pants and navy polo, and walked down Main Street in Cooperstown, New York, to start my day as a curatorial intern at the National Baseball Hall of Fame and Museum. From ages four to fourteen, I spent much of my time on the baseball diamond in the sweltering heat. I played third base, like my favorite player, Chipper Jones of the Atlanta Braves. This love of baseball led me to Cooperstown, where I really reflected on the *Diamond Dreams: Women in Baseball*

Figure 1.2. *Diamond Dreams: Women in Baseball* **exhibit on view at the National Baseball Hall of Fame and Museum.** *Source: National Baseball Hall of Fame and Museum, Cooperstown, New York.*

exhibit. It covered the World War II-era All-American Girls Professional Baseball League, made famous in the movie *A League of Their Own*, and contemporary trail-blazers like pitcher Ila Borders. It was incredible to see these women represented in *the* space for baseball history. There were also exhibits on Black and Latinx players, several objects from the game's greatest Asian athletes, and a few items about disability in baseball. But one thing was glaringly obvious: the lack of queer representation. This omission can no longer be ignored. Museum practitioners have a moral responsibility to promote acceptance through their collections, exhibits, and public programs. Moreover, institutions can achieve these goals through meaningful interpretations of queer sports history.

Sadly, at the National Baseball Hall of Fame and Museum, just as at museums across the United States, the lack of queer sports history interpretation is standard, not anomaly. Since American public schools overwhelmingly ignore both queer and sports history, museums should lead the way in exploring the multitude of roles queer sports have played in society—past, present, and future. Interpreting LGBTQ+ sports history can be challenging because of partisan politics, the hyper-politicization of public education, and deeply rooted antigay and anti-trans beliefs within the sporting culture. The ever-evolving language of the LGBTQ+ community is an additional challenge. But none of these are reasons to ignore queer sports history. The trials and tribulations of queer sporting history are vital for accurately telling our collective past and empowering queer and trans youth.

Public schools and museums struggle to integrate LGBTQ+ voices into their educational practices because of political constraints. Queer and trans people have existed for centuries, but discriminatory legislation and dominant Christian values hindered

American educational and cultural institutions from incorporating queer experiences into mainstream historical narratives until the twenty-first century. Less than twenty years ago, the landmark U.S. Supreme Court decision *Lawrence v. Texas* decriminalized sodomy and sexual activity between partners of the same sex in 2003.[18] Following this ruling, state governments and courts began chipping away at same-sex marriage bans. In the 2015 Supreme Court case *Obergefell v. Hodges*, the justices decided that all state bans on same-sex marriage were unconstitutional under the 14th Amendment.[19] Finally, in 2020, the Supreme Court held in *Bostock v. Clayton County* that Title VII of the Civil Rights Act of 1964 protects queer and trans employees against discrimination.[20]

From this perspective, the tempered pace regarding the inclusion of LGBTQ+ history makes some sense, since societal change is rarely quick in light of legislative and judicial decisions. But queer and trans youth suffer from the lack of representation, and they cannot wait any longer. As of 2021, only five states require LGBTQ+ history in public school classrooms (California, Colorado, Illinois, New Jersey, and Oregon), and just as many states explicitly ban its teaching, actively promoting homophobia and transphobia.[21] In the states that do mandate queer history, students are not learning much. According to a 2019 GLSEN study, only 33 percent of California's students "were taught positive representations of LGBTQ people, history, or events." State governments and school boards continuously fail teachers in the establishment of a queer K–12 curriculum. They give them few resources, set unclear guidelines, and succumbed to fear of political repercussions.

While museums have their own stakeholders and governing boards to appease, they usually have fewer limitations than public school systems in addressing the diversity of their communities, so museums should supplement gaps in the school curriculum with intentional collecting strategies and curatorial policies for not just sports, but all LGBTQ+ history. Still, just like public schools, gender nonconformity and non-heteronormative sexualities have only recently received attention in the standards and best practices of the museum profession. Similar to the British museum field, it is probable that "the law 'protected' museums from having to confront the representation of LGBT communities . . . in their collections and public programmes."[22] It was not until 2014 that the American Alliance of Museums established the Welcoming Guidelines Task Force "to compile preferred practices for museums to use in working with LGBTQ professionals and communities."[23] The task force published guidelines in 2016 and an updated version in 2019.[24] Though museums were slow to consider LGBTQ+ stories, professional standards demand museums make space for these long-ignored voices. Sports history contains some of the most compelling queer and trans perspectives for museums to prioritize in their exhibits and programming—stories that inform the public of political and social issues, the wide spectrum of gender identity, the dangers of toxic masculinity, and the richness of diversity.

Successful exhibition of queer sports history will depend on the museum field's willingness to navigate the historical and present power that the cult of masculinity, homophobia, and transphobia have in sports culture. Amateur and professional sporting activities have a long history in the United States, but the heterosexual-homosexual binary is a modern phenomenon. As Margot Canaday argues in *The*

Straight State (2011), the American government relegated LGBTQ+ people to second-class citizenship through homophobic and transphobic policies related to immigration, military service, and public benefits between the 1930s and 1950s.[25] Thus, instances of prejudice against gender nonconforming and queer athletes in sports became more widely publicized in the latter half of the twentieth century. The historically hostile atmosphere of American sporting culture forced most queer athletes to stay closeted for their own protection. *Out on the Fields*, an international study on homophobia in sport published in 2015, presented historical evidence of discrimination against queer and trans athletes in North America dating back to 1974.[26]

Today's sports remain unsafe for LGBTQ+ athletes. *Out on the Fields* surveyed nearly 9,500 current athletes, mostly in the English-speaking countries of the United States, United Kingdom, Australia, Canada, Ireland, and New Zealand. The study found that 80 percent of all participants and 82 percent of lesbian, gay, and bisexual participants (transgender people were not surveyed in the 2015 study) said they saw and/or experienced some form of homophobia.

These historical and present-day prejudices affect the collecting practices of museums seeking artifacts connected to LGBTQ+ sports. Decades of bigotry have diminished the number of publicly known queer voices in sports, especially professional athletes, so museums will have to rely on their ability to build trust within queer sporting communities to find donors and grow collections. Museum practitioners also need to be creative by developing nuanced interpretation of ordinary objects and experiences. Searching for an artifact or exhibit about professional sports will likely result in frustration and failure. Instead, strive to diversify the queer sports stories by focusing on amateur sports along with coaches, front office staff, and fans.

Club sports, like softball and rugby, were and continue to be imperative to building bonds among LGBTQ+ people and breaking down stereotypes about gay men being unmasculine. Sports have helped define masculinity over time, and "homosexual men were definitely suspect in this macho sports world . . . and lesbians were portrayed as a dominant and corrupting force within women's sport."[27] The main purposes behind club sports as well as the international Gay Games was to "demonstrate to mainstream society that gay people were like everyone else," and gay participation in sports was linked "specifically to the role of gay men" in helping "dispel myths" and affirm their traditional masculinity.[28] Decentering professional sports and giving more space to amateur sports and fandom—arguably the two biggest ways the LGBTQ+ community intersects with sports—will aid museums in telling queer sports history.

The final hurdle public historians and museums face when exhibiting queer sports history is the regular shifts in language and identity within the LGBTQ+ community. Like other groups of marginalized people, queer communities are not monoliths. There are differing political views and social privileges, generational misunderstandings, conflicting beliefs on identity, evolving labels and symbols, and even oppressive behaviors within the community, especially toward transgender and bisexual people. For instance, there may be someone reading this right now who detests that I used "queer" in this essay. Up through the nineteenth century, society used the term *queer* for things considered to be outside the norm, and in the twentieth century it became associated with gender nonconformity or homosexuality.[29] Activists and scholars started reclaiming the word in the 1990s, which led to its mainstream usage today as an umbrella term and a less clunky way to refer to the LGBTQ+ community. Still, for certain generations of people, queer is a slur that needs to be avoided. Documenting and interpreting the history of a community that does not collectively agree on its own acronym can be daunting, but that is not an excuse to undermine the queer community's historical significance and contributions. In present times, such ignorance is a choice; there are plenty of resources within and outside the museum field to guide curators and educators through the nuances and complexities of queer terminology. There are the previously mentioned guidelines from the American Alliance of Museums as well as sites like *Sustaining Places*, an encyclopedia of resources for small historical organizations, which developed a whole page dedicated to protocols for collecting and interpreting LGBTQ+ history.[30] Overall, public historians must face these three major challenges head-on, get comfortable with being uncomfortable, and accept that mistakes will be made as they navigate the complexities involved with queer sporting communities and their history.

Historical and LGBTQ+ institutions have established some common best practices for discussing queer stories and why they matter, especially to queer and trans youth. According to public historian Susan Ferentinos, exhibiting LGBTQ+ (sports) history is essential to accurately tell our collective past, expands audiences for museums and historic sites, can provide context to many current issues in queer sports and prove the relevancy of your institution, and, most notably, "interpreting LGBTQ history can serve as an act of reparation to a group who, until quite recently, has been slandered, ignored, and erased."[31] The museum field's commitment to an intersectional diversity framework that includes queer and trans history is the first step toward properly interpreting LGBTQ+ sports history. Once an institution realizes its gaps and starts the path to reconciliation, what are the protocols for successfully collecting and exhibiting queer sports history?

The next step is for museum administrators to incorporate these readily available guidelines into their strategic plans and the total work culture. AAM's updated "Welcoming Guidelines," published in 2019, defines best practices for LGBTQ+ inclusion in six functional areas of the museum: curatorial, public engagement, guest experience, visitor research and evaluation, human resources, communication, and development.[32] Two of the major practices to keep in mind are hiring LGBTQ+ staff and consulting with members of the LGBTQ+ community when building collections and creating exhibits or public programs.

Working directly with the LGBTQ+ community will build trust with the museum, and provide community buy-in for the museum's queer initiatives. It will also increase the intersectionality of the exhibits since queerness interacts with race, gender, disability, and class, and museums typically do a poor job of balancing these identities in narrative text. The New York Historical Society's online summary of their 2021 exhibit on Billie Jean King discussed King's role in gender equity activism while it completely overlooked her service to the LGBTQ+ community; it would be understandable to assume the physical exhibit ignores her queerness, too.[33] In all fairness, the N-YHS is set to open the American LGBTQ+ Museum in 2024.[34] Portions of the museum field are progressing forward, but searching for exhibitions on LGBTQ+ sports history results in an almost entirely dark void. It is time to step up to the plate.

Museums must never underestimate the power of representation and how much it matters. For me, seeing women in baseball at the hallowed National Baseball Hall of Fame and Museum was both validating and inspiring. It is equally crucial for queer and trans youth to see themselves represented in sports history, particularly today, when trans youth are subject to laws that ban or thwart their participation in athletic competition. The museum space accommodates tough and intricate discussions as well as just about any other institution in our society, and they can make a real difference in the lives of transgender athletes. Exhibitions showing transgender athletes from history paired with current knowledge that breaks down myths about the science and medicine behind transitioning would be powerful. It would instill hope for a better future, and that, for me, is the museum's greatest asset—keeping hope alive.

Yes, museums severely lack interpretation of LGBTQ+ sports history, but there are signs of that changing just as sports are changing, too, with an increasing number of queer athletes living their truth inside *and* outside the locker room. Recently, a few of the women who played in the All-American Girls Professional Baseball League came out as lesbian.[35] What if I had known that as a kid, that some of the female ballplayers I looked up to were queer just like me? It was my childhood dream to one day work at the National Baseball Hall of Fame and Museum. Now, as an openly queer sports fan, it is my adulthood dream to go back one day and see their exhibits discuss sexuality within its historical context, openly display the pain and suffering endured during bigoted times, and provide some hope that it does get better.

CASE STUDY

High Stakes: Designing a Sports Gallery for the National Museum of African American History and Culture

Damion Thomas with Shi Evans

When we began working on the sports gallery for the Smithsonian National Museum of African American History and Culture three years before the museum opened, one persistent question dominated my thinking: can we create a sports gallery for non-sports fans? When I was appointed as the guest curator for the gallery in 2013, this was not the charge that was given to me, but it seemed to be the most appropriate, yet risky way to approach this project. Indeed, I wanted to create a sports gallery for visitors who did not know the difference between a touchdown and a slam dunk. I wanted those visitors to leave the gallery with an appreciation for how and why sports matter far beyond the playing field. Perhaps, my position as the guest curator whose full-time job was as a college professor provided me with the flexibility and job security to be broadminded and a bit daring in my approach. Even as I moved in this direction, I had doubts. I feared that this approach might prove to be foolish. After all, the worst outcome would have been for the museum's sports fan visitors to find the gallery uninteresting and offensive to their nostalgic sensibilities;

and, at the same time, the non-sports fans to find the gallery uninspiring and too difficult to understand. Yet, I was committed to not allowing the sports gallery to be the escape zone in the museum. As a museum that explores the horrors of slavery and segregation, as well as, the resilience of African Americans who fought against and survived those brutal institutions, I did not want sports to be relegated to being the museum's fun, ahistorical, and "feel good" gallery. I saw an opportunity to use sports as the gateway into larger societal issues, particularly race relations, African American cultural identity, gender inequality, access to education, and the impacts of slavery. In doing so, the gallery presents a unique, culturally relevant, and widely impactful interpretation of African American history and culture through the lens of sports.

In many ways, structuring the gallery in this manner meant walking a bit of a tightrope. The goal was to create a gallery that provided a serious, intellectually rigorous discussion of the role of sports in the African American fight for greater access to the American dream while not stripping the gallery of sports as a source of joy. The "joy" emerges from watching our teams win, observing incredible athletes' feats, and seeing our communities' spirits lifted by winning home teams. However, the love of sports is too often amplified by incomplete, culturally sanctioned narratives that circulate around sports. Many of those narratives suggest that sports are an inherently positive and progressive force in race relations; and that inclusion in sports reflects the inevitability of racial progress. To contextualize and challenge these narratives, we moved from history that placed the individual athlete at the center of the story. Instead, we organized the gallery around sports that have had the biggest political, social, and cultural impacts in African American history: boxing, baseball, the Olympics, basketball, and football. To reflect the more intense, solemn subject matter, we chose a black and dark gray color scheme for the exhibit, the darkest in the museum, which many visitors find surprising and unexpected in a sport exhibit.

Despite taking actions to demonstrate the cultural significance of sports, we still wanted the gallery to be fun, but we remained committed to the notion that making the gallery "fun" could not be done at the expense of its larger mission. To that end, we decided to rely upon the gallery's video components to share our messages. Importantly, we interviewed known sports personalities who often shared their expertise and opinions in entertaining ways to narrate several four-minute clips that explain the significance of the sport featured in the video. The music that accompanies the featured videos was selected because it was upbeat and provides a mood infused with hip-hop sensibilities in the gallery rooms instead of the more frequently used soundtracks that tend to dramatize the narration. Additionally, we place several life-size statues of prominent sports figures within the gallery: Michael Jordan, Serena Williams, Venus Williams, Jesse Owens, Jackie Robinson, and others. We knew that the statues, which captured athletes in their action poses, would create photo opportunities for visitors. As we sought the middle ground, we turned to other sources for inspiration.

Striking the proper balance between a serious engagement and a fun experience was crucial because the museum industry's treatment of sports has tended toward nostalgia, which frequently privileges celebration over contextualization. To be guided by the latest research, we began to read the work of scholars that have studied sports and museums. As noted, sports scholar Wray Vamplew contends most sports exhibitions focus on the "concept of 'a golden age'" for a particular sport or team.[36] Many of these exhibitions have offered uncomplicated histories that romanticize sports organizations and athletes. These narratives often divorce sports from the larger cultural, political, and economic forces that shape the context in which sports operate. Because leaders in sports museums tend to "care too much for the image of the sport that they serve to risk it being undermined by historical evaluation," they commit a disservice to their sport by not showing the sport's honest, complete evolution.[37] Yet, the bend toward confirmation of memories and traditions often obscures the history of groups with difficult histories such as African Americans whose collective narratives do not fit conveniently into the triumphant stories peddled by many museums and cultural institutions.[38]

Grappling with these potential pitfalls forced us to make sure that the gallery was grounded in the expectations of those whose efforts helped make the museum a reality namely: Congressman John Lewis, who first introduced the legislation for the museum; President George W. Bush, who signed the legislation in 2003; Lonnie Bunch, the museum's founding director; and President Barack Obama, who presided over the museum's grand opening in 2016. Congressman Lewis told attendees at the museum's groundbreaking ceremony in 2012 that he wanted the new institution to "tell the whole, 400-year story of the African American contribution to this nation's history, from slavery to the present, without anger or apology."[39] At the same ceremony, founding director, Lonnie Bunch, expressed his hope that the museum space would retell U.S. history in ways that challenged visitors to "grapple with these contested memories" and learn "that the African American story is the American story."[40] At the museum's grand opening, President Bush explained that "a great nation does not hide its history. It faces its flaws and corrects them. This museum tells the truth that a country founded on the promise of liberty held millions in chains."[41] President Obama highlighted the tension when he described the African American experience as "one of suffering and delight; one of fear but also of hope."[42] He went on to explain that the NMAAHC "is the place to understand how protest and love of country don't merely coexist but inform each other."[43] Deep reflection on the words of these leaders solidified our decision to tell African American history through sports; rather than create a gallery strictly devoted to sports history.

Perhaps the best example of the exhibit's overarching complex narrative is in its depiction of Jackie Robinson. Within African American history, it is hard to overstate the importance of Jackie Robinson. Our collective knowledge of the extent of Robinson's selection to integrate Major Leagues Baseball, his political activism, and his waning popularity by the time he retired demonstrates that he was a multidimensional athlete. Rather than focusing on his baseball skills, our Jackie Robinson *Game Changers* case provides a case study of the African American commitment to use the country's pastimes as vehicles for increased inclusiveness, spaces to challenge inequality, and as pathways to social mobility.

Sports enthusiasts as well as non-sports fans know Jackie Robinson integrated Major League Baseball in 1947. He was chosen for the "noble experiment" because he grew up outside of the South, played in the Negro Leagues, attended college, and served as a military officer, which seemed to check most boxes of the ideal all-American.[44] Robinson set Major League records and won championships while simultaneously resisting racial taunts and discrimination on the diamond and in his personal life. Despite these indignities, Robinson became one of baseball's most

revered players. He is the only player in U.S. major professional sports to have his number retired by every team in Major League Baseball. Our depiction of Robinson highlights these challenges and triumphs and appeals to a wide variety of visitors while also relating to the cornerstone themes of the exhibit.

The exhibit also engages Robinson's contributions to the Civil Rights Movement in ways that challenge long-held perceptions of his involvement. After integrating baseball, Robinson did not rest on his laurels. He used his public profile to advance equality and justice for African Americans. He was wholly committed to his belief that "the right of every American to first-class citizenship is the most important issue of our time."[45] One of the most challenging moments of Robinson's career was in 1949, when he was called to testify on African American patriotism for the House on Un-American Activities Committee. Robinson assured the committee that, despite the indignities of segregation and Jim Crow, African Americans loved and supported the country. In a masterful speech, Robinson denounced communism and used his high-profile visit to make a "plea to end segrega-

Figure 1.3. The Jackie Robinson case as part of the *Game Changers* exhibit at the National Museum of African American History and Culture. *Source:* Smithsonian National Museum of African American History and Culture. *Photograph by Walter Larrimore.*

tion."[46] His willingness to advocate for African American rights and privileges is an important, often forgotten chapter of Robinson's legacy, one that speaks to the important role sports plays in U.S. history.

Reframing Robinson's role in the ongoing politics of baseball challenges many visitors' long-held perceptions of the sport's integration. As one of the first spaces to give African Americans opportunities to compete on an equal playing field, sports provided athletes of Robinson's generation with a platform through which to engage social issues on and off the field and create opportunities for generations that followed. In our re-telling of Robinson's narrative, we also discuss how his persistent fight to end segregation in baseball and society led to him being one of the most hated men in the sport. After the sport integrated, baseball officials and fans wanted Jackie Robinson to be a silent symbol of progress. Yet, Robinson's persistent critique of baseball's continuing color line and engagement in the Civil Rights Movement frustrated fans. Robinson became known as a troublemaker. He was labeled as "too quick to see racism" and "too grand."[47] Many visitors wrongly assume Robinson's popularity grew over time. And while it is true that the number of African American baseball players steadily increased, his popularity waxed and waned, often with his level of political and social involvement. The museum celebrates Robinson, but also demonstrates the very real cost of Robinson's activism.

Robinson and countless other athletes—some famous and many long since forgotten—centralized the full spectrum of the African American experience into their professional lives. Like Robinson, many athletes use their platform to illuminate their cultural experiences as African Americans. Our gallery honors these efforts, placing their actions in contexts beyond the playing field. This motif challenges visitor sensibilities, just as Black athletes' on-field and on-court protests and demonstrations cause a myriad of reactions from fans. Reactions range from frustration viewing America through a less-than-rosy lens and/or resisting the messages of oppression delivered from sporting arenas to acknowledgment that sports does indeed reflect society. This provides opportunities for conversations on some of the more complex topics of African American history: slavery, Jim Crow, lack of economic and educational access, poverty, and women's rights.

Given the reticence of many cultural institutions to centralize the history of African Americans into their dominant narratives, the National Museum of African American History and Culture has become a safe place for U.S. citizens to discuss difficult histories. As Lonnie Bunch, the museum's founding director noted, it is impossible to "explore African American history without wading into controversy," the sports gallery aims to embrace the Smithsonian Institution's mission to be the "Great Convener:" a place that brings together difficult history, varied intellectual frameworks, and diverse publics to deal with the divisions, failed expectations, and contention over the lessons that sports help teach us.[48] Hence, the gallery supports the museum's mission to take "contested memories [that are] often shoved into dark corners of the American past" and use them as opportunities to educate.[49] By comprehensively and effectively relaying the history and present realities of African American athletes, the sports gallery affirms that sports exhibits can attract even the non-sports fan.

CASE STUDY

Get in the Game: Exhibiting the Fight for Equality in American Sports

Nikki Diller

Since organized sports first became a significant part of American cultural life in the nineteenth century, athletes have championed equal acceptance and participation, both on and off the playing field. Legendary sports figures like Jackie Robinson, Muhammad Ali, and Billie Jean King proved that athletes are not only capable of changing the game, but they can also change society. For museums, sports can be an effective entry point to explore contested histories of race, class, gender, ethnicity, and sexual orientation and identity. The LBJ Presidential Library did just this when it created *Get in the Game: The Fight for Equality in American Sports*, a temporary exhibition. The curatorial staff designed the exhibit expressly to encourage visitors to consider sports as central to ongoing, nationwide conversations about equality and how sports have long served as a vehicle for social change; a task that presented several illuminating challenges. Ultimately, sports in their historical context served as a useful lens for understanding an active dialogue that has long surrounded athletes and social politics. As such, *Get in the Game* explored the pioneering efforts of athletes who dismantled barriers, fought for equality, and advocated for social justice.

In developing *Get in the Game*, staff placed sports within the larger context of American history and illustrated to visitors how sports so often reflect American political, social, and cultural values. *Get in the Game* sought to communicate the role of social justice issues through the lens of sports and present the parallels between racial and ethnic minority participation and treatment in the sports world and the world at large. Although *Get in the Game* could not possibly include every story of influential and inspirational athletes, the library made every effort to be inclusive and honor athletes of every race, religion, gender, ethnicity, orientation, and ability.

To best demonstrate the dramatic evolution of sports and social justice movements, curatorial staff arranged *Get in the Game* chronologically. The exhibit guided visitors from the earliest days of organized sports in post–Civil War America through the current day. One example that is ever present throughout this history is the racial dynamic of sports and athletes. In the 1870s and 1880s, African Americans and other minorities participated in integrated baseball, horse racing, golf, football, prizefighting, and several other sports. After the Compromise of 1877, Jim Crow laws and de facto racial segregation gained power in all facets of American life.[50] By 1896, when the U.S. Supreme Court established the "Separate but Equal" doctrine in the *Plessy v. Ferguson* decision, few people of color were permitted participation in organized sports. Minorities remained in segregated athletic associations and leagues, such as the Negro Leagues in baseball and the American Tennis Association, until after World War II, when the push for integration in all parts of American life gained momentum. The modern Civil Rights Movement, Vietnam War, and atmosphere of protest and civil disobedience of the 1960s spilled over into sports, with Muhammad Ali, Bill Russell, and the 1968 Olympics boycott and protest movement, to name a few. Tennis champion Billie Jean King's fight for equal pay for female tennis players advanced the women's liberation movement. Recent protests and advocacy by athletes such as Colin Kaepernick and Chris Paul mirrored the expanding engagement with social justice issues in American society.

Though planning for *Get in the Game* began several years before the resurgence of athlete activism in America, the timing of the exhibit's debut was fortuitous. When development began, staff did not know how relevant the subject matter would be within the context of contemporary national dialogue. The exhibit team believed that the lens of sports history would not only provide visitors with a new perspective of the present but would also attract an audience that might not usually be inclined to visit a history museum. In fact, the exhibit's significance was wide reaching and attracted not only sports fans and history buffs but also social justice advocates.

While developing *Get in the Game*, the staff encountered several challenges, the most traditional of which was one of the collections. The LBJ Presidential Library does not actively collect sports-related objects. Partnering with a myriad of other institutions ultimately made the exhibition possible, but the process proved to be quite difficult. The museum had to reach out to thirty separate lenders, many of them private collectors, to effectively tell the story. Objects personally used by iconic sports figures are often difficult to borrow because of their uniqueness and value. Any institution that lacks an in-house sporting goods collection should be sure to confirm the availability of objects when developing an exhibit narrative.

Figure 1.4. 1968 Summer Olympic images and artifacts displayed in the LBJ Presidential Library's exhibition *Get in the Game: The Fight for Equality in American Sports. Source:* LBJ Library photo by Jay Godwin.

Given the somewhat fraught nature of the subject—an exhibit that explored the intersection of sports and social politics—attention to language was extremely important. The LBJ Presidential Library took extra care to present the exhibition with even-handed storytelling, inclusivity, and sensitive language. Still, the exhibit does contain some unsettling phrases and terminology. Some of the primary source materials reflected the types of derogatory language and treatment that American athletes encountered while seeking access to athletic opportunities, equality on the field or court, or choosing to use their platform to spotlight social justice issues. As with any difficult subject, the LBJ curatorial staff sought to strike a balance between presenting a historically accurate story. They did this by incorporating contemporaneous language that exposed the often-unsettling nature of the past, while not endorsing or condoning that language. The language in the exhibit proved an effective conversation starter among visitors and led to discussions about the ways that we often talk about personal and group identity in America today.

With the potentially controversial or emotional nature of sports and civil rights, the curatorial staff found it important to give visitors the opportunity to share their perspectives. The subject matter of *Get in the Game* included artifacts related to current and relevant controversial topics and staff anticipated and encouraged visitor feedback. Prior to opening, the museum received consistent input regarding which athletes to include or omit. The exhibit encouraged visitors to use social media to discuss athletes that most inspired them as well as the importance of sports in their personal life experiences. The exhibit also included a specially designed, interactive social media wall near the exit. There visitors could interact with reactions, stories, and photographs from others who engaged with the content.

Combining sports history with politics, social commentary, or difficult histories is not a simple or easy undertaking; nonetheless, the potential benefits far outweigh the possibility of ruffled feathers. The long and winding American sports narrative provides an effective lens for addressing challenging subjects. For many visitors, the context is quite familiar, not foreign or overly didactic. Those who prefer to only peruse the sports memorabilia can do so. By adding rich historical context, visitors also can engage with narratives about which they were previously unaware. Further, an exhibit of this nature can ask museumgoers to consider the important role athletes played in shaping American cultural life and the fight for equality of access, opportunity, and treatment.

As the world becomes ever more diverse and global, museums can present discussions about difficult histories and current affairs that might seem off-putting to some, yet are more easily examined through the lens of sports. By highlighting the stories and voices of a diverse group of athletes, museums can engage new local audiences, establish new partnerships, and increase the overall impact and reach of the museum throughout the community. This is not necessarily easy. In a polarized political climate in which athletes use their voices to express strong viewpoints or stage protests, some visitors might be resistant to looking deeply at the very real sociopolitical influence that sport and athletes have on American cultural life. However, providing that richer context can help visitors think differently and perhaps even appreciate the long tradition of American athlete activism, even if they do not necessarily agree with each political stance. In the experience of the LBJ Presidential Library, visitors to the *Get in the Game* exhibit welcomed a more profound historical perspective that illustrated the myriad ways sports are more than just a game.

NOTES

1. Ira Berkow, "(Human) Athletes and Hero-Worship," *New York Times*, July 25, 1983, https://www.nytimes.com/1983/07/25/sports/human-athletes-and-hero-worship.html.

2. Margaret R. Somers, "The Narrative Constitution of Identity: A Relational and Network Approach," *Theory and Society* 23 (1994): 606.

3. Rebecca Herz, "Can Museums Be Neutral?," *Museum Questions,* December 18, 2017, https://museumquestions.com/2017/12/18/can-museums-be-neutral/.

4. Linda Borish, "Covering all the Bases: Sport and Identity," unpublished essay, March 2018.

5. Charles Curtis, "Colin Kaepernick: I Won't Stand 'To Show Pride in a Flag for a Country that Oppresses Black People,'" *USA Today*, August 27, 2016, http://ftw.usatoday .com/2016/08/colin-kaepernick-49ers-national-anthem-sit-explains.

6. Eric Reid, "Eric Reid: Why Colin Kaepernick and I Decided to Take a Knee," *New York Times,* September 25, 2017, https://www.nytimes.com/2017/09/25/opinion/colin-kaepernick -football-protests.html.

7. Luke Cyphers and Ethan Trex, "The Song Remains the Same," ESPN.com, September 19, 2011, http://www.espn.com/espn/story/_/id/6957582/the-history-national-anthem-sports -espn-magazine.

8. Melanie Schmitz, "How the NFL Sold Patriotism to the U.S. Military for Millions," *Think Progress*, September 25, 2017, https://thinkprogress.org/nfl-dod-national -anthem-6f682cebc7cd/.

9. Elizabeth L. Maurer, "Evening the Score: Interpreting the History of Women and Sports," in *Interpreting Sports at Museums and Historic Sites*, eds. Kathryn Leann Harris and Douglas Stark (Lanham, MD: Rowman & Littlefield, 2023), 39, 36–39.

10. Becky Lee, "The Heroes We Idolize in Sports," *Huffington Post*, May 25, 2011, https:// www.huffingtonpost.com/becky-lee/the-heroes-we-idolize-in_b_223245.html.

11. "Permanent Exhibits," Museum of disABILITY History, accessed May 20, 2018, http:// museumofdisability.org/virtual-museum/society-wing/sports-exhibit/.

12. Sarah E. Calise, "Striking Out: Museums Aren't Interpreting Queer Sports History… But They Should Be," in *Interpreting Sports at Museums and Historic Sites*, eds. Harris and Stark, 40, 39–44.

13. Merriam-Webster Dictionary, accessed June 21, 2018, https://www.merriam-webster .com/dictionary/agency?src=search-dict-hed.

14. Damion Thomas with Shi Evans, "High Stakes: Designing a Sports Gallery for the National Museum of African American History and Culture," in *Interpreting Sports at Museums and Historic Sites*, eds. Harris and Stark, 44–48.

15. "Breaking Barriers: Sports for Change," accessed March 13, 2018, https://www .sports4change.net/#about, accessed.

16. Nikki Diller, "Get in the Game: Exhibiting the Fight for Equality in American Sports," in *Interpreting Sports at Museums and Historic Sites*, eds. Harris and Stark, 49, 49–52.

17. David Berri, "Did Growth of Women's College Sports Cost Men? Data Says No," *Forbes*, January 16, 2018, accessed April 25, 2019, https://www.forbes.com/sites

/davidberri/2018/01/16/did-the-growth-in-womens-college-sports-cost-men-some-might-say-yes-but-the-data-doesnt-agree/?sh=c955df4297a6.

18. Lawrence v. Texas 539 U.S. 558 (2003).

19. Obergefell v. Hodges, 576 U.S. 644 (2015).

20. Bostock v. Clayton County, Georgia, 590 U.S. ___ (2020).

21. Elinor Aspegren, "Kids Aren't Learning LGBTQ History. The Equality Act Might Change That," *USA Today*, March 6, 2021, https://www.usatoday.com/story/news/education/2021/03/06/lgbtq-history-equality-education-act-teachers/6648601002/.

22. Darryl McIntyre, "What to Collect? Museums and Lesbian, Gay, Bisexual and Transgender Collecting," *The International Journal of Art & Design Education* 26, no. 1 (2007), https://onlinelibrary.wiley.com/doi/pdf/10.1111/j.1476-8070.2007.00509.x.

23. "Welcoming Guidelines for Museums," American Alliance of Museums, May 2016, https://www.aam-us.org/wp-content/uploads/2017/11/lgbtq_welcome_guide.pdf.

24. "Welcoming Guidelines for Museums," American Alliance of Museums, May 2019, https://www.aam-us.org/wp-content/uploads/2019/05/2019-Welcoming-Guidelines.pdf.

25. Margot Canaday, *The Straight State: Sexuality and Citizenship in Twentieth-Century America* (Princeton University Press, 2009).

26. "Timeline of Evidence Homophobia and Transphobia in Sport," Out on the Fields, 2020, accessed September 1, 2021, https://outonthefields.com/evidence-timeline/.

27. Caroline Symons, *The Gay Games: A History* (London: Routledge, 2010), 2.

28. Symons, *Gay Games*, 2.

29. Christina B. Hanhardt, "Queer History," *The American Historian*, May 2019, https://www.oah.org/tah/issues/2019/may/queer-history/.

30. "LGBTQIA History in Museums," Sustaining Places: An Encyclopedia of Resources for Small Historical Organizations, accessed August 25, 2021, https://sustainingplaces.com/queering-museums/.

31. Susan Ferentinos, "Interpreting LGBTQ Historic Sites," in *LGBTQ America: A Theme Study of Lesbian, Gay, Bisexual, Transgender and Queer History*, ed. Megan E. Springate (Washington, DC: National Park Foundation, 2016), 4.

32. "Welcoming Guidelines for Museums," 2019.

33. "A Woman's Worth," Exhibitions, New York Historical Society and Museum, 2021, accessed August 28, 2021, https://www.nyhistory.org/exhibitions/womans-worth.

34. Julianne McShane, "American LGBTQ+ Museum Coming to N.Y.C.'s Oldest Museum as Part of Expansion," *ABC News*, July 13, 2021, https://www.nbcnews.com/nbc-out/out-community-voices/american-lgbtq-museum-coming-nycs-oldest-museum-part-expansion-rcna1391.

35. Peter Dreier, "A Lavender League of Their Own," *The Nation*, June 4, 2020, https://www.thenation.com/article/society/women-baseball-gay-history/.

36. Wray Vamplew, "Facts and Artefacts: Sports Historians and Sports Museums," *Journal of Sports History* 25, no. 2 (1998): 270, 275.

37. Vamplew, "Fact and Artefacts," 275.

38. Vamplew, "Facts and Artefacts," 275.

39. John Lewis, "Rep. John Lewis Speaker At Groundbreaking of National Museum He Helped Establish" (speech, Washington, DC, February 22, 2012), quoted in Faun Rice, "National Museum of African American History and Culture: A New Integration?" *Curator: The Museum Journal* 60, no. 2 (April 2017): 254.

40. Lonnie Bunch, "The National Museum of African American History and Culture: The Vision," *Journal of Museum Education* 42, no. 1 (Spring 2017): 8.

41. Lonnie G. Bunch, *A Fool's Errand: Creating the National Museum of African American History and Culture in the Age of Bush, Obama, and Trump* (Washington, DC: Smithsonian Books, 2019), 234.

42. Barack Obama, "Remarks by the President at the Dedication of the National Museum of African American History and Culture" (speech, Washington DC, September 24, 2016), Obama White House Archives, https://obamawhitehouse.archives.gov/the-press-office/2016/09/24/ remarks-president-dedication-national-museum- african-american-history.

43. Obama, "Remarks," 2016.

44. Wall text, *Sports: Leveling the Playing Field*, The National Museum of African American History and Culture, Washington, D.C.

45. Wall text, *Sports: Leveling the Playing Field.*

46. Wall text, *Sports: Leveling the Playing Field.*

47. Arnold Rampersad, *Jackie Robinson: A Biography* (New York: Alfred A. Knopf Publishing, 1997), 271.

48. Lonnie Bunch, "Making A Way Out of No Way," *Smithsonian*, September 2016, 30.

49. Lonnie Bunch, "The Pain and Power of Remembering: 40 Years After the Newark Riots," in *Call the Lost Dream Back: Essays on History, Race and Museums,* ed. Lonnie Bunch (Washington, DC: AAM Press, American Association of Museums, 2010), 57.

50. Following the Compromise of 1877, remaining federal troops were pulled out of the South and the post–Civil War Reconstruction Era ended. Without any federal protection, the social and economic advances made particularly by African Americans in the South were severely curtailed.

Chapter Two

From Local to Global

Interpreting Sports and Globalization

Bruce Kidd and Jenny Ellison

Outside of halls of fame, it may seem as though sports and museums have little in common. Sports are about competition, teams, and fans, whereas museums are typically about preservation, history, and learning. Athletic competitions and exhibition spaces might function with different content, audiences, and purposes, but they share similar histories and organizing principles. Museums and sports are systems that order and classify the human experience. Both have expanded internationally through colonizing processes. Finally, each is globalized, in that we find similar rules, approaches, and commercial impulses shaping production and consumption worldwide. Museums and historic sites can therefore use globalization as a starting point for digging deeper into a sport's shared history. Used this way, globalization provides a lens through which to identify gaps and silences in a collection, evaluate exhibition storylines, and reach out to new audiences and communities.

Key Interpretive Concepts

1. *Globalization is the interaction and integration of communities across national borders*: Globalization is characterized by the adoption or imposition of similar rules and practices, governing bodies, and engagement with international players, audiences, and consumers. Common language and rules can also lead to a breaking down of traditional power relationships between people and cultures.
2. *Institutional silences about the past are a result of ever-shifting global perspectives on relevancy, power relations, and community divisions:* Museum and archive collections preserve history but are rarely fully representative. Museum professionals can seek out artifacts to fill these gaps and diversify collections.
3. *Decolonization is the ongoing process of correcting inequities stemming from injustices of the Imperial period*: In museums, this includes shared authority with community stakeholders, changing the words used for and about Indigenous people and places, and the repatriation of artifacts, among many other things.

Why Globalize Sports Exhibitions?

Globalization is not a simple concept. Rather, it is turbulent and ongoing. As the topic relates to sports museums and exhibitions, traditional museum visitors may be much more interested in local and national sports glories and the heroics of the accomplished athletes than the international context of sport or sports heroes. Sports have helped shape power relationships of class, gender, and ethnicity. The narrative of modern sports is incomplete without some account of these dynamics. Told comprehensively, the history of modern sports is indispensable to the history of the modern period. Museums have important contributions to make in this arena.

Sports were also integral to the history of colonization and the globalization of today. Starting in the 1500s, European nations began colonizing territories across North and South America, Asia, Africa, and Australia. They used sport as a vehicle to assert Western European values on colonized peoples. The soldiers, missionaries, and educators of the British Empire, for example, promoted sports (most notably cricket and soccer) as a way to lead "barbarous" nations and peoples along a path to what they saw as modernity and civilization. Historian J. A. Mangan calls this process "missionary muscularity." The British Empire, Mangan argues, was in part an enormous sports complex, institutionally driven by the military and the church. "Sport traveled the world with the bullet and the Bible," he writes. The result was the presence of sports fields, clubs, and organized teams in every country the British ruled.[1]

The sport of baseball highlights Mangan's principle at work. In particular, the spread of singular, uniform rules over wider geographical areas represents an example of global colonization. In North America, for example, European colonists who became Americans, *canadiens*, and Canadians in the eighteenth and nineteenth centuries, played bat-and-ball games under local rules quite different from today's games. Players negotiated, embraced, and evolved those rules into what eventually became the game of baseball. Local, organic variations of the rules narrowed into one universal set of rules. "*A* particular way of playing became *the* way of playing," argue authors David Whitson and Richard S. Gruneau.[2] This facilitated play across nations and continents. The same process occurred in the traditional Indigenous games that shaped what became hockey, lacrosse, and football. So widespread is the global acceptance of standard rules today that communities vie for the right to be declared the "home," that is, the originator, of a certain sport. Yet, many fail to realize that evidence of play in the "modern" era does not necessarily constitute origins, only that people once played something similar.

In general, Western museums and exhibitions began with similar moral aims as colonialism: to illustrate the path to modernity and civilization. As British sociologist Tony Bennett argues in *The Birth of the Museum: History, Theory, Politics*, institutions displayed technology, imperial history, and natural history to direct visitors toward a "correct" reading of the past. These institutions intended architecture, space, objects, and text to communicate the superiority of European civilizations, thereby casting other populations as weak or exotic.[3] Jennifer Barrett, director of Cultural Strategy at the University of Sydney, maintains that governments established Imperial and colonial museums based on the idea that they "had a purpose and value" to educate the broad public. In the early twentieth century, Canada and the United States began to identify national heritage sites in earnest, and by mid-century, sports museums and halls of fame were established to celebrate and document the preferred narratives of sports history. Heritage preservation and communication aligned with other goals of these relatively young nations, particularly to demarcate a distinct national identity and to provide "rational amusement" to citizens.[4]

Assessing Representativeness

Global histories of sports offer museums and history organizations the opportunity to assess how truly representative their collections and exhibitions are. Knowledge of the shared imperial and colonial history of sports and museums can provide a starting point for this evaluation. "Memory relies on the continuing existence of the physical traces produced by members of society in their activities," archivist Rodney G. S. Carter writes. Since collective memory typically relies on keeping collective records, Indigenous communities, racial minorities, and women are frequently institutionally underrepresented. The museums and archives of the past simply ignored their stories. Silence has also resulted from the failure to recognize different record-keeping traditions (e.g., the written word versus oral traditions).[5]

For incomplete or missing stories, finding new perspectives through the collection of artifacts, archival files, or oral histories can expand the institution's interpretation beyond the "victors" and toward a more expansive view into the ways and places other groups historically played a sport. South Africa's history of colonialism and apartheid resulted in the dearth of artifacts and knowledge of Black communities in collecting institutions. Sports existed in racial silos during the apartheid era and Black community organizations were relegated to the margins. To more effectively tell the stories of Black South Africans and sports, the District Six Museum in Cape Town had to build new community partnerships. These relationships provided theretofore untold, new perspectives on South African sporting history. This process required not only community-based research but the ongoing institutional reflection on holes in the story and attempts to fill these gaps.[6]

Shifting Perspectives

Shifting the narrative of sports requires more than just adding a section or exhibit case on diversity. Adding to the main story or isolating a particular group in a separate section reproduces long-standing hierarchies of museum display because it decontextualizes the shared history of all groups. For this reason, the International Tennis Hall of Fame in Newport, Rhode Island, moved from a chronological to a thematic approach. This approach offered a broader, more global picture and allowed the museum to more completely present the diverse, multifaceted history of the sport.[7]

For museums seeking to shift perspectives, a challenge may arise if relevant material culture is unavailable. In 2014, the Art Gallery of Ontario hung a contemporary cartoon sketch of Métis hero Louis Riel in a room alongside Victorian art. In the accompanying label, the gallery acknowledged Indigenous art was not part of its historic collection.[8] Juxtaposed against the Victorian artworks, the cartoon reminded visitors that other groups were present and making art at the same time as the paint-ings' creations. For sports-exhibiting institutions, this creative use of photography and design could serve a similar function and therefore highlight the accomplishments of individuals and groups for whom there is limited material culture. The Canadian Mu-seum of History added images to their exhibitions when artifacts were not available, as a way to demonstrate how diverse groups played the game.

Another approach is to connect sport to other global issues. Drawing on common themes like worship, ritual, and rivalry, the Amsterdam Museum orchestrated *Foot-ball Hallelujah!*, an exhibit that compared football to religion and toured five other European cities. The project not only decentered the focus on "greats" but also encour-aged reflection on aspects of football that happens off the pitch. *Football Hallelujah!* included the perspective of fans, for example, as a connection to the culture of global football. Using this method proved effective at acknowledging the important role that fans play in sport and also opened the door to critical reflection on consumption, fan violence, and rituals. *Football Hallelujah!* also included local stories as a means to illustrate the dynamics between individual teams, universal experiences, and emo-tions that shape sporting culture. By incorporating these perspectives, the museums included in the tour welcomed new audiences comprised of visitors who could see themselves in the project.[9]

Decolonization

Following World War II, a steady wave of decolonization—the realization of inde-pendence by a large number of Asian, African, and Caribbean countries—created new impulses for globalization. In most of those countries, the leaders made the decision to promote the sports of their former colonizers and try to "beat their former masters at their own games."[10] They did so by participating in the Olympic Games, soccer World Cup, and other international competitions.

This phase of globalization was also enabled by the creation of a new international order inspired by the Universal Declaration of Human Rights, the creation of the United Nations, and the UNESCO International Charter of Physical Education and Sports in which UNESCO stated, "The practice of physical education and sports is a fundamental right for all."[11] This declaration was a profound shift in approach from the missionary muscularity of the colonial era. It recognized sport's contributions to social, political, and global relations.

Sports-exhibiting institutions multiplied exponentially in the Cold War era. Com-bined with decolonization movements that began to sweep the globe, the Cold War destabilized international power relationships. In nearly every sphere of life, the Cold War bitterly divided the world into a capitalist bloc led by the United States and a communist bloc led by the Soviet Union. It was only natural that the rivalry extended into sports. Thus, international events were tense with competition, intrigue, charges, and counter-charges. The Olympics in Moscow in 1980 and Los Angeles in 1984 precipitated tit-for-tat boycotts.[12]

In Canada, Britain, and the United States, scholars Deborah McPhail, Christopher Dummitt, and Sonya Rose describe a crisis of masculinity that led to the creation and promotion of physical fitness programs aimed at maintaining people's physical strength in this increasingly affluent era.[13] Sports halls of fame are one part of this broader cultural phenomenon, historian Eldon Snyder argues. These institutions, with their focus on the best players and most memorable wins, also represent a response to the need for collective and personal nostalgia at times of social dislocation and identity crisis, two outgrowths of the Cold War and decolonization.[14] The National Baseball Hall of Fame and Museum in Cooperstown, New York, founded in 1939, was the first of these institutions; numerous other sports-specific local and national halls of fame followed. Many of these institutions remained stuck in the spirit of their creation and have not kept abreast of changing historiography and museum practices. While professional historians since the 1990s have been reevaluating global sports, sports scholar Wray Vamplew argues, "Sports museums in general and halls of fame in particular" continue to reflect "the part of the sporting world that is obsessed with winners and winning."[15] Promoting nostalgia and celebration is more difficult when looking at histories of race, class, and gender or difficult subjects like violence and doping.[16]

A powerful example of this historical shift is the role of sport in South Africa's anti-apartheid movement. Sport played a major role in ending the system of white minority rule in South Africa. A group of Black South African sports leaders in exile formed the South African Non-Racial Olympic Committee (SANROC). The Black sports movement within South Africa and sports leaders of newly independent nations in Africa, Asia, and the Caribbean all supported SANROC and initiated an international campaign to isolate white South Africans in the sporting world. They succeeded in preventing the apartheid nation from competing in the Olympics and other international competitions and eventually stopped foreign athletes from competing in South Africa altogether.[17] While the movement was ultimately successful, its impact has been mixed. Exhibiting the sports history related to the legacies of apartheid at the District Six Museum proved intrinsically political. Community members challenged the museum's approach, funding sources, and even its storytelling.[18]

Difficult Discussions

For museums, decolonization movements and impulses toward globalization have had major ramifications for collecting, exhibitions, and community relationships. In the immediate post–World War II era, American museums continued to focus on collecting, cataloging, and research. Public access remained a secondary concern. This changed as the Baby Boom generation came of age. Education was increasingly seen as a way to foster democracy and civic engagement. Youth of this era, therefore, were among the best-educated generations in Canadian and American history. Many believed learning should extend beyond the classroom, including in museums, and that experts should engage more deeply with the general public.[19] These factors combined with changes in thinking about the traditional "establishment" and the rise of a counterculture that embraced more liberal attitudes toward sex and social relationships to create a new dynamic for museums and public institutions.[20]

Many museums, therefore, adapted their practices in response to changing attitudes toward education and social relationships.[21] One particularly important shift that resulted was the transformation of exhibitions about Indigenous peoples. Many early museums represented Indigenous people as savage, racially inferior, and/or exotic. They placed emphasis on tools and production and treated Native culture as a scientific specimen. In *Decolonizing Museums: Representing Native America in National and Tribal Museums*, scholar Amy Lonetree offers in-depth case studies that explore efforts to share authority with Indigenous people. She shows how Indigenous activism has led to critical shifts in the representation of Native peoples, the incorporation of Native groups into museum project planning, the repatriation of artifacts, and the shared authority and ownership of artifacts with community-based museums. Museums can look to studies like Lonetree's, or guidelines published by museum and professional associations, to initiate repatriation and community partnerships with Indigenous peoples.

Relying on external activism is insufficient, however. Curators must also accept a revised role in the process. Rather than having full authority over the content, the new ideal is to become "more involved in the distribution of multi-voiced information originating elsewhere," museum consultant Elaine Heumann Gurian writes.[22] If curators accept other perspectives, shared authority is possible. Thus, exhibitions and artifacts may be seen, as Senior Research Fellow at the Institute of Culture at the University of Sydney Fiona Cameron writes, "in entirely different ways from those imagined under the guise of curatorial authority or heritage significance, value, and certainty."[23] Decolonizing institutions requires collaboration with groups the museum has previously excluded and/or utilized solely as objects of the museum. Representation is political, and achieving change requires consultation and partnership with Indigenous groups.[24]

Museums as Fourth Estate

Sports offer a point of entry for talking with and about groups that experienced past events differently. The idea of contextualizing sports in light of decolonization and globalization may, however, seem untenable, overly intellectual, or even unnecessary. Or, it may be that museums and history organizations face challenges from stakeholder groups that envision a celebration of the past that does not acknowledge colonial histories or the global scope of most sports. For example, critical exhibitions about war like "Bomber Command" at the Canadian War Museum and the *Enola Gay* atthe National Air and Space Museum (Washington, D.C.) have confronted controversy when strong veteran stakeholder groups challenged the alternative, non-nationalist viewpoint presented in the projects. In both exhibitions, veterans felt their sacrifices were undermined by discussion of the impact of bombing campaigns on enemy nations during the war.[25] As sports scholar Murray G. Phillips has argued, more research is needed on museums and history organizations about sport and their audiences.[26] Nonetheless, research suggests audiences are open to museums discussing controversial and sensitive topics, provided that the institution presents multiple sides of a story. Jenny Ellison's study of audiences and journalists in Canada, the United States, and Australia, "Controversies in Context," found that museums were seen to have a role akin to journalisms' Fourth Estate in that audiences wanted museums to present multiple perspectives and felt that they had a responsibility to present challenging stories to the public.[27] Because audiences expect and want sports to be fair, presenting evidence that some athletes have been treated differently is one way to start a conversation about controversial issues.

Globalization and Equity

Since 1990, the resurgence of global capitalism and migration dramatically accelerated globalization. The broad liberalization of international trade, the dramatic spread of the mass media through cable television, the vast transformations wrought by the Internet, and the steady increase in international migration all paved the way for rapid change in sports and museums. To participate in this new global context, players and teams must now find additional revenue streams to support salaries and travel. At the same time, globalization has also facilitated efforts to foster greater equity and accessibility to sports. Many global sports bodies and corporations have sought to use their reach to help develop sports across the globe. The International Olympic Committee (IOC), to cite one such example, contributes a significant share of its revenue to sports development around the world. Between 2013 and 2016, Olympic Solidarity spent $439,870,000 on programs focusing on athlete, coach, and leadership development. The largest share went to the poorer countries of the Global South. In 2014, the IOC outlawed discrimination on the basis of sexual orientation in the "fundamental principles" of the Olympic Charter. Nevertheless, the extent to which globalization has encouraged greater equity needs qualification. In the first place, men from Europe and North America still dominate leadership in the organizations that govern sport. Athletes from the Global North still enjoy far superior resources than those from the Global South. Secondly, even when international bodies, such as the IOC or the United Nations, approve equity policies there can be national and local noncompliance and resistance. We are still a long way to realizing genuine equity in sports around the globe.

Inequities in the sports world have impacted collecting decisions and representations of athletes. In sports, girls and women are still significantly underrepresented as participants and decision-makers, and generally, receive much less (and typically inferior) media coverage than males. In addition, while a few sports provide equal prize money in major events, like World Cup Alpine Skiing, World Championship Figure Skating, the London, Boston, and New York Marathons, World Cup Snowboarding, and some tennis events including the Australian Open, Wimbledon, U.S. Open, and French Open, women generally receive less for their efforts than men.[28] Men's sponsorship opportunities outside sport also dramatically increase their earnings. The IOC has recommended that the international federations close the gender gap in prize money by 2020.[29]

The issues of reduced access and participation, inequity in pay, and social mores that attempt to limit female participation in sports make interpreting women in sports a challenge. Many hope women will gain much greater equality of access, benefit, and decision-making in the years to come. However, while women have long pushed for greater opportunities to participate in sports, scholar Bruce Kidd reports that some factions of global society have justified limits on female involvement based on the false premise that sports and fitness have a detrimental impact on femininity.[30] Women continue to fight for the right to participate and for equal pay in sport.[31] As Ellison writes in her review of the Canadian Museum of History's exhibit *Hockey*, locating artifacts is not easy, and institutions must actively seek out female athletes and coaches to recover their stories.[32]

Identities

Beyond economics and competition, history organizations and museums working with sports topics must think about globalization in terms of identity. Decolonization and new technologies have led to a splintering of identities and concepts of nations. In North America, the museum designer and consultant Paul Williams writes, globalization has shifted "the understanding of collective memory from the unified, chronological narratives of nationhood to the episodic, affective narratives of groups."[33] It has allowed people to communicate across national and linguistic borders, and it has resulted in greater knowledge of global differences.[34] Museum audience members bring with them multiple, global identities; they often may not identify first as a member of a national community, but by their gender, sexual orientation, or ethnicity. This is an important consideration for museums and history organizations.

The rapid growth of information technology is another factor that influences and accelerates change. Fiona Cameron argues that this has shifted the flow of information in museum and heritage sites. Even local museums, she maintains, operate in global networks because of the availability of information. Tony Bennett has identified these institutions as part of an "exhibitionary complex," one designed to impose a worldview on audiences. Access to information and technology may mean it is now even more controversial to refuse to acknowledge complicated histories than to remain silent. Institutions, even smaller ones, must necessarily reflect upon and reevaluate their roles to respond to new information and its possibilities and pitfalls.[35] The approach depends on the type of institution and its goals.

Strategies for Change

Simple changes can also disrupt the audience understanding of sport. For halls of fame, making the member selection process transparent and with clear criteria is an effective strategy. Explaining to visitors the member selection process provides space for reflecting on the institution's purpose.[36] Institutions with permanent displays on sports should also reconsider how they have told their stories. This requires pondering fundamental national and global sports narratives. For example, consider what we mean when we say, "hockey is Canada's game" or "golf is an elite sport." Addressing silences and reorganizing and regrouping artifacts is another way to fundamentally shift how visitors understand sports. In the hockey exhibition at the Canadian Museum of History, the *Football Hallelujah* traveling exhibition, and the permanent displays at the International Tennis Hall of Fame, exhibition teams included different perspectives into the same space, intentionally challenging a hall of fame model.

Rather than focusing exclusively on great wins, the curatorial staff contextualized sport in this space by including new material that added historical and cultural context. Their interpretive methods also involved adding material on sports aspects that have not always been recognized—like fan culture, Black leagues, women's leagues, and sport for people with disabilities. By comparison, the more linear narrative of the World Golf Hall of Fame in St. Augustine, Florida, used a global view to illustrate the history of the sport worldwide. In its attempt to provide more context to the role of sports in history, the District Six Museum undertook a large institutional shift that required extensive community collaboration.

Ultimately, all decisions depend on the goals, stakeholder relationships, and available artifacts. Regardless of approach, a wider, global perspective can help expand community relationships and reach out to new audiences. This is relatively easy to do because the historical forces of globalization—immigration, forced migration, depopulation, and industrialization—touch most citizens of the contemporary world.

Replicable Practices for Interpreting Sports and Globalization

- **Evaluate silences in a museum or archival collection:** Whose experiences with sports are represented? Can you graphically illustrate the sources and diffusion of sports in the way museums such as New York City's Ellis Island and Pier 21 in Halifax, Nova Scotia, have been able to do when showing patterns of immigration?
- **Learn about Indigenous sports and games in your region:** How are they similar to the games of European settlers? Where do they diverge?
- **Consider how people organized teams and tournaments in your region:** Were they divided along ethnic, gender, class, or religious lines?
- **Interpret the social and cultural relations of sports:** Given that most sports, teams, and leagues were initially organized along strict ethnic/racial, gender, and class lines and only recently became integrated (often through political struggle), can you show examples of these different practices and outline the history of integration? Can you present a history of sports as community building through such a lens?
- **Contextualize your collection or project in relation to global movements of people, ideas, and sports:** Is there evidence of evolutionary thinking in existing approaches to this topic? Can you decolonize the way you approach sports?
- **Develop a strategy for addressing gaps and silences in your collection:** Can you identify those who have traditionally been excluded and invite their representatives to contribute artifacts and stories?
- **Include different types of stories and artifacts about sports in an exhibition to demonstrate complexity:** Leagues and teams organized by women, non-white people, and people with disabilities can add context to halls of fame dedicated to elite and professional sport.
- **Discover ways you can illustrate the relationships between the globalization of sports and changes in technology**: Different forms of equipment, rules, and record keeping help to show that sport changes across time and place.
- **Discussion Starters: Reading Against the Grain:** Sports winners, greats, and/or the best of the best of a community, state, or nation often appear as the predominant

subject matter of institutions that collect and interpret sports. Review aspects of your collection to see whose stories are represented. How does this compare to the demographics of your audience or region? Read your sources against the grain to discern what stories are missing. Most groups are engaged in sports already; actively look to find evidence of their participation? Consider what stories are hidden behind the public face of a great player or victory. Who were the trainers? Who sewed the uniforms? Is it possible to make interpretive connections between your collection and the communities not normally represented in halls of fame? How can you connect these peripheral stories into your exhibitions or institutional activities?

CASE STUDY

Aces and Places: Serving the Globe at the International Tennis Hall of Fame

Nicole F. Markham

Preserving, documenting, presenting, and celebrating tennis' global history and impact are central to the mission and day-to-day activities at the Museum at the International Tennis Hall of Fame in Newport, Rhode Island.[37] Tennis has a storied history rooted in inspirational players, impactful innovators, and memorable moments that have influenced history, on and off the court. Few sports have as deeply extensive or more globally relevant history than tennis. Dating from the Middle Ages, where tennis began as a game of kings and clergy, the sport spread beyond castle and cloister walls. Over centuries, it developed into a constantly evolving present-day mega-sport that spectators and participants experience in a multitude of settings—from schoolyards to private clubs and public courts to the world's biggest stadiums. As compelling as this story is, telling it purely in date order led to a more singular, linear storyline. Shifting from a chronological to thematic approach, the International Tennis Hall of Fame staff utilized the museum's extensive collections to present inclusive and complex narratives through exhibitions, research projects, programming, and other initiatives that allow for an expansive global audience reach.

Why collect, interpret, and share objects and stories about any sport, let alone tennis? Well, sport is not extraneous to the human experience; it is intrinsic to it. Its richness, variety, beauty, passion, and rewards are undeniable. Sport is an element of nearly every culture. The forms sport takes, and the objects made for and about it, represent cultural expression. All human beings play, and play (in the form of sport) provides an avenue to learn about competition, cooperation, and the limits and capabilities of our own bodies, minds, and spirits. Because of this, sport can transcend, and even break down, cultural and societal barriers, allowing us to understand and appreciate what we share in common. Uncovering tennis's history through its tangible material culture, which appears in various mediums—fine and decorative arts, trophies, equipment, clothing, player memorabilia, oral histories, still and moving images, books and serial publications, letters, manuscripts, and other primary sources—allows the museum staff to document, present, and share the personal, emotional, historical, and technological aspects of the sport. This material culture both expresses and influences tennis's evolving economic, social, and cultural milieu.

While the sport of tennis may appear timeless and elitist to some, the same social, cultural, and historical forces that transformed the world also impacted and interacted with tennis. Some of the ways in which tennis has evolved may have been predicted a century ago—better equipment, improved athleticism, more comfortable clothing. Other changes were likely less foreseeable. Few might have predicted the types of changes that mimicked twentieth-century social progressions: expansion of tennis courts beyond the realm of private estates and country clubs to public parks, the rise of professionalism and the decline of the amateur ideal, the emergence of great female athletes, the erosion of racial barriers, the commercialization of sport and the role of athletes in popular culture, the use of ever-developing science and technology to aid and educate players and spectators, the influence of the media, or the global reach of the sport. These changes revolutionized the game and impacted not only tennis' primary stakeholders (the sport's governing bodies and officials, players, fans, facilities, and sponsors) but larger society as well.

In the modern era, tennis has produced a continuous series of international personas that influenced society beyond the lines of the court via their accomplishments, struggles, demeanor, leadership, tenacity, and generosity. France's Suzanne Lenglen introduced her daring fashion in the post–World War I years. American Althea Gibson broke the racial barrier in the 1950s. Billie Jean King pushed for equality and the Title IX legislation. Andre Agassi developed a school in Las Vegas to serve low-income students. This list reflects but a small sampling. The global reach of tennis contains innumerable examples of the sport's socially important impact on the world.

Socioeconomically, the modern game repeatedly changed in significant ways that mirrored and drove social movements. The game evolved in the 1950s with the belated entry of African Americans into the highest levels of competition around the world, in 1968 with the long-over-due advent of "open" tennis,[38] in the late 1970s with the development and growth of wheelchair tennis,[39] and again in 2007 when Wimbledon Championships became the last major event to offer equal prize money to men's and women's singles champions.[40] All of these pivotal moments provided more opportunities, equality, and growth in the sport. The democratization of sport, the emergence of mass culture, changes in fashion, evolving ideas about lifestyle and physical fitness, the women's movement, and the civil rights struggle all reflect larger cultural phenomena that were happening both outside of and within the sport. Tennis's international appeal meant a global audience experienced these same cultural shifts through worldwide media markets.

In 2012, the hall of fame staff began planning for a nearly complete renovation of the museum's permanent exhibition areas during which the implications of the sport's storied social history and the global impact were seriously contemplated. The project was long overdue, as the last renovation and reinterpretation of the museum occurred in the mid-1990s. The museum approached the project with several leading goals: to present a more engaging, consistent, and globally relevant tennis history narrative through a thematic rather than chronological approach while utilizing more of its expansive holdings than previous exhibits. In order to display and use more of the

museum's collection, a media content management system was installed, which provided flexibility for continuous updating and content additions alongside digitization
of the existing collections. The museum staff also created a more socially participatory
experience and increased the focus on the global nature of the game. To achieve this,
interactive components were added—such as a *Tennis & Culture* table[41] and a *Call the
Point* desk[42] along with numerous touch-screen components and audio guides in multiple
languages for both adult and youth visitors.

To address a key part of the museum's mission, we needed to tell the story of the international game through the experiences of hall of famers and other recognized figures
in the sport.[43] We aimed to contextualize their experiences—both struggles and accomplishments—relevant to the part of the world and period of time in which they played.
Many recreational players and fans of the sport look to these individuals as role models,
and the impact of those figures' life experiences is part of the history and evolving story
of the sport.

The renovated museum reopened in 2015 with a design that appeals to dedicated tennis
fans and casual visitors alike. The updated museum exhibitions present the evolving social and cultural history of tennis—from its origins through the present day—and feature
a range of material culture documenting the impact of tennis on the world and vice versa.
The museum's permanent exhibits are split into three main areas: *The Birth of Tennis
(1874–1918)*, *The Popular Game (1918–1968)*, and *The Open Era (1968–Present)*.

- *The Birth of Tennis* section explores how the sport evolved from court tennis, the
  rise in popularity of lawn tennis in the late 1800s, the development of international
  tournament tennis, the involvement of women in the game from its earliest days, the
  impact of war on the sport, and early infusion of tennis in pop culture.
- *The Popular Game* highlights growing worldwide interest in the sport, and how
  tennis became intertwined in popular culture in the fashion, technology, media, and
  decorative arts industries. Themes explored in this area focus on the early pro tours,
  the rise of a celebrity among athletes, the impact of technological advances on the
  sport, and the sport's early forays into social matters, such as furthering opportunities for African American players and growing the women's game.
- *The Open Era* explores the period of time in which tennis experienced its most
  significant growth and success including an examination of the roles that the men's
  (ATP) and women's (WTA) professional tours and the International Tennis Federation have on furthering the global reach of the sport.[44] This section also features
  content on how journalists and the media support and document tennis, the growth
  of wheelchair tennis and its full integration into the sport, the role of tennis in larger
  sporting events such as the Olympic and Paralympic Games, the involvement of
  outside interests, businesses, and sponsors, as well as continuing discussion on
  popular culture themes and technological advancements in the game.

In addition to the newly renovated museum, the staff developed numerous projects
as a means to engage with a wider audience. A series of traveling exhibits bring the
museum's content to a larger, global audience and addresses topics in more detail than
could be physically displayed in the galleries. These exhibits travel to various venues

around the United States, as well as abroad (including Brazil, the Czech Republic, Greece, Mexico, Russia, Switzerland, and Spain). The *Passing Shots: Photographers' Perspectives on Tennis* exhibit shared some of the most emotional tennis moments captured by internationally recognized tennis photographers from the 1940s to today. In *Breaking the Barriers: The ATA and Black Tennis* the museum chronicles the history of African American tennis, including the American Tennis Association (ATA), and spotlights many of the unheralded early Black tennis champions. The history of African American tennis is discussed within the greater context of American History, focusing on the years from the founding of the ATA in 1916 to Arthur Ashe's historic Wimbledon win in 1975.

Working on this exhibit allowed us to make connections with numerous individuals and to incorporate the greater story of African American tennis history into the museum renovations as well as expand the collection. We explored the Latino tennis world in *¡Vive el Tenis! Common Threads, Different Peoples*, which also allowed us to partner and develop relationships with numerous individuals and organizations in Central and South America and the Caribbean. The museum presented the story of the international tennis community's commitment to a free and safe world in *Serving Their Countries: Tennis and War*. In *Home Court: The Family Draw*, we featured distinctive stories about numerous tennis families from locations around the world where the impact of tennis has spanned generations. *Tennis and the Olympics* allowed us to partner with the Summer Olympic and Paralympic Games and showcases some of the most successful

Figure 2.1. This display case within the Museum at the International Tennis Hall of Fame is located within our Global Tennis Gallery and focuses on the Olympic and Paralympic events in the sport of tennis. *Source: Kate Whitney Lucey/International Tennis Hall of Fame.*

and interesting tennis Olympians/Paralympians in history and highlight the appeal of tennis as one of the most international sports.[45]

In exploring options for further outreach to individuals and communities, the Hall of Fame staff determined that both a digitization project and a curriculum-based education project would provide the museum with tools and opportunities to inter-act with an even wider audience on a more global scale. In spring 2017, the ITHF began a ten-year digitization project, with the goal to use digital assets via multiple platforms to engage a global audience about the organization, its hall of famers, and the history of tennis. We are currently working on projects to use digitized assets in an enhanced website and an online searchable collections database.[46] We are also considering plans that include adding enhanced and updated interactives within the museum, retail product development, and virtual and augmented reality. The museum has also been focusing on the development and implementation of curriculum-based educational programs that include topics and themes such as tennis and war (history/ social studies), tennis art (arts), growth of tennis around the world (geography), and nutrition/health/exercise (science/physical education). Future plans include expanding programs to a wider audience via distance learning opportunities.

From the museum's founding in 1954 to today, the International Tennis Hall of Fame has continually expanded its mission and interpretive goals to tell a more inclu-sive story of the sport. Globally, tennis is considered a sport for a lifetime. Anyone can participate. Whether one is a young child or an elderly adult, able-bodied or wheelchair-bound, man or woman, professional player or recreational player, there are opportunities for all in the sport of tennis. By using the collections and internal resources, looking outward, and working with various partners around the world, the curatorial staff can engage with and connect tennis to the larger society.

The museum preserves and promotes the history of tennis and celebrates its cham-pions, thereby serving as a vital partner in the growth of tennis globally. Utilizing the updated thematic museum exhibits with features that highlight the globalization of the sport allowed the curatorial staff to expand on this commitment. We created traveling exhibits that cover a wide variety of global topics, developed an online platform that utilizes the museum's digital assets accessible to people all over the globe, and imple-mented educational initiatives and programs for a wide audience. The museum has now become an instrumental and influential player in the global impact of tennis, a result of inclusively and thematically sharing the experiences and stories of interna-tional figures in far-reaching ways.

CASE STUDY

Football Hallelujah!: A European Traveling Exhibition

Annemarie de Wildt

In the Western world, the stadiums are getting fuller and the churches emptier. Is football[47] fandom fulfilling needs and longings that were previously met by religion? Is football actually a new religion? These thoughts inspired *Football Hallelujah!*, an international exhibition project. The curatorial staff aimed to link global football rituals and expressions of fandom to a variety of local situations and practices. The Amsterdam Museum in the Netherlands and the Basel Historical Museum in Switzerland initiated the project and developed the exhibition concept. The exhibit premiered in the Amsterdam Museum in 2014 and toured five other European cities and ethnographic museums over a four-year period.[48] To this end, three-quarters of the exhibit explored a worldwide perspective and remained relatively unchanged at each location, while the remainder analyzed football culture local to each respective city on the tour. Exhibit content throughout explored the similarities and differences between football and religion in terms of heroes, rituals, faith, and superstition.

Football and Religion

In developing the exhibit, the concept team primarily looked to the European sporting landscape and scholarly research. We were surprised to learn that despite the myriad of possibilities found by connecting local expressions of football fandom to ways of believing in football, none of the European city museums had previously explored the somewhat controversial subject of football and religion. *Football Hallelujah!*'s theoretical groundwork thus emerged from an exploration of several leading scholars. In his work, *The Soccer Tribe*, Desmond Morris offers an ethnographical lens on the sport. Through his sociological interpretations, Simon Kuper explores soccer's universal essentials and compares various local political and religious differences. Journalist Franklin Foer describes the intersection of football, globalization, and the persistence of tribal rivalries.[49] As the United States is a much more secular country than most of Europe, the American literature was less helpful. American sources primarily focused on sports having religious characteristics, but not so much coopting religious functions. In one of the first American works on the subject, *The Joy of Sports: End Zones, Bases, Baskets, Balls, and the Consecration of the American Spirit*, Michael Novak goes so far as to describe sport as a "natural religion," but does not allude to sport replacing religious practice.[50]

Amsterdam and Basel curators organized the exhibit into six major themed sections, *Help from Above*, *Saints and Idols*, *Places of Worship*, *Rituals*, *From Cradle to Grave*, and *Symbols*, each of which explored a different facet of the intersection between football and religion. Throughout the exhibit, religious and football symbols sat juxtaposed in order to demonstrate how they are similarly utilized. For example, a football cup placed next to a Roman Catholic chalice reflected the appropriation of religious symbols as sports trophies. Each section reflected this methodology in a unique way.

- Content in the section *Help from Above* addressed how fans evoke gods in hopes of influencing the game. Photos of fans praying together and videos with superstitious gestures portrayed fans' widespread use of these ritualistic practices. An altar made by Togolese voodoo priest Serge Hounpatin, on loan from the Soul of Africa Museum in Essen, bore material witness to the belief that casting spells on an adversary and invoking spirits can influence a game's outcome. Next to it was a glass case with an orange bra worn during matches by a Dutch woman, who believed this would help the Dutch team to victory.

- The section entitled *Saints and Idols* contained a replica of an altar for Maradona created by Bruno Alcidi, who keeps the original in his Bar Nilo in Naples. This altar serves as a testimony to the godlike status of the Argentinean player among the Napoli population. True Roman Catholic style relics, including hairs of Maradona that Alcidi collected from an airplane chair, sit at the centerpiece of the altar.
- The theme *Places of Worship* showed how the impressive architecture of football stadiums designates them as modern-day cathedrals. These places become holy ground for football fans.
- Another section, *Rituals*, exhibited the ways fans collectively prepare for matches through marches to the stadium, songs, and fireworks. Imagery and objects highlighted the similarities between a football crowd and a church congregation: standing up and sitting down, chanting, using smoke, and marching in procession to places of worship.[51] Crowd behavior is a key to understanding what goes on in religious revivals and football games. According to psychologist Serge Moscovici, crowd behavior is a form of secret-secular religion in its own right.[52]
- The *From Cradle to Grave* section included commercial and club merchandise, including baby rompers, T-shirt, bras, and even condoms in club colors. These objects exemplified the ways in which passionate football supporters demonstrate football affiliation during deeply meaningful and spiritual phases of life. A coffin adorned with a club logo showed how even in death fans pay tribute to one of their life's greatest passions.
- Cultural and religious imagery covered the walls of the *Symbols* section. Club fervor inspires many fans to cover their bodies in football-related tattoos, thereby adopting the team's identity as part of their physical being. The exhibit featured a video that juxtaposed the use of fan tattoos from throughout the world.

In an effort to explore the complicated comparison of football and religious rivalries, the exhibit included cut and re-sewn professional football jerseys, pieces from designer Floor Wesseling's controversial "Blood in Blood out" art.[53] The artist creates new shirts by sewing together jerseys of rival clubs and using the graphic language of heraldry. The result is a visual image of football archenemies, such as the Netherlands and Germany or the three clubs in Istanbul, combined in one shirt. Most of Wesseling's pieces depict club and city rivalries, as supporters tend to feel a deeper love and passion for their club and city teams than those at the national level. They support their local teams all year, not just around the European and World Cup tournaments. Some of these rivalries even originate in religious oppositions; the Protestant-based Rangers fans, for example, still support their team as a means for venting hatred toward the Catholic-based Celtic fans in Glasgow, Scotland.[54] Wesseling designed this art to express his sentiment that "we will all be a mixture soon anyway," suggesting that crossing sport rivalries and cultural or religious loyalties is acceptable, perhaps inevitable.

Fittingly, at least one conjoined jersey elicited a public outcry among Dutch fans after a Feyenoord fan used Facebook to post an image of Wesseling's Feyenoord/Ajax jersey made from the combination of the two local rivals: the Ajax club from Amsterdam and the Rotterdam club Feyenoord. After it was posted, Feyenoord fans released a string of insults and even threats. More than five hundred angry and threatening

Figure 2.2. *Football Hallelujah!* **exhibition with the "Blood in Blood out" shirts by Floor Wesseling.** *Source: Kathryn Leann Harris.*

comments flooded the post, prompting the museum to hire additional security. This incident validated the intense, cultlike, emotional connection found within football rivalries. While no trouble occurred, the impassioned reaction underscored the exhibit organizers' assertion that "Football is passion, football is war, and football is god." The shirts traveled Europe with the tour, and Floor Wesseling created new shirts for each new city. The Ajax-Feyenoord outcry was the most intense response from any city on the tour.

Local and Global

In an ever-globalizing world, football is one avenue by which people cling to something local and familiar. Franklin Foer called football a "secular nationhood" in his groundbreaking work *How Soccer Explains the World.*[55] The world surrounding the sport contributes to the formation of narratives, rituals, images, and symbols, which reflect and contribute to national identity.[56] National teams playing in the UEFA European Championship and the FIFA World Cup evoke strong nationalist feelings and display an exuberant use of national colors. *Football Hallelujah!* invited and encouraged visitors to explore issues of adoration, cultlike identity, and religious fervor on both a global and local scale, thus urging them to think critically about football's interconnected impact.

Creating a European traveling exhibition was a way to explore the overarching theme from various international angles while diminishing costs through collaboration. As Amsterdam would be the first venue, its museum hosts played a prominent

roleein conceptuelizing, researching, and selecting objects and photos. Marie-Paule
Jungblut, director of the Basel Museum, and Amsterdam Museum director Paul Spies
involved four other city museums: Bremen (Germany), Lyon (France), Luxembourg
(Luxembourg), and Liege (Belgium). Representatives from each museum participated
in at least one of the intercity meetings to give input.

The exhibit was designed with a global audience in mind with space left for each
institution to cater to its own local audience. Designer Thomas Ebersbach used
a system of frames, panels, and glass cases to make the exhibition adaptable for
various spaces. This design was very important because the exhibit spaces ranged
from a former orphanage, the Amsterdam Museum, to former churches in Basel and
Liege. Each site on the tour could adapt to the themed sections by including local
additions. Roughly three-quarters of the twenty-two panels approached the themes
from various international perspectives, showing, for instance, a collage of various
stadiums, football processions throughout different countries, and the video with
football tattoos from all over the world. Each panel featured a backdrop of close-
up faces that reflected the range of emotions found inside the stadiums. Ebersbach
worked with the partner museums to add local stories and objects in the remaining panels. Fittingly for an exhibition of global impact and importance, all panels
included texts in the local language(s) and in English.

Local Passions

Due to the exhibition's global/local concept, all host cities needed to contact nearby
football communities to identify themes, objects, and stories for the local portions of
the exhibition. Amsterdam Museum staff discovered deep interests and patterns as
we engaged in authentic interactions with football fans. During the 2014 World Cup
in Rio de Janeiro, we found ample opportunities to conduct fieldwork with fans. The
staff met orange-clad fans in bars, homes, and the Amsterdam streets to inquire about
local passions and rituals. Also, in Basel, and other cities, the exhibit curatorial teams
established a deep rapport with the local football worlds. In Lyon and Liege, expert
sport journalists participated in exhibition creation.

Local football fandom research uncovered objects that communicated directly to
the heart of religious fervor for the majority of visitors. In Amsterdam, the exhibit
included the costume of the Oranje Ootjes, an all-male supporters' group from
Spakenburg, a fishing village in the Netherlands. Fans tweaked the local traditional
female costume, replacing the black skirt with an orange cloth while wearing the
white crocheted women's bonnet. On a screen next to the costume, a father and
son from the group spoke about representing the Netherlands with their attire at
matches, in their village, at home, and abroad. The son, adopted from Colombia,
expanded upon his loyalties toward teams from both countries. In Liege, the exhibition included analysis and objects related to the myth of the Red Devils, the
nickname for the Belgium national team. In Lyon, an anthropologist researched and
constructed a series of interviews with divergent soccer fans.

During the research and fieldwork, we faced challenges as we extended our
hometown contact zone to the Amsterdam Football Club Ajax stadium, cafes, and

even courtrooms (to witness a case against football hooligans). F-Side, named after a section in the stadium, is a group of very passionate Ajax fans; critics call them hooligans. In Ronald Pieloor, the current fan representative for Ajax, we found a gate-keeper to this superfan group. He openly shared his knowledge and networks. Pieloor has enjoyed a fascinating fan career, starting as one of the founders of the F-Side in 1976. During matches, they become a pulsating body-singing, chanting, playing drums, and lighting (forbidden) fireworks and flames. He has his own YouTube channel on which he posts videos of matches, preparations, and Ajax fan commentary. He allowed us to use his recordings in the exhibition.[57] Pieloor also introduced us to F-Side members, from whom we sought personal artifacts, such as banners and clothing, to use in the exhibit. Before they trusted us, the F-Side wanted to know how the museum would portray them.

The appropriation of the nickname Superjews was one of the most controversial topics regarding Amsterdam's most passionate fans. Two panels containing a short description of Feyenoord fans' use of anti-Semitic slurs against Ajax parsed the complex relationship between Europe's cultural history, the role of the Nether-lands during the Holocaust, and contemporary football fans' adoption of traditional scapegoats as proxies for their rivalries. This is part of a long and complicated story about Amsterdam and its Jewish community. Complete with Star of David tattoos, Israeli flags, and Hebrew marching songs, the symbolism reflects a comprehensive appropriation of Israeli and Jewish religious symbols. The use of these symbols obviously needed to be included in the narrative. At our first encounter, while sharing beers in a bar, the F-Side delegation requested we use a different symbol of football and religion, the Greek hero Ajax. In the 1990s, an older logo of Ajax was replaced by a more stylized version; better suited for merchandise. "Ajax is a god, isn't he?" the F-Siders asked while requesting their old beloved icon be featured in the exhibit. To them, he certainly is. Together we decided to include content about both the fans' fight for the old Ajax logo and the Superjew controversy in the local Amsterdam panels. Fragments from a documentary that contained interviews with "Superjews," including Ronald Pieloor, and real Amsterdam Jews gave depth to this complicated history.

Interactive

The curatorial teams and the designer grappled with the idea of developing interactive elements that could travel with the exhibition. During a workshop, the Basel and Amsterdam teams worked on generating game experience concepts that would be engaging to visitors. A Dutch company, ID Guide, worked with the museum staff to develop the interactive tour. All visitors received a free handset, and we invited them to form teams (red or blue) at the exhibition entrance. The teams could take a photo, which was sent to their email address, and compete at answering questions about the themes. In most of the exhibition venues, sports journalists were used as audio tour narrators. They spoke with an engaging inflection rather than the common neutral museum voice. Halfway through the exhibition, visitors could try their hand at a virtual goaltender's game. The Basel Museum created a box where visitors could vote to indicate whether they were "very," "quite," or only "a little" passionate about football, or not at all. In each city, the exhibition ended by asking visitors to consider whether they thought football was a religion. Interestingly enough, yes and no votes were nearly equal.

Engaging

The greater football community's involvement was essential for the success of the exhibition. As the exhibit competed with the attraction of the stadium, getting fans to the museum was not always easy. Once there, fans tended to regard the exhibition as fun, but also thought provoking. Many found it illuminating to see a passion for their own local club mirrored in that of another city's football fans. For some non-football- fan visitors, the exhibition exposed them to a whole world in which people have near-religious feelings about football, to the extent that they want to be buried in a coffin with the club colors.

Working on this international experience was rewarding for the public historians involved. The exhibition did not tour sports museums and instead appeared at six different cultural museums. Staff at each institution, therefore, gained insight into the football cultures of its own and the other cities. The staff also benefited from exchanging museological ideas and practices. For example, collaborative and inter-active events, like a football tattoo competition, are added to each museum's digital collection. Visitorship at all host locations expanded to include a football fan base, and all of the museums added interesting objects to their collections.[58]

CASE STUDY

Hockey: Challenging Canada's Game

Jenny Ellison

Canada's deep hockey history and public affection for the game posed a challenge in preparing *Hockey*, a comprehensive exhibition presented at the Canadian Museum of History in 2017. While hockey is a sport with global history, many Canadians believe it to be *their* game.[59] Hockey is something from which Canadians legiti-mately derive much pleasure. An estimated 700,000 Canadians register for hockey each year, and millions more keenly follow professional and Olympic hockey.[60] Hockey is a common symbol in advertising, television, music, and art.[61] In the exhibition, the museum sought to capture this spirit while also pointing audiences in directions they may never have previously considered.[62] The Canadian Museum of History chose to focus on the social and cultural significance of hockey in Canada instead of a traditional chronological narrative, which required an understanding of the global, postcolonial history of the game.

Institutional history and context matter for sports exhibitions. As sports historians Vamplew (1998) and Phillips (2007) show, there is a perception that sports history is about nostalgia.[63] A narrative model that emphasizes great wins, celebrated teams, and incredible players has been predominant in sports exhibitions. Audience and stakeholder expectations of a national history museum are different from those of a hall of fame. The Canadian Museum of History's mandate is to enhance the public's "knowledge, understanding, and appreciation of events, experiences, people, and objects that reflect and have shaped Canada's history and identity, and also to enhance their awareness of world history and cultures."[64] Internal research suggests the museum's audience understands this approach. In a 2014 survey, visitors reported that they saw the museum as a place to discover new things about Canadian history, including sports.[65] The museum staff was encouraged by this feedback; however, the public's interest in deep history and unexpected content presented the *Hockey* exhibition team with unique challenges. Men's professional hockey dominates the public conversation and many sport history exhibitions. While internal research suggested audiences wanted something more diverse from the museum, it was not clear if this would hold true for a sports exhibition about Canada's game.

To balance audience expectations with the museum's mandate, the exhibit team decided to focus on the social and cultural aspects of the game. A simple message was crafted: hockey is more than just a game. Creative development specialists worked with curators to define what this meant. Three subthemes were chosen to answer the question: *how* is hockey more than just a game? For this project, the exhibition teams determined that "hockey is more than just a game" because of the game's role in diverse communities, its place in Canadian popular culture, and the ways in which the sport is in constant evolution. Throughout the development process, the exhibition team tested artifact selection, messaging, interactive elements, and learning programs against these core themes and cut exhibition elements that did not meet the criteria. The approach was intentionally thematic: "more than just a game" allowed the exhibition team to create an experience around ideas rather than a chronology of hockey. It also permitted the museum to talk about hockey in a Canadian context without resorting to truisms and stereotypes about Canada's game.

Hockey's Canadian origins are the subject of national and international debate. Seven Canadian towns and cities claim to be hockey's birthplace. International scholars have scrutinized these claims and come to different conclusions. In *On the Origin of Hockey*, Carl Giden, Jean-Patrice Martel, and Patrick Houda argue that documentary and artistic representations of field hockey, bandy, and hurley in Europe predate the colonization of Canada and that *ice* hockey first appeared in England.[66] Though *On the Origin of Hockey* offers an important global perspective on the game, it ignores the postcolonial literature on the sport in Canada. Indigenous peoples across what is now Canada played various forms of hockey long before contact with European settlers. These Indigenous games and technologies, including the use of sticks and pucks, likely shaped settler versions of hockey.[67] Focusing only on the origins of hockey overlooks the ways the game has been shaped by social dynamics and power relations.

Rather than focus on what makes hockey Canadian, the exhibition addressed global themes and how they are reflected in a national context. The exhibit team organized the sport's history into eight thematic sections: earliest players, the locker room, behind the bench (trainers and coaches), professional hockey, media,

Figure 2.3. "Hockey" at the Canadian Museum of History emphasized that diverse groups have always played the game. The first artifact grouping in the exhibition featured a hockey stick made in an Indigenous style and used by a settler boy (c. 1830) in front of a mural of female hockey players (c. 1885). *Source: Canadian Museum of History.*

memorable moments, fans, and popular culture. The exhibition team rejected the idea of organizing the project around types of hockey (i.e., men's and women's, professional and amateur, national and international) because such divisions reinforced the idea that skill and wins and losses should be the primary criteria for understanding sport.

Instead, the exhibit emphasized the cross-cultural history of hockey and the ways it shapes everyday life. The museum set this tone with its very first artifact grouping and mural in the exhibition. Situated in front of an oversized mural of a female hockey player on an outdoor rink, visitors encountered one of the oldest-known hockey sticks. Carbon-dated to the 1830s, the stick belonged to a settler boy. It is distinctive because it is carved in a Mi'kmaq style.

Stories in the exhibition focused on Canada. This was a practical decision reflecting the fact that about 75 percent of the museum's visitors are Canadian. Knowing this impacted the exhibition team's approach to storytelling. The goal was to balance well-known with less familiar, but equally significant, hockey histories. Events and teams that were lesser known illustrated important points about the history of the game. The Colored League of the Maritimes, for example, was an all-Black hockey league that formed circa 1895 because of Black players' (informal) exclusion from other leagues. In existence until 1930, the league was never remotely as popular as the National Hockey League (NHL). Nonetheless, the story illustrated the racial dynamics of hockey for the first half of the twentieth century. The inclusion of stories such as this made *Hockey* unique.

Another strategy was to group artifacts from different times and places into each themed section. This juxtaposition reinforced the exhibition's theme: hockey is more than just a game. In some sections, "more than" referred to cultural elements of hockey. In others, it meant "more than" what visitors might think. For example, in the section entitled "Centre Ice" artifacts representing teams and events that have garnered the most public attention—those of the NHL and men's Olympic hockey—shared space with objects representing women, people with disabilities, fans, amateur players, and coaches. Visitors encountered the most well-known (and valuable) hockey jersey in history—Paul Henderson's sweater from the 1972 Canada-Russia Summit Series—as well as sweaters from iconic Para Ice Hockey and women's hockey players.[68] Because visitors might make a pilgrimage to the museum to see the Henderson jersey, but may not know about other important victories, bringing these objects together in one space was a way to draw a parallel without being overly didactic.

The institution selected some exhibition elements to appeal to international visitors and even those unfamiliar with hockey. Interactive elements, in particular, offered alternative points of entry into the sport. The media section featured a 1979 cartoon of Peter Puck, a character the Canadian Broadcast Corporation created to explain the rules of hockey in plain language. Originally aimed at children, this content was equally useful as an introduction to the game. In the same section, a video karaoke machine gave visitors a chance to call famous hockey games. An element that appealed to different types of learners and people with disabilities was the interactive on the evolution of equipment. Visitors to the locker room section could lift, touch, and feel equipment from different eras. Authentic historical and contemporary equipment provided a tactile, interactive learning experience for visitors.

Neither hockey's global history nor contemporary international hockey history was explicitly part of the exhibition. Initially, a section called "Hockey Diplomacy" included Olympic and world hockey events. The exhibition team cut the section because it did not fit easily within the exhibition's subthemes: community, popular culture, and the evolution of hockey. Some artifacts about international hockey were redistributed to areas where they better supported the messaging. For example, France St. Louis's 1990 Women's World Ice Hockey tournament jacket appeared in a subsection on "Team Colors." The label explored the decision to dress Team Canada in hot pink at that tournament. Beyond that, the development of the first international women's hockey event was not discussed in detail. Part of the process of planning the project was accepting that the exhibition team could not include all stories in the exhibition. With some topics, the exhibit team let go of depth and breadth to allow other stories to shine. Research on international hockey undertaken for the exhibition was incorporated into other projects including social media, blog posts, and an academic collection entitled *Hockey: Challenging Canada's Game/Au-delà du sport national.*[69]

Using global and postcolonial sports research as the basis for decision-making allowed the Canadian Museum of History to tell a more nuanced story of "Canada's Game." Rather than a chronological history or one highlighting sports records, the institution articulated hockey's social and cultural importance. Using "more than just a game" as a core message allowed the exhibit team to focus on the social and cultural dimensions of hockey history. By the end of the exhibition, Canadian and international visitors hopefully left with a better sense of the role of hockey in Canada. The sport is more than just a game because of its ubiquity in Canadian life and culture. The simple core message allowed the museum to bring star artifacts together with unexpected hockey stories. Choices were made with an understanding that there is more than one way to tell the story of hockey. Hockey is a topic that the Canadian Museum of History is likely to address again in the future because it is a historically rich and culturally relevant subject.

Acknowledgment: Ideas discussed in this article were the product of a multidisciplinary exhibit team that included Dean Oliver, director of research, Jennifer Anderson, historian, and Dominique Savard, creative development specialist and the author.

NOTES

1. J. A. Mangan, "Christ and the Imperial Playing Fields: Thomas Hughes's Ideological Heirs in Empire," *The International Journal of the History of Sports* 23, no. 5 (2006): 777–804; the quote is from Markku Hokkanen and J. A. Mangan, "Further Variations on a Theme: The Games Ethic Further Adapted: Scottish Moral Missionaries and Muscular Christians in Malawi," *The International Journal of the History of Sports* 23, no. 8 (2006): 382.

2. Richard Gruneau and David Whitson, *Hockey Night in Canada* (Toronto: Garamond, 1993), 39.

3. Tony Bennett, *The Birth of the Museum: History, Theory, Politics* (New York: Routledge, 1995), 105.

4. Jennifer Barrett, *Museums and the Public Sphere* (Oxford: John Wiley and Sons, 2011), 9–50.

5. Rodney G. S. Carter, "Of Things Said and Unsaid: Power, Archival Silences and Power in Silence," *Archivaria* 61 (Spring 2006): 219–20.

6. Chrischené Julius, "Recalling Community at the District Six Museum," in *Interpreting Sports at Museums and Historic Sites*, Kathryn Leann Harris and Douglas Stark, eds. (Lanham, MD: Rowman & Littlefield, 2023), 160–168.

7. Nicole F. Markham, "Aces and Places: Serving the Globe at the International Tennis Hall of Fame," in *Interpreting Sports at Museums and Historic Sites*, Kathryn Leann Harris and Douglas Stark, eds. (Lanham, MD: Rowman & Littlefield, 2013), 64–68.

8. Murray Whyte, "Art Spiegelman and the Triumph of 'Low Art,'" *Toronto Star*, December 19, 2014.

9. Annemarie de Wildt, "*Football Hallelujah!*: A European Traveling Exhibition," in *Interpreting Sports at Museums and Historic Sites*, Harris and Stark, eds., 68–74.

10. UNESCO, "International Charter of Physical Education and Sports," 1978, accessed May 12, 2017, http://www.unesco.org/education/pdf/SPORTS_E.PDF, accessed May 12, 2017; a revised Charter of Physical Education, Physical Activity and Sports was approved in 2015; see, accessed May 12, 2017, http://www.unesco.org/new/en/social-and-human-sciences/themes/physical-education-and-sports/sports- charter.

11. UNESCO.

12. Douglas Booth, *The Race Game: Sports and Politics in South Africa* (London: Routledge, 1998).

13. Deborah McPhail, "What to Do with the 'Tubby Hubby?' 'Obesity,' the Crisis of Masculinity, and the Nuclear Family in Early Cold War Canada," *Antipode* 41, no. 5 (November 2009): 1021–50; Christopher Dummitt, *The Manly Modern: Masculinity in Postwar Canada* (Vancouver: University of British Columbia Press, 2007); Sonya O. Rose, *Which People's War? National Identity and Citizenship in Britain, 1939–1945* (New York: Oxford University Press, 2003).

14. Ellen Snyder, "Sociology of Nostalgia: Halls of Fame and Museums in America," *Sociology of Sport Journal* 8, no. 3 (1991): 228–38.

15. Wray Vamplew, "Facts and Artifacts: Sports Historians and Sports Museums," *Journal of Sport History* 25, no. 2 (1998): 272.

16. Murray G. Phillips, *Representing the Sporting Past in Museums and Halls of Fame* (New York: Routledge, 2012), 250.

17. Booth, *The Race Game.*

18. Julius, "Recalling Community at the District Six Museum."

19. Jennifer Sandlin, Michael O'Malley, and Jake Burdick, "Mapping the Complexity of Public Pedagogy Scholarship: 1894–2010," *Review of Educational Research* 81, no. 3 (September 2011): 338–75.

20. Bryan Palmer, *Canada's 1960s: The Ironies of Identity in a Rebellious Era* (Toronto: University of Toronto Press, 2009), 216–18.

21. Stephen Weil, *Making Museums Matter* (Washington, DC: Smithsonian Institution Press, 2002), 28.

22. Elaine Heumann Gurian, "Curator: From Soloist to Impresario," in *Hot Topics, Public Culture, Museums*, Fiona Cameron and Lynda Kelly, eds. (Newcastle upon Tyne: Cambridge Scholars Publishing), 98.

23. Fiona Cameron, "Introduction," in *Hot Topics, Public Culture, Museums*, Fiona Cameron and Lynda Kelly, eds. (Newcastle upon Tyne: Cambridge Scholars Publishing, 2010), 5.

24. Carter, "Of Things Said and Unsaid," 222; Amy Lonetree, *Decolonizing Museums: Representing Native America in National and Trivial Museums* (Chapel Hill: University of North Carolina Press, 2012), 5–17.

25. Norman Hillmer, "The Canadian War Museum and the Military Identity of an Unmilitary People," *Canadian Military History* 19, no. 3 (Summer 2010): 25; Richard H. Kohn, "History and the Culture Wars: The Case of the Smithsonian Institution's *Enola Gay* Exhibition," *Journal of American History* 82, no. 3 (December 1995): 1041.

26. Phillips, *Representing the Sporting Past*, 2.

27. Jenny Ellison, "Controversies in Context: Communication, Hot Topics, and Museums in Canada," in *Hot Topics, Popular Culture, and Museums*, Fiona Cameron and Lynda Kelly, eds. (Newcastle upon Tyne: Cambridge Scholars Publishing, 2010), 187.

28. BBC, "Prize Money in Sport—BBC Sport Study," BBC.com, June 19, 2017, https://www.bbc.com/sport/40300519.

29. IOC, Gender Equality Review Project Recommendations, Lausanne 12 October 2017, p. 26.

30. Bruce Kidd, *The Struggle for Canadian Sport* (Toronto: University of Toronto Press, 1996).

31. Jenny Ellison, "He Would Like to Settle the Matter: Behind the Scenes of the *Blainey v. OHA* Decision," *Findings/Trouvailles*, August 31, 2017, accessed May 11, 2018, https://champlainsociety.utpjournals.press/findings-trouvailles/2017/08/behind-the-scenes-of-the-blainey-v-oha-decision.

32. Jenny Ellison, "Hockey: Challenging Canada's Game," in *Interpreting Sports at Museums and Historic Sites*, Harris and Stark, eds., 74–78.

33. Paul Williams, "Hailing the Cosmopolitan Conscience," in *Hot Topics, Public Culture, Museums*, Fiona Cameron and Lynda Kelly, eds. (Newcastle upon Tyne: Cambridge Scholars Publishing), 228.

34. Williams, "Hailing the Cosmopolitan Conscience," 228.

35. Cameron, "Introduction," 4, 6.

36. Bruce Kidd, "The Making of a Hockey Artifact: A Review of the Hockey Hall of Fame," *Journal of Sports History* 23, no. 3 (Fall 1996): 329.

37. The Museum at the International Tennis Hall of Fame (ITHF) was founded in 1954 to complement the newly sanctioned National Lawn Tennis Hall of Fame, later to become the International Tennis Hall of Fame (1975). The ITHF is housed at the Newport Casino, the first major commission of the American architectural firm McKim, Mead & White, the location of the first U.S. National Championships (US Open), and a National Historic Landmark. Over its sixty-plus years, the museum has professionalized and grown into one of the finest sporting museums in the world. In 2013, the museum achieved accreditation by the American Alliance of Museums (AAM), becoming the first sports hall of fame to do so. In 2017, the ITHF became an official Affiliate of the Smithsonian Institution in Washington, D.C., becoming the first independent sports hall of fame to earn this prestigious recognition.

38. Prior to 1968, the major tennis events around the world, including the Australian National Championships, French National Championships, Wimbledon, U.S. National Championships, Olympics, Davis Cup, Wightman Cup, and Federation Cup, were accessible to amateur players only. Players that turned professional for economic reasons were forced to compete on separate tours without the support of their countries' tennis governing bodies or the International Tennis Federation.

39. Wheelchair tennis began in the late 1970s when Brad Parks (International Tennis Hall of Fame Class of 2010, https://www.tennisfame.com/hall-of-famers/inductees/brad-parks) hit a tennis ball from a wheelchair during rehabilitation for a skiing accident that left him paralyzed. Wheelchair tennis is now played in approximately one hundred countries, with more than 150 tournaments in more than forty countries, and is fully ingrained in the global governing body for the sport. To learn more: https://www.itftennis.com/wheelchair/organisation/about-the-sport.aspx.

40. The major tennis events that occur each year are the Australian Open, the French Open, Wimbledon, and the U.S. Open. The U.S. Open was the first to institute equal prize money in 1973, while the Australian Open and French Open did so in 2001 and 2006, respectively.

41. The Tennis & Culture touch table presents a dynamic bird's-eye view of an active tennis court. Visitors can approach and engage the table from any direction, and depending on where they step up to the table, various interactive features are available. The two ends prompt visitors to compete in a Tennis & Culture Trivia game (either against the computer or a human opponent), while the sides enable visitors to access six different Tennis & Culture modules that are related to the content themes featured in the gallery. Both the Trivia Challenge and Interactive Modules leverage content featured in the museum in the following themes: pop culture, technology, games, fashion, accessories, and decorative arts.

42. The Call the Point interactive lets visitors play the role of a well-known announcer for a thrilling tennis moment. Visitors take a seat at the desk, which features a touch screen monitor and microphone. A large monitor is mounted on the wall in front of the desk. Visitors select one of the classic moments to watch and hear a live call with transcription. After watching the original call, visitors can then record their own version. Once complete, they can listen to their recording along with the video of the selected moment and email themselves said recording.

43. As of 2019, there are 257 hall of famers representing twenty-fournations (https://www.tennisfame.com/hall-of-famers/eligibility-voting-process).

44. The ATP (Association of Tennis Professionals) World Tour is the men's professional tennis tour (www.atpworldtour.com). The Women's Tennis Association (WTA) is the women's professional tennis tour (www.wtatour.com). The International Tennis Federation (ITF) is the world governing body of tennis, overseeing the following five areas of the game: administration and regulation; organizing international competition; structuring the game; developing the game, and promoting the game (www.itftennis.com).

45. This particular exhibit continues to be updated to remain relevant to the Olympic movement, including traveling to the 2016 games in Rio de Janeiro and hopefully the upcoming 2020 games in Tokyo.

46. The International Tennis Hall of Fame has fully digitized and shared two curated collections via its website, with plans for additional ones. "Courting Fashion" was completed in 2018 (https://www.tennisfame.com/courting-fashion) and "Tins, Cans, and Cartons" launched in Spring 2019 (https://cans.tennisfame.com/).

47. In this context, the term "football" is interchangeable with "soccer."

48. Thanks to Marie-Paule Jungblut, Tom van der Molen, Paul Spies, and Jean-Louis Postula for providing comments.

49. Desmond Morris, *The Soccer Tribe* (London: Jonathan Cape, 1981); Simon Kuper, *Football Against The Enemy* (London: Orion, 1994); Franklin Foer, *How Soccer Explains the World: An Unlikely Theory of Globalization* (New York: HarperCollins, 2004).

50. Michael Novak, *The Joy of Sports. Endzones, Bases, Baskets, Balls and the Consecration of the American Spirit* (New York: Basic Books, 1976).

51. Martyn Percy and Rogan Taylor, "Something for the Weekend, Sir? Leisure, Ecstasy and Identity in Football and Contemporary Religion," *Leisure Studies* 16, no. 1: 37–49. Percy and Taylor state that the etymology of religion comes from 'to bind.'

52. Serge Moscovici, *The Age of the Crowd: A Historical Treatise on Mass Psychology* (Cambridge: Cambridge University Press, 1986), 183.

53. *Blood in, Blood out*, accessed July 26, 2018, www.bloodinbloodout.nl.

54. Bradford Plumer, "How Soccer Explains the World. Franklin Foer on the World Cup and Our Ever- Shrinking Globe," *Mother Jones*, August 4, 2004, accessed October 15th, 2017, http://www.motherjones.com/politics/2004/08/how-soccer-explains-world.

[56] Foer, *How Soccer Explains the World*.

55. Foer, *How Soccer*.

56. Gary J. Armstrong and Richard Giulianotti, *Football Cultures and Identities* (London: McMillian, 1999).

57. Pieloor presents on YouTube as Pi Alfa with over 6 million views: https://www.youtube.com/user/rapie1960. The images show much less violence than mainstream images of hard-core fans because Pieloor's focus is more on fan behavior. However, he also did this as to not risk persecution of F-siders nor their objection to his filming.

58. For further exploration see these sources: Armstrong and Giulianotti, *Football Cultures and Identities*; Foer, *How Soccer Explains the World*; Kuper, *Football Against The Enemy*; Simon Kuper, *Ajax, The Dutch, The War: Soccer in Europe During the Second World War* (Orion: London, 2003); Novak, *The Joy of Sports*; Moscovici, *The Age of the Crowd*; Morris, *The Soccer Tribe*; Percy and Taylor, "Something for the Weekend," 37–49; Bradford Plumer, "How Soccer Explains the World." Websites Accessed: https://hart.amsterdam/nl /page/31279/voetbal, https://www.hmb.ch/fussball_glaube_liebe_hoffnung.html, http://www .gadagne.musees.lyon.fr/index.php/history_en/Histoire/Expositions/Expositions-temporaires /Archives/Divinement-foot, http://www.provincedeliege.be/fr/node/11792, http://citymuseum .lu/exhibition/football/.

59. See: Jason Blake, "From Fact to Fiction-An Introduction to the Mythology of Ice Hockey in Canadian Life and Literature," *Elope* 1 (2004): 81–94; Carl Giden, Patrick Houda, and Jean-Patrice Martel, *On the Origin of Hockey* (Stockholm and Chambly: Hockey Origin Publishing, 2014); Gruneau and Whitson, *Hockey Night in Canada*; Jack Jedwab, "Giving Hockey's Past a Future: Identity Meets Demography in Canadian Sports," *International Journal of Canadian Studies* 35 (2007): 191–214; Garth Vaughn, *The Puck Starts Here: The Origin of Canada's Great Winter Game Ice Hockey* (Fredericton: Goose Lane Editions, 1996).

60. Jedwab, "Giving Hockey's Past a Future," 201.

61. Tim Elcombe, "Hockey New Year's Eve in Canada: Nation-Making at the Montreal Forum," *International Journal of the History of Sport* 27, no. 8 (2010): 1287–312.

62. Nancy Bouchier and Ken Cruickshank, "Reflections on Creating Critical Sport History for a Popular Audience: 'The People and the Bay," *Journal of Sport History* 25, no. 2 (1998): 309–16.

63. See: Phillips, *Representing the Sporting Past*; Wray Vamplew, "Facts and Artefacts: Sports Historians and Sports Museums," *Journal of Sport History* 25, no. 2 (1998): 268–82.

64. "About the Museum," Canadian Museum of History, https://www.historymuseum.ca/about/the-museum/#tabs, accessed July 24, 2018.

65. Public Research and Evaluation, "Summative Evaluation of the *Empress of Ireland* Exhibition at the Canadian Museum of History," Canadian Museum of History Corporation, 2014. Research based on a survey administered to 303 museum visitors in summer 2014.

66. Giden, Houda, and Martel, *On the Origin of Hockey*, 3–16, 36. Hurley is an adaptation of the Irish field sport hurling that appeared in Canada in the late eighteenth century. Hurling sticks have long necks and curved, paddle-like ends. The object of the game is to hit a ball through a goal post. It is played on the ice. The game was played at some Canadian boys' schools. Bandy is an on-ice version of field hockey. Players used curved sticks and a ball.

67. Stewart Culin, *Games of the North American Indians* (Toronto: General Publishing Company Ltd, 1907 (1975)), 561, 616–17, 621–29, 632, 642; Michael Heine, *Dene Games: A Culture and Resource Manual* (Yellowknife: Sport North, 1997), 2–181–184; Vaughan, *The Puck Starts Here*, 139–46.

68. The Canadian Press, "Paul Henderson's Jersey Sells for Record $1.2M: Auctioneer," *CBC.ca.*, March 2, 2012, accessed March 14, 2018, https://www.cbc.ca/sports/hockey/nhl/paul-henderson-s-jersey-sells-for-record-1-2m-auctioneer-1.1191588.

69. Jenny Ellison and Jennifer Anderson, eds., *Hockey: Challenging Canada's Game/ Au-delà du sport national* (Ottawa: University of Ottawa Press, 2018).

Chapter Three

Fans, Coaches, Athletes, and Participants

Interpreting Sports and Identity

Kathryn Leann Harris

Museums face fierce competition as they wrestle with an ongoing struggle for relevance, and—perhaps most pressing—face an ever-increasing demand to create engaging guest experiences. Curators of sports-themed exhibits and museums face an added challenge: the present. Sports are an all-consuming, active, ongoing presence in American society. While a sports museum or exhibit can be an extension of the sporting event excitement, they should also offer experiences that are at once celebratory while simultaneously placing sports in the context of cultural history and contemporary society. A lively base of engaged fans, coaches, athletes, participants, and stakeholders have more than a simple interest in how institutions interpret sport history. Their involvement and agendas complement the efforts of museums even as they add complexity. When crafting a sports museum or exhibit, it is paramount to consider the influence of these participants and grapple seriously with ways to involve and challenge their voices.

Key Interpretive Concepts

1. *Personal Identification:* Let fans, coaches, athletes, and participants see themselves in the story in a balanced way while remembering they are highly invested stakeholders.
2. *Consider Both Direct Experience and Historical Context:* The immediate attraction to sports lies largely in the excitement of live competition while exploring the past elicits a different kind of pull. Offer both, in unexpected ways, for optimal results.
3. *Balanced Commemoration:* Remember you are talking about humans who are neither gods nor villains. Honoring legacy with a balanced approach is rooted in a pragmatic image of humanity.

Presence

Nearly all organized sports in America trace their genesis to the mid-to-late 1800s. Popularity and participation grew at a slow pace until the early part of the twentieth century when the birth of professional sports organizations brought a sea change in the sports landscape. Interest ballooned and then exploded, leading to the well-funded, highly attended, and expertly organized sports culture that exists today. Locked within this culture lies a century's worth of fans who are ever-increasing in size and energy, coaches, and personnel whose livelihoods were or are connected to a particular game or team, and players that range from amateurs to the most elite players in nearly every category.

The personal identities, lives, and legacies of coaches and athletes are deeply woven into the fabric of their respective sporting cultures. Many, if not most, athletes and coaches remain connected to their sport long after retirement. They often maintain relationships with active participants and desire prosperous futures for those involved in a game they grew to love. This can be true even when a coach or athlete has a falling-out with the sporting community connected to their sport. In fact, their interest in the narrative may increase as they work to protect or rebuild their reputation or to redirect their efforts toward meaning making and contributing. In any case, the initial love for the sport they played or coached rarely wanes significantly in one's lifetime. This is a very important consideration.

Fans likewise contribute to sports in such great measures that it is nearly impossible to separate them from the game. They invest on many levels—financially, emotionally, and mentally—as well as with their time, resources, attention, and physical presence. While sports can exist without fans, fans contribute mightily to their size and scope. It is a mutually beneficial relationship. Spectator revenue and support lead to larger stadiums and arenas and extends into television, radio, and online broadcasts. Fan opinions drive social media interest, newspaper and magazine writing, and talk radio conversation. Generations of enthusiasts bring team loyalties into homes and family legacies. They care deeply about their beloved sports figures or teams and often find a great deal of pride or disgrace in the choices and achievements of those they follow.

Competition is deeply ingrained into the American character, and sports is one arena in which this manifests itself most clearly. Athletics have become so pervasive in national life that they often touch, influence, and/or affect even those who do not care about them. Simply put, sports are nearly impossible to ignore. Games are an unavoidable sideshow, ever present in the backdrop of restaurants and family gatherings, often central in professional banter and social conversation. Many find joy and inspiration from attending, participating in, and creating family rituals around sports. For those who cringe at the space, place, and ways that sports inhabit American life, the opportunities for political engagement are replete and ever present. Sports, and the competition-at-all-cost mentality associated with a sports-centric culture, often expose the seedy underbelly of society through issues like "pay to play" in college programs, drug use in baseball, sexual abuse in gymnastics, and bullying, racism, and anti-LGBT sentiments in a number of sports.

With a topic so central to a people, no one is ever truly sitting on the sidelines. Sports offer windows and insights into everyday life that the public is craving to explore, opportunities for meaningful engagement to take root and flourish. Sports museums and historic sites should embrace the cultural and social issues around engagement, topics and issues that matter most to stakeholders no matter their interest level in sports. Begin with the assumption that most of those connected to any given sport care to see the sport thrive. Stay committed to a central, heartfelt purpose that elevates the whole rather than undercuts or disenfranchises some. Avoid shying away from the voices and perspectives of the ever-evolving conversation about the role of sports in our lives. Embrace them instead. Actively engage participants in the narrative. Grant them their agency. Give their stories a place to shine. At the same time, embrace the difficulties of interpreting something that means so much to society; lean into them.

Personal Identification

In January 2013, a Montreal newspaper's large cover image showed an artist's rendition of a child staring out at a frozen pond donned in a hockey uniform. The caption read, "THIS IS WHO WE ARE."[1] It was the morning of the Montreal Canadiens' return to the ice upon resolution to the NHL strike. Inherent in the image and caption is the weighted impact of the sport upon the local population. An extended absence from the game cut at the heart of the Canadian's identity. Returning brought them back to something central to who they are as a people, who they always were since children playing on the open frozen waterways in their communities, and who they remain throughout their lives as fans and amateur players at virtually all stages of their lives. As with all fans, "who they are" is not a one-dimensional aspect of their lives. Humanity is messy and multifaceted, just like sports. Both hearken to something innocent and primal, while at the same time mature and complex. That is what makes life, and sports, so interesting and enthralling. Knowing this, and capitalizing on it, is a rich opportunity and significant responsibility. Fans and participants offer a passionate audience that is central to sports museums and exhibits. Their invested interest gives museums reason to generate new and updated sports-related content. This does not necessarily equate to the proverbial philosophy "If you build it, they will come." It is an open secret that many sports museums often sit empty.[2] Yet, sports history is relevant to the lives of those most involved with each team or sport. For this reason, it is paramount to include them as part of your rollout strategy, and to do so with a clear understanding of their invested interest.

Considering identification becomes very personal when the exhibit's subject is living and breathing, a consistent theme with sports history interpretation. The majority of figures featured in history museums will never know what is said about them because they are no longer living. The exact opposite is true with sports. Given the short timeline of their development in America, virtually all major sports histories connect either to someone alive today or are no more than three generations removed from someone who is alive. This adds an interesting and important constraint for museums. Central subjects might walk through the institution's front door and stand in the galleries while reading a review of themselves. In many cases, staff might aim to attract the attention and interest of athletes, actively recruiting to engage them in the process or promotion. In other examples, the museum might be acutely aware that they are treading into some dicey territory with their chosen analysis. A local historical society may, for example, choose to discuss and display the complicated history of a local beloved sports figure, past or present, that captivates the hearts of the community. In either case, it will serve the institution well to consider the impact of their interpretations on the very person about whom they are reporting and to remember they (or someone very close to them) will be personally affected and impacted.

When sports fans and participants visit a history exhibit, they do so with a vested interest, one that is emotionally and often financially tied to major commercial sports entities. This matters, sometimes quite a lot. Money talks, and the people closest to a sport or team are also the ones who spend their hard-earned dollars to support the ones they love. They are loyal and opinionated; this loyalty is part of what makes the exhibits relevant and well attended. If your museum or site decides to challenge hagiography or take on a tough issue, be aware that you might conflict with the perspectives of loyal fans and participants. Also, know that no team or sport's fan base functions as a singular bloc. Like any group, they comprise a nuanced mix of societal, cultural, and political perspectives. There is a delicate, and important, balance to strike here. When choosing to take on tougher issues such as safety concerns or societal ills, keep in mind the perspective and interest of fans and participants. Then use it as motivation to find new and creative ways to generate engaging conversations.

Museums know visitors are likely to attend or not attend an exhibit based on its content, which can have a big impact on what the staff chooses to include or ignore.[3] This is particularly true when sports are the central subject matter. Fans, coaches, and athletes alike often rally around the public display of their team's history, even claiming a stake in the discussion of collective identity and how individual memories play a role in its interpretation.

Focusing on a popular figure or omitting unpopular narratives are common sports museum practices expressly because of the presence of loyal followers. The Alabama Sports Hall of Fame in Birmingham, Alabama recognizes more than three hundred inductees from a wide range of sports, including world-class athletes like Jesse Owens, Hank Aaron, Mia Hamm, and Charles Barkley. Individual cases feature a selection of objects from each inductee's career. Included among them is the state's most historically revered college football coach, Bear Bryant, for whom the museum exhibits a disproportionately high number of objects and images. Engaging the University of Alabama fans in this way is a draw for the large and impassioned base. The Patriots Hall of Fame in Foxboro, Massachusetts, appealed to their fan base by implementing selective interpretation. An exhibit on Malcolm Butler's much-discussed Super Bowl XLIX interception, which led New England to victory, excluded any mention of the "deflate-gate" scandal that famously and publicly rocked the franchise during that same year.[4]

These practices are rampant throughout the field and in need of review. As Wray Vamplew notes, "many sports museums, even at the elite level, eschew the controversial; they are reluctant to give the whole picture and deliberately omit things from history. World champions are presented without blemish, and world championships are presented without political context. Halls of Fame in particular are driven by 'the ever-present emphasis on finding heroes . . . [which] . . . overshadows the less showy need for historical accuracy.'"[5] Moreover, these methods are widely accepted, even expected where sports content is involved. Industry perspectives suggest that these practices are "brought on by the belief that the fans of the sport might be upset by the intervention of real history into the fantasy world of nostalgia."[6] The idea that fans want to see a "happy ending," however, is not a foregone conclusion, meriting exploration for common practices such as those at the Alabama Sports Hall of Fame or Patriots Hall of Fame.[7]

Exhibit text written *for* the fans can result in two museums describing the same event in very different ways, as is the case with the University of Washington's Hall of Fame and the Bear Bryant Museum at the University of Alabama. Both discuss the 1926 Rose Bowl. The University of Washington's museum has a section dedicated to the school's many appearances in the Rose Bowl—both wins and losses. The 1926 game was a loss for Washington. In their interpretation, the museum praises the team for being favored, leading the game throughout the first half, and losing by only one point after their starting quarterback was injured at the start of the second half despite his fourth-quarter rally. For the University of Alabama, the 1926 Rose Bowl was not only their first bowl game but also the first bowl appearance for any team from the Southeast. Being invited and then winning, even by one point and even with a hurt player on the opposing side, was a marquee moment that changed the trajectory of college football in the South—facts the Alabama fan base knows well. Thus, the Bear Bryant Museum celebrates the glory of the moment, including the larger story behind the win, and omits the finer details of the game that the University of Washington includes. Each retelling caters specifically to their fan bases. Neither is incorrect. Both are incomplete. This can be a successful strategy for promoting a team and exciting a fan base. While these are not egregious omissions, they do speak to the easy pitfalls of interpreting only one side of a sports story. Well-balanced text at both institutions could invite visitors to get outside a singular mindset and consider the impact on both communities. This method promotes complexity of thought, inclusivity, connectivity, and accuracy.

Catering to a fan base is a tactic that affects a museum's interpretation of sports history facts—offered here as both a strategy and a cautionary tale. There is a delicate balance to strike. The fan voice is important; a museum is wise to not overlook this factor. Involving fan and participant perspectives can bolster the relevancy and intrigue of your content, involve your audience in an excited and connected way, and possibly expand your reach. Still, getting intricately connected to constituents can compromise a museum's identity, particularly if the goal is to create a reciprocally beneficial relationship.

When nurturing participant or fan connections causes a museum to avoid addressing politics, going after the jugular, or slanting and omitting information, the museum needs to consider whether they are sacrificing integrity and wider impact. Vamplew explains, "the tendency of museums is to celebrate the rise of a player from rags to riches but barely dwell on his or her slide to obscurity, alcoholism, poverty, or social dysfunction. Revelations that famous players were also physically abusive to spouses or were recreational drug abusers or rapists receive the response that this occurred off the field and was not related to their sporting performance. Yet, he goes on to say, "[certainly some] . . . fans prefer the true picture to the sanitized version."[8] Keeping visitors in the dark about what is really happening does not necessarily best serve them or the museum. Some topics are important to bring to light, and balanced commemorative practices welcome healthy, productive discourse about them. Alternately, placing an emphasis on one sports figure among many can appear as placating or pandering to a specific collective interest. Narrative omissions may speak to an institution's obligations and appease certain constituents, yet the public at large is nonetheless aware, and may find the exhibit lacking credibility due to glaring oversights.[9] By displaying disparate narratives with equity and inclusivity, institutions can uphold professional ethics, attract a wider reach, and offer opportunities for visitors to engage in meaningful conversations.

Examining the interpretation of culturally appropriated mascots offers a particularly important, and likely challenging, opportunity to explore accuracy and myths. Mascots hold a unique place in historical understanding due to the nature of sports. They are central to a team's identity. Yet, myths and misinformation often encircle mascot stories that are only loosely connected to historical facts. Without proper context, too much accuracy is lost, which can be dangerous when presented improperly. As former NMAI Director Kevin Gover has observed, the Chicago Blackhawks or Illinois Illini, for example, do not recite the accomplishments of Black Hawk or Illini before each game. Why? For starters, the middle of a sports event is not really the best place to learn history. Mainly, because historical accuracy is not the primary goal at that moment; promoting the team is. Some organizations *try* to redefine the mascots through creating origin myths. This is also problematic, for many reasons, namely the fans. When discussing the challenges associated with recontextualizing Native mascots rather than eliminating them, Gover attested, "What they could not control was their fans, and that's the problem. Once you open Pandora's box, fans simply cannot be trusted to behave as fair-minded human beings."[10] Even with redefinitions and updates, a sizable collection of fans will usually remain loyal to the previous branded images until trusted organizations explain the cultural responsibility of eliminating offensive caricatures and imagery. This is where museums must intervene and hold a consistent position that educates the public with accuracy and inclusivity, despite fan yearnings.

Let visitors know that sometimes the best way to protect an entity is by giving voice to more unseemly areas that need to be reformed, or at least explored. This is particularly relevant to topics of safety. While some of the governing factions of the football world prefer to look away from the risk of concussions in football, the sport itself will ultimately suffer if the museum continues to ignore it. Players will continue getting injured, parents will stop allowing their children to play, divisions may arise within organizations, and ultimately the government may have to act. Museums and historic sites are well positioned to present a balanced perspective and thus provide an ideal setting for the type of discourse that helps communities grapple with these tough subjects before they become toxic to society. As an ongoing standard practice, stay true to the institution. When considering a potentially controversial topic, remember to align with your institutional values and mission rather than defaulting to releasing only the most palatable content.

When writing about sports, know that you are writing for a highly knowledgeable audience, but one whose understanding is neither necessarily consistent nor altogether accurate. As it turns out, most visitors will already know much of the information you are presenting, and many will want to tell you what is missing, their own experiences, or even what they think your exhibit should be. Fans tend to remember sports history in a variety of ways, sometimes incongruent with historical accuracy. Many carry a wide swath of knowledge and often know more or different information than the museum, information they relish retelling. Your institution will face all types of input and critique from visitors who remember stories exactly the same (or even completely differently) than you have reported it, sometimes stories that are central to their tight-knit fan community or even their identity. Provable facts will not actually satisfy everyone's appetite; still, make certain every figure, statement, and statistic is accurate and current. Facts keep your reputation intact and give you the confidence to confront any challengers with a listening ear and engaging attitude.[11]

Keep the fan and participant interest and passion top of mind, and continue to innovate and create relevant reasons for them to show up again and again. They will likely relish the opportunity to participate. Consider specific ways to involve them in the creative process—engage their voices in the exhibit or program development process and find reasons they might visit and/or participate. Those who are closest to the game can serve as resources for information, events, collaboration, and promotion. Tap into their direct and personal experiences and let them tell you what they know. Use this to foster dialogue among similar or even disparate fan bases and teams. With some of these tools, the museum space can even be used to create lasting memories, particularly for annual museum events that coincide with popular live sporting events. For example, a history museum or local or state sports museum in Kentucky may hold a pregame gathering the night before the Kentucky Derby that features special guests such as previous jockeys and team coaches. Coming to an event like this could become a new tradition that fans and participants associate with a treasured competition.

Direct Experience vs/and Historical Context

Sports reside in two distinctly different places in our cultural consciousness: the past and the present. This creates a challenge. In theory, sports museums and exhibits should have a sizeable, consistent built-in audience. In reality, many sports museums struggle to generate large attendance numbers. The lure of the past is often what draws sports visitors to the museum, while the thrill of a live sporting event keeps their attention. Institutions should provide a combination of historical intrigue and game day excitement. Many sports museums create exhibitions almost entirely rooted in historical facts, figures, and details. While informative, they lack pizzazz and a sense of play. An exhibit based on giving visitors the "game day experience" can be a lot of fun but can also seem contrived. Visitors may leave questioning the added value of visiting the museum, when they can attend and experience the excitement of a live game, discuss the impact of sports history through media outlets, play the games they enjoy, or collect their favorite objects in their own home. The most successful models combine the past and the present in creative ways.

Simulating the game day experience is a challenging, and worthy, endeavor that also helps engage visitors in the lure of the present sporting world. Large interactive modules serve as a consistent draw, but re-creating a live event can require a lot of space, technology, and money. The NASCAR Hall of Fame features a racing interactive in which visitors can experience the thrill of driving a race car. Features like this are costly, require planning, and utilize museum staff as attendants—and they are worth the effort. Visitors flock to museums for these types of immersive and unique experiences that connect to the thrill of attending an event of the sport they love or let nonfans get a glimpse of the excitement. Once drawn to the museum, NHOF attendees can explore the museum's rich participant-centric content and connect exhibition driving experiences to the professional lives of athletes and crew.[12]

The Chick-fil-A College Football Hall of Fame in Atlanta provides another example. In an immersive experience, their opening video takes visitors directly into the exuberance of football stadiums around the country. Galleries invite visitors into the Saturday game day experience with sights, sounds, and activities. Fans select their team upon entering and wear a badge that personalizes the guest experience. They can sing their team's fight song and represent their school in a virtual ESPN College Gameday video. Exhibits feature life-size images of excited fans in packed stadiums as well as iconic mascots and marching bands, cheerleaders, teams, and significant games and achievements. Fans can enjoy the virtual experience of standing in the middle of any college stadium. The museum experience ends with a half-sized football field and a chance to attempt to kick a field goal. Altogether, these individual pieces re-create the game day experience for a college football fan in an engaging way.

Remember that sports are a social activity, practiced in groups, which opens a large door for museums to attract expanded audiences.[13] The sporting world offers countless opportunities for museums to access a much more diverse audience. Think creatively about topics that appeal to different groups at different times. Give them reasons to bring a friend to explore sports history together from personally applicable perspectives. This replicable practice is easily accessible, something you can use throughout the year to target various audience subsets. Athletics are such a central part of everyday life that virtually every demographic group is well represented, which can and should be reflected in the museum space, including current notable gaps.[14]

Another way to engage fans is to interweave current events, news, and highlights. Create space in a permeant exhibit to alternate current events and create museum programming that addresses ongoing sports and political conversations from media outlets. This can be a unique way to tie together pieces from the past with pieces of the present. During the global COVID-19 pandemic, the International Tennis Hall of Fame created a digital exhibit named *When Tennis Stopped*. The exhibit reviewed the times that professional tennis halted due to global catastrophic events, namely World Wars I and II. To encourage engagement while the museum was closed, fans could have their name and picture added to the digital exhibit by donating to the hall of fame.[15] This method works for most ongoing news stories as they overlap with sports: national debates, social media trends, and updates connected to participants, coaches, and players. Overlay today's discussions with relevant historical topics to add depth and interest. Then, allow visitors a chance to interact with the display or discussion to further the conversation and/or impact.

In many ways, the mystique is missing from sports museums because the games are so accessible. Sure, fans often want to kneel at the altar of a precious object, play the fun games, and/or relive the past. But this low-hanging fruit is not as much of a draw as you might think. In some cases, a well-known story or a specific set of objects will move many visitors to make a pilgrimage and enter your doors. This is usually most true when a deep sense of passion is involved within a fan base. The National Baseball Hall of Fame and Museum serves as a pilgrimage site that attracts many annual visitors in part precisely for an impassioned, must-see visit of America's favorite pastime.[16] This is not true for all sports or objects. While it is a unique experience to see certain objects or certain collections in person, many are now easily available to view on the internet or simply not worth a trip to the museum. Moreover, objects alone will not often merit a repeat visit or lead visitors to encourage others to attend. To make it interesting, sports museums or exhibits must go far beyond the known quantity. Keep it fun and exciting. Highlight the unexpected objects at unexpected times, partner with known and/or nonconventional entities, let fans and participants see themselves in the content, give visitors chances to participate in the storytelling, and, most importantly, turn the sports narratives on their end by challenging long-held understandings.

Giving your audience an opportunity to interact with and generate content that combines sports objects, public discourse concepts, and their personal perspectives can create an illuminating and inspiring experience for everyone involved. This is a place and space where the museum can begin to go beyond a standard history exhibit or tour and play with experiential opportunities. Robert Saarnio, director of the University of Mississippi Museum, seized a rare opportunity that was innovative, creative, and appealed to his sports-crazed audience in a new way. He acquired a collection of helmets from *Fashion Touchdown*, an artistic collaboration between Bloomingdale's, the Council of Fashion Designers of America, and the National Football League (NFL) Foundation to honor Super Bowl XLVIII, the first ever played in New York City. Fashion designers including Vince Camuto, Diane von Fürstenberg, and Donna Karan creatively decorated forty-eight white football helmets.[17] Saarnio saw an art exhibit in the designer helmets. The museum obtained three of them, plus images of the remaining helmets and one looping video of all the objects, which it displayed as a single collection. The exhibition acted as the cornerstone of the museum's seasonal family kickoff event. Children designed their own helmets using milk jugs, pipe cleaners, and other embellishments. The result? Families who typically spent their time tailgating before a game poured into the galleries, celebrating the start of their favorite season in Oxford: football.[18]

The objects themselves represent a powerful exercise in crossing sports equipment with artistic creativity, current events, and personal perspective. Each designer's helmet spoke to a personal or political angle associated with professional football. The exhibition offered guests a complex set of messages in its marriage of fashion's "soft" side with football's violence. It was a unique avenue for artistic expression, and, in some cases, an outlet for cultural commentary. Designer Kenneth Cole used his art to focus on problems surrounding head injuries in the NFL. American fashion designer and sculptor Gregory Rogan took a theoretical approach to think outside the box by placing a solid white box over the helmet with only the face guard showing. Most of the designers chose to focus on the juxtaposition of the feminine meeting the masculine in an ironic twist on gender.

This type of activity could also be extended to a museum's more traditional audience, giving fans and participants a unique chance to artistically combine their love of sports and personal worldview. While *Fashion Touchdown* tapped a high-level collection of designers, an artist lies in everyone. A museum could extend this idea to the everyday visitor, soliciting the public for decorated helmet submissions. If your institution is affiliated with a specific team, you could, for example, ask participants to only use the Pantone colorway colors of the school or organization. This could also include lesser-known colors, symbols, or phrases that the team used at various times throughout history. Make a contest of it, choosing submissions for exhibition and combining them with historically relevant interpretations based on the subject and expression of each design. An idea like this can cross into many terrains—including virtually every type of sports object or sports-related topic. The key is to take the nuts and bolts of the games into the abstract and encourage your audience to think far outside the expected box, court, or field.

Balanced Commemoration

Approach sports commemoration with great consideration and care. Commemoration solely in the name of honoring a person or achievement often leaves gaping holes in interpretation. In these instances, visitors can worship or revere the jersey or trophy to honor players or teams for their stats and accomplishments. This is a consistent, time-honored commemorative practice, particularly in Western cultures, and it has its place. Sports figures who accomplish great feats inspire others to explore the expansive limits of the human body and believe in the joy of accomplishing personal goals and dreams. But it also lacks balance. Sports figures are not gods or superheroes. They are human beings. A society that places athletes on a pedestal merely because of their physical achievements runs the risk of villainizing them for their human failings. Museums that exploit this practice perpetuate an insidious trend, most notably because imbalanced commemoration practices leave no room for culturally relevant and evolving issues.

Exposing the imbalances in commemoration is a trend that permeates the museum field at large and is central to conversations surrounding virtually every sports museum or exhibit. In his edited compilation, *Commemorations: The Politics of National Identity*, John Gillis explores the commemoration practices that have taken root in Western culture. These practices, Gillis explains, began with the country's genesis just after the American Revolution, to break with the past and solidify a national identity. In that pivotal moment, the new Americans cultivated remembrance methods designed to cast the nation's foundational ideals in bronze and stone, and, later, in the interpretive text found in museums and at historic sites. At the very base of this concept lies the notion that each historical moment of import contains an objective statement to be codified into a national consciousness by firmly placing it in the public eye into perpetuity. However, Gillis posits, "memories and identities are not fixed things, but representations or constructions of reality, subjective rather than objective phenomena."[19] As Tom Engelhardt states in *The End of Victory Culture*, America's victory-based identity, the notion of a perpetual morally superior victory narrative that started with the Revolution, began to erode in the mid-twentieth century with the use of the atomic bomb. Thus, came the beginning of the end of a unified and innocently understood American victory narrative that was firmly affixed to a glorified, white-centric society. In its place grew a much more nuanced, subjective understanding of history, overall.[20]

Still, objectively affixing sports history to the overarching victory narrative has, in many ways, remained embedded in interpretive practices. Sports, perhaps more than any other subject, lends itself to this. Games can provide attendees and players with a joyous escapism from the challenges of a rapidly changing social consciousness while sports history offers a chance to nostalgically remember the glory days of the past. To remain relevant, embrace opportunities for updating the commemoration practices that surround athletics-based exhibits to reflect the public history field at large.[21]

Sports figures are often larger-than-life characters whose athletic accomplishments exceed the abilities of everyday people. This is part of the appeal of sports and athletes: they provide inspiration for physical, mental, and emotional stamina. Fans often choose athletes as role models. Still, the life of a professional athlete is beyond the reach of most people. Bridge this gap by offering more than just images and narratives of athletic achievements. Remember, like your visitors, athletes are people who also had a childhood and now have homes, families, and jobs. Use these stories to find ways to allow visitors to see a reflection of themselves in the lives of the players and see the players' humanity. Childhood Little League pictures and stories of triumph *and* struggle, for example, provide context for an athlete's everyday life. They also reflect your visitors' own personal histories.

Honoring a person does not always mean ignoring their personhood, and blind celebration can certainly cause dishonor to the sport and society at large. Such is the case at the Chick-fil-A College Football Hall of Fame, which fails to acknowledge Hall of Fame coach Joe Paterno's alleged inaction in the face of decades of child sexual abuse by one of his assistant coaches. The Hall of Fame has yet to produce an exhibit about the scandal at Penn State or the issues the story raises that affect college football. Paterno is an inductee. Current commemorative trends suggest that the very purpose of his placement in the Hall is one of honoring and that delving into systematic concerns of being "too big to fail" or other topics highlighted by the scandal would run counter to this aim. This, at its very core, is willfully blind commemoration that protects the honoree at the expense of others. It is common at many sports museums that omit the more difficult stories associated with their sport.[22] This type of practice perpetuates a perfect hero mindset that is dangerous for society as a whole. Instead, use in-depth exhibits or forum discussions to better address controversial issues with nuance. Invite guests to consider the topic with thought development activities in collaborative, open settings.

The key is to recognize that, when needed, both credit and candor can happen simultaneously. In commemoration at its best, celebration and historical relevancy intersect. An inductee or subject of a sports exhibit need not have a spotless personal record, few do. At the same time, history need not be whitewashed, particularly when the blights are connected to systemic issues, such as racism and misogyny, within their sport and/or society. The FC Bayern Munich Museum hails the history of the world-famous soccer team. Glory stories of the club's championship seasons are juxtaposed with candid explanations of their intersections with Nazism. The exhibit details the ways the Nazi regime harmed Jewish citizens and intersected with the Bayern Munich organization. Discussing racism so openly in a commemorative-based museum space is one way to maintain inclusive dialogue and discourage prejudice from permeating their club and soccer or sports at large.

Feeling seen and represented is paramount for historically underrepresented populations and offers a healing opportunity for everyone. At the 2020 Olympics (held in the summer of 2021), Michael Phelps made an impassioned plea for a safe place where sports figures can address mental health associated with athletic competition. Museums can answer this call. In doing so, public history institutions would, at the same time, give voice to a large, deeply closeted demographic and invite all visitors into an empathetic, humane conversation centrally connected to the nation's core value system.[23] Holistically embracing athletes' physical and mental states while also considering the impact of competitive sports on identity and the psyche is a long-overdue, intricate, and nuanced conversation that belongs in public exhibition spaces.

Speak candidly. Sometimes the best way to honor and support a sport, athlete, team, or fan base is to highlight that which is threatening to its existence. Know you are protecting the sport by calling it to a higher standard based on historical patterns and information. Avoid pure commemoration and glory stories. At the same time, avoid overtly calling out or attacking with angry speech. Take careful consideration and use a measured approach to highlight that which will best educate your constituents while acclaiming the sport. Instead of only asking "who is the GOAT?" ask questions like "what does 'greatest' mean?" Invite your visitors to consider this and to explore skill, character, endurance, grace, and other qualities that contribute to excellent athleticism. The more we, as a culture, can humanize sports participants, the more agency we give sports figures by placing their voices in its proper place, just like we do with other historical actors. Humanizing athletes by celebrating without worshipping and exposing without denigrating sends a message to visitors that no matter the accomplishments, we are all just human beings.

Otherwise, provide few easy answers, and give visitors participatory options to explore subjectivity, claim their own perspective, and share with one another. There are many occasions upon which audiences may benefit from open reflective space in a gallery, including when the subject is an ambiguous topic with little to no shared narrative, when an exhibit elicits intense or raw emotions, or when the content examines a fairly recent event. All three of these factors impacted the curator's interpretive decisions for the *Dear Boston: Messages from the Marathon Memorial*, a reexhibiting of the memorial that arose in the days following the 2013 Boston Marathon bombing. Instead of attempting to craft a definitive narrative just one year after such a tragic event, the exhibit staff offered a space for healing—one that gave visitors a chance to interact with emotionally weighty objects, participate in reflective exercises, and draw their own conclusions. Each object display was accompanied by contemplative questions rather than long text. In the final section, people could participate in both collective and personal response activities such as a communal reaction wall and a space to write a reflection message of hope.[24] When considered and implemented with intention, the strategy of using mostly objects, less text, and reflective opportunities can have a profound impact. This works when the space is designed to invite subjectivity, facilitate the unfolding of each person's unique perspective, and allow corporate space for responsive interaction.

Conclusion

Fans, coaches, athletes, and participants give museums a reason to present sports history in a fun, interactive, engaging, and challenging way. They are the backbone of an ongoing sporting world, consistently breathing new life into the storied history of humanity's need to seek movement and engage in competition. Games played by real people involve more than escape from daily life. In fact, they reflect society's most surface and deepest issues. Mining this treasure trove of interpretive storytelling with the participants in mind is a gift, a responsibility, and a challenge for the public historian all at the same time—one to handle delicately and with a sense of balance.

With all sports-related content, maintaining a healthy balance while catering to—but not placating—fans and participants makes for a better overall experience. Include the fun, excitement, and joy that sports bring into the lives of those who attend and play games. Shed light on glorious triumphs and sports folklore while carefully qualifying them as such. At the same time, do not shy away from exploring the more difficult topics related to your content that may be less popular yet equally as important to explore. Celebrate alongside a team or sport's ardent supporters while resisting the urge to be intimidated by your perception of their perspectives or agendas. There is an opportunity here to help people understand what it means to be "a fan" and whether it changes the way they view events when they have a team af- filiation. To be a fan can be to breed an uncritical mindset. Roots of fan affiliation run deep—often connected to family, region, a special player, or a need to belong. Using sports interpretation to dig into this kind of fan psychology can help fans think more critically and fairly and invite all visitors to explore a complex concept that sits at the heart of sports history.

Replicable Practices for Sports and its Participants

- **Growing Up a_____Fan:** Provide rival fans a chance to explore how fandom is passed from one generation to another. Offer activities for each age demographic during the week two rival teams in your area play each other. Assign each day to a different age-group starting with young children on the first days, teenagers in the middle days, young adults later in the week (maybe with an evening mixer event), and older adults at the end. Create activities where each age-group can share how they became a fan of their team and engage with the other fans. Encourage them to dress up in school colors. Offer a contest or competition for each rival fan base that would build throughout the week.

- **Accuracy Matters:** Build into the exhibit a method for updating facts, figures, and statistics to remain accurate and current as data changes.
- **Choose a Perspective:** Carefully consider whether to provide specific details that cater to a certain audience or present an all-inclusive story.
- **Mine Available Treasure Troves:** To access the coveted stories held within the minds of your audience, create an opportunity for them to gather at your site for a storytelling event. Record their dialogue and collect oral histories to later use in the exhibit space.
- **Create Interactive Storytelling Modules:** Offer digital platforms in the museum space where visitors can type their memories. This could be an organic experience whereby each person can see the other submissions and expound upon them.
- **Let the Visitors See Themselves:** Create a "day in the life" exhibit of an athlete showing their daily routine as a child, teenager, young adult, and working adult. Juxtapose that to the life of various non-athletes that reflect your visiting base, keeping diversity, inclusivity, and empathetic humanity in mind.
- **Use Objects Wisely:** Keep some of the most prized objects off the main exhibit floor and reserve them for an annual viewing event that draws the most ardent fans.
- **Lean In:** Challenge conventional narratives in inclusive ways by mining your collection for objects that reflect diverse perspectives on a widely accepted narrative. Combine this with a forum series or digital exhibit that features fans and participants who add their voices to the anthology of the sport.

CASE STUDY

Exhibiting the Mental Game: Empathetic Sports Conversations

Kathryn Leann Harris

In mid-2020, Paul Piwko and Alexandra Orlandi formally launched the National Museum of Mental Health Project, whose mission is "strengthening mental health literacy through the arts nationwide by bringing the exhibition to you."[25] The launch came at a timely moment, as the COVID-19 pandemic was bringing mental health starkly into the public consciousness. This discussion extended to the world of sports, where a robust mental health discourse emerged during the Olympic Games of summer 2021. Tennis champion Naomi Osaka and gold medal-winning gymnast Simone Biles each removed themselves from the competition, citing mental health concerns. In support of their decisions, former Olympic champion swimmer Michael Phelps rose to the defense of his peers. Phelps, who now operates the Michael Phelps Foundation, a nonprofit organization dedicated to water safety and mental health, pled publicly for safe places, *any* places, where athletes could meet and discuss their mental health.[26] While many fans applauded these athletes for their candor and strength, a strong contingent saw these decisions as unacceptable, asserting that high-level competitors should maintain an unwavering mental strength. Thanks to the advocacy and openness of these athletes and many others, we are witnessing the emergence of a more holistic understanding of mental health and wellness that encourages destigmatizing these vital components of overall well-being in sports; this is a conversation that belongs in museum spaces.

Phelps's personal story reflects that of many athletes, highlighting both the positive and negative mental effects of sports. When he received an ADHD diagnosis as a child, he and his mother sought an outlet to help focus his brain. Swimming became part of his answer.[27] By the time he retired in 2016, he had faced a serious battle with anxiety and depression while under the immense pressure of being an elite athlete and becoming the most decorated Olympian of all time. Upon retirement, his depression was further overwhelming as he faced the opposite, a life without the daily drive to compete. An advocate for fellow athletes, Phelps speaks candidly about his personal struggles: "The hardest thing to understand is you can't just put your mental health on a timeout."[28] Instead, he contends, athletes need support to weather their mental challenges.

Museums could be at the forefront of that solution. Mental illness is common, yet those who suffer, particularly sports figures, face an uphill battle against negative public perceptions that must be confronted and corrected. The public needs renewed and revised understandings of mental health, and athletes need safe spaces to discuss the topic. *Museums can and should fill this gap.* The intersection of mental health and sports history is a crossover opportunity that hits right at the heart of our shared humanity. Our institutions are uniquely poised to become brave, empathy-forward spaces of conversation about sports and mental health in the public sphere.

Putting Stigma Out of Bounds

How can museums be part of the solution? Interpretation must begin with the awareness that the stigma of mental illness is particularly strong in the arena of sports. In total, 35 percent of professional athletes experience a debilitating mental crisis at some point in their careers, often accompanied by a painful public rejection.[29] Athletes exist in a hypercompetitive world, one that demands personal sacrifice in the name of victory. While many fans and sports figures excuse physical injuries, mental illness is not as easily tolerated, and rarely even discussed. The Cleveland Clinic reports that for athletes, "depression and anxiety are not diagnoses evident on an X-ray or MRI, but they can be every bit as limiting or debilitating as a physical injury. Too often, however, these issues are ignored in the name of grit."[30] Fans, the general public, and even competitors themselves see athletes as modern-day gladiators who simply *will* themselves to the finish line despite any adversity. Complicating that challenge, high-level athletes rely on their mental game as a significant component of their overall competitive edge. When they struggle mentally, they often struggle to compete. Any weakness—mental or physical—becomes an enemy. This cycle feeds upon itself, heightening the tension of a hypercompetitive environment. Sport becomes both the cause and effect of an athlete's mental health struggles.

A shift in focus is much needed. Piwko and Orlandi, co-developers of the National Museum of Mental Health Project, propose an empathetic, accessible approach to mental health interpretation that produces the kinds of spaces athletes desperately need—learning environments that teach and reinforce that mental illness is real, treatment is available, and prevention is often possible. Handling the subject matter with knowledge and sensitivity is essential. Mental health history is fraught, rife with controversial and outdated treatment modalities, alienating verbiage, and misdiagnoses with devastating effects. Past depictions of mental health in museum spaces have often drawn on images, narratives, and ideas that can re-stigmatize mental illness and those who experience it. Museums have at times played up aspects of mental health history that emphasize otherness and the seemingly bizarre, or invite mockery at past patients and medical practices. Uncritically presenting "insane asylums," leaning on a "freakification" paradigm, or even treating respectable yet recently dismissed therapy modalities as unenlightened does little more than perpetuate a "fixed" idea of mental illness as a permanently debilitating identity.

As public history practitioners, we do not want to reinforce ideas that do more to maintain outdated tropes than foster compassion in the present. As a society, we have witnessed a dramatic change in understanding of cognitive processes over the last two hundred years, with significant developments occurring in even just the past twenty years. Recognizing the dramatic shifts in both medical and public understandings of mental health in recent decades, Piwko and Orlandi suggest a hybrid exhibit approach that incorporates knowledge of past constructions and treatments while taking care to acknowledge the modalities, mindsets, and treatment options for mental health today. Good interpretive practice, they argue, will draw on the very core of the discipline of history: understanding change over time. Rather than fixating on dismal stories of the past—risking the repetition of harm to people with mental health challenges—interpretation can demonstrate advances in the understanding and treatment of mental health. Museums need to shift the collective focus toward prevention, proper treatment, and empathetic, supportive care—to shine a light on what *is* working *now* rather than telling historical tales that cast mental health stories in a negative light. Often, the most gripping part of mental health exhibits is the stories of everyday heroes who can and do speak out about their experiences. That is where the most powerful work is to be done: highlighting advocates, communities, family, and friends; supporting, embracing, and accepting those closest to us while they face and manage their illnesses.

Exhibiting a New Image of Mental Health

To help change the narrative on mental health, many museums are reaching beyond the traditional vocabulary of fixed permanent exhibits. Instead of creating a single physical museum location, the National Museum of Mental Health Project plans to remain a primarily online entity, producing virtual, traveling, and "in your face" exhibitions installed in unexpected places. Virtual exhibits are available to anyone who has a computer and internet, providing a global reach. Traveling exhibit models are effective in disseminating information to a large portion of the population, offering access to people who might not otherwise be able to travel to a single national museum. "In your face" style exhibitions pop up where the public can encounter them unexpectedly—airports, libraries, colleges, hospitals, and hotels . . . or stadiums, ballparks, and arenas. In these public spaces, people can stay as long as they like and go at their own pace. They are also more financially accessible, as most are either inexpensive or free. These strategies are all well adapted to intersecting with the topic of sports.

Instead of segregating mental health topics in specific institutions, placing exhibits where people are passing through in everyday life can help to normalize mental health topics. The groundbreaking exhibit *Deconstructing Stigma: Changing Attitudes About Mental Health* debuted in 2016, produced by McLean Hospital (Harvard Medical School's largest psychiatric affiliate). Aiming for widespread visibility, McLean installed the exhibition in airports around the world, starting with Logan International Airport in Boston; it has now appeared in ten locations across the United States and on all inhabited continents except Australia.[31] *Deconstructing Stigma* humanizes mental health through a selection of case studies from a cross section of the population, helping viewers rethink their attitudes and move beyond stigmas; as the exhibit explains, "1 in 5 Americans will experience mental illness in his or her lifetime. It is something that affects us all."[32] The exhibit's floor-to-ceiling panels present life-size photographs of people who have experienced mental illness—whether short term or lifelong—accompanied by personal interviews. Every participant in the project has a story of stigmatization associated with their mental illness, acknowledging a polarizing experience that tends to exacerbate the underlying issues.

Figure 3.1. Boston Logan visitors pass the exhibit positioned down a long narrow hallway. *Source:* **Kathryn Leann Harris.**

The introduction to *Deconstructing Stigma* reminds viewers that the people who volunteered their stories for the project "are more than just statistics or nameless faces. They are mothers, fathers, wives, husbands, lawyers, doctors, engineers, musicians" and athletes.[33] Sports figures are not immune. Brandon Marshall, one of several athletes featured in *Deconstructing Stigma,* was diagnosed with borderline personality disorder while playing for the NFL. In 2011, he simultaneously announced his illness and his dedication to mental health advocacy. As a third-generation survivor of mental illness, he chose to speak out and share how he found a path forward for his own life. While a patient at McLean, Marshall received dialectical behavioral therapy, which allowed him to regulate his emotions and continue investing in his professional and family life. Marshall turned his toughest life experience into his greatest life's work: "Football is my job, but being a mental health advocate and changing how mental illness is perceived and treated are my calling."[34] He is featured in the Boston Logan Airport installation of the exhibit alongside several amateur athletes who cite exercise as a valuable outlet and coping skill for managing their symptoms.

Another project, *Mental Health: Mind Matters*, is a traveling exhibit produced by the Science Museum of Minnesota. Adapted for North American audiences from The Science Center in Helsinki's exhibit *Hureka Goes Crazy*. This immersive experience is designed to raise awareness about mental health, promoting the message that mental illness affects everyone, can happen at any time, and is treatable.[35] Just like physical health, treating mental ailments requires attention and nurturing. While this is not a sports-centered exhibit, it does reference the importance of moving the body, including creative movement. Minnesota Science Museum also houses *Sportsology*, a permanent exhibit that brings together science (including cognitive science) and sports. Exhibits and associated online videos address topics like the intersections between eating disorders and sports, how sports and games can help hone mental skills and build mastery, and the effects of concussion on the brain. Visitors can take an interactive cognitive test that replicates a baseline concussion exam, physically interacting to see how the brain and skull react when an athlete experiences a concussion.[36]

Empathy-Centered Interpretation

These exhibits help point the way to supportive, empathetic, and respectful interpretations of mental health and sports. The importance of grounding interpretation in empathy is well established, and especially vital when interpreting topics so prone to stigma and misunderstanding. As public history practitioners, it is important to listento and engage empathetically with those with lived experience, then use their stories to help others see themselves or someone they love in a new light. We must begin to really hear what people with mental health conditions are experiencing inside their bodies and how it affects their outside realities.

Remember that a mental health event can happen to anyone at any time in their life—whether related to sports or not. Museums must take care to not treat mental illness as something that only happens to others; most people know someone who is living with a mental illness. At the same time, interpretation should recognize that sport environments pose unique challenges. Athletes may have encountered mental or physical abuse or experienced a prolonged lack of listening, understanding, compassion, or concern for their needs.

Interpretation should not overlook the positive mental effects of sports—both in terms of prevention and treatment. Exercise is a healthy outlet and coping skill for many people, from those who face mild anxiety or depression to those who are struggling with more severe chronic or acute ailments. Sports can offer opportunities to improve mental health through exercise, camaraderie, belonging, and excitement. At the same time, exercise or strenuous activity can cause additional stress on the mind and body. Attitudes surrounding competition or success, even on the level of pursuing personal goals, may feed the very issue someone is trying to treat. Be mindful to interpret all sides of the mental health spectrum in relation to a sports topic.

Museums must be sure to humanize the people at the center of mental health narratives by looking at the full self, not simply the struggling self. Mental illness can affect someone at any stage of their life or career—even athletes—without necessarily hindering their opportunity to live a full, satisfying life. Confronting long-ignored conversations around mental wellness will most certainly fly in the face of central, culturally held tenets that are ripe for re-interrogation. Allow those threads to be pulled by giving a voice to the athletes who struggle against cultural silences and stigmas.

Be thoughtful when choosing images and language in interpretive work. Do not use images that reinforce stigma or have the potential to re-traumatize viewers. Use current language and respectful descriptors. Most importantly, consider portraying mental health not as a permanently fixed state, but as a fluid experience that changes over a lifetime. Older models of mental health imagined it as a fixed brain state that holds a person captive or labels them as defective or weak, and limits their access to parts of society that make a life worth living. More contemporary models recognize that mental health, like physical health, emerges from a process of constant change. In all communities, there are organizations and industries that work on mental health and wellness issues. Reach out and engage community partners in these spaces. Their knowledge, contacts, and feedback can help you ensure your project reaches its potential.

Finally, remember that museums *can* and *should* play this all-important role in addressing the causes and effects of sports on mental health, both positive and negative, and provide safe and brave spaces for the athletic community to see themselves and understand their experiences in historical context. With mental health exhibits of any kind, the goal is to get to a place where your visiting audiences can say "I get it." By presenting new models of mental health, and revealing the skills and tools that those who actively practice mental health management and recovery use daily, museums can open the door to conversations about therapeutic options that work. From those who are "coming out" with their diagnosis to those who do not yet have a strong understanding of brain science or psychology, museums can be a safe space for everyone to build understanding, express feelings and ideas, heal, and gain greater awareness of mental health.

CASE STUDY

Experiences for All: Participant and Fan Engagement at the NASCAR Hall of Fame

Daniel J. Simone

The NASCAR Hall of Fame, ideally located in Charlotte, North Carolina, the center of one of the largest racing communities in the world, maintains strong relationships with NASCAR insiders (participants) and outsiders (fans), allowing the staff to cultivate a memorable museum experience. When designing exhibits, its curators strive to create visitor relevance by answering the question: "What does stock car racing teach us about ourselves?" Defining the "*us*" and "*ourselves*" in that statement is an intricate challenge. NASCAR-sanctioned stock car racing is wildly popular in the United States, with a vast array of people and positions affiliated with the sport.[37] Representatives from all associated categories remain actively engaged with the museum, forming a significant, yet not exclusive, part of the visitorship. When at all possible, historical interpretation at the NHOF is intended to have appeal across a spectrum of passionate fans, NASCAR participants, casual guests, and youngsters. The NHOF aims to help all visitors understand and connect the various components that keep the NASCAR wheels in forward motion while also relating the content's meaning to their *own selves* and place in history.

The NASCAR Hall of Fame staff also continuously fosters a reciprocally beneficial relationship with this motorsports community, which adds to the value of

Figure 3.2.   The NASCAR Hall of Fame in Charlotte, North Carolina, opened its doors in May 2010. *Source:* **nascarhall.com.**

the museum's collection and ultimately the exhibits and visitor experiences. The NASCAR fan and participant base is vast and far reaching yet also functions as a close-knit network. Because of this, the museum staff can build relationships and develop collaborative partnerships with personalities that reach far beyond the sport's inner circles. They are also able to procure artifact donations from such a deep and wide collective. Once the staff conceives an exhibit idea and drafts a summary, curators alert fans and participants with a request for object acquisition, which they readily fill. At a macro level, this increases the size of the NHOF's permanent collection. In turn, as the collection grows and the access to fan objects remains accessible, the exhibits team can plan, develop, and build future exhibits with a larger pool of data from which to select. Fans, participants, and all visitors then benefit from more comprehensive, complex, and interesting museum content.

Due to the very active, present position sports occupy in American culture, halls of fames and museums interpreting sports stand to benefit from recognizing current accomplishments, storylines, and milestones in their interpretation, programming, and special events—a methodology the NASCAR Hall of Fame staff understands and implements with great consistency. The curatorial staff stays readily connected to the sport's annual calendar and emerging technological updates. They then offer ongoing opportunities for fans to connect motorsports history to the ways they are experiencing the sport in real time. Failing to do so would result in missed opportunities to celebrate with and educate a present-day audience through a historical lens.

Thus, the museum's exhibits team carefully plans and develops proactive and reactive exhibits. Proactive exhibits require an exhibit treatment focused on identifying a historical topic or theme, such as the museum's deep probe into NAS-CAR's 1948 inaugural season. Reactive exhibits are developed based on relevant NASCAR events, anniversaries, and milestones, which often manifest as contemporary developments within the sport, and typically include context that takes the visitor beyond the thrill of the moment. One such reactive exhibit celebrated Hall of Famer Richard Childress's fiftieth anniversary as a NASCAR competitor with a heavy exploration of his family, team, and philanthropic work. Implementing this combination strategy allows curators to honor historic topics while engaging fans with current and fresh- off-the-track content.

Probing beyond names, dates, places, and races, the exhibits team tries to maintain focus on the unique and complicated nature of automobile racing. This is a team sport where success requires the collective effort of a pit crew, strategists, mechanics, engineers, technicians, fabricators, aero dynamists, and other specialists—many of which do not work at that track or in the garage. Interpreters must also consider the people who create and manage competition tracks, race cars and other competition vehicles, and racing events themselves. A loyal base of fans connects all these moving parts. As a whole, this community is quite invested in the sport's history—and present. They passionately and religiously attend and watch races, follow their favorite drivers' lives, and connect to one another inside and outside of the sporting events.

Accessing a historically relevant and presently recognizable platform for connecting NASCAR participants with fans, the hall of fame's staff utilizes an important characteristic long associated with America's motorsports, "fan accessibility." Stock car racing facilitates a great deal of fan interaction with drivers and race teams. On race weekend, fans have much more access to the sport's participants in comparison to the NFL sidelines or MLB bleachers. On race day, hundreds, sometimes thousands, of fans purchase pit passes, granting them the opportunity to step onto the actual racing surface and walk through the NASCAR garages and pit stalls. The NHOF staff is mindful of this tradition and promotes special events and autograph sessions with the drivers and crewmembers. This requires collaboration with numerous partners. The NHOF staff works in tandem with NASCAR and the sport's participants to facilitate press conferences, live, on-site television shows, and other sponsor and/or team-related functions.[38] These types of programs place the museum as a valuable asset for the sport and its teams.[39]

Motorsports fan loyalties represent a diverse base of interests within the sport, a complex factor unique to NASCAR that the exhibits team actively considers in their design processes. Some fans have team allegiances, while others root for a specific automobile brand. Most are devoted to a particular driver. Enthusiasts extend their loyalty by ardently supporting their favorite drivers at races and in their lives beyond the track. Fans consistently plan travel decisions or product purchases that reflect their favorite drivers' current brand, sponsor, or marketing campaigns. These factors are markedly different from other stick-and-ball team sports because race cars serve as billboards with the capacity to travel at 200 mph. The institution realizes and recognizes this notion of star power by devoting significant space to artifacts and interpretive material related to the hall of famers and other popular drivers. The inductees, five of which are elected each May and enshrined the following January in the Hall of Honor section, stand as the primary subject matter of a hall of fame.[40] Maintaining this focus means that ardent fans and participants, as well as casual fans and general visitors, can easily find recognizable and memorable personalities, moments, and artifacts.

To provide a richer visitor experience, the star power of hall of famers comprises only a portion of exhibits and content—the NASCAR Hall of Fame also highlights lesser-known stories that connect the sport with American history. Like other sports, NASCAR has a cast of characters that serve as unlikely candidates for enshrinement but made significant contributions to the sport's history. One such "hall of fame worthy" accomplishment was Ron Bouchard's thrilling victory in 1981 at Talladega Superspeedway. This was the Massachusetts native's only career NASCAR Cup Series win. It was a big day for Bouchard and his fellow New Englanders because, at that time, his was one of the biggest top-division wins of anyone from the region. Thus, the NHOF commemorates this moment with the fire suit Bouchard wore on his way to victory. These types of stories really pique the interest of the sport's most ardent fan base and knowledgeable participants.

The voting process and related exhibits at the NASCAR Hall of Fame are rather unique in the ways they provide participants and fans with an interconnected involvement. The voting process occurs in two stages. Each February, a designated nominating committee consisting of roughly twenty to twenty-five members meets and votes in Daytona Beach, Florida, to select twenty nominees worthy of being placed on the ballot, from which a larger panel consisting of roughly fifty-five to sixty members votes in May. On the Wednesday before Memorial Day weekend, the larger panel convenes at the Charlotte Convention Center adjacent to the NASCAR Hall of Fame.[41] Each voter lists five names for induction. The Voting Panel consists of members from the nominating committee plus former drivers, owners, crew chiefs, manufacturer representatives, media members, and the current reigning NASCAR premier series champion. Interestingly, the panel technically consists of one additional (fan) member each year. Once again, noting NASCAR's important fan connection, an online voting process allows fans to select their choices for the new class. They pick from the list of twenty predetermined nominees. The fan vote is tabulated, and the top five vote getters appear on a final submitted ballot. An outside entity tallies the committee votes plus the solitary fan vote that same afternoon, and the five newest inductees are announced at the Hall of Fame later that day with television crews and media on-site to cover the live news.[42]

After the new class announcement, the exhibits team immediately begins designing a yearlong exhibit slated to be unveiled roughly eight months later with content related to the five new hall of famers' careers, each organized in a distinct case layout. In addition to working with the new inductees (if still living) these exhibits require contributions from a network of individuals willing to provide artifacts, photos, and research assistance. The exhibits team presses a complicated rubric into action, as inductees and their friends, families, and colleagues participate in the selection of objects used to commemorate each inductee's career. Situated in the middle of the Hall of Honor are five exhibit cases that contain graphics, photos, captions, and roughly one to two dozen artifacts. These cases sit next to a platform that displays a well-recognized race car associated with each inductee. A seven-foot-tall spire with an etched portrait, engraved biography, and video serves as the inductee's permanent hall of fame marker. A little over a year later artifacts are returned to various lenders, and the curators work further with these individuals moving forward. The exhibits team remains committed, ongoing, to displaying inductee-related artifacts in other proactive and reactive exhibits throughout the museum. A NASCAR hall of famers is always given a special designation and artifact captions always include interpretive text that places an inductee's date of induction after their name.[43]

When designing each Hall of Honor case, the exhibits team aims to cater to die-hard and casual fans through the presentation of a well-rounded discussion of the inductee's career. Some artifacts depict major wins and championships. At the same time, in order to deepen the content, curators also include some of the more rare or untraditional artifacts and lesser-known stories.

Casual NASCAR fans primarily know 2017 inductee Mark Martin for his forty career NASCAR Cup Series wins and five runner-up championship points finishes. The NHOF tends to primarily highlight NASCAR-related honors, yet many ardent fans know that Martin also won four American Speed Association (ASA) titles. The museum chose to feature one of Martin's ASA winner's trophies in his Hall of Honor case.[44] Martin's case also included a plaque recognizing his five International Race of Champions victories.[45] The one-year exhibit showcased a broad range of Martin's career accomplishments, providing hard-core fans and casual visitors alike an experience that highlighted his regional and national impact in motorsports.

Understanding NASCAR through in-depth contextualization stands as a central component of the curated NHOF visitor experience, for merely stressing statistical accomplishments such as wins and championships presents a vastly incomplete and insufficient narrative. Instead, the staff crafts exhibit interpretation in thematic topics that highlight stock car racing's incalculable technological, cultural, social, corporate, and environmental connections and impact on American society. To satisfy the expectations of the most knowledgeable and passionate fans as well as create a holistic experience for all kinds of visitors, curators delve into intensive research reinforced with the "*why*" question. For example, they ask: *Why* does a certain car represent a technological advancement? *Why* did so many successful drivers hail from the tiny town of Dawsonville, Georgia? *Why* was a certain track built where it was? This method results in rich and complex content that relates visitors to the personal, human experience of a wide variety of participants associated with the sport.

The exhibits team also understands and gives credence to the importance of nostalgia in relationship to motorsports. Gazing through the sport's history, numerous NASCAR personalities, teams, cars, or innovations remain as fan favorites. Remembered histories of other sports—such as the NFL—function in much the same way; many memorable players and teams did not win a championship, but fans lovingly look back at the players, coaches, teams, and stadiums with affection. Quarterback Dan Pastorini, Coach O. A. "Bum" Phillips, and the Houston Oilers who played in the iconic Houston Astrodome in the late 1970s are well remembered and beloved by their old-time fans—despite never making it to a Super Bowl. Popular and successful driver Ken Schrader holds a comparable position in NASCAR lore. Schrader never won a Daytona 500 or a championship, but he competed in motorsports for decades as an extremely popular driver among fans and within the motorsports industry. The NHOF displays Schrader's winner's trophy from his first career victory in 1988.

Sense of place is another extremely powerful force that resonates with NASCAR participants, fans, and even nonfans—a force to which the museum staff connects and then depicts, often in unexpected but deeply impactful ways. When guests from the west coast visit the NHOF, they are typically interested in artifacts and stories that commemorate west coast races, such as the 1972 Miller High Life 500 at Ontario (California) Motor Speedway, while taking less interest in who won a particular event or which type of car someone drove. A guest may not be familiar with race winner A. J. Foyt, whose winning 1972 Miller High Life 500 trophy is on display but might be captivated by the fact that a 2.5-mile track superspeedway existed in San Bernardino County, California, in the 1970s. Canadian Earl Ross, who in 1974 became the first foreign-born driver to win NASCAR Cup Series rookie of the year honors, represents another place-based story of import. He is not entirely well known in the motorsports community, yet the NHOF designates space to display a fire suit from his rookie season, commemorating this impactful achievement.

Unique to NASCAR is a particularly long and rich family heritage dynamic among its participants, which the museum can effectively utilize as a profoundly contextual connection point for visitors. Since its inception in 1948, NASCAR has remained a privately owned company. William H. G. "Big Bill" France founded the entity. Over seventy years later, NASCAR is still maintained by members of the France family. Their familial-centric culture trickles into every facet of the sport, most notably the race teams. The Pettys stand as one of the most prominent families in motorsports. Richard Petty, one of the five inductees in the 2010 inaugural class, won two hundred NASCAR Cup Series races and earned the nickname "the King." His brother and engine builder, Maurice Petty; his cousin and primary crew chief, Dale Inman; and his father Lee Petty (also a driver and owner) are NASCAR Hall of Fame inductees as well. Richard's son Kyle, a former winning NASCAR driver and current television analyst, is a driving celebrity in his own right. In celebration of Richard's eightieth birthday in 2017, the curatorial team developed a six-month exhibit, which permitted visitors a deep exploration of the King's family, taking guests beyond the Pettys' success on the racetrack. During the exhibit development process, the King, Kyle, other family members, and their staff were available and willing to entertain artifact and interview requests at the Pettys' headquarters in Level Cross, North Carolina, conveniently just ninety minutes from the museum's location in Charlotte.

Although curators did not ignore the record book, they concentrated most of the Petty exhibit content around noncompetition-based accomplishments and contributions that spoke to the heart of the family's spirit. At the insistence of the King, who stressed that his family be the focal point, the exhibit recognized public service, charitable work, and innumerable off-track contributions. Panels that spoke of the legacy of Richard's grandson and Kyle's son, Adam, delivered an especially poignant message. Before Adam tragically died in 2000 while competing at New Hampshire Motor Speedway, he dreamt of building a camp for ailing and terminally ill children. Richard, Kyle, and other members of the family oversaw the construction of the Victory Junction Camp in Randleman, North Carolina, in 2004. The camp continues to operate successfully, touching the lives of hundreds of children and their families each year—none of whom pay to attend. As an extension of the family's core values and long-standing commitment to the spirit of Adam's life, the Petty family, along with their various charitable entities and operations, are dedicated to raising the funds necessary to support the campers. This multi-themed and dynamic exhibit gave the curators an opportunity to dive into deep and heartfelt content that really spoke to the visiting fans. Like the Pettys, many other of the sport's partakers have deeply entrenched family roots. At the hall of fame, those families, along with the fans, can access, connect, and explore the meaning of this impactful thread that runs throughout the NASCAR experience.

The NASCAR Hall of Fame exhibits team endeavors to commemorate motorsports with an understanding that they, like other sports halls of fames and museums, must preserve the past while considering current accomplishments, storylines, milestones, and technologies—and the fans, coaches, and participants that actively drive the sport with invested interest. These visitors carry with them the heartbeat of the sport and relay it in a way that gives meaning to the past and the impact of the present. The curatorial staff at the NASCAR Hall of Fame recognizes this and continuously offers participants and fans opportunities to connect the sport's present and past to relevant aspects of the American historical landscape, their *own self* and place in history, and the reciprocal nature of the two.

CASE STUDY

Dear Boston: Messages from the Marathon Memorial

Dan Yaeger

> *How an Exhibition Helped Heal Fans and Athletes:*
> *Acts of terrorism have a profound and lasting impact on communities in which they occur. The effects of the 2013 Boston Marathon Bombing also rippled well beyond the city itself. Because the race is an internationally familiar sporting event, runners, and fans from around the world joined local Bostonians in their need to heal from the tragedy that killed three and wounded more than 260. I asked museum professionals Rainey Tisdale and Matt Kirchman to reflect on the exhibition they developed for the one-year anniversary of the bombing, a complicated and emotional project that charted new territory for sports interpretation.*

When the bombs exploded on Boylston Street that April day in 2013, Rainey Tisdale and Matt Kirchman had no idea that exactly one year later they would find themselves immersed in efforts to support the city's healing process. As pandemonium engulfed the fans and runners of the 117th Boston Marathon, they could not imagine the journey they were about to undertake. They could not foresee the looming hopes, disappointments, red tape, and, ultimately, professional satisfaction they would experience. As they witnessed the tragedy on television with millions of others, all they knew was that they wanted to do something to help.

As museum consultants, Tisdale and Kirchman were keenly aware that objects have the power to help people make meaning of historical events, their everyday lives, and even an act of terrorism. They closely observed this phenomenon in Boston. In the days following the tragedy, that power was on full display in Copley Square, a public park near the marathon finish line. Runners and fans alike deposited flowers, teddy bears, T-shirts, hats, and handmade signs, ultimately leaving thousands of objects. "There were multiple layers of meaning at the makeshift memorial," said Tisdale, a curator and international expert on city museums.

> Some of these layers were ones you find at other memorials for major tragedies—like condolences for those killed, support for the injured, and gratitude for the people who helped that day. But then there were also layers that you don't see at other memorials, the ones that reflect what it meant that this tragedy happened in the middle of a major sporting event.[46]

Figure 3.3.   Displayed in the center of the exhibit was a selection of sneakers left by mourning visitors in the weeks after the bombing. The concentrated re-exhibiting of such personal objects strikingly infused the sense of community spirit that permeated the Copley Square bombing memorial a year prior. *Source:* Kathryn Leann Harris.

Runners from all over the world brought objects and notes expressing solidarity with Boston marathoners. Many items at the memorial used the language of running such as "Lace Up Your Shoes" or "Finish the Race" to express solidarity with those injured. Boston Marathon runners left objects from the 2013 race: their medals, bibs, and, most poignantly, their shoes. These objects signified the many ways the bombing deeply affected their personal experience of the race.

When she first walked through the memorial, which expanded with each passing week, Tisdale thought, "Who is going to collect all this?" She realized the importance of preserving the objects for the historical record and, possibly, for a future exhibition. She also knew from her long experience with Boston museums that the city's collecting institutions did not typically focus on contemporary artifacts. Two weeks after the bombing, the New England Museum Association (NEMA) organized a conference call with roughly twenty-five Boston-area museum professionals from different institutions. Everyone on the call wanted to see a substantive response from Boston's cultural community, but no one felt their institution had the capacity to formally lead such an effort. The meeting resulted in the formation of an ad hoc group of institutions and individuals who each offered what they could.

With NEMA's support, Tisdale coordinated the project's efforts and found the necessary additional resources. Mayor Thomas Menino decided the City of Boston's archives should preserve all memorial objects, even though such items normally would be outside the institution's collecting scope. Historic New England volunteered to fumigate the objects, which had been exposed to rain and pests while outdoors at Copley Square. Polygon Group volunteered professional drying services.

With the objects stabilized, Tisdale embarked on a fundraising odyssey to garner interest in organizing an exhibition and related programming at the 2014 Boston Marathon. She hoped this would help with survivors' ongoing healing processes. "We knew from past tragedies that the anniversary would be a really important moment for the city where a lot of raw emotion would surface," Tisdale said. "People could either face that emotion alone, in isolation, or they could face it together in civic spaces that supported collective healing, so it was important to at least try to create something that could do the latter."

NEMA agreed to help with fundraising and logistics. In summer 2013, Tisdale and I visited Boston's foundations and corporations seeking support for the project. While there was a lot of interest, no one was willing to fund the exhibit as most had already committed their philanthropy to other projects long in the works. As summer cycled into autumn, Tisdale eyed the first of October as the go/no-go date to secure funding. That would provide six months for project development, an aggressive timeline that afforded very little margin for delay. As that date came and went without a sponsor, it seemed that the idea would not come to fruition. Tisdale consoled herself by reflecting that at least the objects themselves were preserved and safe in storage.

In early January 2014, she called me with a "good news/bad news" conversation. She said that a funder had stepped forward. Iron Mountain, the records storage company based in Boston, offered to sponsor the project in its entirety. However, we would have to plan the exhibition at a breakneck pace. "We had seven weeks from contract to delivery," said Kirchman, who focused on the exhibition's content development. "But we were determined to make it happen." Tisdale and Kirchman pulled together a team of independent professionals including graphic designer Helen Riegle, project manager Anne Starr, and graduate interns who cleared their schedules to work virtually 24/7 on the initiative. They secured a commitment from the Boston Public Library as host. This guaranteed maximum visibility, as the library is located proximate to the finish line, makeshift memorial location in Copley Square, and bombing sites on Boylston Street.

Tisdale and her team crafted an exhibition concept that spoke to the heart of the city and race participants. "We decided that we would focus on race fans, runners, and Bostonians as our primary audiences," Tisdale explained.

> Tragedies have concentric circles of impact. There were, by then, many support mechanisms in place for the marathon bombing's inner circles—the survivors and families of victims—and museum exhibitions aren't a great fit for their needs anyway. But a lot less was available for the outer circles, who also need to grieve and find meaning, albeit with less intensity. We hoped the exhibition would help them.

Tisdale and Kirchman organized the exhibition plan around an emotional arc, using photographs of and objects from the makeshift memorial to prompt visitors to explore their own memories and feelings. "We made a conscious decision to maintain a light curatorial voice," Tisdale said.

> We didn't do a lot of explaining, but instead wherever possible allowed the objects to speak for themselves. We provided a platform and structure for visitors to interact with the objects but wanted them to be able to make their own meaning. We knew that at

the anniversary everyone would be dealing with a lot of raw emotion, and therefore it wouldn't be productive to inflame or anger people with editorializing, or to try to impose a unified historical narrative of the event when one didn't exist yet. Our goal was to provide the city with a safe space to promote healing and move forward together.

The City of Boston tightly scrutinized that goal. Because the exhibition topic was controversial and so high profile and the venue was the city-operated public library, the exhibit required an intense approval process. "About a dozen people in various departments of the city government had to review the concept and text, and everyone had different ideas of what the exhibition should feel like," Kirchman recalled.

> Some of them wanted us to be more forceful and polemical, using graphic language like "explosions," "perpetrators," and "manhunt," while others wanted completely different approaches—very formal language, or very soft and passive language. The approval process pushed us to get really clear on what visitors needed from the exhibition, and to work hard to keep those needs front and center.

Through a series of compromises, the team produced an exhibition that passed muster with stakeholders while also maintaining the exhibition team's vision.

Central to the exhibit's theme was a concept of embodying the experiences surrounding the tragedy; physicality was laced throughout the entire space. Visitors were invited to step into a selected re-exhibition of the Copley Square memorial, just across the street from where it was originally laid. Glass cases displayed objects collected from the site: hats, medals, bibs, running clothes, handwritten notes from children to law enforcement and emergency crews, and white crosses laid as markers for those who lost their lives. Against a life-size backdrop depicting the memorial, curators placed a sizeable stack of teddy bears, flowers, signs, sneakers, candles, and flags, selected from the stored objects. The exhibit's centerpiece was an enormous display of running shoes left at the memorial, arranged in rows on a low platform. "The shoes faced outward toward the viewer so you could almost imagine this group of marathoners standing there wearing them," said Tisdale. "With this composition we wanted to evoke a Greek chorus, which in classical tragedies acted as a witness, and said out loud the things the main characters couldn't say." At the end, visitors encountered a reflection table with a chance to write messages of hope on white cards and hang them together on a bare tree growing out of yellow tulips, an homage to messages of hope left hanging on a tree at the memorial site.

Visitors entered a solemn space that encapsulated the emotional outpouring and impact of the marathon bombing and invited them to mourn and reflect in solidarity. The words "Boston Strong," the world's emboldened unified response to the bombers, peppered the space. Installations throughout housed condolence letters and signs written by mourners for the grieving families. A banner hung above the exhibit with the quote, "Lace up your shoes and run for those who can't," a harkening to the pop-up runs that sprouted across the world in the wake of the bombing. Perhaps the most poignant message came from slain eight-year-old marathon spectator Martin Richard, "No More Hurting People: Peace." Richard wrote this on a sign in school while studying social justice. His wish virally spread throughout the world in the days following the tragedy that took his life.

Dear Boston: Messages from the Marathon Memorial, opened on schedule on April 7, 2014, attracting a crowd of dignitaries and invited guests. The state's U.S. senators joined Mayor Martin Walsh to mark the occasion. Media coverage was extensive, with an estimated 140 million impressions internationally. The exhibition won awards from the American Alliance of Museums and the American Association for State and Local History. The impact was far reaching as almost 52,000 people visited the space in the thirty-four days the exhibition was on display.

Sports interpretation often deals with slow-moving narratives: the evolution of a game over time or the careers of storied athletes. Except for record-setting accomplishments or the occasional high-profile scandal, sports exhibitions rarely respond to breaking news. This project made meaning out of a contemporary event that sparked raw emotions in athletes and fans globally. It is perhaps fitting, then, that the exhibition came together with such urgency and with restrained curation. After all, that is how the makeshift memorial evolved in the first place, with honesty, authenticity, and the unmediated humanity of fans and runners who contributed the objects.

NOTES

1. Article seen by the author in Montreal Canada, January 2013.
2. Mike Dodd, "Sports Museums Struggle to Draw Fans, Turn Profit," *USA Today* November 1, 2011.
3. Smithsonian Institution Office of Policy and Analysis, "Exhibitions and their Audiences: Actual and Potential," Smithsonian Institution, September 2002, https://www.si.edu/content/opanda/docs/rpts2002/02.09.exhibitaudience.final.pdf, accessed July 16, 2022.
4. Wikipedia, "Deflate-gate," https://en.wikipedia.org/wiki/Deflategate, accessed July 17, 2022.
5. Wray Vamplew, "Facts and Artefacts Sports Historians and Sports Museums," *Journal of Sport History* 25, no. 2 (1998): 274.
6. Vamplew, "Facts and Artefacts," 275.
7. Vamplew, "Facts and Artefacts," 275.
8. Vamplew, "Facts and Artefacts," 274–75.
9. For more on visitor perspectives on incomplete exhibitions, see Margaret Lindauer, "The Critical Museum Visitor," in *New Museum Theory and Practice: An Introduction*, ed. Janet Marstine (Oxford: Blackwell, 2006).
10. Kevin Gover, Under Secretary for Museums and Culture at the Smithsonian Institute and former director of the National Museum of the American Indian, interview with the author, July 28, 2021.
11. Museum research on inclusion shows both strong public demand for more comprehensive narratives, and ways of framing museum information to demonstrate that it is evidence based. See Susie Wilkening, "Value of Museums, Part IV: Understanding and Social Justice," The Data Museum, https://www.wilkeningconsulting.com/datamuseum/category/inclusion, accessed July 17, 2022 and "Audiences and Inclusion: a Primer for Cultivating More Inclusive Attitudes Among the Public," American Alliance of Museums, February 9, 2021, https://www.aam-us.org/2021/02/09/audiences-and-inclusion-primer/, accessed July 17, 2022; and

"Reframing History," American Association of State and Local History, https://aaslh.org/reframing-history/, accessed July 17, 2022.

12. Daniel J. Simone, "Experiences for All: Participant and Fan Engagement at the NASCAR Hall of Fame," in *Interpreting Sports at Museums and Historic Sites,* Kathryn Leann Harris and Douglas Stark, eds. (Lanham, MD: Rowman & Littlefield, 2023), 101–107.

13. See Nina Simon, The Participatory Museum (Santa Cruz: Museum 2.0, 2010), https://www.participatorymuseum.org/,accessed July 17, 2022.

14. Comprehensive resources for developing more inclusive interpretation are included in the MASS Action (Museums as Sites of Social Action) Toolkit, available at https://www.museumaction.org/resources.

15. Joel Drucker, *When the Tennis Stopped,* International Tennis Hall of Fame website, 2020, accessed December 2021, https://www.tennisfame.com/tennisstopped.

16. Michael Patrick Allen and Nicholas Parsons, "The Institutionalization of Fame: Achievement, Recognition, and Cultural Consecration in Baseball," *American Sociological Review* 71, no. 5 (October 2006): 800–25.

17. Christopher Inoa, "Super Bowl Fever in Haute Couture 'Fashionable' Football Helmets on Display at Bloomingdale's," *Untapped New York*, accessed July 10, 2022, https://untapped-cities.com/2014/01/20/superbowl-fever-in-nyc-haute-couture-fashionable-football-helmets-on-display-at-bloomingdales/.

18. Sharon Morris, "University Museum Scores Fashion Touchdown," *Ole Miss: University of Mississippi News*, August 8, 2014, accessed July 10, 2022, https://news.olemiss.edu/university-museum-scores-fashion-touchdown/.

19. John Gillis, ed., *Commemorations: The Politics of National Identity* (Princeton: Princeton University Press, 1994), 3.

20. Tom Engelhardt, *The End of Victory Culture* (Amherst: University of Massachusetts Press, 2007), 5.

21. See Bill Adair, Benjamin Filene, and Laura Koloski, eds., *Letting Go? Sharing Historical Authority in a User-Generated World* (New York: Routledge, 2011) and Gail Anderson, ed., *Reinventing the Museum: Historical and Contemporary Perspectives on the Paradigm Shift* (Lanham, MD: Rowman & Littlefield, 2004).

22. Additional examples include the National Baseball Hall of Fame and Museum and steroid use, the Basketball Hall of Fame and gambling scandals of the 1950s, and the Pro Football Hall of Fame and the difficulties associated with the life of OJ Simpson.

23. Kathryn Leann Harris, "Exhibiting the Mental Game: Empathetic Sports Conversations," in *Interpreting Sports at Museums and Historic Sites*, Harris and Stark, eds., 96–101.

24. Dan Yaeger, "Dear Boston: Messages from the Marathon Memorial," in *Interpreting Sports at Museums and Historic Sites*, Harris and Stark, eds., 108–112.

25. "Our Mission," The National Museum of Mental Health Project, https://www.nmmhproject.org/mission-vision.

26. "Who We Are," Michael Phelps Foundation, https://michaelphelpsfoundation.org/; "Michael Phelps Speaks on the Importance of Mental Health (Part 1)," interview with Lester Holt on NBC, July 29, 2021, accessed July 11, 2022, https://www.nbcnews.com/nightly-news/video/michael-phelps-speaks-on-importance-of-mental-health-part-1-117596229869; "Michael Phelps Speaks on the Importance of Mental Health (Part 2)," interview with Lester Holt on NBC, July 29, 2021, accessed July 11, 2022, https://www.nbcnews.com/nightly-news/video/michael-phelps-speaks-on-importance-of-mental-health-part-2-117594693944.

27. Judy Dutton, "How Swimming Saved Michael Phelps: An ADHD Story," *Additude*, July 28, 2021, accessed July 13, 2022, https://www.additudemag.com/michael-phelps-adhd-advice-from-the-olympians-mom/.

28. Kathy Gurchiek, "Make Mental Health a Priority, Olympian Michael Phelps Urges," Society for Human Resource Management, September 10, 2021, https://www.shrm.org/hr-today/news/hr-news/pages/shrm21-annual-conference-michael-phelps-mental-health.aspx.

29. Robin Kuik and Suzanne Potts, "Mental Health and Athletes," Athletes for Hope, May 2022, accessed September 25, 2021, https://www.athletesforhope.org/2019/05/mental-health-and-athletes/.

30. "Athletes and Mental Health: Breaking the Stigma," Cleveland Clinic Health Essentials, August 10, 2021, https://health.clevelandclinic.org/mental-health-in-athletes/.

31. Deconstructing Stigma, https://deconstructingstigma.org/, accessed September 20, 2021.

32. "The Campaign," Deconstructing Stigma, accessed September 20, 2021, https://deconstructingstigma.org/.

33. "The Campaign," Deconstructing Stigma, accessed September 20, 2021, https://deconstructingstigma.org/.

34. "Deconstructing Stigma: Revealing Leads to Healing," McLean Hospital, October 4, 2017, https://www.mcleanhospital.org/news/deconstructing-stigma-revealing-leads-healing.

35. Cari Dwyer, Director of Exhibit Project Management at the Science Museum of Minnesota, interview with the author, July 28, 2022; The Science Museum of Minnesota modified the exhibit for the United States and prepared it for tour. For more information, see "Mental Health: Mind Matters," Mayo Clinic, accessed August 25, 2021, https://communityengagement.mayoclinic.org/mind-matters.

36. Interview with Dwyer.

37. NASCAR: The National Association for Stock Car Auto Racing.

38. As of 2020, the top NASCAR national touring series is primarily known as the NASCAR Cup Series. The two other national divisions are the NASCAR Xfinity Series and the NASCAR Gander Outdoor Truck Series.

39. The NHOF also provides monitors, which provide in time standings in the three national touring series. Monitors also display highlight and audio from the previous weekend action.

40. The date of the induction ceremony varies. In 2018 it took place in early February.

41. The NASCAR Hall of Fame has two votes in this process.

42. More than a mere token, that lone fan ballot matters because the voting can and has been extremely close over the years. Note: Content in this essay was written in 2019, after which the NASCAR Hall of Fame revised their voting process along with various exhibits and programs. Visit www.nascarhall.com for further information regarding current structure and offerings.

43. For instance, Dale Earnhardt (2010) or Jeff Gordon (2019).

44. ASA still exists. It is a regional stock car racing entity based primarily in the Midwest, which enjoyed its heyday in the 1970s and 1980s.

45. The IROC Series existed from 1974 to 2006 and pitted top drivers from various racing series competing in equally prepared cars built for the sole purpose of the series. Martin was proud of the fact that he beat the best of the best on five different seasons and wanted this acknowledged in his Hall of Honor case. Curators were more than happy to oblige.

46. Interview with Raney Tisdale and Matt Kirchman on April 27, 2017, in Watertown, Massachusetts. Raney Tisdale is a museum consultant specializing in interpretive & strategic planning, content and collections curation, institutional capacity building, and igniting the creative process, according to her website www.raneytisdale.com. Matt Kirchman is the principal of the consulting firm ObjectIdea, which plans visitor experiences for cultural attractions by researching content, developing exhibitions, and serving as a visitor advocate, according to his website www.objectidea.com.

Chapter Four

Finding Authenticity with the Voice of Influence

Interpreting Sports and Branding

Erin Narloch

When interpreting sports history, museums and historic sites often find it necessary to work with, as an extension of, alongside, or in consideration of a sports brand. A sports brand is defined as a commercial organizer or producer of sport products that holds both business and sport objectives.[1] Many sports museums are chartered by or directly affiliated with at least one, if not several, corporate partnerships. Even museums and historic sites that function outside of a sports corporation must consider the impact and presence of brands when approaching a sports exhibit. Establishing a relationship with a corporate brand may be a useful and, in some cases, unavoidable part of interpreting sports history in public spaces. Conversely, a history institution may find it necessary to develop an interpretative sports plan without establishing a brand partnership, which could happen for any number of reasons ranging from mismatched scheduling to conflicting narrative objectives. This essay will explore the intricacies of working with sports brands when interpreting sports history at a museum or historic site as well as the process of deciding how and when to best leverage a brand–museum relationship and under which circumstances an institution should consider working independently.

Key Interpretive Concepts

1. *Strategic Positioning*: Consumption in a digital age affects the way museum audiences view, consume, and reimagine sports history before ever entering a historic institution, a key concept to understand when attempting to interpret balanced history while also attracting and engaging a wide audience that is undoubtedly inundated with brand messaging.
2. *Benefit from the Brand Relationship*: Establishing a strong brand relationship can bring a lot of potential benefits for a museum or historic site. In order to navigate this partnership, museums need to proactively consider how to best utilize key components of the sports brand/museum relationship.
3. *Interpreting Independently*: Choosing to interpret sports history without a brand relationship may be necessary for your institution and may also be tricky to navigate and require careful consideration.

Principles that lie at the heart of sports branding are not merely twentieth- or even twenty-first-century concepts; in fact, they have evolved in human consciousness for more than fifteen centuries. Giving financial rewards for superior sport performance dates to 590 BCE.[2] The first European Cup took place in the 1950s. The Scottish Team, "Hibernia" saw approximately €34,000 in revenues.[3] In the 1970s, corporations embraced televised sporting event sponsorships as a form of "buying eyeballs." The primary goal was simply to gain widespread exposure to larger audiences. Today this concept is dead. A more modern-day concept of sport brands gained significance throughout the industry and in contemporary popular culture over the past two decades. Sponsorships and sports marketing activities are no longer simply focused on touchpoints and exposure. Brands now seek to tap into passion points to build stronger connections with audiences that are seeking authenticity.[4] This idea is reflected by strategic brand entities dedicated to the promotion, management, and growth of a sports-related identity (think: Nike, adidas, Manchester United Football Club, Green Bay Packers, FIFA, and National Basketball Association, etc.) that connects to consumers at a cultural level.[5]

Like many businesses, global sports brands have discovered that mining their corporate history opens the door to a deeper connection with the consumer. Historic roots bring a certain sense of authenticity to the present. Therefore, many sports corporations have history-related corporate holdings, archives, history departments, or museums. Story stewards are at work in many brand archives. They are constantly looking for context, layering in research, adding to the historic record, and working with colleagues to make informed product and marketing decisions.

> Brand-controlled stories have an inherent marketing function because brands, by definition, have a bias that protects and builds their legacy and identity over time.

Virtually every brand decision is focused on their target athlete and, by extension, target consumer, which is, in part, driven by the demands of the open market. Most brands are affixed to publicly held corporations that are accountable to shareholders. Thus, they are designed to consistently generate quarterly profit. In 2017, the second largest producer of sport products, adidas, saw sales rise to more than twenty billion euros, an increase of 17–19 percent over the previous year.[6] adidas keeps a close eye on their market share, the result of a well-oiled profit-generating machine. Sports brands are big business. That's just the name of the game. Corporate sports brands attract consumers through highly developed relationships with sports figures, which they contractually hold as company *assets*.

This business agenda can become problematic when it intersects with history interpretation. A brand-told story is almost never one hundred percent inclusive of the historic record. Rarely do corporations portray a straightforward, linear, or entirely consumer-facing narrative. Looking to the past to make sense of the present creates pitfalls of skewed perspective and inherent desired outcomes. In some cases, such as with controversial sports figures like O. J. Simpson, exploring the past could interfere with profits generation by highlighting a sullied brand story. When properly designed and implemented, a corporate archive distills a vast inventory of historical data into a carefully curated catalog of content that can help an organization see where it has been and where it is headed. This is usually told through a positive lens that combines the brand narrative with the targeted consumer's interests.[7]

Because of the conflicts of interpreting the historical record, museums and historic sites that function independently of a brand can lend their expertise instead of relying on sports corporations to function as the monolithic storyteller. Historic institutions serve as third-party validators of a brand's story through scholarly research, exhibitions, and audience intersections in a noncommercial environment. They have more freedom to investigate and illuminate stories that might otherwise go untold. In these environments, the "everyman's shoe" can be interpreted in a balanced, fair manner and visitors have the time and appetite to consume the content.[8] *Out of the Box: The Rise of Sneaker Culture*, took all the brands of athletic footwear and presented them together within a larger narrative. The Bata Shoe Museum skillfully presented the variety of the sneaker brand landscape and with this exercise the museum created an exhibition where all visitors could find their entry point.[9] This becomes more problematic when the brand and museum are the same entity, as is the case with a lot of sports museums. However, regardless of locale, all museum professionals can insert their trained expertise when partnering with or working in spite of sports brands to interpret balanced history for a modern audience.

Strategic Positioning

Consumer obsession is a current global enterprise concept that brands utilize to generate a constant dialogue with their target audience. The focus is placed squarely on a relationship between brand, athletes, and *consumer* (or fan). Under this concept, all business decisions would ideally prioritize the purchaser, thereby creating a seamlessly personal experience between brand and consumer. The more heroic a brand can make an athlete appear, the more they can market their products to consumers. Brands can more easily sell a "hero shoe" than an "everyman's shoe" because the *hero* archetype is less complex than the collective *everyman*. The hero is one of Carl Jung's seven archetypes in storytelling and is overwhelmingly the most accepted form of athlete, worldwide. Nike has undoubtedly created more hero shoes and heroic athletic worship scenarios than any other sports brand in existence. Perhaps their most famous campaign was the April 1985 *Jordan Flight* commercial, which showed the superhuman transcendence of a "flying" Michael Jordan.[10] Brands could greatly benefit from the perspectives of a cultural historian or museum professional to explore the *everyman* narratives. They could examine objects, sights, and sounds that expose humanity's underlying emotions and anxieties. However, doing so with the intent to sell more shoes can prove to be incredibly difficult.[11] Complex humanity is difficult to package and deliver in succinct, high-impact ad campaigns that produce impulse purchasing.

Because of their business marketing agenda, sports brands contextualize history in a far different way than museums and historic sites. Sports brands interpret their histories quickly and in real time. During monumental events, brands will often choose to make interpretive connections to previous heritage moments to strengthen and reinforce the significance of the brand. This content is compelling, incredibly succinct, and geared toward consumer consumption. Sports brands need to tell their story to millions of people through messaging that's aligned, crisp, and strategic. In order to get there, brands must be connected to their brand identity, vision, and values—defined by who they were, who they are currently, and who they want to be in the future. Internally, sports brands can breed authenticity in their culture when they generate true consistency and leverage it within a long-term strategy. Externally, the threshold for consistency and accountability is low, very low. A sports brand can mention one moment consistently for decades until it becomes an authentication milestone that identifies a company or team to an external audience through a red thread connecting the past, present, and future. The message of that thread is then often undoubted by consumers. The corporation can use this thread to formulate a relationship with the public and then repeatedly reinforce the same concept to reconnect buyers to the brand's identity. Maintaining this consistency throughout time is *unrealistic*, especially when it lacks authenticity.

The business strategies that global brands execute are carefully guarded and multifaceted orchestrations. These strategies incorporate various company departments and disciplines: brand marketing (marketing, communications, content, public relations, social media, assets, and events), product (creative direction, life cycle, go-to-market), digital, finance, sales, and global operations (logistics, sourcing, production). At least twice a year brands go to marketand release thousands of products for global distribution. Internal organizational departments handle dedicated categories that can range from team and league sports to worldwide sports competitions and specialized sports. In the world of sport product production, the likelihood of working alongside a former athlete or coach is greater because they have intimate knowledge of the needs of the athletes, organizations, and competitions. A product's release is activated through the brand's marketing and communication plans. These campaigns operate at the global, market, regional, and, finally, the local level. Sports brands utilize an exhaustive selection of marketing channels. Marketing activations commonly include special campaigns, television commercials, advertising during competitions, hashtags on social media channels, influencers who carry social currency, or even promotional discounts at a key retailer. A brand's content strategy creates the hierarchy of messaging and produces the key indicators of performance that will measure a specific launch or campaign's success.

A brand archive rarely has enough time to fully explore the breadth and depth of the historic record. Brands do well to get the consumer hooked, but often drop the ball when it comes to delving into rich and layered historical narratives. The type of research that is required to truly unpack an object or historic narrative takes considerable time. Cultural historians and museum professionals are tasked with diligently unpacking an object from a 360-degree view. In the mid-2000s, Pete Samis coined the term "Visual Velcro" to describe the visual "hooking" power contained in a piece of art.[12] After a viewer is captivated by the aesthetics of the work, they can begin unpacking and contextualizing the item by asking questions like: "What was the artist thinking" and "Why did she/he make it?" Samis's concept also applies to the feeling that can be generated from viewing sport history artifacts in that we, the viewing public, can become "hooked" by an object. After we love it, we want to learn more and continue unpacking it. In the fast-paced world of global marketing, brands often default to rapidly evolving content production, thus eliminating the opportunity for more meaningful and impactful historical contextualization.

Brands can resolve this issue by making an intentional ongoing effort to partner with history interpretation professionals in order to improving contextualization over time. Building a full historical narrative takes time and concerted effort. Brands stand to offer significant benefits to both internal and external researchers alike by investing in a comprehensive, long-term evolutionary exploratory process. This commitment will build upon itself, adding to the richness of the storytelling opportunities for sport brands. Cultural historian Elizabeth Semmelhack, a senior curator at the Bata Shoe Museum, often says, "Rigor makes right!"[13] By this, she posits that while the ship cannot be righted overnight, museums can add sustaining value by consistently and continuously mining an archival collection and progressively stacking context. Trained public historians can then partner with brands to fill in some of the historic gaps and explore effective interpretive strategies for a consuming public that include an authentic representation of the historic record.

A brand archive can lead the pursuit of constant contextualization and understanding of the 360-degree story internally, while a sports museum or historic site leads the pursuit of constant contextualization and understanding of the 360-degree story externally. For the story of Reebok's Instapump Fury, a running shoe first released in 1994, the Reebok Archive led the research of the shoe's inception—its origin story, its internal story. When it came to how the Fury went on to become an iconic fashion model, the Archive acted as a partner in the research with the publication *Sneaker Freaker*, as the storyteller.

The Reebok Brand Archive created and uses the model below for internal audiences who have limited experience with the humanities, scholarly research, and a dynamic archive concept.[14] When utilized in presentations, animations illustrate a compelling argument for the value of a dynamic, multitiered Brand Archive. The desired outcome for each collection layer is found on the right-hand side. On the left-hand side, the elements of the brand collection are "blown apart." Creating strata upon which the brand's history is continuously contextualized, researched, and made more and more relevant. This model gives heightened value to knowledge and narrative, essentially creating the argument for seeing the interconnectedness of the brand's story through their product, makers, players, and audience. This is an evolved corporate archive model because the archive professional's responsibility is to continually build relevant context for colleagues without it becoming bogged down with perceived irrelevant data or antiquated language. When successfully implemented, a brand's cultural practices will include acquiring knowledge within the archive and throughout the organization by producing elevated brand experiences, storytelling modalities, archive visits, authentic brand strategies that include evidence, brand-level authority about corporate heritage that is highly contextualized, sophisticated, relevant, and emotive. When a brand is committed to this type of work internally, it can better support similar external pursuits and collaborative efforts performed by sports museums or historic sites.

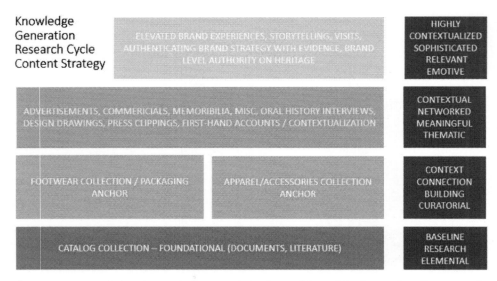

Knowledge
Generation
Research Cycle
Content Strategy

ELEVATED BRAND EXPERIENCES, STORYTELLING, VISITS, AUTHENTICATING BRAND STRATEGY WITH EVIDENCE, BRAND LEVEL AUTHORITY ON HERITAGE

HIGHLY CONTEXTUALIZED SOPHISTICATED RELEVANT EMOTIVE

ADVERTISEMENTS, COMMERICIALS, MEMORIBILIA, MISC, ORAL HISTORY INTERVIEWS, DESIGN DRAWINGS, PRESS CLIPPINGS, FIRST-HAND ACCOUNTS / CONTEXTUALIZATION

CONTEXTUAL NETWORKED MEANINGFUL THEMATIC

FOOTWEAR COLLECTION / PACKAGING ANCHOR

APPAREL/ACCESSORIES COLLECTION ANCHOR

CONTEXT CONNECTION BUILDING CURATORIAL

CATALOG COLLECTION – FOUNDATIONAL (DOCUMENTS, LITERATURE)

BASELINE RESEARCH ELEMENTAL

Figure 4.1. Knowledge Generation Research Cycle model used for internal audiences at the Reebok Brand Archive illustrates the value of connecting the brand's story through products, makers, players, and audiences. *Source:* **Erin M. Narloch.**

Public historians, both inside and outside of sports brands, must be diligent in the search for transparently rewriting entrenched sporting myths that distract from an authentic understanding of the past. While museum professionals can often delve into difficult topics in ways that brands cannot, all cultural historians have a responsibility to find ways to push the sports cultural envelope. Interpreters working inside sport brands and at museums and historic sites are highly trusted by all audiences. When brands choose to ignore the myths or perpetuate them, they are risking their brand story, authenticity, credibility, and relationship with audiences—externally *and* internally. The same holds true for museums and historic sites. Ignoring the more difficult parts of the past can breed distrust among the public, constituents, and employees. In the converse, corporations, museums, and historic sites can foster trust within their organizations and with the public by embracing the full breadth and depth of the brand's history and the historic sporting narrative. Moreover, they can mitigate potential risk or crisis manage by owning their own history before someone else owns it for them.

Depending on the sensitivity of the topic, a demand for authenticity can become monumentally daunting and risk institutional and societal destruction; yet, it is vitally important for the organization to stay the course. Any institution may find it intimidating to tackle political topics, especially when those topics intersect with sports, fame, race, gender, and ego. The competitive nature of sports, professional athletes, sporting events, sport brands, and big business often thwarts the drive for authenticating sports history. Conversely, credibility is a direct outgrowth of authenticity and transparency. Regardless of the size and scope of the legendary saga, sport brands must be aware of and embrace their entire history. If left unchecked, entrenched, long-held myths around sporting history grow exponentially. Public historical consensus sometimes self-corrects by exposing a myth and validating a more historically accurate and culturally proper version. This type of movement can actually result in a sports culture shift that happens outside of the brand or museum. Yet, these moments of cultural movement are exceptional and rare and are usually accompanied by negative pushback from an inquisitive, and then often untrusting, public presence.

In 2019, adidas launched the highly anticipated four-hundred-page academically produced book, *Playing the Game: The History of adidas,* in which the corporation exposed new layers of the company's seventy-year history. adidas partnered with Die Gesellschaft für Unternehmensgeschichte (the Organization of Company Historians in Germany) and four independent historians to conduct a multiyear in-depth research project in hopes of uncovering previously unpublished pieces of the company's full historically accurate record. Most notably, the company's updated written history included new research about their founder, Adi Dassler, and his pre-adidas affiliation with the German National Socialist Party during the years leading up to and during World War II. Previous adidas histories omitted these details. This book launch provided adidas with the opportunity to tell richer, more complex historical stories and own the more complicated parts of their corporate history. Going forward, they can become a standard bearer for embracing a challenging sporting past and using it to inspire a better future.[15]

Today, sports brands are more motivated toward authenticity because consumers are driving them there. Presenting accurate content, hard evidence, and primary research findings provides the necessary context for the consumers of today. Millennials are specifically demanding this in all of the consumer goods categories. At a 2018 consumer analyst group industry conference, Emmanuel Faber, chief executive of Danone, declared, "Consumers are looking to pierce the corporate veil in our industry and to look at what's behind the brand. The guys responsible for this are the millennials." He went on to say that millennials have a completely new set of values, "they want committed brands with authentic products."[16] Museums and historic sites can partner with brands to enrich and enliven the impact of this cultural shift.

Any time a sports brand releases elements of their story, they have the opportunity to engage in a rich and meaningful discussion about being present in a global sporting experience shared by millions globally. Historic sports moments generate a collective memory experience that provides an entry point for brands, museums, and historic sites to engage with the public. This happens in a museum through exhibitions and special events. Museum visitors deliberately buy a ticket to see an exhibition or attend a community event in person, demonstrating genuine interest in the presented content. When they leave the museum halls, they often want to continue learning and are eager to share their experience within their spheres of influence. Museums generate these limited events after years of planning, and then the content disappears. It is often relegated to the "previous exhibitions" section of a museum's website. Sports brands generate a similar experience during marketing campaigns, such as an exclusive sneaker drop. Sneaker companies create devoted fans by implementing marketing ploys like online leaks with hyped teasers. Consumers often form lines to see the latest event or cop a glance at the hottest new shoe drop. The whole experience lives online, in social media channels like Instagram stories, tags, and Twitter retweets. The top sneakers fans in the world have tens and in some cases hundreds of thousands of followers. They are known as influencers who help brands and consumers connect with one another through content channels that were never seriously considered until recently. Museums and historic sites can be aware of the hype created by marketing campaigns and find ways to intersect with the brand in order to generate awareness around historical content during moments of high brand visibility.

Benefit from the Brand Relationship

Creating a symbiotic relationship between a brand and a museum requires concerted effort, but holds exciting potential for both entities. At first glance, the world of global sports marketing may appear antithetical to the museum field's highest ideals. Upon closer inspection, the two can and often do intersect at a place that fosters an authentic reflection of the historic record, contemporary and timeless critical analysis on societal issues, and balanced commemoration. With *Out of the Box: The Rise of Sneaker Culture*, the Bata Shoe museum's curator Elizabeth Semmelhack demonstrated the value of symbiotic museum–brand relationships that can produce a unique and relevant blockbuster exhibit. She saw a gap in the museum's collection and sought to fill it. She quickly learned that she would need to contact and partner with major global sports brands in order to procure the objects she needed for the exhibit. She found the sporting brands to be quite willing to loan the objects she requested, and they did so without much, if any, limitation on historical interpretation. As a result, Semmelhack created and toured the first international traveling exhibition on sports footwear and wrote engaging, historically relevant, and accurate exhibit copy without compromising her institution's mission, values, or vision.[17]

Nonbrand-connected museums and historic sites may find it necessary to navigate or even partner with a global sports brand when attempting to interpret the sporting past. Branding, either historically or in the present, influences most sporting subjects. The very presence of global sports marketing impacts the way a consuming public views an athlete, sport, or team, for better or worse. Beyond this more ephemeral barrier, museums and historic sites will often need to garner the permission of a major sports company before interpreting some specific historical narratives. Corporations or sport brands often own the rights and trademarks to certain historic objects, information, sports figures, or teams, which places them as gatekeepers to the past. Thus, museum staff must carefully plan a sports interpreting project and consider a multitude of factors when fostering a brand relationship.

Some brand-connected or -owned museums, who have little choice as to whether or not they work alongside the corporation with which they are affiliated, have discovered ways of effectively utilizing the brand/museum relationship. The Green Bay Packers Hall of Fame, for example, navigates a very unique relationship that exists between the community and the franchise. The Packers is the only professional sports community-owned franchise in the United States. They are also the only professional team that has sold out *every* home game, at the famed Lambeau Field, since 1960. The

Green Bay Packers Hall of Fame and Museum must, and does, find meaningful ways to engage with the brand, *because it is also the community*. This presents some unique challenges for the museum, as Krissy Zegers and Justine Kaempfer explain, "The museum has to determine how to fulfill its obligations to those constituents without jeopardizing the brand, vision, and story." Through careful research, they identified a thematic approach that descriptively encapsulates the rich and authentic ways that both the brand and community identify with the team's storied history.[18]

When a museum or historic site decides to create a sports exhibit, they may find it nearly necessary to intersect with a brand, a process that very well may result in a multitude of mutual benefits. Consider, for example, the various ways a city's historical society might encounter brand relationships when developing a sports-related exhibit. Imagine a fictional example in which the Atlanta Historical Commission crafted a plan to produce a one-year comprehensive sports exhibit in honor of the 150th anniversary of the first sporting event in Georgia's largest city. They would need to coordinate with all of the city's professional sports teams, each managed by a corporate brand. They may also want to partner with the official USA Olympic team and the official Olympic Games organization, which are also both managed as individual brands. Each of these affiliations would function with annual competition and marketing schedules, with which the museum could align so as to attract the highest attendance. Some of the current or previous high-profile athletes may have contracts with global sports apparel brands. The museum staff could examine the design campaigns, check the historical relevance of a specific item, and/or possibly coordinate exhibit features with an iconic object anniversary or market introduction. The brands would possibly loan valuable, historically relevant, or highly sought-after objects for the museum to display in the exhibit. The acquisition of those objects may or may not come with interpretive restrictions based on the brand's image standards. Each brand would be able to communicate their expectations. Ideally, the museum would be able to add rich historical value and context to objects that are more often worn or sold than culturally interpreted. Even if the objects are on loan from a brand-affiliated museum, the historical society may have more interpretive leeway than the corporate museum and may be able to dig deeper and attract a wider audience.

Equipped with the knowledge that sports brands are big business, museums and historic sites can often fulfill their institution's sports interpreting needs by plugging into a brand's established assets, marketing strategies, and messaging. Historic institutions can potentially tap into a global market, access brand assets, and instill enduring corporate relationships. Sport brands also stand to benefit from a relationship with the museum or historic site. A corporation might be able to garner scholarly research, third-party validation, and a viable corporate social responsibility (CSR) partner. In order to navigate this partnership, museums need to proactively consider how to best utilize key components of the sports brand/museum relationship.

Know Your Partner

Thoroughly preparing your staff with information about the brand, their objectives, the corporate structure, company objective and strategies, and their history will put you in a solid position to know how to approach them and communicate how the relationship will be viable for your both organizations. Conduct baseline research. If the brand is publicly held, read their recent annual reports, search their corporate website online for organizational structure or a foundation. What do they currently sponsor? Who are their top executives? Someone from your development department may be able to help you connect with someone within the organization. Make contact through a corporate communications liaison or mine your professional network for the proper connection. Remember that brand archives and historians sit in a variety of locations within an organizational structure including but not limited to: the legal department, sport marketing, brand communications, and brand strategy departments. In short, do your homework: determine the best department to contact, work your connections, understand how their organization operates, and be able to clearly communicate how they might be able to intersect with your institution's objectives in a mutually beneficial way. And when all else fails—if you don't know, just ask.

Key Considerations for Developing New Narratives, Perspectives, and Audiences:

- Consider the brand's agenda: What might a brand need to make a partnership with your institution work for them?
- Find a way to work with the brand's agenda: What can your institution gain from working with their agenda?
- Evaluate how your institution can add to the brand's perspective.
- Think broadly: Which historic figures in your institution are connected to a sport? Which current community members affiliated with your museum are connected to a sport? Who might want to help you cross promote your institution's historic interests with a sports brand?
- Utilize brand resources, this could include an online press room, grant programs, field offices, and so on.
- Request and acquire objects and assets from the brand's holdings.
- Access the brand archive for research.
- Have the brand sponsor an exhibition, publication, or event.
- Bring brand ambassadors or insiders for an appearance or panel discussion.
- Provide in-kind donation of product for museum programming, for instance, shirts for campers or sport shoes that could be customized by participants at a museum program.

Requesting Brand Objects or Assets

Once a museum or historic site's staff determines which part of a corporation's history or holdings will help make their exhibition's story more compelling or complete, the next step is to extend an *ask* to the brand archive. This is corporately known as a brand request: an inquiry to secure an object loan, gain access to an internal archive for research, or garner assistance in contacting a brand partner on behalf of your institution. Brand requests can be conducted in one of three ways:

1. *Simple Request*: This would be a great place to start when trying to garner a single object loan, image use, or access to research material. Clearly and simply articulate what is needed, by when, and why.
2. *Strategically Relevant Request*: A request that clearly amplifies the brand's key messaging. Articulate, in depth, what you need, by when, and why. Take the time to connect the objectives of the museum/historic site's project to the sports brand, finding synergies between both.
3. *Ongoing Partnership Opportunity*: A brand can assist a museum or historic site with access to its history and can also provide access to experts. In addition to artifact loans, or donations, a sports brand has a global network of experts in athletic footwear, apparel, equipment production, historical artifacts, brand-related assets, teams, athletes, coaches, and other participants. Curators can, for example, learn from shadowing a cobbler or asking questions about the parts of an early twentieth-century ice skate from an expert. They can also intersect with research processes, public or private events, and ongoing asset swapping.

Key Considerations for Brand Collaborations and Brand Requests

- Articulate the project's benefit to the brand: Anticipate visitor numbers, reach of the project, target audience overlap, and so on.
- Provide realistic project timelines up front: Keep in mind that certain external requests require sign-off from various internal stakeholders; this process can take additional time.
- If requests involve individuals that once had a relationship with the brand (e.g., athletes), determine if that relationship is active. If not, be diligent to establish a relationship with the sports figure before you contact the brand.
- Clearly identify any potential conflict of interest with the brand: Do not expose them without proper communication. External loans are built on collegial trust.
- Be aware of any PR-related needs and credit the brand when appropriate.
- Invite proper brand ambassadors to museum events.
- Request cross-channel marketing and promotion support.
- Make sure you've secured all copyrights, trademarks, and intellectual property.
- Plan for enough review time for publications. Note: it's common practice to have the brand's legal department review all publications featuring brand content prior to sign-off. Do not feel nervous about this step; it happens often.

Interpreting Independently

A global sports brand is serious business and working with a brand is not always the best solution for museums or historic sites. While working with one brand, or several at once, can provide an incredible opportunity that amplifies the work of local museums and historic sites, sometimes the agendas or directions of each institution counteract. Brands, at their core, are designed and centrally operate to turn a profit while museums and historic sites are often nonprofit entities with invested donor bases whose primary objective is to drive educational, communal, and/or socially oriented content. Sometimes, just the introduction of a third party can prove more cumbersome than helpful, as the particulars of the two entities simply may not mesh in terms of time, money, logistics, or purpose. Corporations move on a scheduled routine in a fast-paced world, which will not always fit the rhythm of a public history institution. Museums or historic sites may be seeking financial support or content approval that the corporation is unable or unwilling to provide in the stated time frame or for the institution's stated reasons.

Public historians are increasingly exploring complex and contested narratives, including sports narratives; at times, deconstructing the foundation of previously accepted societal norms in ways that might be presently conflicting for a sports brand. In the Forward to Julia Rose's *Interpreting Difficult Histories at Museums and Historic Sites,* historian Jonathan Scott Holloway describes the current climate of collective historical reflection, "We find ourselves in a new moment in which we are wrestling with our pasts, our ethics, our obligations to share our most painful stories with our present and future. This is not easy work. Indeed, it is often profoundly unsettling work."[19] This *call* is affecting, at least in some way, nearly every facet of society—even corporations. Yet, rarely is this particular type of work undertaken by major sports brands. Exploring difficult histories can be unearthing, devastating, and even traumatic for individuals or entire communities or nations. Navigating this space is a delicate and tenuous endeavor that can prove challenging for even seasoned public history professionals. Moreover, as Rose later states, "The rising trend and demands to interpret difficult histories has serious consequences on reshaping of collective memories."[20] This type of foundational change is often met first with resistance, something a brand might not be ready to embrace. If your institution is charging toward an exhibit of this kind, you may find yourself forging a new, isolated path or delving into territory that your subject's applicable brand is unable to face and/or endorse, for any variety of reasons. Turn instead into your extended community to find allies, utilize your museum as a third space to activate that community, and use the expertise of others to create new meaning.

Working within a stated organizational structure can provide clarity to everyone at your institution and help you set the foundation to proceed independently—without the connection to a brand—when developing a sports exhibit. Mission-driven projects with clear communication and strategic management plans outlined from the onset provide museum staff with supportive frameworks. These frameworks support effective decision-making and efficiency. Being transparent with an institution's objectives holds them accountable. In many cases, organizations place their strategic plan online, as was the case with the Carnegie Museum of Natural History. Their staff clearly presented the museum's growth, development, and content objectives for the duration of two years. They explained how those objectives would affect the annual business plans, performance agreements (with project management chart inclusion), and even the review and promotion of staff.[21] This type of practice may be standard for your institution. If not, you may want to consider garnering this type of focused clarity before confirming which direction you want to go—with or without a brand relationship—when developing a brand-related sports exhibit.

Next, reflect upon the particular exhibit or program in question in light of your institution's central mission in comparison to that of the brand. From a simple methods perspective, you may be seeking either a more complex or simplistic project than the brand would prefer or could support. In macro terms, carefully explore and consider the brand's larger agendas and measure that against your institution's goals, values, and objectives. If they are a mismatch, it may be best to explore other options. Be diligent in the exploratory process. Not all brands are the same. Some are transparent or working toward being transparent about who they were, are currently, and strive to be in the future. Some are not. Some may share your institution's political or social agendas or want to partner on a campaign. Some clearly may not. Others may even work in opposition. In these situations, you may find yourself approaching an historical interpretation project that borders on a social action campaign in a way that challenges a long-held sports trope or engrained cultural or corporate identity. Working with a brand in these situations may, by definition, run counter to your institution's broader objectives.

Following institutional conviction can offer a platform for inciting change within a brand. In support of their constituents and core mission, the Smithsonian Institute National Museum of the American Indian (NMAI), led by the then-Director Kevin Gover, confronted professional and amateur sports teams' use of Native American symbols. NMAI museum staff engaged their community in two symposia that empathetically explored the historical roots of sports teams culturally appropriating Native symbols. The symposia's impact was far reaching, eventually leading the local Washington R*dskins franchise, among others, to part with their mascot name and caricature.[22] When speaking in opposition to a brand becomes the necessary direction for your organization, maintain a purposeful stance grounded in scholarship, cast a wide net of influence, and maintain distance from the brand unless or until collaboration becomes palatable for both organizations.[23]

Consider your audience. The brand may not care about what you are trying to say. You may not care about what the brand is trying to say. Your audience may not care about what either of you is trying to say. It is your job to mitigate these considerations and decide how to proceed with or without following what comes affixed to a brand. Moreover, it is imperative to consider if your institutions are ready to welcome the new audiences that will come when you align with a sports brand. In a traditional organization with a fixed mindset, would museum leadership be prepared to open the aperture on museum visitorship? It could be that partnering with a specific sports brand will be a positive way to cast a wider net for museum visitors, a chance to change the heart and minds of someone who might have previously thought the museum had "nothing for them." Confronting a brand for inaccuracy, cultural appropriation, disrespect, or a lack of inclusivity will impact your audience. Some may become enlivened by the discussion while others may feel challenged. Consider if your current audience has the interest and/or if the institution has the capacity to generate and sustain the exhibit or program you are trying to create. Then, look at your long-term capacity—after this exhibition closes, how might your institution sustain repeat visitorship? Check all of this against your institutional values and the direction you intend to represent or lead your audience.

Think about internal resources, particularly time, timing, and money. A corporation may offer resources, either time or money, that support an exhibit with which they align. However, sometimes working with a brand can cost time and money your institution does not have. Working on a brand request or responding to the brand's legal requirements could require more time resources than available. Moreover, a brand may attach strings to the money they offer, strings your institution cannot abide. Carefully consider timing. Ask whether it is the most effective time to raise a certain issue or topic for your institution, audience, and the public at large. If it is, then further consider how raising that topic might affect a current or future beneficial relationship with a brand.

Above all, stay committed to aligning with the message and agenda that best fits your institution. Start by diligently exploring other interests or interested parties that may conflict. Think about your board members, donors, or any part of your institution that might have overlapping or conflicting interests. Then consider how these perspectives may or may not align with a brand's mission, perspective, or agenda. If you are approaching a particularly controversial issue, carefully explore the ways in which all of the parties may be affected by taking a path that either bumps up against internal constituents or external forces. Conversely, working independently may give your institution an opportunity to highlight a topic of societal import that unifies seemingly conflicting parties, even some brands while not others. Museums and historic sites are uniquely positioned to bridge societal gaps through diplomatic public historical analysis, which is often quite challenging work. Staying true to your mission may put your institution in the best position to make a real difference by presenting sports history in a way that is unique to public interpretive branches regardless of how large, financially backed corporations might react.

Questioning Authenticity Forward

The generations coming into adulthood are requesting more and more transparency from brands and this desire will not be going quietly into the night. These sophisticated audiences call out "signaling" when they see it, they can tell what is and isn't real or authentic. What practitioners at sports museums and historic sites can do is question the authenticity of the narratives they're telling, the brands they are aligning with, and the research they're conducting. Who is holding the keys to the narrative? In the case of the Green Bay Packers, their brand is so intimately connected to the community of Green Bay. In many ways, the community is writing the brand's story; they demand both authenticity and collective memory concurrently. When it pertains to sports history, museums and historic sites could engage audiences in dialogue, listen, and share the theoretical microphone with a variety of audiences to engage in discourse and share in constructing a more complete view of the subject at hand. It would be a revolution. Question authenticity forward.

Converging Paths—Brand & Museum Connections: Replicable Practices

Working with a brand shouldn't be a daunting task. The list of practices below is designed to get you started, from ideation into action. Remember that the best way to start a discussion is to be open and forthright about your intensions. When in doubt, starting with the phrase, "Would you consider" is polite and offers an extended hand to a partnership, even if that hand is to a giant global entity.

- **Follow sports and brands:** Track world sporting events and brand engagement on social media as well as follow the actual brands on social media—namely Instagram and Twitter. You can search their handle and follow it or a common hashtag. Set a Google alert for the brand you want to work with, so that you have the most current information and reference it in your research—and continue throughout the project. Watch sshareholders' deadlines and avoid contacting organizations during those time periods.
- **Think about the calendar year:** Schedule different global and regional sporting events that matter to your target audience—that have an intersection with key brands or a variety of brands that you want to talk about or have represented in your collection. Reproduce or replicate an event—like what happens with March Madness—against different objects in your collection.
- **Engage younger visitors:** Post about cool events that happened the night before and use that to educate and interpret based on your collection and content, or even encourage your younger audiences to post and engage with their peers and followers.
- **Interpret names within a brand:** Explore the history of symbols, icons, and logos (like Run-DMC or Stan Smith). Think about the knowledge behind the brand.
- **Consider career paths of figures other than athletes:** Provide behind-the-scenes tours or panel discussions that explore the career paths of coaches, trainers, or sports media figures that are sponsored or promoted by a certain brand.
- **Hack History:** Remake the Air Jordan '85 or design your own jersey, where kids can have fun, learn about history, and play.
- **Target sports figures in your community:** Design a history exhibit around them that considers their brand relationship throughout their career and how you might partner.
- **Attract a brand:** Think about creating an exhibit where the brand *wants* to participate with you so that you can benefit from their resources (PR, money, notoriety).
- **Think about how to create a sustainable brand relationship with longevity:** Create a relationship model—maybe one that fulfills their corporate CSR while matching some aspect of your strategic plan, the commitment to one another's organization could grow over time. A fundraiser one year could turn into a fundraiser and panel the following, into a community activation plan. You might build more traction without a highly developed brand relationship from the beginning and then allow it to grow: proof of concept, pilot, full-on partnership.
- **Engage the brand, regardless:** If you choose to *not* work with a brand still ask them for a comment, invite them to the opening, ask them to share it with their employees, and link them on social media.
- **Think globally about the reach of brands:** Consider all of the various ways they cross over throughout the world—where people work, various perspectives based on identity and nationality, what is popular where, who likes it and who doesn't,

and so on. "If you were in ____ city, you would likely buy a ____ shoe from this ____ brand."

- **Get local:** Track discounts and create a scavenger hunt in the gallery that leads to a discount at a store in the community (general stores like Dick's or even a specific brand store). Ask to be on local sports calendars. Ask to make announcements during local games or on social media.
- **Look to collectors:** Memorabilia stores, collecting conventions, and major worldwide collectors—these are the people who are tracking objects, third-party authenticators. Invite influencers to review the exhibition with you. Ask them to post and comment online throughout the exhibition's run.
- **Legalese:** If you want to work in opposition to a brand, or to expose some thesis about them, get legal help, know copyright law, understand the difference between legal courtesy, enforceable legal law, and opinion.

CASE STUDY

Playing Nice: The Making of *Out of the Box: The Rise of Sneaker Culture*

Elizabeth Semmelhack

In 2011, the Bata Shoe Museum in Toronto, Ontario, began developing *Out of the Box: The Rise of Sneaker Culture*, an exhibition on the history of sneakers from their mid-nineteenth-century incarnation to contemporary sneaker culture with a specific focus on shifting constructions of idealized masculinity. There was great enthusiasm for the project, but there were also several obstacles. One of the most significant was the limited number of contemporary sneakers in the Bata Shoe Museum collection making loans that were of paramount importance for the viability of the exhibition. A number of important sneakers were borrowed from the Northampton Museum and Art Gallery in the UK, but the majority needed to come from individual collectors and sneaker brand archives. The Bata Shoe Museum is committed to creating exhibitions that explore complex and challenging issues such as cultural appropriation and identity, racism, and sexism. Considering these goals, we were concerned that brand lenders would hesitate or place restrictions on the academic integrity of the project. We quickly discovered that historical accuracy, nuanced analysis, and academic integrity were of central importance to both the private collectors and the brands that lent to the exhibition. One of the greatest challenges arose when the exhibition began to travel in 2015. Some art museums wanted to exhibit the sneakers as "art" without the extensive didactics and images central to the exhibition. Ultimately, the curatorial narrative of *Out of the Box* prevailed, and the contextualizing content went on to be a highly valued aspect of the exhibition as displayed at the Bata Shoe Museum and as it traveled globally to art museums.

Research and Making Connections

At the start of the project, it became evident that there was scant academic research on sneakers—from their origin in the middle of the nineteenth century to their

Figure 4.2. *Out of the Box: The Rise of Sneaker Culture* at the Bata Shoe Museum, 2013.
Source: 2019 Bata Shoe Museum, Toronto (Photo: Philip Castleton).

current importance in the construction of masculinities. Therefore, significant primary research was conducted. This included extensive surveys of historic newspapers, trade publications, patents, and advertisements as well as field research and consultation with a small group of sneaker culture advisers, including Dee Wells from Obsessive Sneaker Disorder, Dion Walcott from Toronto Loves Kicks, and Mayan Rajendran a well-connected sneaker collector.

This research resulted in an exhibition dense with information. Section 1, Rubber Revolution: Physical Culture, Urban Anxiety and the Origin of the Sneaker, discussed the development of leisure culture and established sneakers as signifiers of privilege in the middle of the nineteenth century. It also positioned sneakers on the vanguard of material and manufacturing innovation, while considering the exploitative nature of rubber cultivation. In addition, this section addressed increasing social anxiety around growing urban populations and the hope that exercise would address ideas of both moral and physical contagion as well as the associations established between sneakers and criminality. Section 2, The Body Politic: Sneakers, Statehood, and Sporting, traced the increased importance of physical fitness following World War I and the role fascism played in the democratization of the sneaker. It also charted how sneakers lost all association with status in the immediate postwar period to become the footwear of childhood in the 1950s and 1960s. Section 3, Sports Stars and Status Sneakers: Fashioning Fitness, addressed the reemergence of the sneaker as a status symbol important for both fitness and fashion in the 1970s and 1980s. This era also saw the relationship between sneakers, urban culture, music, and basketball cemented when Michael Jordan signed with Nike and Run-DMC signed with adidas. In addition, this section addressed the highly problematic and often racist positioning of sneaker culture in the media at the time. Section 4, Fresh Out the Box: Sneaker Culture and Shifting Masculinities, looked at the explosion of sneaker culture and the concomitant increase in companies and fashion houses producing sneakers in the 1990s to the 2000s. It explored how sneakers have inculcated men into the fashion system and considered how they have become central to expressions of masculinity. This section also featured clips from the documentary *Just for Kicks* (2005). Finally, the last stand-alone section examined the work of a select group of renowned sneaker designers including Steven Smith, Tinker Hatfield, and Eric Avar.

Securing Loans

With a complex storyline in place, the next step was to secure loans. Not only did the exhibition require original sneakers that could illuminate the stories in insightful ways, but it also needed examples of the iconic sneakers that sneaker connoisseurs would expect to see—in addition to welcomed surprises. Unfortunately, many of the desired sneakers were extremely rare and often in fragile condition. The museum requested loans from all the major sneaker brands but was concerned that the nature of the highly competitive commercial sneaker market would leave brands reluctant to lend.

With an overwhelmingly positive response, the exhibition opened at the Bata Shoe Museum in 2013 with 122 artifacts. In addition to the Northampton Museum and Art Gallery, loans came from all the major brands including Reebok, PUMA, Nike, adidas, Ewings, and Converse as well as private collectors. No brand sought to exert control over the curatorial content, and in fact, brand archivists, especially Sam Smallidge at Converse and Martin Herde at adidas, were dedicated to promoting accurate histories even if the facts challenged long-standing myths embedded in sneaker lore. A few companies did request to read text related to artifacts that they had lent, but any requested changes were minor.

Exhibition Design and Traveling of *Out of the Box*

The Bata Shoe Museum is a material culture institution, not an art museum, and, although aesthetics is central to the success of the museum's exhibitions, each exhibition's curatorial *messaging* and supported cultural context are critical. The museum commissioned Karim Rashid for the design of the *Out of the Box* exhibition. His aesthetic was fresh, but in the earliest stages of the design, there was little room for contextual material. This issue was resolved with the addition of touch screens containing in-depth text, historical footage, and images placed throughout the exhibition. As the exhibition evolved into a traveling exhibit, the tensions between content and design resurfaced.

Out of the Box became a traveling exhibition under the auspices of the American Federation of Arts.[24] Working with the AFA was essential to the success of this venture, as the Bata Shoe Museum is a small institution which, at the time, had a curatorial staff comprised of a senior curator, a collections manager, and a conservator.[25] In addition to enabling the exhibition to expand and travel, working with the AFA also allowed for a large exhibition catalog to be copublished with Rizzoli. Although the opportunity to reimagine *Out of the Box* as a traveling exhibition brought new opportunities, it also presented some challenges. The design of the original exhibition was extremely site specific to the Bata Shoe Museum so the exhibition needed to be reimagined at each venue. In addition, the size of the exhibition increased— the number of lenders grew from twenty-six to thirty-eight for the multicity tour.[26]

The biggest challenge, however, involved fitting a cultural history exhibition into art museum settings. Many contemporary sneakers occupy a liminal space between art, fashion, and material culture. Some institutions expressed the desire to display them simply as "art" without the extensive wall and label text, contextual images, and videos. Ultimately, the content was retained and became central to the success of the traveling exhibition.

Between 2015 and 2017, *Out of the Box* traveled across the United States and to Australia, stopping at the Brooklyn Museum, Toledo Museum of Art, High Museum of Art, Speed Art Museum, Oakland Museum of California, and the Art Gallery of Western Australia and attracting more than 500,000 museum visitors—receiving considerable positive feedback at each venue, often directly related to its contextual content. The content was also central to the promotion of the exhibition through social media which expanded the exhibit's reach dramatically. Many posts featured sneakers in the exhibition, but gratifyingly many also featured the text panels, artifact labels, and contextual images. The online comments and discussions that accompanied these posts often specifically contained expressions of appreciation for the exhibit content. Likewise, many articles about the exhibition also focused on the stories that contextualized the sneakers. The opportunity to exhibit sneakers in art museum settings encouraged people to appreciate their aesthetic value, but the inclusion of contextual information allowed visitors to understand their cultural importance more fully.

In the end, the exhibition's pedagogy turned out to be critical in obtaining the enthusiasm of lenders, central to capturing the interest of the general museum audience, and key to attracting wide-ranging media coverage. Examining the history of sneakers through a critical sociocultural lens helped borrowing institutions justify the display of sneakers in "serious" museums. Most importantly, the context provided in the exhibition didactics, imagery, and footage demonstrated respect for the sneaker's cultural importance. Ignoring this would have been a serious misstep and rightfully would have alienated many of the exhibition's most enthusiastic visitors.

CASE STUDY

Green Bay Packers Hall of Fame: Telling the Story of this Historic Brand

Krissy Zegers and Justine Kaempfer

As the Green Bay Packers football team celebrated more than one hundred years of history, many in the organization referred to the team's legacy as the greatest story in sports. The team's overall success is evidenced by thirteen National Football League (NFL) Championships, twenty-five Pro Football Hall of Fame inductees, countless legendary players and coaches, including one for whom the Super Bowl trophy is named, Vince Lombardi. With over a century's worth of history, there were certainly a lot of branding options from which to choose. Forty years of storied history precede the introduction of the Green Bay "G" logo and the team's green-and-gold color combination, some of the most iconic team symbols in the sport. The team's on-field success could have easily become the organization's (and by extension the museum's) primary focus of pride and glory; it is by no means insignificant. Yet, the small-town team in a working-class community speaks to something richer than records and trophies. The Green Bay Packers are interlaced with a hardworking rugged heritage, a local spirit that is critical to the team's identity and the fabric of the community. As such, the Packers Hall of Fame's mission is to challenge the museum's staff and visitors to see beyond the victory moments and take pride in the team's survival, resilience, and unique relationship with that very community.

The Green Bay Packers have a particularly unique relationship with the public. With more than 361,000 shareholders, the Packers are the only community-owned professional sports franchise in the nation. Furthermore, the football games have been sold out since 1960. The waiting list for season tickets is over 130,000 people long. There is very little turnover since tickets can be passed down to the next generation. Fandom functions as an inheritance for Packers families, which perpetuates a deep familial-based community connection to the team.

The team is inextricably linked to the city. Without the Packers, Green Bay would likely be like any other small city in Wisconsin. The team literally defines the community's identity, perhaps most exemplified by the mascot. Rather than some fearsome beast or mighty warrior, the team is named after the meat-packing company for which its founder worked. This fundamentally reinforces a blue-collar ethic associated with both the city and the organization. Green Bay is also the smallest market in the National Football League and has been for most of the Packers' existence. Because of this, it is impressive that the team and brand continue to maintain consistent financial success. The threat of market saturation is very real. Imagery of the Packers is not just visible at Lambeau Field, it is everywhere in Green Bay. Residents and visitors can see the team's history in city street names, Packers Heritage Trail, Packers history bus tours, and Packers exhibits at other local museums, among many other places. Conversations about the team also dominate the local news media, social media, bookstore books, and magazine racks.

Claiming affiliation to the "G" symbol and the team's legacy is both advantageous and challenging. As a museum run by the organization it represents, the Green Bay Packers Hall of Fame brand is tied directly to the team brand, which is tied directly to the community. The museum represents a respected brand that is immediately recognizable worldwide. However, this also means brand protection is paramount. Moreover, the museum has to work hard to differentiate its message from the onslaught of external Packers commentary. A loyal and devoted fan base and community create an irreplaceable invested collective with a deeply embedded and interconnected brand-based identity. The museum has a responsibility to both represent that relationship and respond to it. This becomes quite challenging, however, with such an enormity of voices and stakeholders in the mix. The museum must determine how to fulfill its obligations to those constituents without jeopardizing the brand, vision, and story.

Despite the local and widespread popularity of the Green Bay Packers, attracting visitation can be quite a challenge for this brand-affiliated museum. In many ways, the museum benefits from being connected to such a high concentration of locally invested individuals and businesses. The small community is a significant part of the brand's identity and growth; however, this does not translate into opportunities for high tourism traffic into the hall of fame. Since the city is constantly inundated with Packers imagery, it is challenging to attract and appeal to local repeat visitors. Attracting out-of-town visitors is not much easier. Lambeau Field is a bucket list destination for many sports fans, but not exactly conveniently located. Factoring in these conditions, the museum seeks creative and innovative ways to appeal to guests beyond rehashing successes. This translates into emotionally meaningful exhibit content, membership offerings, customizable group sales options, technology integration, social media interactivity, alumni experiences, and special programming.

When redesigning the Packers Hall of Fame beginning in 2013, the staff sought a more abstract vision to truly encompass the brand *and* its community as a whole rather than limiting the scope to people, places, and/or events. The staff asked deep questions about the type of story to tell, how to appropriately mix the early history with the more-recent history, the interconnected meanings between the team and the fans, and the methods that might help visitors emotionally experience that symbiotic relationship. From these discussions emerged a collection of descriptive words that became the central starting point for the exhibit; words that correlated to a gallery either to designate a characteristic of an era or an aspect of the organization's history: commitment, community, resilience, discipline, love, pride, championships, and

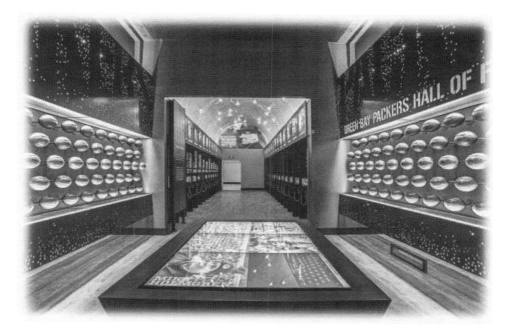

Figure 4.3. Excellence Gallery at the Green Bay Packers Hall of Fame. *Source:* **Green Bay Packers.**

excellence. These each represented an attribute adopted not only by the organization and team, but also by the players, coaches, employees, and broader community.

The exhibit design team consistently considered aesthetic value, but prioritized historically authentic interpretation in all of their decisions. Specific historically relevant touches were added to the design of each gallery. The replica Hagemeister Park fence in the Resilience gallery illustrated the ways the community rallied to support the team in its infancy. Originally, the Packers' first home field was simply an open lot. The community volunteered to build a fence around it so the team could charge admission to the games. The fence design also featured special knotholes to pay homage to the "knothole gang" stories about a group of children who would peer through the holes of the fence to watch the game. The trophy room, or Championship Gallery, was strategically placed as the last gallery that guests will visit. All trophies were located in one spot, partly to create a memorable experience, but also to allow space throughout the rest of the museum to focus on content that went beyond the victory moments.

While interpreting more than one hundred years of brand building, the Green Bay Packers Hall of Fame works with a duty of protecting and maintaining the history as well as conveying it in a relevant way. The museum must pay respect to the team's history while also keeping an eye on the present and future. As a museum directly connected to the team it represents, the public expects the Packers Hall of Fame to stand as the authority on the team's history. The museum represents the front line for fan interaction and often serves as a fan's first insider contact. As challenging as it is for the museum to consistently work to "get it right," these mandates present a welcomed opportunity to explore the complications and intricacies of the team's legacy.

During the design phase, the museum encountered challenging conversations about the organization's history. The hall of fame used the renovation as an opportunity to more accurately interpret and clean up the team's history, to "get it right." With one hundred years of history comes a considerable amount of mythology and lore. The exploratory process exposed the ways that history is alive, the brand does not just exist in the past, and nostalgia cannot be relied upon as factual data. The early years were especially rife with misinformation since founders, Calhoun and Lambeau, both of whom had a propensity for exaggeration, influenced most of the known content. This meant revisiting primary sources, involving the team historian and stadium tour guides, and consulting the best historical resources. Even among the experts, however, many of the "facts" and tales from the early years were left to interpretation. The staff had to be willing to admit when the narrative challenged them, be comfortable with certain topics remaining messy, and ultimately be able to move forward with only the stories that possessed the most factual evidence. This proved to be an ongoing exercise for the museum; the staff continuously adjusts the story as new facts and findings come to light.

Once the Hall of Fame was open, the staff was charged with exploring history in greater detail while engaging the local community. Educational programming, temporary exhibits, and historic programming instill more of an interactive connection between a guest's museum experience and the organization itself. This allows the brand and history to come alive for the fans. Guests can handle artifacts, learn about the collection, and explore topics like team traditions, uniform and equipment evolution, and how players become members of the greater Green Bay community and often evolve into local business owners. These program offerings are guided by the principles of the brand. They offer a method to explore the intricacies of the brand's history and organization.

While the museum has new ideas for exhibits and programs, it is important that the ideas fit with the overall mission of the organization. Other departments, such as football operations, administration, or public relations, typically examine and offer feedback on program ideas and exhibit changes. This occasionally leads to constraints on some of the more experimental ideas. It also confirms the commitment, support, and investment from all levels of the organization. All levels of the organization understand the need to tell the Packers' story accurately and in a way that compels fans to identify with and enroll in the team's storied history.

Ultimately, sustaining success at the Packers Hall of Fame depends on a clear understanding of the assets and support system. The museum has a team of historians and curators that find ways to incorporate innovative design and story elements with realistic operational functionality. A strong understanding of the brand gives the museum staff direction and helps avoid the pitfalls of listening to too much feedback and too many voices. The museum knows which type of story it wants to tell and has identified the significant people, places, and events that meaningfully connect with visitors and the greater community member's memories. This often includes complicated stories or periods of struggle. When a brand and its museum are willing to recognize some of the more difficult content, they breed trust and garner the public's confidence. Further, they maintain honesty within the organization and among visitors, which is especially important when working alongside an actively engaged community of fans. Concurrently, a corporate sports museum must work diligently to stay relevant in the active sports world in which they inhabit. As the brand, organization, and fans change, the museum must stay rooted in the past, while also adjusting to trends of the present and future. By doing this in Green Bay, we are allowing the Packers' history to stay at the forefront of the community and central to the fans that so actively drive the brand identity.

CASE STUDY

Challenging Branded Appropriation by Uncovering Native Mascot Origins

Kathryn Leann Harris

On July 13, 2020, the owners of the NFL Washington football team announced the formal retirement of their mascot, a Native American caricature named R*dskin (renamed the Commanders in 2022).[27] This decision came after decades of increasingly intense social and corporate pressure to eliminate the symbol long endorsed by the team and its fans. The mascot retirement reflected a deep shift in cultural perspectives, but that shift did not happen all by itself; museum education practice played a critical role in raising awareness of the roots, impacts, and effects of racist mascots in sports. Two influential symposium programs organized by the National Museum of the American Indian, held in 2013 and 2018, were significant turning points in the movement to retire racist mascots. Then-museum Director Kevin Gover, a citizen of the Pawnee Tribe of Oklahoma, recognized the power of the museum platform to expose the implicit racism and cultural appropriation found in the adoption of Native mascots by professional and amateur sporting teams. The educational programs he and his team devised and led helped drive the mascot discussion into the limelight, correct long-held inaccurate historical interpretations, and incite real change. The NMAI's leadership with these projects demonstrates how museum education programs can serve as a catalyst for wider cultural change and the reevaluation of harmful branded sports traditions.

Origins of the Issue

In the late 1980s and early 1990s, a robust public debate began to circulate around two opposing Native mascot views. One side held that American Indian mascots were a way to honor Native cultures; the other argued that these symbols were racist and deeply damaging.[28] In 2005, the American Psychological Association published a recommendation that all athletic teams remove American Indian imagery. That position, their website explains, "is based on a growing body of social science literature that shows the harmful effects of racial stereotyping and inaccurate racial portrayals, including the particularly harmful effects of American Indian sports mascots on the social identity development and self-esteem of American Indian young people."[29] In ensuing years, this perspective was validated and reinforced. Historian Jennifer Guiliano corroborated this point, noting that the harm of stereotyping can affect all children: "History matters because it has contemporary consequence; What psychological studies have found, is when you take a small child out to a game and let them look at racist images for two hours at a time, they then begin to have racist thoughts."[30] The movement to eliminate racist mascots was endorsed by the U.S. Commission on Civil Rights in 2001 and addressed in 2012 by the U.S. Senate Committee on Indian Affairs.[31] In 2005, the National College Athletic Association (NCAA) required thirty-three member teams to evaluate their mascots for potentially offensive imagery or names; fourteen schools eliminated those names and images, while another eighteen continued to use Native American references.[32] Supporters of the mascots continued to argue that franchises and universities were honoring Natives and their principles by taking on their likeness. Historical research tells a different story.

A historical exploration of appropriating Native symbols as mascots traces to the early 1900s, when American Indians were no longer considered a threat because they were removed, controlled, and eliminated by white prevailing society. "Government policy and popular culture assumed that, certainly by the end of the twentieth century, there would be no more Indians," Gover wrote in response to a U.S. Senate Committee on Indian Affairs hearing.[33] It was in this environment that sports teams felt comfortable exploiting Native culture. Gover later unpacked this historical overlap further:

The mascots come into being really at the very nadir of Indian life. They had been confined to reservations and were terribly oppressed . . . in an aggressive effort to assimilate their tribes and deny them their existence as Native Americans. So, it was weird—at the same time the government didn't want Indians to be Indians, sports franchises were deciding that they wanted to brand their enterprise using Native American imagery or Native American people.[34]

Central to this practice is the reality that brands *used* Native American people and imagery in a way that could only happen in a time when Natives were stripped of their agency. "It is no surprise then," Gover explained, "that as Indians gain power in both the political and economic life of the country that these mascots are starting to fall and that these brands, so carefully built up over such a long time, have begun to be devalued."[35] In the confluence of these societal factors, the NMAI engaged public discussion around the origins of Native mascots that led the Washington football team to remove their mascot.

2013 Symposium

When Gover stepped into the role of museum director of the NMAI in 2007, he consciously confronted a public steeped in misinformation about Indigenous North Americans. He understood that visitors come to the museum woefully misguided by formal education and commonly held dominant cultural beliefs, including ideas about Native American imagery in sports. Central to his work was the dismantling of these myths and the bolstering of agency and respect for Native people.

In this spirit, Gover and the NMAI decided to engage the discussion of Native mascots through a symposium, a very public-facing and high-profile museum education platform.[36] In 2013, at least twenty-six college teams and seven major professional league sporting teams in the United States, along with hundreds of high-school teams, were still using Native imagery to represent their teams' identities.[37] The Smithsonian's daylong program, *Racist Stereotypes and Cultural Appropriation in American Sports*, featured a robust slate of panelists, including writers, educators, and representatives of Native nations and the NCAA.[38]

Before a capacity audience, they explored the "mythology and psychology of stereotypes in sports, the history of ethnic 'identity theft,' and recent efforts to both retire and revive 'Native American' sports references" at various universities "despite the NCAA's policy against 'hostile and abusive' nicknames and symbols."[39] Dr Philip J. Deloria (Standing Rock Sioux), the author of *Playing Indian* and *Indians in Unexpected Places*, engaged a marquee selection of local voices in a conversation that explored the origins and removal of the local Washington, D.C., NFL team's name and mascot.[40] The museum made a live webcast available to the public and asked viewers to use the hashtag #RacistSportsLogos in a Twitter discussion.[41] Representatives from the Washington franchise chose not to attend and remained committed to maintaining their logo, with the support of NFL commissioner Roger Goodell, maintaining that their choice to adopt the Native mascot was one of honor.[42]

Intersecting with larger inclusivity and equity movements, the symposium became the impetus for Native mascot removal. The media took notice, and the debate often reappeared in the news after the event. Looking back, Gover reflected that "The 2013 symposium re-lit the fuse to get rid of the mascots. Black Lives Matter made a big difference in that happening when it did."[43] The #blacklivesmatter movement emerged in 2013 after the killer of seventeen-year-old Trayvon Martin was acquitted. The two discussions overlapped in the national consciousness and built a momentum that fed a larger movement toward valuing historically undervalued American lives. He also believed the change was inevitable; Native American agency had expanded in recent decades.[44] In this atmosphere, Gover initially thought the Washington team's name change would come quickly. It would take seven more years and another symposium to incite the final change.

2018 Symposium

In 2018, The Smithsonian National Museum of African American History and Culture cosponsored a symposium with the National Museum of theAmerican Indian titled *Mascots, Myths, Monuments, and Memory*. This event examined the history and overlap of Confederate monuments, Native mascots, and related public memorials of contested histories.[45] The multiday event was held at NMAAHC's Oprah Winfrey Theater and broadcast on YouTube, where it remains for public viewing. The symposium began with a film trailer screening from the documentary *More Than a Word*, a film that analyzes the Washington football team and their use of the derogatory name. Featuring interviews from people on both sides of the issue, *More Than a Word* "presents a deeper analysis of the many issues surrounding the Washington team name," according to the filmmakers' website.[46] The day also included a panel session entitled "Contested Symbols in Sports and American Culture," which asked "Why were racist mascots selected to represent American sports teams? Who is invested in holding on to them? How are communities recognized or misrecognized historically? Who stands to gain from the misrecognition of others?"[47]

The symposium established clear overlaps between American racist monuments and mascots. A majority of the nation's overtly anti-Black monuments were erected by white Americans during the same period that Native mascots emerged, between the 1890s and 1915, a period historians have called the nadir of race relations in the United States.[48] In an article on the symposium appearing in *Smithsonian Magazine*, Lonnie Bunch explained that

> these monuments were really created as examples of white supremacy—to remind people of that status where African-Americans should be—not where African-Americans wanted to be. For Native people, rather than see them as humans to grapple with, [there was an effort to] reduce them to mascots, so therefore you can make them caricatures and they fall outside of the narrative of history.[49]

The Cleveland Indians baseball team, for example, assumed its name in 1915 and actually "became more racist over time, culminating in the insanely grinning, red-faced Chief Wahoo."[50] In 2019, the movement successfully urged Cleveland to cease their use of the Native caricature, changing their name to the Cleveland Guardians and introducing a new mascot. The Washington, D.C., football team did not

Figure 4.4. EA group protests the Washington Redskins name across from Levi's Stadium before an NFL football game between the Redskins and the San Francisco 49ers in Santa Clara, Calif., Sunday, Nov. 23, 2014. *Source:* **AP Photo/Tony Avelar.**

immediately follow suit, despite urging from President Barack Obama. Participants of the event remained in "general agreement on the psychological harm, especially to African American and Native American children, perpetrated by the unquestioned presence of these images in our midst," sending a strong unified message from a discourse rooted in informed educational content.[51]

Perhaps the greatest challenge and opportunity in this work is guiding individuals to see exactly how and why these images have in fact become part of their identity through recreational sporting outlets. Ray Halbritter of Change the Mascot spoke at the 2018 symposium, explaining his objections to the Washington team's name. "Racism and bigotry are not simply expressions of hate and animosity. They are instruments of broad political power. Those with political power understand that dehumanizing different groups is a way to marginalize them, disenfranchise them, and keep them down," he stated.[52] Halbritter illuminated the truth beyond the myth—that the name originated with one of the team's previous owners, George Preston Marshall, who held segregationist views. "This team's name was an epitaph screamed at Native American people as they were dragged at gunpoint off their lands," Halbritter explained. "The name was not given to the team to honor us. It was given to the team as a way to denigrate us."[53] He added that the team was the very last to sign African American players, and that its name remains offensive to many, particularly Native Americans.

This symposium underscored the importance of driving the narrative, rather than allowing fandom lore to remain as the authoritative voice and the danger of leaving them unchallenged. Author Ibram X. Kendi stated, "Historically, when racist ideas won't subdue Black people, racial violence is oftentimes next. . . . So those who adore Confederate monuments, those who cheer for the mascot are effectively cheering for racial violence."[54] Instead of leaving errant narratives exposed to violent ideologies and behaviors, public sports discourse can illuminate fans' and brands' blind spots and help soften their hearts and minds to changing long-held, beloved symbols that have become engrained in their personal identities.[55]

Responsible Sports History Influence

When interpreting Native American history and sports, begin by discovering the overlap of the two in your own community. Encourage brands and organizations with Native imagery to partner with the museum and stakeholder communities—to get beyond the myth, tell the direct true story, and remain committed to engaging in an ongoing reciprocal relationship with American Indians relative to the franchise. Native people have a story to tell that is rarely, almost never, adequately told, particularly in relation to sports. Embrace an open, cooperative spirit that welcomes their voices, understanding that Native people are not a monolith. Mindfully create cohesive, accurate, and relevant sports narratives that reflect these new understandings of a complex, shared Native past.[56]

Do this work with the sense that this is your history as well, because it is. Many people are unaware of the extent of their contributions to mainstream culture. Gover sees this as an oversight that detracts not only from Native history, but that misses the point on all history. He wants to see Native history examined as human history, belonging not just to Native Americans, but to everybody, emphasizing that "there is no part of the country that doesn't have a Native history. This is your history as well. These people that were here before you did things that influence life in your community now."[57] Native influence is all around, from landscapes to food to placenames to traditions of government. Despite this, he states, "most often it's notable for its absence."[58] Native people are made invisible culture wide, and subsequently at historical institutions.

Be diligent in finding that history, particularly in regard to team mascots. Underlying the original choice to use that symbol is a reason that goes deeper than the leading story. "When people say 'it is part of our heritage' they are not wrong," Gover explains, "it really kind of is. But they are misunderstanding the *meaning* of that heritage."[59] Ask: Who chose this mascot, when, and why? What did they write down in terms of their thinking? What was the design process that created the imagery? Calling attention to these gaps can educate a misled public, create a personal connection to real Native people and their history, and foster a kind of respect that renders offensive caricatures unacceptable.

Gover believes that historical institutions can and should take a more active role in reframing Native representation by explaining the nation's history differently, more accurately and inclusively. "The obvious thing to me was that when you have a platform like a Smithsonian Museum dedicated to the interest of Native Americans, you are to use it to their advantage and tell stories in ways that are advantageous to them,"[60] he reflected. He thus backed the two mascot symposia with institutional investment and leveraged his contacts to produce high-profile expert speakers that created a landmark conversation. Taking a stand, as an institution, comes with the position of authority granted to museums by the public. The mascots issue gained traction when the resources of the Smithsonian amplified its voice.

Removal of the Washington R*dskins mascot happened due to the confluence of the right timing, cultural agency, public outcry, *and* museum influence. The story of these two symposia is a bit about being in the right time and place. Gover and the NMAI responded to sports concerns while they were circulating in the wider culture. In the preceding decades, Native Americans had been deploying their agency to occupy a greater role in the nation's political and economic life. They increased the public consciousness and awareness of the nation's historical and ongoing mistreatment of Native communities. Various influential institutions took an inclusive and respectful stance regarding the cultural appropriation of Native imagery. In the midst of this environment, Gover used his trusted seat of authority at the NMAI to lead a national discussion and influence a course correction in the public's historical understanding of Native Americans. As a result, a major corporate sports team confronted their relationship with mythical and offensive branding, and chose a new path forward.

Museum voices matter to the public. Programs are often thought of as ephemeral, unlike exhibitions or publications; yet, with the benefit of institutional investment, programs can instill a deep and lasting impact. They bring context and thoughtful interdisciplinary review that can challenge brands and their consumers to reconsider entrenched beliefs built on myths. They surface the roots of present-day debates and work to build an understanding of the impact of past and present choices. Respectfully and courageously embracing the responsibility of public trust opens pathways for visitors to incite change. Gretchen Jennings, founder of the blog *Museum Commons* and a member of The Empathetic Museum group, echoes this sentiment,

> As I listened to the discussion, I realized that there could have been a fifth "M" in the *Mascots, Myths, Memorials, and Memory* title: Museums—a subtext for much of the day. Although this program focused on nationwide issues, any museum could examine memorials in its local community, partnering with other museums, parks, preservation groups, and historical societies.[61]

Indeed, public discourse events place the museum directly in the center of a search for historical accuracy, bringing together disparate factions of controversial and contested topics. Once illuminated, the mere presence of updated narratives implores sports organizations to reconsider their use of cultural representations. Remain committed to advocating for your audience, vigilant of cultural shifts, and prepared to confront narratives that are misaligned with your institutional values and historical record.

NOTES

1. Ulrik Wagner, Rasmus K. Storm, and Klaus Nielsen, eds., *When Sport Meets Business: Capabilities, Challenges, and Critiques* (London: SAGE Publications, 2016), 76–77.

2. Wagner et al., *When Sport Meets Business*, 44.

3. Wagner et al., *When Sport Meets Business*, 44.

4. Rezwana Manjur, "Sports Marketing Report: The Evolution of Sports Marketing," *Marketing-Interactive.com*, June 12, 2015, accessed December 30, 2018, https://www.marketing-interactive.com/features/sports-marketing-report-evolution-sports-marketing.

5. Wagner et al., *When Sport Meets Business*, 45.

6. "adidas Sales Grew to More than $24 Billion in 2017, Says CEO," *Footwear News*, February 28, 2018, https://footwearnews.com/2018/focus/athletic-outdoor/adidas-sales-2017-earnings-q4-ceo-kasper-rorsted-508729/.

7. Bruce Weindruch, *Start with the Future and Work Back: A Heritage Management Manifesto* (Lanham, MD: Hamilton Books, 2016), 28.

8. Seema Rao, "Appetite for Content by Visitor Segment," Brilliant Idea Studio, June 21, 2018, https://brilliantideastudio.com/art-museums/appetite-for-content-by-visitor-segment/.

9. Elizabeth Semmelheck, "Playing Nice: The Making of *Out of the Box: The Rise of Sneaker Culture*," in *Interpreting Sports at Museums and Historic Sites*, Kathryn Leann Harris and Douglas Stark, eds. (Lanham, MD: Rowman & Littlefield, 2023), 130–133.

10. Robert Goldman and Stephen Papson, *Nike Culture: The Sign of the Swoosh* (London: SAGE, 1998), 47–48.

11. Michael Conway, "The Problem with History Classes," *The Atlantic*, March 16, 2015, https://www.theatlantic.com/education/archive/2015/03/the-problem-with-history-classes/387823/.

12. Beth Harris and Steven Zucker, "Just What is Visual Velcro?" *Smart History*, May 30, 2009, accessed April 14, 2019, https://smarthistoryblog.org/2009/05/30/just-what-is-visual-velcro/.

13. Elizabeth Semmelheck, Senior Curator at the Bata Shoe Museum and cultural historian, personal interview with Erin Narloch, April 27, 2017.

14. Erin Narloch, *Knowledge Generation Research Cycle*, internal image at Reebok Archive, 2018.

15. Rainer Karlsch, Christian Kleinschmidt, Jorg Lesczenski, and Anne Sudrow, *Playing the Game: The History of adidas* (Munich: Pretsel, 2019), 68.

16. Scheherazade Daneshkhu, "How Millennials' Taste for 'Authenticity' is Disrupting Powerful Food Brands," *Financial Times*, June 19, 2018, https://www.ft.com/content/09271178-6f29-11e8-92d3-6c13e5c92914.

17. Semmelheck, "Playing Nice."

18. Krissy Zegers and Justine Kaempfer, "Green Bay Packers Hall of Fame: Telling the Story of this Historic Brand," in *Interpreting Sports at Museums and Historic Sites*, Harris and Stark, eds., 134, 133–137.

19. Jonathan Scott Holloway, *Interpreting Difficult Histories at Museums and Historic Sites*, Julia Rose, ed. (Lanham, MD: Rowman & Littlefield, 2016), inro, ix.

20. Julia Rose, ed., *Interpreting Difficult Histories at Museums and Historic Sites* (Lanham, MD: Rowman & Littlefield, 2016), 18.

21. "Strategic Plan 2017–2019," Carnegie Museum of Natural History, accessed July 10, 2022, https://web.archive.org/web/20190506182732/https://carnegiemnh.org/visitor/about/strategic-plan/.

22. The owners of the Washington D.C. NFL football team redacted the original mascot, Redskins, on July 13, 2020. The change came in response to intense social and corporate pressure related to misappropriation of Native symbols. The team was known only as the Washington Football team until 2022, at which time the owners added a new mascot named the Commanders. For further explanation of this topic, refer to Kathryn Leann Harris, "Challenging Branded Appropriation by Uncovering Native Mascot Origins" in *Interpreting Sports at Museums and Historic Sites*, Harris and Stark, eds., 137–143.

23. Kathryn Leann Harris, "Challenging Branded Appropriation by Uncovering Native American Mascots," in *Interpreting Sports at Museums and Historic Sites*, Harris and Stark, eds., 137–143.

24. The Brooklyn Museum and the Toledo Museum of Art opted to shorten the title to *The Rise of Sneaker Culture*.

25. The museum added an assistant curator/project manager in 2015.

26. The final brand partnership list comprised thirty-eight lenders, many of which donated sneakers to the Bata Shoe Museum's permanent collection for inclusion in the traveling exhibition.

27. Refer to endnote #22 for more information.

28. Stephanie A. Fryberg, Hazel Rose Markus, Daphna Oyserman, and Joseph M. Stone, "Of Warrior Chiefs and Indian Princesses: The Psychological Consequences of American Indian Mascots," *Basic and Applied Social Psychology* 30, no. 3 (2008): 208–18.

29. "Summary of the APA Resolution Recommending Retirement of American Indian Mascots, Symbols, Images, and Personalities by Schools, Colleges, Universities, Athletic Teams, and Organizations," American Psychological Association, September 2005, accessed July 14, 2022, https://www.apa.org/about/policy/mascots.pdf and https://www.apa.org/pi/oema/resources/indian-mascots.

30. Jennifer Guiliano as quoted in Alison Keyes, "Two Museum Directors Say It's Time to Tell the Unvarnished History of the U.S.," *Smithsonian Magazine*, March 5, 2018, accessed July 14, 2022, https://www.smithsonianmag.com/smithsonian-institution/two-museum-directors-say-its-time-tell-unvarnished-history-us-180968341/; See also Rick Cohen, "Bullying Native American Children Through Racial Mascots," *Nonprofit Quarterly*, October 8, 2014, accessed July 14, 2022, https://nonprofitquarterly.org/bullying-native-american-children-through-racial-mascots/.

31. "Statement of U.S. Commission on Civil Rights on the Use of Native American Images and Nicknames as Sports Symbols," US Commission on Civil Rights, April 16, 2001, https://www.usccr.gov/files/press/archives/2001/041601st.htm; "Reclaiming Our Image and Identity for the Next Seven Generations," Hearing before the Committee on Indian Affairs United States Senate, 112th Congress, 2nd Session, November 29, 20212, accessed July 14, 2022, https://www.govinfo.gov/content/pkg/CHRG-112shrg78924/pdf/CHRG-112shrg78924.pdf.

32. "NCAA Executive Committee Issues Guidelines for Use of Native American Mascots at Championship Events," National Collegiate Athletic Association, August 5, 2005, accessed July 14, 2022, http://fs.ncaa.org/Docs/PressArchive/2005/Announcements/NCAA%2BExecutive%2BCommittee%2BIssues%2BGuidelines%2Bfor%2BUse%2Bof%2BNative%2BAmerican%2BMascots%2Bat%2BChampionship%2BEvents.html. See also: Markus et al., "Of Warrior Chiefs" and the "Native American Mascot Policy," National Collegiate Athletic Association, August 2005, https://americanindian.si.edu/sites/1/files/pdf/seminars-symposia/NCAA-Mascot-Policy.pdf; http://fs.ncaa.org/Docs/PressArchive/2005/Announcements/NCAA%2BExecutive%2BCommittee%2BIssues%2BGuidelines%2Bfor%2BUse%2Bof%2BNative%2BAmerican%2BMascots%2Bat%2BChampionship%2BEvents.html.

33. Kevin Gover, "Native Mascots and Other Misguided Beliefs," *American Indian Magazine* (Fall 2011), 10–13, accessed July 14, 2022, https://americanindian.si.edu/sites/1/files/pdf/seminars-symposia/Fall2011-Director.pdf; See also: List of resources examining the origins of Native American mascots and the history of Native American resistance available at "Mascot Resources," Program in American Indian Studies, University of Illinois at Urbana-Champaign, accessed July 14, 2022, https://ais.illinois.edu/resources/mascot-information/mascot-resources.

34. Kevin Gover, Under Secretary for Museums and Culture at the Smithsonian Institute and previous director of the National Museum of the American Indian, interview with the author, July 28, 2021.

35. Interview with Gover.

36. "Program Agenda for Racist Stereotypes and Cultural Appropriation in American Sports," National Museum of the American Indian, February 7, 2013, accessed July 14, 2022, https://americanindian.si.edu/sites/1/files/pdf/seminars-symposia/RacistStereotypes_Agenda .pdf.

37. "List of sports team names and mascots derived from indigenous peoples," Wikipedia, accessed July 14, 2022, https://en.wikipedia.org/wiki/List_of_sports_team_names_and _mascots_derived_from_indigenous_peoples#American_football.

38. "Program Agenda."

39. "Native American Mascot Controversy Takes Center Stage at the National Museum of American Indian," National Museum of the American Indian, January 24, 2013, accessed July 14, 2022, https://www.prnewswire.com/news-releases/native-american-mascot-controversy-takes-center-stage-at-the-national-museum-of-the-american-indian-188184031. html. See also: Paul Lukas, "Native Americans Speak on Imagery," ESPN.com, February 13, 2013, accessed July 14, 2022, https://www.espn.com/blog/playbook/fandom/post/_/id/18144 /native-americans-speak-on-sports-imagery.

40. Hon. Judith Bartnoff, deputy presiding judge of the District of Columbia Superior Court's Civil Division; Rev. Graylan Hagler, of the Plymouth Congregational United Church of Christ and the former president of Ministers for Racial, Social and Economic Justice; Mr. Robert I. Holden (Choctaw/Chickasaw), deputy director of the National Congress of the American Indians; Erik Brady, a sports reporter for *USA Today;* and Mike Wise, a sports columnist at the *Washington Post* joined in the community discussion about the Washington, D.C., NFL team symbols, as referenced in "Native American."

41. Native American.

42. "Mascot Symposium: 'Redskins' Racists," *Cherokee Phoenix*, February 11, 2013, accessed July 14, 2022, https://www.cherokeephoenix.org/news/mascot-symposium-redskins -racist/article_2e191484-aeb3-5c83-b32f-d8c13f1de371.html.

43. Interview with Gover.

44. "Entities Opposing 'Indian' Sports References," compiled by The Morning Star Institute, October 2009, accessed July 20, 2022, https://americanindian.si.edu/sites/1/files/pdf /seminars-symposia/Sports-References-Support.pdf.

45. "Mascots, Myths, Monuments, and Memory," *National Museum of African American History and Culture*, February 23, 2018, accessed July 14, 2022, https://nmaahc.si.edu/explore /stories/mascots-myths-monuments-and-memory.

46. "More Than a Word," MoreThanAWordFilm.com, September 2017, accessed July 14, 2022, http://morethanawordfilm.com/about-the-film/.

47. "Mascots, Myths"; Presenters included: Kevin Gover, Ray Halbritter (Oneida National Enterprises), Jennifer Guiliano (Indiana Purdue University), Mike Wise (ESPN Undefeated) as referenced on "Mascots, Myths."

48. Keyes, "Two Museum"; Rayford Logan as referenced in Mark V. Tushnet, "Progressive Era Race Relations Cases in Their 'Traditional' Context," *Vanderbilt Law Review* 51, no. 4 (1998), accessed July 14, 2022, https://scholarship.law.vanderbilt.edu/vlr/vol51/iss4/6/.

49. Lonnie Bunch, founding director of the National Museum of African American History and Culture, as quoted in Keyes, "Two Museum."

50. Gover as referenced in Keyes, "Two Museum."

51. Gretchen Jennings, "Monuments, Memorials, and Mascots: What Is a Museum's Role?," *Museum Commons*, March 19, 2018, accessed July 14, 2022, https://museumcommons.com/2018/03/monuments-memorials-mascots-museums-role.html.

52. Halbritter as quoted in Keyes, "Two Museum."

53. Halbritter as quoted in Keyes, "Two Museum."

54. Ibram X. Kendi as quoted in Keyes, "Two Museum."

55. Linda M. Waggoner, "On Trial—The Washington R*dskins' Wily Mascot: Coach William 'Lone Star' Dietz," *Montana, The Magazine of Western History* (Spring 2013): 24–47; See also: Case No. 339242, William Henry Dietz, Investigative Case Files of the Bureau of Investigation, FBI investigation for the 1919 trial of Dietz, as referenced in Waggoner, "On Trial."

56. For guidance on engaging Native perspectives, see Raney Bench, *Interpreting Native American History at Museums and Historic Sites* (Lanham, MD: Rowman & Littlefield, 2014).

57. Interview with Gover.

58. Interview with Gover.

59. Interview with Gover.

60. Gover as quoted in Keyes, "Two Museum."

61. Jennings, "Monuments."

Chapter Five

Connecting to Your Community

Interpreting Sports and Place

Kathryn Leann Harris and Terence Healy

Sports is somewhat unique in its ability to unite communities of disparate people. Multiple generations of players, coaches, and fans (on both sides of the ledger) connect through experiences that encapsulate their shared love of sport. These sporting communities form bonds that at times appear to be familial. This high degree of connectivity means museums should leverage sports content to attract well-established local, national, or global populations. At the same time, communities, and even families, can differ or split due to competitive outcomes, rivalries, level of interest, and sports-related politics. Sports history presents the opportunity to bridge any number of gaps that seem to prevent notions of a shared past. Creating experiences at museums and history organizations is by nature a collaborative endeavor, one that can, and often does, support different agendas and visions. These institutions are thus well positioned to interpret disparate sports-related agendas in the same space, provide unifying events and activities, or cover larger societal issues that their identified communities experience. When an institution carefully considers community relevance, connections to place and space, and inclusion opportunities, they can craft a well-developed sports project that attracts varied audiences, solidifies old and reimagines new communities, ignites impactful discussions, and provides growth experiences for the engaged staff.

Key Interpretive Concepts

1. *Community Relevance:* Define the community in relation to a proposed project or goal. Determine their expectations and gaps in awareness. Create a plan that aims to deliver, connect, and illuminate content relevant to that community.
2. *Connections to Place and Space:* Think creatively about ways to attract and engage the identified community by placing them in spaces that inspire personal reflection and ignite collective memory.
3. *Community Participation:* Consider ways to create and foster inclusive involvement opportunities for identified constituents.

Benefits of Using Sports History to Connect a Community

Creating a sports project geared toward a certain community can be challenging. Limited resources and competition for an audience's attention require institutions to become very clear about whom they are trying to attract and for what reason, lest they fail to develop buy-in or connection from their audience. The sports-enthused community is eclectic and tends to be somewhat tribal—resulting in a varied yet ardently unified assemblage. Creating and developing a singular yet complex project considering this combination can be difficult to navigate. Government agencies' agendas, stakeholder expectations and visions, funding sources, and the process of establishing a viable collection can, and likely will, emerge as barriers.

When an institution becomes and remains clearly focused on their engagement objectives, crafting a sports-related exhibit or program can have a highly rewarding outcome. Sports history is as vastly complex as the human experience itself. The average sports fan yearns to share what they know and glean new information from their fellow enthusiasts. Museums and historic sites can facilitate space for this fusion of ideas and information while contributing historical context that enriches collective awareness. With a focused engagement plan, museums can channel the scholarship into a sports-related exhibit, discussion, or program that engages new and diverse audiences—including sports fans and non-sports fans alike—and provides their community with opportunities to navigate conversations that both validate and challenge long-standing perspectives.

Determining Your Community

The word "community" conjures images of neighborhoods, towns, cities, counties, states, nations, and the global world—all outlets from which sports groups emerge. They form at ballparks and stadiums, parks and pools, social media outlets, and even museums and historic sites. As in museum endeavors, institutions creating a sports exhibit or program need to initially identify its audience, community interest, and relevance. This creates a more thoughtful experience for the visitor and establishes criteria for community engagement for future decisions. A community's connection can be based on place, people who hold shared beliefs, or through communication and socialization.[1]

Navigating these factors requires passion, clarity, and perseverance. A museum development team in Green Bay, for example, could create a Wisconsin experience that presented the broad heritage of all types and levels of sporting competition. Theoretically, by adding cultural depth, this concept would draw many, varied guests. Museum planners may find the concept appealing due to the famous Green Bay Packers football team fan base. Yet, the content of this experience may be too broad for that specific market and thus not pique the interest of the professional football fan who may have provided the initial inspiration for the project.

Determining whom exactly you hope to attract may be an easy first step or a complex question to revisit throughout the research and development process. Your institution's targeted audience might be inherent and consistent. Crafting a sports project, however, might inspire staff to think outside of the expected norm. Take time on the front end to establish audience parameters.[2] Then, walk through the process outlined here. Consider the larger questions you are trying to target and to whom they apply. Consider where your institution might best intersect with those groups. Consider ways they can participate in achieving the stated goals. Throughout the process, keep revisiting the audience question. Think creatively, complexly, and abstractly. The meaning and relevance of sports is rapidly evolving throughout the world, and your institution can participate in addressing and shaping that evolution through innovated approaches to community definition.

Community Relevance

Sports museum projects can demonstrate relevance by mimicking the places where sporting communities grow and develop: print media newspapers, sporting events such as games and competitions, and online publications. A newspaper can provide all the necessary information, images, and statistics. Publishers document and report sporting events and athletic accomplishments in their community; subscribers evince interest in the outcome of yesterday's games. The sports event provides engagement and activity; fans demonstrate their interest by choosing which to attend. Online publications invite consumers to engage and follow their own interests while watching videos, reading columnists, following a virtual conversation, and contributing their own thoughts. The sports section of a newspaper has an interpretive hierarchy similar to a museum exhibition, appealing to the three types of readers: Speeder, Grazer, and Expert. It starts with a headline and first paragraph for the Speeders, those who appreciate the major themes and messages. The Grazers will relax and take their time to read every story from beginning to end. They will connect different stories to each other in a much more sophisticated way. Finally, experts will not only read all the stories but also will study the box scores and compare an infinite amount of player information in the minutia.

Institutions can find rich inspiration by studying the ways communities facilitate tight connections through sports bonds. Sports transcend generations and have gradually become more integrated, inclusive, and prevalent in American life. Their ubiquity permeates many facets of collective life and fosters a consistent point of connectivity.

A soccer club in Takoma Park, Maryland, is representative of community engagement. For the past three decades, families in Takoma Park have awoken every spring and fall, from either their winter hibernation or self-imposed air-conditioned environments, to meet on city soccer fields. The ritual surrounds the activities of Takoma Soccer. It is part of both the history of the community and the city's identity. Takoma Park players start as early as preschool; parents volunteer to serve as coaches. Participation hones the young athletes' skills and game knowledge, teaches skills such as teamwork and preparation/practice, and expands their social circles. Something as simple as an article of clothing can become a central visual symbol that instantly inspires a sense of unity. Athletes in Takoma Park receive a T-shirt as their uniform. A palette of bold colors identifies their team as one unit. As they emerge through the school ranks, the players create a multicolor banner of their shirts, which identify them and their place in their community. The right to wear one of these T-shirts functions as a rite of passage in Takoma Park. In wearing them, the athletes pronounce they belong to something bigger than them (the soccer club) and the specific team to which they belong. But this soccer club is not only about the youth. The parents also build common bonds that grow stronger annually. These bonds reinforce a community of involvement and activism and confirm a sense of place in Takoma Park.

In today's media-driven environment, the online newspaper and cable sports channels have created yet another community that can be both a great resource and time competitor for a sports exhibition. Subscriber bases can be so large that members do not know each other yet their need to know the latest sports news binds them together. Online publishers thus create the equivalent of an online exhibit experience daily. They change and update sports news on an ongoing, often hourly, basis. This sports community could be an institution's largest, most diverse, and most knowledgeable audience. But the competition is fierce, comprising all the pleasures of home: the couch, television, time-of-day, snacks, computer, napping, among other options.[3]

Crafting a museum project that appeals to your target community and bonds them together can happen by filtering sports through a lens of cultural relevance. While it may seem counterintuitive to promote a sports rivalry, fans often spend all year talking about what happens when they come together for the big game. They know well the history and passion that drives the feud between the teams. Whether your local community contains one or both teams in a contested rivalry (as in statewide college football rivalries), your institution can create a project that is unifying by speaking to that which the fans know best and giving them a reason to engage around it. The Tennessee Sports Hall of Fame in Nashville exhibited both Vanderbilt University and the University of Tennessee football programs to speak to the storied rivalry between the only two major in-state schools. This gave fans a reason to be in the same space at the same time to compare, contrast, and even compete over various versions and tribal agendas connected to historical memories.

The key here is to choose a neutral site to give both sides an equal stake in the story. At the Chick-fil-A College Football Hall of Fame, rivalries are celebrated throughout the space at various levels: game day experiences with the fans, competition on the field with players, and the legacy shown through accomplishments over the many decades. Combining this information in such a commingled and high-profile public arena invites fans to explore their rival teams in a safe space, even among other visiting fans.

This same concept pertains to the cultural significance of advocating for a need. Consider the history and demographics of your community, and then find a sports-related topic that connects the two. For example, in 2015, the Minnesota History Center explored local Native American history through an outdoor lacrosse tutorial using historical gear and rules. Meeting the community at a place of need can also attract and connect various types of individuals or groups by drawing awareness to issues that thwart community connectivity: increases in ticket prices or violence among fans in stadiums and arenas. Advocacy that helps the masses tends to bring people together. Sports provides this in abundance.

Place and Space

Determining the most effective place or space to connect your community with a sports-related exhibition is vital. Institutions should not simply follow the instructions of the voice Ray Kinsella (Kevin Costner) hears in *Field of Dreams:* "If you build it, he will come." Museums cannot write their own Hollywood endings. This concept is not an effective strategy for crafting an interpretive experience, especially when success is measured through attendance. Do not assume popularity alone will draw visitors.

Sometimes it is helpful to place a sports exhibit near a major sporting team, fan base, venue, event, or in the places sports are played: stadiums, arenas, ballparks, natatoriums, even the great outdoors. The experience can be more powerful within or close to the place that generates ongoing connectivity. Fenway Park, the famed historic home of the Boston Red Sox, chose to memorialize the team's history in the place their community most often gathers: the stadium itself. Instead of building a separate historical interpretation space, the organization interpreted in place. Fans read Red Sox history on panels as they walk to their seats, view World Championship displays in historic ticket booths, commiserate over tales of those hard losses and recount incredible victories—all while eating their Fenway Frank with their friends and family en route to watching the next season's players make their marks in the history books.

A museum or historic site might select a location based on a geographic theme. The Georgia Sports Hall of Fame in Macon created the museum to honor athletes from the state and provide an exhibition experience for general visitors centered around the interpretive theme: "Sports throughout Our Lives." As visitors entered the exhibitions, they heard famous athletes comparing their earliest sports recollections in Georgia to their later experiences. Subsequent galleries noted the achievements of high-school, college, Olympic, and Special Olympics events and athletes. Its final galleries included exhibitions about professional athletes and sports connected to the Peach State, including motorsports, golf, and its professional teams.

The place-based sports museum theoretically has a built-in community yet can still struggle to find ways to adequately connect with their audience. For the Georgia Sports Hall of Fame and Museum, residents from Georgia comprised a major part of its audience, as did anyone who was connected to a Georgia sporting event or player. To boost the economic redevelopment efforts of Macon, local government officials appealed to the museum to choose their town as its home over a more populous city such as Atlanta. The strategy was economically beneficial for the local community; yet, the locale created a geographic barrier because its exhibits barely related to the city in which it stood. Instead, the exhibits presented stories of major universities hours away, professional sports and the 1996 Olympics based in Atlanta, and golf in Augusta. All these factors contributed to visitation struggles. Although Macon's downtown community grew tremendously, once the hall of fame opened, the larger sports communities still had to drive at least an hour each way to visit.

The Tennessee Sports Hall of Fame, originally located on the campus of the University of Tennessee in Knoxville, was later integrated into Nashville's newly constructed Bridgestone Arena in hopes of creating a well-attended experience in the centrally located state capital. In part, the parties were drawn to the location because the space was readily available. City leaders also believed the arena operators could use the hall of fame as a value-added experience for fans and events. The hall of fame organizational team and government officials felt the arena destination would assist in connecting communities across the Volunteer State. They recruited the Tennessee State Museum to develop culturally relevant content through collections and interpretation. Collections and related media productions reinforced the thematic interpretive experience. Tennessee Sports Hall of Fame inductee information did not focus solely on athletic achievements but aligned with the current interpretive design philosophy of presenting a broader picture of sports and their influence on the community. Museum curators crafted exhibits that centered on the cultural aspects of sports, rather than just highlighting specific marquee players and their accolades. For example, the exhibit featured the football rivalry between the Tennessee Volunteers and the Vanderbilt Commodores, the famous Pyramid home floor of the National Basketball Association's Memphis Grizzlies, and outdoor sports representing Middle and East Tennessee.

Placing the museum in a highly visited space was helpful for visitation, but not a clear-cut solution for attendance woes. Like its Georgia neighbor, the Tennessee Sports Hall of Fame was another example of a failed *Field of Dreams* strategy. They built it, but attendance never met expectations. The synergy between sports events at the arena and the hall of fame never really materialized. Visitation from fans attending the National Hockey League Nashville Predators' games and other sporting events was not an accurate gauge of the museum's actual attendance. Since hockey was relatively new to both Nashville and the South, the sport was unrepresented in the hall of fame. And hockey fans were not necessarily interested in discovering the history of Tennessee football, track and field, or Olympic swimming and boxing. As single-sport fans, they represented the hockey community, and when attending games, were more interested in keeping with their own interest rather than visiting a museum that presented a broad selection of sports. Visiting basketball fans and other collegiate sports teams also had no connection to the Tennessee sports community or the specific sports in Tennessee.

The Virginia Sports Hall of Fame and Museum underwent a transformation in the early 2000s specifically to better connect with its surrounding community. Unlike many other sports halls of fame built during this era, the institution already had a building, museum, and existing staff (the hall of fame was housed in a renovated church, perhaps an apropos place of reverence). The institution's policy of recognizing each inductee with a biography panel *and* individual display case with images and personal artifacts prompted a crowded exhibition experience and a repetitive presentation technique that appealed only to a small group of people, mostly fans or family and friends of inductees. In response, the museum opened a new museum in 2004 as part of a business and retail district redevelopment in Portsmouth.

The new project connected with the community in two important and positive ways. First, the new building was across the street from the Virginia Children's Museum, which had an annual visitation of approximately forty thousand guests. The geographic partnership resulted in a cultural district in the heart of historic Portsmouth. The museums' visitation complemented one another. As the youngest visitors aged out of the children's museum, they were naturally drawn to the sports hall of fame. Second, the director implemented a strong education program to align the interpretive experience and activities with the Commonwealth of Virginia's Standards of Learning.

Exhibit content attracted different sports communities from across the Commonwealth. First-floor cases featuring the hall's inductees greeted visitors. An orientation film featured Virginia's rich sports heritage, and various communities throughout Virginia used the formal presentation theater for public programs. The museum used a rotating exhibition space for educational programming and children's camps during the year. Themed galleries on the second floor highlighted the state's broadcasting, collegiate sport, motorsport, Washington's NFL and golf histories. The facility also included an activity area where guests could compete with one another and test their sports skills.

The changes meant the institution became financially sustainable by securing multiple communities of visitors—primarily the local, regional, education, and tourism markets—combined with state and municipal funding and annual sponsorships, a promising model that ultimately did not last. Commitments to each of these revenue streams dwindled over time. The final blow came when the City of Portsmouth eliminated the museum funding and investments altogether—effectively saying that tax dollars better served the community in other ways. After fourteen years of operation, the hall of fame closed its doors. The institution was simply not fully sustainable without the city's assistance. Still fulfilling their mission of connecting to the public, the content was dispersed into various locations throughout the downtown Virginia Beach business community.

Creating a sports museum or exhibit can be complex when considering the quantity of sports, diversity of audiences, and reach across a geographic area. During the planning phases, it is important to remember that reducing from a thousand-piece puzzle to a ten-piece puzzle will increase the degree of success. Sports is so broad; it does not mean you have to be broad with it. The Tennessee, Georgia, and Virginia state halls of fame were trying to be assets to their communities by including all topics. A better presentation in a more concise way might have been more of a strength than what is often perceived as a weakness. They each successfully developed a sense of pride for their resident communities. Unfortunately, the locals did not materialize as paying customers twice a year, and the messages were not concise enough to attract a sizeable broader audience. A temporary art exhibit, *The Art of Baseball*, at the Concord Museum produced different results. By narrowly focusing the content on baseball, they attracted a nontraditional and expanded audience from their typical art museumgoers. Red Sox fans from around the area, including nearby Boston, flocked to the museum in larger numbers than usual. Choosing a relevant place and space is as important as understanding your audience and narrowing the content focus in a way that fosters connectivity.[4]

Community Participation

Rather than relying on outside funding opportunities, internally promoting participation and engagement with your visitors is the primary way to emotionally connect the sports community to your institution. Sports communities often reflect the active and competitive nature of the sports they enjoy, and museums should follow their lead. The sports exhibit experience or project should be an anchor of community engagement. When attending a high-school basketball, college football, or Major League Baseball game, people can feel the mounting tension, pounding excitement, and immersive sense of competition. Community swim team members and families enjoy the premeet festivities, socialization, food, and pageantry. Spectators witness the competitors' eagerness and a wide range of emotions: fear, disappointment, struggle, exuberance, the thrill of victory, and the agony of defeat. A player's effort, leadership, and skills are all on display. If these competitions were not called sports, games, or races, they could otherwise be called reality television. Sporting events are entertaining precisely because they invite spectators to immerse themselves into the place, time, and emotions. Re-creating the authenticity of these moments is important when planning a sports exhibition experience.

While capturing the athlete's emotions and the atmosphere of great sports temples can be difficult, it is an extremely important way to attract visitors who wish to connect with their sports-related passions. When sports exhibitions first debuted, they were usually aligned with a hall of fame. Institutions utilized their inductees as a core focus and interpretive priority. Earliest versions of these museums selected interpretations that reflected a more curatorial and authoritative voice supported by collections and memorabilia on view. The collections were indeed authentic, but the interpretation was aligned with that of museum advisors and staff, rather than the wider sports-loving community. That these museums rarely updated interpretation or refreshed their exhibit experiences led to major struggles with attendance. Most importantly, these museums failed to deliver anything that approximated, much less matched, the authenticity of the experience on the field, between the bases, on the ice, or in the water.

Learning from their peers' experiences, national sports halls of fame that have opened in the 2010s have since evolved into major tourist destinations. These institutions, particularly as single-sport museums, can leverage sponsorship partnerships, their brands, and fan communities to generate public and private funding for multimillion-dollar experiences. Recently added examples include the NASCAR Hall of Fame and Museum and Chick-fil-A College Football Hall of Fame plus major renovations and additions to the Pro Football Hall of Fame, Naismith Memorial Basketball Hall of Fame, and National Soccer Hall of Fame. Even with the ability to generate large amounts of funding, none of this can exist without defined fan and visitor participation opportunities within the museum experience.

Often, sports museums or museums looking to install a sports exhibit can partner with an existing community asset to become more sustainable and relevant. The North Carolina Sports Hall of Fame renovated its exhibit experience in partnership with the North Carolina Museum of History, which provided the hall of fame more than three times its existing space. It was a great opportunity for both institutions. The history museum collaborated with the hall of fame to create programming and educational goals in the sports exhibition space and incorporate the history of North Carolina sports into the larger brand of the North Carolina Museum of History. The

Sports Hall of Fame had a permanent home and did not have to risk financing a new building. History museum staff incorporated programming, collections rotation, and new visitor experiences into the existing and previously successful operations. Because of the partnership, the sports museum enjoyed a more varied audience than it would have if it were a standalone attraction.

Non-sports-related museums and historic sites could also interpret sports to help draw new communities to their institution. Using sports allows museums to cross boundaries, build bridges, and connect with new audiences in their larger community. The Henry Sheldon Museum of Vermont History captured a passion for bicycling in the exhibit *Pedaling Through History: 150 Years of the Bicycle*. The museum created and developed this exhibition to commemorate the fiftieth anniversary of the 1866 first patent for a pedal bicycle. Then director William F. Brooks Jr. matched his own interest in riding with the collection of Glenn Eames. In curating an exhibit of bicycles, equipment, and art, they created a connection to the local and global riding communities. Members of the local community participated in the installation process, promoted and marketed the exhibit, and offered public programs for community engagement. Ultimately, *Pedaling through History* was a great success for the museum.[5]

Sports content can be used to foster pride as well as raise awareness. Seemingly disparate groups can gather to discuss shared interest or debate contested political topics illuminated through historical or present-day sports narratives. While producing two football-related exhibits, the District Six Museum in Cape Town, South Africa, invited previously unengaged factions of their audience to enliven dormant memories and then carefully constructed a critical understanding of their shared past. Work on the 1996 exhibit *Displaying the Game* resulted in uncovering abandoned histories and exposing systematic untruths about the lack of a sporting presence and impact during apartheid. In their 2008 exhibit, *Fields of Play*, they revealed systematic partnerships between the sporting communities and the apartheid regime that underscored and perpetuated racism. In both cases, the museum navigated contested narratives by deepened community engagement practices and examining a challenging political and social past.[6]

Going beyond traditional community history exhibits, museums can also use sports history to present contemporary interpretations and collections. The Heard Museum in Phoenix, Arizona, creatively encouraged their visitors to use sports as a lens for linking Native pragmatism and artistic expression to community development. The museum's 2014 exhibit *Beautiful Games: American Indian Sport and Art* highlighted the ritualistic nature of sports, showing how sports offer fertile ground for fostering a sense of community centered on sacred human values. Coinciding with the 2015 Super Bowl in Phoenix, *Beautiful Games* attracted and connected a variety of audiences and communities, both local and nonlocal, traditional and nontraditional.[7] Similarly, the Customs House Museum and Cultural Center in Clarksville, Tennessee, includes a rotating art exhibit called the Challenges and Champions Sports Gallery. This exhibition highlights athletes who were born or raised in the region, including sports legends such as hall of fame basketball coach Pat Summitt, Olympian Wilma Rudolph, and NASCAR driver Jeff Purvis. The museum developed the exhibition to connect to the region's sports community and to instill a sense of pride in the center's younger visitors. Visitors identified with and emotionally connected to these more contemporary stories from their community. The exhibit also included skill activities for younger audiences that reinforced historic content and created memories with a new community of visitors.

Museums can combine their exhibition space, a sporting event, and community to transform history and heritage into a celebratory experience. The State Historical Museum of Iowa has included sports stories and presentations in many of their recent exhibit galleries as a way to better attract and engage a wider base of visitors. *Riding through History* opened in 2013 and highlighted Iowans' love affair with bicycling. The museum focused the interpretation on the Register's Annual Great Bicycle Ride Across Iowa (RAGBRAI), commemorating the fortieth anniversary of the event. Over those forty years, the ride has become an Iowa tradition. It began in 1973 when John Karras and Donald Kaul, *Des Moines Register* reporters who were also avid bicyclists, proposed to ride across Iowa for a week and write about the Iowans they encountered along the way. They invited readers to join them on their six-day journey from Sioux City to Davenport. During the week, Karras and Kaul submitted articles about the people they met, places they visited, and events of the day. Readers gravitated to the daily news, many wondered if the ride would take place the following year and called for a formal announcement early enough to allow greater participation. The number of riders varied from day to day with approximately 300 joining on the first day, a maximum of 500 riders on one single day of the ride, and 114 completing the entire trek. In year two, 2,700 riders participated. That number grew to 7,500 by 1983. The largest daily rider count in the past forty years was 23,000 from Boone to Des Moines. Today, the race caps riders at 8,500.

In the forty-plus years of the Ride, riders have passed through 780 communities and stayed overnight in another 125 host towns. In these moments, sport and community intersect. Though it is not a race or competition, Iowans supported the riders in several ways. They feed, entertain, comfort, and congratulate the athletes. For a few hours, the number of riders dwarfs the population of the towns they ride through. The greatest result of the Ride is how community organizations unite for greater causes. While supporting the riders, they fundraise from souvenir, water, and food sales—especially food-on-a-stick, pies, and baked goods. These funds ultimately pay for local building renovations, field and ballpark scoreboards, fire emergency equipment, and care for the less fortunate.

The State Historical Museum of Iowa sought to capture the spirit of the wide and passionately connected RAGBRAI community. In addition to the fortieth anniversary celebration opportunity in 2013, the event represents a symbol of pride for the state's residents. The museum wanted to leverage that pride to emotionally connect to a broader audience of the state. At the beginning of the development process, the museum held advisory meetings and asked some of the initial riders to share memories and opinions on the stories and presentations to include. From these meetings, the museum partnered with the *Des Moines Register* and the Register's Annual Great Bicycle Ride Across Iowa for content assets (images, film, and memorabilia) and to connect the institution to past riders who loaned and donated personal objects. This gave the museum the opportunity to expand the breadth of its collections beyond the 1950s to today. Since the fortieth-anniversary ride traveled through Des Moines as an overnight town, the museum provided events and programs as well as opened the exhibition to the riders. Thus, sports provided the material for one of the museum's first exhibitions that looked beyond their traditional collections to present an exhibition that was highly relevant to the interests and concerns of present-day Iowans.

Conclusion

Using sports history to build connections between your institution and your community can be successful, rewarding, and fun. The process is similar to completing a jigsaw puzzle. Though main interpretive pieces must fit together to create a successful and valuable asset for your community, the foundation will always stand on intentionality and relevance. Connecting to a new community of audiences requires your institution to thoroughly understand your expected audience. Determine the best place for the experience, a space for it to occupy, and how to give visitors a way to participate within the experience whether or not they are sports fans, general museum visitors, or members of your institution. The key is to keep connecting with the people coming through the door, to make sure the experience is engaging and impactful for them, whoever they are, and give them a reason to find commonality, conversation, and emotional connection. This is all easily attainable when dealing with America's favorite sporting pastimes.

Replicable Practices for Interpreting Sports and Community

- **Get them competing!** Sports fans love to play to win. Give visitors a chance to play a trivia game where multiple people can compete while learning and testing their memory about sports history and fan culture.
- **Put the visitors in a moment or scene:** Think of a place where the fans have always dreamed that they wanted to be. Visually or literally put them in a ballpark, a locker room with the coach, or on the sideline with the players. Let them experience it together.
- **Let the visitors touch and play with objects as much as possible:** Find a few meaningful objects that can be touched, the Louisville Slugger Museum, for example, allows visitors to pose with actual game-used bats. Use these objects to create an in-exhibit competition or game.
- **Start a conversation to which visitors can contribute:** Sports fans love to talk about what they think is most important and what they think they know more than others about their favorite team or sport. Allow them to have that conversation, to express their thoughts, or share what they know. Hold a forum or discussion event, place Post-it Notes on a wall where they can add their input, or create a digital wall with an ongoing and real-time engaging conversation. Even better, expand the above conversation to a social media feed.

- **Offer special events with celebrities or athletes:** Hold a press event where people can ask questions instead of a talk or lecture. Athletes are well versed in handling this type of event and it is more engaging for the community.
- **Do not lose touch with the angle of entertainment:** Remember that sports are, at their core, entertaining. Speak to that and give experiences that allow people to unite around the fun.

CASE STUDY

Recalling Community Through Sports at the District Six Museum

Chrischené Julius

The District Six Museum in Cape Town, South Africa, interprets the living memory of former residents of District Six, a neighborhood previously located on the slopes of Table Mountain. Against the backdrop of apartheid, football clubs and associations developed in racial silos that gradually became more fixed, building to a crescendo before Apartheid's end was marked by the 1994 appointment of Nelson Mandela as the nation's first democratically elected and first Black president. The museum thus noted sports history as an important catalyst for considering and representing societal structures as they had existed during apartheid and within the politics of the present. Community relationships informed and challenged two football-related exhibitions at the museum, *Displaying the Game* in 1996 and *Fields of Play* in 2008, which then further contributed to an important community-wide examination of the impact of apartheid on football organizations and informed adjustments there within the sport and the museum.

Convergence of Movement: Apartheid, Football, and District Six

From its establishment in 1867, District Six was home to a multicultural community that included the descendants of Dutch and British colonists, workers from different parts of South Africa, emancipated slaves, and Eastern European immigrants. By the 1960s, this area was home to a largely working-class, vibrant community characterized by sporting and music clubs, religious communities, and political activism. In 1966, South Africa's racially segregation-based apartheid regime designated District Six a White Group Area—a designation that led to the ultimate dissolution of the community and physical destruction of the residential area between 1968 and 1981.

The eventual destruction of District Six has its origins in 1948 when the National Party, an Afrikaner nationalist party, came to power and introduced the policy of apartheid. Apartheid enforced the separate development of racial groups through a series of laws that restricted movement and ownership of land. The state's policy of separate development was embodied by the Group Areas Act of 1950, which set in motion a series of forced relocations that materially shaped Cape Town and South Africa's landscape. In tandem with the Population Registration Act, which officially classified South Africans into racial groups, the Group Areas Act mandated the division of neighborhoods into racial group areas. In Cape Town, the state classified prime areas around Table Mountain as "white." District Six residents were displaced to the undeveloped coastal plains beyond Table Mountain, known as the Cape Flats, which extended thirty kilometers away from the city and were set aside for populations designated "colored," "Indian," and "African." The apartheid state's classification of Black people further rested on a sliding scale where to be classified "African" restricted movement and land tenure rights, while being classified "colored" or "Indian" afforded nominal benefits above others. This separate development legislated and entrenched longer social processes of segregation and racial classification introduced by colonialism.

Forced removals between the 1950s and the late 1980s resulted in waves of involuntary migration throughout Cape Town, severing many communities' ties to places and spaces of collective memory. In the case of District Six, up to 60,000 people were forcibly removed to the Cape Flats, outside Cape Town. In her work on the impact of displacement under urban renewal schemes in U.S. cities in the 1960s, American social psychiatrist Mindy Fullilove dubs this type of movement as "root shock," which she describes as, "the traumatic stress reaction to the destruction of all or part of one's emotional ecosystem."[8] For District Sixers, that ecosystem was a "web of connections" that tied them to a place and intimately bound them to their environment in the way they navigated streets, familiar landmarks, and their homes. Displacement severed those ties.

This oppressive political culture was the milieu within which many South African sporting codes evolved over the second half of the twentieth century. Notably, sporting codes had already been impacted by racial segregation implemented under British colonial and municipal administration prior to the 1948 establishment of the apartheid state. In 1908, the twenty-one football pitches at the Green Point Common in Cape Town, where South Africans first played the game, were rigorously allocated according to a racial hierarchy, which placed "white" associations and clubs at the top and "colored" and "Indian" clubs at the bottom. "African" football associations were not considered at all.[9]

Concurrent with the first waves of relocations in the 1960s, increased political activity and armed resistance to the apartheid government resulted in violent state suppression. This forced political movements underground for several years until trade unions and various anti-apartheid organizations brought a resurgence of political activity in the 1970s broadly known as the "congress movement." It was in this latter period that opposition to the apartheid state went through a period of tactical consolidation—engaging political, religious, and sporting communities on all fronts. Sports, therefore, became a political tool to fight the state. This resulted in the formation of the South African Nonracial Olympic Committee and the South African Council on Sport (SACOS) and a demand from the South African Soccer Federation that FIFA, football's international governing body, expel the whites-only Football Association of South Africa. For younger generations, the history of their clubs was indelibly linked to forced removals, which scattered teams to far-flung areas, resulted in the loss of their home grounds, and inevitably pitted them against a state intending to destroy their communities.[10]

In the 1970s, local sports clubs and associations increasingly affiliated themselves to SACOS and its dictum of "No normal sport in an abnormal society." As part of the nonracial sports movement, SACOS called on clubs and associations to reject the apartheid state's policy of multiracial sports, whereby teams classified "African," "colored," "white," and "Indian" competed against each other only within their defined racial groups. In Cape Town, where SACOS was strongly rooted, affiliated clubs and associations boycotted any government-sanctioned sports facilities and competitions and organized their own nonracial leagues and sports festivals.

Though SACOS framed its work as part of the liberation movement in general, it refused to align with specific political parties that formed part of the congress movement, which was led by the African National Congress (ANC).[11] SACOS resisted talks of unity when the Afrikaner Nationalist government and the ANC negotiated the end of apartheid in the late 1980s. It argued against negotiations while South African society was still wholly structured along racial divisions. The organization also expressed dissatisfaction that broader consultation within the nonracial sports movement and affiliates had not taken place. Some SACOS members, who disagreed with the organization's policy of nonalignment and instead favored negotiations, openly aligned themselves with the ANC. They broke away from SACOS and formed the National Sports Council, effectively entering talks to create unified national sporting bodies for an envisioned democratic future.

The rupture within SACOS was far reaching and post-1994 could still be felt in the curatorial and research practices for two exhibitions at the District Six Museum: *Displaying the Game* and *Fields of Play*. Spaced roughly a decade apart, both exhibitions highlighted issues of identity formation, the hidden histories of apartheid (both in terms of sports and the apartheid geography of the city), and the political nature of sports before and after 1994. Both exhibitions thrived in the contestations of what it meant to be a South African citizen in the present, relying on a framework for representing communities, rather than sports histories, over time.

Displaying the Game: A Celebration of More than a Century of Sport, 1996

In 1996, a former District Six resident and footballer, together with a member of SACOS, lobbied the museum to hold an exhibition on Black sporting history in Cape Town. Bolstered by funding and support from the Metal and Electrical Workers Union of South Africa (MEWUSA), the museum undertook to gather and exhibit the hidden stories of Black sporting communities across a range of sports—such as rugby, cricket, swimming, darts, and fencing (to name a few). The museum, which was not state funded, had recently opened with a popular exhibition about District Six and welcomed the additional funding and opportunity to layer new information into the existing exhibition. While the focus on sporting histories seemed "out of place," the museum noted important linkages between the displays in that the sports clubs had flourished and enjoyed a proud history in District Six. Further, the staff was encouraged by the notion that football history could be told by communities themselves.

The aim of the partnership between the museum and MEWUSA was to frame sports exhibitions as more than a display of "boots, balls, badges, and blazers," and instead as a means to "reflect and comment on the political and social role of sports clubs in community life and [the] social and political context which shaped the course of the history of sports clubs and organizations."[12] Doing so, both partners sought to highlight the long-standing tradition of sports in local communities. Reporting on its work in 1996, the curatorial team embedded their practice in a critique of sports development after the first democratic election in 1994, noting that the unification of sports bodies that had started in the late 1980s had simply led to the demise of community clubs and associations. For the sportsmen involved in the exhibition process, unified sporting bodies had not promoted the development of sporting skills in Black communities and had merely created the impression that sports had not existed in these communities prior to democracy. The partnership between the museum and MEWUSA actively countered this impression and sought to acknowledge that community structures and sports *had* existed pre-1994.[13]

Displaying the Game became a political statement that mobilized memory and foregrounded forgotten histories in the community space of the museum, which itself was forging a collective history of District Six at the time. This statement, in the context of a young democracy, was crucial as national debates about reconciliation, restitution, and justice took center stage with the Truth and Reconciliation Commission (TRC), which was set up to investigate human rights abuses during apartheid. The TRC placed heavy emphasis on individual testimony and stories by "ordinary" people to pull back the veil on the personal impact of apartheid on South Africans. This turn toward bearing witness to the past and taking ownership of one's life history complemented the

Figure 5.1. *Displaying the Game* exhibition, 1996. *Source:* District Six Museum collection.

museum's mission. Sports became another lens through which to document the impact of apartheid on everyday lives.

Methodology implemented by the District Six staff in *Displaying the Game* proved significant in the context of the new South African museology, in which apartheid-era museums had yet to transform and display inclusive historical narratives of the past. In order to build the exhibition narrative, the museum facilitated a series of workshop discussions with sports administrators and players to support an examination of sports development after 1994 and to counter the perception that local club histories and structures did not exist prior to 1994. An introductory pamphlet for the exhibition, *Sport: A Community Definition*, foregrounded this active participation of administrators, players, and communities and called for, "imaginative reconstruction of sporting life and cultural heritage of all communities in the Western Cape affected by forced removals."[14] The institution encouraged participants involved in the exhibition research to embark on a process they denoted as, "discovery, reconciliation, and renewal," toward an understanding of how sports clubs and communities were products of each other.[15]

Moreover, the museum accessed personal and institutional archives of administrators, clubs, and sportsmen, which provided far more than a glimpse at family albums. Indeed, an examination of the research materials unearthed broader issues such as class formation, identity politics, the ability to thrive despite apartheid, and how the active presence of various sports impacted the formation of community identities. The photographic and archival record took center stage in the final exhibition, which thoroughly documented sporting life prior to 1994 through photographs of clubs and associations and objects en masse in the museum space. The wealth of displayed images and memorabilia provided crucial documentary evidence of the long-standing community structures that sustained various sports. This emphasis on visual representation as *evidence* was especially groundbreaking and impactful in a museum climate in which the documentary and photographic evidence of Black sporting communities was neither collected nor displayed.

Fields of Play: Football Memories and Forced Removals in Cape Town, 2008

Twelve years later, in 2008, the museum developed the football exhibition *Fields of Play: Football Memories and Forced Removals in Cape Town*, which focused on the history of the sport in Cape Town between 1862 and the mid-1960s. In this exhibition, the museum sought to help visitors understand how, through football, "people (have) organized themselves, formed bonds of solidarity, and created forums in which they exercised their citizenship, particularly in a society that sought to dehumanize them," the staff explained in the exhibit catalog.[16] Museum staff developed the exhibition along four themes: "Playing the Game," "Visualizing the Game," "Contesting the Game," and "Rupture." "Playing the Game" followed the histories of the home grounds and football associations that formed along racial lines before and during apartheid. "Visualizing the Game" explored women's football and fan culture in Cape Town. "Contesting the Game" delved into the dynamics of administering football during apartheid, the nonracial sports movement, and the development of

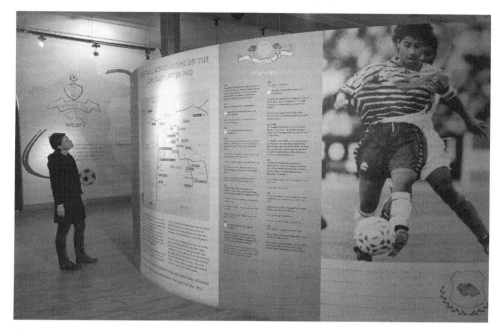

Figure 5.2. *Fields of Play* **exhibition, 2008.** *Source:* **Photographer: Paul Grendon, District Six Museum.**

professional football in the city. "Rupture" highlighted three-ways forced removals in the city affected football clubs.[17]

Local government officials from the Department of Economic Development and Tourism initiated the *Fields of Play* exhibition as a result of their commissioned study of Cape Flats tourism opportunities during the 2010 FIFA World Cup. These officials saw the role of the tourism industry as being able to "play a spatial reconciliatory role in the re-integration" of the Cape Town metro.[18] They further saw the existing research, content, and network established during *Displaying the Game* as key assets for developing a potential sports museum and tour route that would conceptually and physically connect Cape Flats' sporting histories to the Green Point Common, the site of the World Cup stadium precinct. The Department of Economic Development and Tourism asked the museum to design an "interactive narrative of football in the city" placed within the larger context of the underdevelopment of the Cape Flats areas due to apartheid.[19]

The museum decided to bolster the tourism-driven approach with a community-led process, which led the exhibition team into some challenging and revealing areas of exploration and resulted in content that was quite different from their previous sports exhibit. A close network of football administrators, players, researchers, and museum staff shaped the *Fields of Play* curatorial intention—a critical reflection of the politics between clubs during apartheid, the impact of apartheid era restrictions on the game, and the personal impact on communities that resulted from forced removals. Whereas during the process of developing *Displaying the Game* the curatorial staff sought to recover forgotten histories, broaden the museum's collections, and develop oral histories to underline the broader contribution of communities' defiance of apartheid, during *Fields of Play*, they more explicitly sought to highlight the ways in which sporting associations were complicit with the apartheid state.[20] They attempted to, as artist and curator Fred Wilson states, "push the outer edges of what it means to be in any particular community, to challenge stereotypes and to explore issues that might not immediately seem relevant to the community in question, but that engage identity from multiple perspectives."[21] They devised a series of public forums and focus groups as well as site walks to grounds and neighborhoods where clubs were once based—all of which were designed to explore the complexities of identity formation and the impact of apartheid on football and communities.[22]

In examining these complexities, curators were challenged to confront the prevalence of racist attitudes among sportsmen, dissension in the footballing fraternity as a result of the politicization of the sport in the 1970s, and community members with nostalgia-based perspectives who refused to acknowledge anything but a romanticized view of the past. The museum staff willingly listened to conflicting stories and asked difficult questions about the impact of prejudice within the game (not only from the apartheid state). They discovered and ultimately illustrated how private identity formation was interwoven with club identities and often reified racial classification. They then used archival and official records sourced from state and museum archives to illuminate these subjective histories rather than simply creating an objective, linear experience of apartheid.

In pushing the outer edges of what it meant to be a footballer during apartheid, the museum received two significant responses from the Cape Town football community that affected the exhibit's form and function. First, an older generation now spoke more freely about the early discriminatory policies of some clubs that often denied membership based on race, religion, and class. Thus, the museum focused on the histories of those clubs who prevented membership based on appearance—where, for example, "pencil tests" were administered to check the coarseness of hair or membership was restricted to Muslim, Christian, or a certain class of players. Voices reflecting the second key reaction exposed a perception that the museum was complicit with local government funders. Sportsmen and administrators interviewed by the museum often expressed how the process of unifying different racial sports bodies under new democratic, nonracial sports associations failed.

Despite unification, former Black associations felt under resourced and unsupported by the post-1994 government, and because the exhibition received significant government funding the museum received sharp rebuke. Some players frowned upon the reuse of sports memorabilia previously collected during *Displaying the Game,* as the context in which the memorabilia was displayed was viewed as support for the state that led to the demise of community clubs and structures. The museum chose not to reject government funding; electing instead to refine the methodology of *Displaying the Game* by establishing a reference group to mediate a critique of the research process and to suggest how this critique could inform and guide the staff in directing content. Interviews, focus group sessions, and site walks no longer became spaces for nostalgic remembrance of the past, but spaces for interrogating participants in regard to personal ambitions (and if they led to active moments of collaboration with the apartheid state), attitudes about women's football, and players' motivations in joining particular clubs (namely if membership would raise one's social and econ omic standing in communities). Curators also accepted some donors' refusal to have their memorabilia displayed or even be interviewed while simultaneously calling pub lic meetings to address concerns and reiterate the museum's position of presenting the different layers in the city's footballing history.

The *Fields of Play* exhibition content did not overtly rely on the biographies of players or club mythologies, thus producing an important sports narrative—one that did not easily fit into a typical hall of fame approach replete with league tables, championship wins, and player biographies. Rather, the depiction chronicled a deeper history of the game and the sites at which they were played. Historical accounts of the sites proved nuanced and highlighted a web of connections between communities and clubs. They became key factors in presenting the legacy of Apartheid's spatial planning, as many home grounds fell within declared White Group Areas or had to contend with substandard grounds on the Cape Flats. Linked to these site histories were complex club histories. The forced displacement of clubs from their grounds impacted their team's chances at survival. Some clubs were obliterated due to dwindling and dispersed membership, others reinvented themselves by branching into new sporting codes, while other clubs rallied and saw an increase in membership after displacement. Popular player and administrator stories were highlighted; yet, they were featured alongside oral histories from club supporters, players' wives, and journalists who were active during the period.

Despite the layered narrative approach, museum curators were still concerned that they were presenting a sanitized history and omitting key areas of research. They worried about not including enough voices from SACOS and the nonracial sports movement, as well as women's football. They also wondered if they used oral histories most effectively—in hopes of ensuring interviewees had not only helped the museum shape a football narrative but were also presented as having more holistic life histories. To accomplish these goals, the curatorial team intentionally appointed researchers with a vested interest in sports histories and narratives alongside museum staff and trustees whose curatorial approach was rooted in a memory methodology that placed subjective experience as the basis of historical narrative. The distance between *Displaying the Game* and *Fields of Play* spanned twelve years, and each exhibition was opened at two varied points in the museum's organizational history, as well as the unfolding of the democratic process in South Africa. *Displaying the Game* was largely driven by the efforts of community activists, artists, and sports men who were motivated by the activism and solidarity that drove anti-apartheid struggles in the 1980s.

Their belief that communities were authors of their own histories and held their own archives (through stories and personal records) informed a methodology that sought to place Cape Town's Black sporting history on the broader map of South African history. For a newly established community museum comprised largely of volunteers, this task involved recovering the first layer of history—the record of experience. Twelve years later, *Fields of Play* did the same but took a far more critical approach to that record, interrogating the everyday experience of apartheid and emphasizing that "hidden histories" were complex ones, not merely stories perpetuating the generalized apartheid narrative of "victim and perpetrator."

Digging deeper into these hidden histories during the creation of *Fields of Play* resulted in a number of lessons for the museum. By 2008, the museum was streamlined into distinct education, exhibition, and archival departments and staffed by members who had no familial ties to District Six. In this context, the scale of holding together a community-driven exhibition process highlighted shifts in how the museum defined itself as a "community museum." Staff members constantly debated the integrity of community-authored exhibition narratives in relation to a museum-directed exhibition narrative. They repetitively asked: Who truly is the author of the community histories the museum is presenting? To answer this question, the museum deepened their engagement and consultation with the public and then assumed a more critical stance, no longer merely acting as the archival repository for hidden sports histories. Players occasionally challenged, and ignored, the museum's authority to critically reflect on footballing history. In this crucible, a more complex notion of the past was forged—one the museum sought to retrieve under all conditions; accepting the many ways, both with and in opposition to others, in which communities make history known.

CASE STUDY

The Art of Baseball at the Concord Museum

Carol L. Haines

The Concord Museum, a history museum that serves as a gateway to the remarkable town of Concord, Massachusetts, began planning in April 2014 for a special sports exhibition in its 1,000-square-foot Wallace Kane Gallery. The exhibition was drawn from an exceptional private art collection of period objects related to baseball— paintings, sculpture, prints, textiles, and memorabilia. For nearly forty years, New York collectors Millie and Bill Gladstone searched for artistic expressions of the game of baseball, gathering up the best examples they could find in galleries, antique shops, and flea markets. They generously agreed to share their collection with Concord Museum visitors in *The Art of Baseball*, for which then-Concord resident Doris Kearns Goodwin served alongside the museum staff as Honorary Curator. Baseball meets at the intersection of a timeless American experience—the connection of neighborhoods, childhood, and summer. For generations, the game has challenged artists to capture some of this magic. With *The Art of Baseball*, the Concord Museum created an engaging exhibition that celebrated this intersection of baseball and culture, attracted new audiences, fostered community connectivity, and increased the public understanding of the importance of baseball in American life.

Founded in 1886, the Concord Museum is a center of cultural enjoyment for the region and a gateway to the town of Concord for visitors from around the world. The museum's outstanding collection of 50,000 objects includes American icons such as the famed Paul Revere lantern; Ralph Waldo Emerson's study; the desk on which

Henry David Thoreau wrote *Walden*; and exceptional furniture, silver, ceramics, and needlework. Visitors of all ages learn about the principles of freedom, self-government, environmentalism, and our shared cultural heritage—and baseball is certainly part of that heritage.

Concord is like many small towns in America in that its own share of baseball history can be found in the games that are played by young and not-so-young athletes on its grassy fields. This historic Boston suburban town sits just eighteen short miles from Fenway Park, the home of the Boston Red Sox. None other than one of America's most influential authors and thinkers, Henry David Thoreau—a true Concordian—remarked about baseball in Concord in his journal on April 10, 1856: "Some fields are dried sufficiently for the games of ball—with which this season is commonly ushered in. I associate this day, when I can remember it, with games of base-ball played over behind the hills in the russet fields toward Sleepy Hollow where the snow was just melted & dried up."[23] A review of the twentieth-century oral histories in the Concord Free Public Library uncovered similar memories. While not as famed as Thoreau, the Concordians interviewed were equally heartfelt in their remembrances of the baseball games played in town. At the time of the exhibit, Concord was also home to Pulitzer Prize–winning historian Doris Kearns Goodwin. Goodwin is a lifelong baseball fan and author of the book *Wait Till Next Year*, a touching memoir of the childhood love of her family and baseball. She generously agreed to serve as Honorary Curator for the exhibition and to work with the staff to create a video statement for use in the gallery and online. As she articulated in the exhibition video, "I think the reason why baseball has played such a large role in American history is that it really connects families over time; one generation hands its love of baseball—or baseball memorabilia—on to the children . . . and on to the next children."[24]

Based on the formative research, the exhibition team, consisting of the curator, director of education, collections manager, and manager of exhibitions and design, developed the goals of both the exhibition and the related programs. The team worked with a mission to examine and celebrate the intersection of baseball and culture, bring in new audiences—particularly baseball fans—to the Concord Museum, and increase public understanding of baseball's impact on American life. They contracted with Jay Hurd, a baseball historian who was also one of the museum's education staff, to conduct topic research and community outreach. Staff reviewed past visitation statistics and found that attendance from the Greater Boston area increased when the museum presented interdisciplinary exhibitions (such as *Building Thoreau's Boat*), considered themes beyond Concord history (such as *Annie Leibovitz: Pilgrimage*), or related the past to contemporary issues (such as *Early Spring: Henry Thoreau and Climate Change*). Accordingly, the museum expected that *The Art of Baseball*, which combined art, history, and popular culture would cross boundaries and attract not only traditional audiences, but also those with an interest in art, baseball, and the Red Sox.

Developing a fundraising campaign for the exhibition served as an opportunity to connect various key diverse audiences from the wider community in a way that underscored the museum's central goals for the project. Special exhibitions are not funded through the Concord Museum's operating budget, but through specifically targeted sponsorships. BNY Mellon Wealth Management was the lead sponsor for this exhibition. Major foundation support was received from the Yawkey Foundation. Both the Boston Red Sox Foundation and their then-Class A Affiliate, the Lowell Spinners, joined the project as promotional sponsors. Seven additional corporations, foundations, and individuals helped to underwrite the exhibition. This financial support of the Greater Boston community was key to enabling the museum to connect to the larger community and expand our visitation to audiences outside of Concord.

Baseball fans are passionate about their home teams, and American artists have responded to America's national pastime in kind. In addition to unknown folk artists who were inspired by the sport, the exhibition featured several acclaimed artists— including John Marin, Robert Rauschenberg, John Sloan, and William Zorach—in its fifty featured works from the Gladstone Collection. Highlights included:

- *Saturday Afternoon at Sportsman's Park*, by Edward Laning (1908–1981); about 1944; Oil on canvas. This scene is a game from the 1944 World Series played in St. Louis, Missouri.
- *Fastball*, by Lou Grant (born 1934); 2004; Oil on canvas. Grant's animated scene captures his memories of the Negro League games he attended as a child in Brooklyn, New York.
- *Weathervane*, Artist unknown; 1930–1940; Sheet iron. The main figure is not a horse or a cow, but a ball player, and doesn't stand on an arrow, but a bat. The directional indicators are not the usual N, W, S, E (North, West, South, East), but 1, 2, 3, H for first, second, third, and home.
- *Box Office Sign,* by Theo I. Josephs; about 1890; Painted wood. The sign painter decorated the "O" in "Office" as a baseball with a bat in its center—a clue for those fans who might not be able to read.
- *Baseball Player,* by William Zorach (1889–1966); 1940; Bronze. The catcher and his position are conveyed in the sturdiness of bronze by Lithuanian American Zorach.
- *Back Out*, by Robert Rauschenberg (1925–2008); 1979; Silkscreen. Rauschenberg was one of the most influential American artists of the post–World War II generation. He combined elements of sculpture, painting, and printmaking into his works, often employing found objects and images.
- *Bat Spinning at the Speed of Light*, by Claes Oldenburg (born 1929); 1975; Lithograph. Oldenburg is renowned particularly for his public sculptures that depict ordinary objects on a large scale.

In choosing which works to include, Concord Museum Curator David Wood looked to those that reflected the passion of both the artist and the fan and would connect those communities. Wide-ranging examples in a variety of media explored not only the playing field, the positions, and the equipment, but also the fans, the color barrier, and the involvement of women in the sport.[25] Combining these works of art with memorabilia generously on loan from the National Baseball Hall of Fame and Museum in Cooperstown, New York, gave the exhibition a bonus appeal. Merely mentioning the names Jim Rice, Carlton Fisk, Carl Yastrzemski, and Ted Williams was enough to bring a gleam to the eyes of Red Sox fans, but the oppor-

Figure 5.3. *The Art of Baseball* in the Wallace Kane Gallery at the Concord Museum. *Source:* Photograph by Mary Orr.

tunity to display a bat, glove, cap, and catcher's mask associated with these heroes, as well as three Red Sox Championship rings, proved irresistible.

The intergenerational conversations among visitors that took place in front of these objects provided anecdotal evidence that the goals of the exhibition were being met. New faces visited the museum, especially on the days that the museum admitted youth baseball and softball players, coaches, and families free of charge. The Red Sox memorabilia and the World Series rings transfixed both young and old visitors. A grandfather was overheard sharing a story with his granddaughter about his first Red Sox game. Adults of all ages were particularly drawn to the 1944 painting, *Saturday Afternoon at Sportsman's Park*, by Edward Laning, which put the observer right in the stands. Conversations in front of this painting ranged from "I remember sitting right there" to "What's your favorite thing to eat at a ballpark?"

To build an audience for *The Art of Baseball*, the Concord Museum implemented an extensive marketing program, engaged in promotional partnerships, and offered the Greater Boston community a wide range of high-quality, free programming. The marketing program included a regionally distributed rack card, an active public relations effort, a media sponsorship with *The Improper Bostonian*, and an interview of Doris Kearns Goodwin by Jared Bowen of WGBH, Boston's local NPR affiliate. A special membership drive using a three-town, all-resident postcard mailing aimed to gain new members for the museum. Promotional partnerships with the Red Sox Foundation and the Lowell Spinners increased the marketing reach of the free programs and brought in Spinners team members to read stories to children at the museum, as well as a "Meet the Spinners" day. Over twenty programs and events were held, many of which were free, including outdoor baseball movie nights, gallery talks, an appraisal day with leading sports memorabilia appraiser Leila Dunbar, a sports trivia night, and vintage baseball games on Concord's own Emerson Field, which drew crowds from surrounding towns. As a finale to the exhibition's five-month run from April 16 to September 21, 2015, the Concord Museum held a special program entitled "Talking Baseball with Doris Kearns Goodwin and Ken Burns." This free event attracted four hundred people to hear Goodwin and award-winning documentary filmmaker Ken Burns share their personal stories and current thoughts on baseball. Moderated by Jeff Idelson, president of the National Baseball Hall of Fame and Museum, the sold-out program was a huge success and received press coverage in *The Boston Globe* and other media outlets.

In terms of community expectations, managing the Ken Burns/Doris Kearns Goodwin program was challenging for the museum's small staff. While the event was free, reservations were required, and museum members were given priority registration. To accommodate a much larger audience than the museum can hold, the event was held at the Fenn School in Concord. Tickets sold out within three hours, requiring the museum to maintain a waiting list of more than two hundred people. Although the museum has presented events with other popular cultural figures in recent years, this event necessitated a delicate balance between creating a unique evening for as many community members as possible and managing the disappointment of those who could not attend. Staff addressed this challenge by carefully handling expectations, lists, and logistics to make for a very successful evening. Many attendees expressed delight and appreciation to have been in the audience for such a special event.

Another challenge to the success of the exhibition—and one over which the museum staff had no control—was the 2015 Red Sox season! The run of the exhibition purposefully coincided with baseball season, but unfortunately 2015 was not a good year for the Red Sox. They finished last in the five-team American League East with a record low of seventy-eight wins to eighty-four losses. But, as one exhibition reviewer noted, "The Red Sox might be in the cellar, but America's national pastime is still thrilling fans at the Concord Museum."[26]

By combining art with sports history and maintaining the museum's mission-driven focus on object-based learning, the Concord Museum connected to the Greater Boston community—and beyond—in a fresh way that increased its engagement with visitors. This was evidenced by the following results:

- During the run of the exhibition, the Concord Museum experienced a 5.3 percent increase in visitors compared to the previous year
- Over 14,000 people saw the exhibition and participated in the associated programs and events
- The museum attracted sixty-five new memberships, an 18 percent increase from the same period the previous year
- Museum staff reported an increase in family interactions among generations in the gallery as they discussed the art, their own personal experiences, and baseball memories

- More than in previous exhibitions, younger visitors used the family guides, scavenger hunt, and hands-on table with its make-your-own baseball card activity
- *The Art of Baseball* continues to engage viewers in an online exhibition at www .concordmuseum.org, where exhibition highlights are accompanied by a chapter about Concord's own baseball history

In his documentary *Baseball*, Ken Burns reminded us that the game is "a repository of age-old American verities, of standards against which we continually measure ourselves, and yet at the same time a mirror of the present moment in our modern culture."[27] *The Art of Baseball* at the Concord Museum succeeded in presenting to a national audience this intersection of baseball and culture. Whether it was a young boy in his baseball uniform meeting a favorite player from the Spinners, a millennial enjoying a sports trivia night with friends, or an art lover from the local senior center following along on a curator's gallery talk, *The Art of Baseball* enabled the Concord Museum to foster community connectivity through sports history. As one visitor from Maine wrote of the exhibition in the museum's guestbook: "Super! A Home Run!"

CASE STUDY

Pedaling Through History: 150 Years of the Bicycle from the Collection of Glenn Eames

William F. Brooks Jr.

The Henry Sheldon Museum of Vermont History in Middlebury was founded in 1882 to document and exhibit the history of Middlebury, Addison County, and the Mid-Lake Champlain Region. During the summer and fall of 2016, the museum presented *Pedaling Through History: 150 Years of the Bicycle*, a vintage bicycle exhibit to coincide with the 150th anniversary of the first pedal bicycle patent issued in New Haven, Connecticut to Pierre Lallement. *Pedaling Through History* featured historic bicycles, photographs, and related material from the collection of bicycle historian Glenn Eames of Burlington, Vermont. Eames participation brought great acclaim and interest to the project because of his already established reputation as a curator, speaker, cycle shop owner, bicycle rider, historian, and storyteller. Riding culture is quite prevalent in Vermont and the neighboring states of New York and New Hampshire. A great many cyclists gather to participate in annual events that include three prominent fundraisers: a ride in memory of a Middlebury College staff member killed by a drunken driver, the Kelly-Brush ride dedicated to making active lifestyles a reality for anyone with a spinal cord injury, and The Vermont Gran Fondo, a noncompetitive ride through Vermont's Green Mountains. Due to this high level of local and regional biking interest, many surrounding townspeople and cyclists banded together with great community effort to create and promote the exhibit alongside the Henry Sheldon Museum and Eames. In addition to attending the exhibition, residents, cycling enthusiasts, and bicycle riders of the Lake Champlain region and greater New England played a paramount role in the exhibition's development, installation, fundraising, promotion, and attendance.

As the Henry Sheldon Museum Executive Director, I developed the concept for *Pedaling Through History* alongside Eames, my fellow cycling enthusiast. I became a serious biker when I turned forty years old. Cycling quickly took a prominent place in my life, as I used it as a substitute for a previous smoking habit. This new activity led me to compete in triathlons; a bicycling trip in England, Scotland, and Wales; and a twenty-day cross-country ride from Huntington Beach, California, to Currituck Sound, North Carolina, in 1986. Before relocating from Maryland to Vermont, I regularly spent two-week summer vacations touring the Green Mountain State on organized rides of Vermont Bicycle Tours.

Eames's passion for bicycles and biking began even earlier than my own. But we shared one thing in common; Eames also quit smoking when he started riding. *Vermont Sports* magazine chronicled his passion for cycling in summer 2016:

> "I was in my twenties, a smoker and not particularly healthy when I first started riding," said Eames. "Cycling probably literally saved my life." He also met an avid cyclist named Mary Manghis. They began touring by bike, first making forays into Vermont and around

Figure 5.4.   Penny-Farthing Bicycle, 1884–1885. Pope Manufacturing Co., Hartford, CT. Collection of the Henry Sheldon Museum, Middlebury, VT. *Source:* **Photograph courtesy of The Henry Sheldon Museum.**

New England, and then trips to Europe, Asia, and Africa. Eventually, the couple sold their respective businesses, put their belongings in storage, and set off on a two-year bike trip around the world. When they returned, they moved to Burlington and in 2000 founded the Old Spokes Home bicycle shop. Its second floor served as a space to exhibit Eames's ever-increasing premier collection of historic bikes, related equipment, and memorabilia.[28]

Eames and I formed a strong team that combined his cycling connections with the Sheldon Museum's vision for the exhibition and community connections. This collaboration together with the local passion for cycling enabled us to attract a great many early investors and participants. Eames's extensive leadership in the Vermont bicycle community attracted former employees, customers, vendors, and bike club members who stepped forward to offer their financial support and counsel. Local community members joined forces in the early phases of research, development, and installation. Caroline and Gregg Marston of Vermont Bicycle Tours (VBT) Bicycling and Walking Vacations and Wynne and Tony Ridgway, a college fraternity brother of mine who'd previously toured with VBT, led the fundraising efforts. The support of the Marstons and Ridgways brought in an additional fifty individual and business donors. All told, the museum raised $10,000 from community businesses and avid bicycle riders, which covered the exhibit costs.

The exhibit gained other community support as well. Central to the installation of the exhibit were Sheldon Museum Associate Director Mary Manley and three interns from nearby Middlebury College: Grace Bryan, Matt Brophy, and Vanessa Dikuyama. Three local community members offered expertise for the installation. Greg Hancock, a logistical engineer, positioned the bicycles for the exhibit. Will Blanchard, a cabinetmaker, crafted wooden bases for display. Woodworker Patrick Johnson provided exhibit installation insights and the use of his shop where Eames modified hardware for stanchions. Hunt Manley, Mary's son who had worked for the Old Spokes Home as a bike mechanic and salesman, volunteered to help with publicity.

Vermont landscape and outdoors lifestyle, Eames's well-developed cycling community, and interested local citizens drew a wide range of objects to the museum's effort. Hunt Manley offered the Fat Bike from the high-end Budnitz Bicycle of Burlington.[29] Anja Wrede and David Black of *RAD Innovations: Mobility Solutions*, a nearby company that operates out of a converted dairy farm, lent several bikes adapted for disabled riders. Canadian collector Lorne Shields provided historic bicycle photographs and memorabilia. The museum community pitched in as well. Regional heritage organization Historic New England lent vintage bicycle shoes. The nearby Shelburne Museum offered stanchions. Vermont artist Martin McGowan brought a feminist dimension to the exhibit with his metal sculpture titled *A Woman Needs a Man Like a Fish Needs a Bike*.[30] Ed Koren, Vermonter, avid bicyclist, and celebrated cartoonist from *The New Yorker*, lent three of his bicycle drawings to the exhibit. Collecting objects from individuals outside of the institution instilled a certain amount of ownership to the Sheldon Museum's extended community and demonstrated the deep appeal of the exhibit's subject matter.

Surpassing all previous records, visitation to *Pedaling through History* reached roughly three thousand during the exhibit's run and included widespread support from within the Vermont community as well as all fifty states and several foreign countries. Thousands of visitors who already enjoyed an avid cycling lifestyle attended the exhibit, and many more were inspired to begin, renew, or accelerate a personal bicycle habit. Bicycle historian Carey Williams arranged for a busload of conferees to visit the Sheldon Museum as part of the International Cycling History Conference held nearby in New Haven, Connecticut. In September, six New England members of the Wheelmen, a national nonprofit organization dedicated to the heritage of American cycling, historical restoration and use of early models, and promotion of riding as part of modern living, drew added attention to the exhibit. They displayed their historic bicycles on the grounds of the museum, answered guest questions, and embarked on a ten-mile round trip ride into the rolling hills of the countryside.

Increased interest in the Sheldon Museum's *Pedaling Through History* exhibit was due in part to the local and regional lure of cycling but also to a well-crafted, community-focused effort on the part of all those who participated in the creation and promotion of the exhibit. Eames's collection was central to creating a captivating exhibit. The specialty objects garnered from around the area and region enhanced this collection and provided an opportunity for other cycling enthusiasts to participate. Gallery talks and demonstrations included several sold-out presentations by Eames and University of Vermont Professor Luis Vivanco, who explored the fascinating early history of the bicycle in Vermont. The museum also benefited from community-supported promotion. Owners of the nearby Frog Hollow Bikes rental, sales, and repair store, David Tier, Chas Lyons, and Carl Robinson encouraged their many customers to visit the exhibit and attend special events. Swift House Inn owners, who are also cyclists who host bicycle tour groups, recommended the exhibit to their guests, as did their other innkeepers. All told, the cycling focus facilitated a rousingly successful exhibit for the Sheldon Museum, as it gave the community a connection and bonding point that reflected a widely experienced local year-round pastime—attracting them with a deeply enjoyed activity and providing a quality reason, the Eames collection, to participate in expounding upon the regional sporting passion.

CASE STUDY

Discovering Strong Medicine: Native American Healing Rituals and Sports

Kathryn Leann Harris and Marcus Monenerkit

An artist's work, like an athlete's, is value based, intuitive, curious, active, and progress oriented. Both art and sports build healthy individuals and well-balanced communities. Drawing on Native principles, Marcus Monenerkit, director of community engagement of the Heard Museum in Phoenix, Arizona, and member of the Comanche Nation, links art, sports, and ritual by bringing a unifying Indigenous perspective to all three. He believes that "sport and art are one and the same," an idea woven together through existentially pragmatic Native artistic principles.[31] Practicing the arts and playing sports each guide the participant through a holistic experience, one that moves between structure and fluidity. Both embody an artistic purpose, allowing for a sense of experimentation and comfort with imaginative expansion. In 2014, Monenerkit united these ideas in the Heard exhibition *Beautiful Games: American Indian Sport and Art,* exploring the intersection of sports and art to demonstrate how artists act in community with common communication and purpose.[32] *Beautiful Games'* message centered around a sense of respect for diversity in experience and in community, a social phenomenon common in Indigenous cultures and motivations, and revealed visibly in sports. The exhibit framed sports as a conduit for interpreting the most sacred of humanity's values and principles. Monenerkit accomplished this by displaying artistic expressions that modeled athletic endeavors. Using sports as a lens, *Beautiful Games* showed how any individual or community can foster artistic values and seek expressive excellence regardless of their path in life. By doing so, the Heard Museum was able to attract, educate, and connect with both their local and broader communities.

For a museum that focuses on the value of American Indian art and cultural experience, a sports exhibit was a natural idea. Sports are extremely important in American Indian communities. Local to the museum, the Arizona High School State Basketball Tournament draws more than ten thousandpeople when Native teams play in the downtown Phoenix arena. There is a real competitive tradition at these predominantly Native high schools. Hopi High School, for example, has won twenty-five straight Arizona State High School Cross Country championships, a national record. But athletics are more than just an expression of young energy. Indian Country has a rich history of public sporting moments. Competitive tales are common within many Tribal creation stories and consistent with Native values. Current Native athletes grow up participating in ceremonies and events that sometimes incorporate acts of athletic prowess—like the Navajo coming-of-age ceremony, Kinaaldá, in which a young woman runs daily greeting the spirits, informing them she is coming into the world with energy and strength.[33]

The ethnographic, fine art, and archival materials housed within the Heard Museum reflect this ritual presence of competition and community sporting values. These concepts and objects played a key role in conceptualizing and crafting *Beautiful Games: American Indian Sport and Art.* The Heard Museum houses around 45,000 artifacts, among them hundreds of sports-related items, many of which had never been displayed. The collection includes sculptures created by famed American Indian artists, such as Allan Houser, and more simple objects like a bundle of sticks used in Native guessing games. Monenerkit had worked with the collection for over a decade and had intimate knowledge of its contents and potential. In a normal work day, he would come across items ranging from archeological stone balls to ethnographic games to fine art paintings depicting sporting rituals. The sheer amount and quality of available objects stirred his imagination.

Upon hearing the 2015 Super Bowl would be held in Phoenix, Monenerkit became further inspired to produce the exhibition to coincide with an impending influx of sports fans. He selected works that demonstrated that the breadth and depth of Native sport experience is more than meets the eye, a message often omitted from sports histories. Most do not teach that the 1912 Olympics included multiple American Indian athletes who came directly from the boarding school experience; that the 1916 Pendleton Round-up rodeo champion Jackson Sundown, who won at the age of fifty-two, was a Nez Perce Native; that the only person to win U.S. Olympic gold in the 10,000 meters was Ogalala runner Billy Mills in 1964; or that the first person to carry the U.S. flag in the winter Olympics opening ceremony (1924) was an Ojibwe hockey player named Taffy Abel. Those are legacy stories of excellence for generations to recognize, know, and learn, from which Native people can derive pride and the general public can gain awareness of the value of Native contributions in sports as in all other social realms.

When weaving together this intersection of Native philosophies, art, and sports, the Heard interpreted a wide range of athletic topics. *Beautiful Games* covered three galleries totaling four thousand square feet. The main gallery provided remarks about the sporting heritage of Indian communities and background as to how sport-like or physical activities are involved both in everyday life and also in the telling of tribal creation histories. The exhibit proceeded with one of the most universal of competitions, running—an activity that needs few accouterments but was a critical skill for early groups in hunting, communication, and/or warfare. The Heard featured lacrosse and stickball games with items ranging from contemporary uniforms, stone sculpture, an Oneida cradleboard with applique and carved lacrosse imagery, and early American paintings by George Catlin. The main-floor exhibit continued with boxing and rodeo stories followed by American field games, football, baseball, women's basketball, and golf. The mezzanine gallery introduced surfing and positioned it as a predecessor for skateboarding, a more recent introduction into tribal communities that has become popular among the younger members. Also, in an adjacent educational gallery were two-dimensional items representing games and sports from the collection. These were accompanied by an interactive area with tops, game boards, an electronic buffalo hunt, and a reading area for extended learning.

One of the highlights of the related exhibition programming was "American Indian Stereotypes in Sports." This program functioned as a public conversation (filmed by C-SPAN) that included Susan Harjo (Cheyenne and Hodulgee Muscogee); Amanda Blackhorse (Navajo); Leo Killsback (Northern Cheyenne); and Jim Warne (Oglala Lakota Sioux). Kevin Gover (Pawnee), then-

Figure 5.5. *Beautiful Games: American Indian Sport and Art* showcases boxing and rodeo within the exhibit. *Source:* Heard Museum, Phoeniz, Arizona.

director of the National Museum of theAmerican Indian, moderated.[34] Together, the panel navigated complexity and nuance, allowing the Heard to provide a place to have a conversation, a place where the community could communicate and exchange ideas without resorting to hateful speech and actions, an exercise in pluralism.

Through the exhibit research process, Monenerkit discovered anew the critical connections between Native philosophical principles and the interpretive intersection of art and sports. Many Native sports have origins in healing rituals. "That is strong medicine, sports," he contends.[35] Rituals are powerful both for the community and the person who benefits. Someone grounded in ritual, identity, and activity is connected to and learning core tenets of the human experience and the complex art of association. Both sports and art apply similar approaches to learning: practice, reflect, and then adapt, while maintaining time-tested principles of fairness and equity. With art as with sports, participants think with intuition, novelty, and confidence. And like a new piece of art, every game is a completely original experience, and yet it has its patterns of continuity and consummation too. Both have a start and an end—artistic productions and competitions all come to completion. That kind of ritualistic movement demonstrates how effort can be pleasant: the toil of work, research, integrity, and creation can become methodically soothing while deeply enriching.

Monenerkit also found many connections regarding the role of leadership in sports. Native American leadership philosophies are often based on community and deliberation—being sensitive to the social environment. Critical Indigenous theory suggests communities benefit most when functioning pragmatically and with collective principles of respect, reciprocity, responsibility, and relations. In his work *Native Pragmatism*, Scott L. Pratt describes this through four domains that guide Native conversations and action: pluralism, interaction, community, and growth.[36] Pluralism, for example, posits that each perspective is valid to a group or organization, to its future and collective growth. "Most people live by life themes that are dubiously habitual and dualistic," Monererkit observes. "It's them against the world. Their problems and solutions either drown community or uphold it. The acceptance of pluralism is a key element to building community—key in life and sports."[37] American Indian spirituality allows for both individual connection and a community-centered mindset, where each person can develop authenticity and build character through risk taking, self-discovery, empathy, and understanding.

Native pragmatism provides valuable insight for interpreting sports history. Popular narratives often unrealistically portray heralded singular heroes whose stories are told from a one-dimensional perspective, placing the leader on a pedestal, gifted and all-knowing. Sports leadership, in actuality, almost never comes in the form of an isolated individual. For the most part, every leader has a team, and the leader depends not only on interaction but on interdisciplinary insight and interrelationships. Even in a single-person competition, the participant has a support crew. Through these engagements, the practicing leader creates a shared culture with all involved, founded on sound decision-making practices, strategy, innovation, experimentation, critique, and sharing. The importance of a leader's ability to surrender their ego to criticism is often overlooked in public discourse. A strong sporting actor is one who regularly undergoes evaluation, is open to dissent, and remains sensitive to alternative perspectives. Their receptiveness to otherness creates an adaptive, entrepreneurial spirit, which is a required attitude when the goal is to make an equitable and mutually beneficial difference.

Acting with deliberative appreciative inquiry and sensitivity increases awareness and aids in artistic expressive acts be they sports, business management, or museum interpretation. Healthy organizations grow iteratively, consistently generating new and adaptable concepts around value planning and result evaluation. Inherent to these ideas is the concept of being flexible and comfortable with contingency. Sensible, personal, and communal, this values-based approach teaches teamwork, taking risks within the confines of the rules, and changing parameters by petitions, process, and deliberation. It teaches how to be more comfortable in uncertain situations and create sensitivity to a perceptually differentiated approach. People can then feel open to express themselves innovatively without someone else gatekeeping or censoring their connection to the working group.

As the Heard proved, socially active and experiential sports themes easily connect with museum missions and curriculums to enable genuinely educative experiences. Sports, games, and play leave an indelible impression on individuals and societies and provide a strong alternative model for organizational management. Sports, Monenerkit says, provide lessons for interpretation and association at work and in daily life, making it a useful topic for exhibitions and discussions. The universality of sports positions it as what Frank DeFord, longtime sportswriter and social critic, once referred as a "lingua franca," a common language, shared among almost everyone.[38] The cooperative principles of sports offer a lens of shared evaluation. When viewed through the lens of Indigenous philosophy, sports interpretation can provide generative examples of leadership to help shape institutional success and group excellence. In a time and place where it is difficult to find truth, sports help communities find a sense of authentic connectivity through the physical embodiment of shared goals and standards. Traditional Native practice has much to offer in this regard—a source of medicinal healing in a time of great need and a conduit for honing artistic values and expressive excellence.

NOTES

1. For an in-depth discussion of forging connections with diverse audiences, see Nina Simon, *The Art of Relevance* (Santa Cruz: Museum 2.0, 2016), http://www.artofrelevance .org/, accessed July 17, 2022; also see MASS Action Toolkit, https://www.museumaction.org /resources, accessed July 17, 2022, and Margaret Kadoyama, *Museums Involving Communities: Authentic Connections* (New York: Routledge, 2018).

2. For information on surveying your audience, consult "Who's Coming: Respectful Audience Surveying Toolkit," Ofbyforall, https://www.ofbyforall.org/resources/survey-toolkit, accessed July 17, 2022; Judy Diamond, Michael Horn, and David H. Uttall, *Practical Evaluation Guide: Tools for Museums and Other Informal Educational Settings* (Lanham, MD: Rowman & Littlefield, 2016) and Marcella Wells, Barbara H. Butler, and Judith Koke, *Interpretive Planning for Museums: Integrating Visitor Perspectives in Decision Making* (Walnut Creek, CA: Left Coast Press, 2013).

3. See Colleen Dilenschneider, "Growing Competitor for Visitation to Cultural Organizations: The Couch (DATA)," *Know Your Own Bone*, January 4, 2017, https://www.colleendilen .com/2017/01/04/growing-competitor-for- visitation-to-cultural-organizations-the-couch-data/.

4. Carol L. Haines, "The Art of Baseball at the Concord Museum," in *Interpreting Sports at Museums and Historic Sites*, Kathryn Leann Harris and Douglas Stark, eds. (Lanham, MD: Rowman & Littlefield, 2023), 168–173.

5. William F. Brooks Jr., "Pedaling Through History: 150 Years of the Bicycle from the Collection of Glenn Eames," in *Interpreting Sports at Museums and Historic Sites,* Harris and Stark, eds., 173–176.

6. Chrischené Julius, "Recalling Community at the District Six Museum," in *Interpreting Sports at Museums and Historic Sites*, Harris and Stark, eds., 160–168.

7. Kathryn Leann Harris and Marcus Monenerkit, "Discovering Strong Medicine: Native American Healing Rituals and Sports," in *Interpreting Sports at Museums and Historic Sites*, Harris and Stark, eds., 176–180.

8. Mindy Thompson Fullilove, *Root Shock: How Tearing Up City Neighbourhoods Hurts America and What We Can Do About It* (New York: Ballantine Books, 2005), 11.

9. *Fields of Play: Football Memories and Forced Removals in Cape Town* (Cape Town: District Six Museum and Basler Afrika Bibliographien, 2010), 23. Exhibition catalog.

10. For cricket associations, the development of the game in Black communities was linked to this past of relocation and displacement. See Mogamad Allie, *More than a Game: History of the Western Province Cricket Board 1959–1991* (Cape Town: Cape Argus and Western Province Cricket Association, 2000), 112.

11. *Western Province Council of Sport: 16th Annual General Meeting*, November 19, 1989, 12. Brochure. District Six Museum collection.

12. *Sport: A Community Definition* (Cape Town: District Six Museum Foundation, 1996). Introductory pamphlet to the sports exhibitions process. District Six Museum collection.

13. *Report on Status of Exhibition* (Cape Town: District Six Museum Foundation, 1996). District Six Museum collection.

14. See *Application for Funding: Sport, A Community Definition* (Cape Town: District Six Museum Foundation, 1996). District Six Museum collection. *Sport: A Community Definition* (Cape Town: District Six Museum Foundation, 1996). Introductory pamphlet to the sports exhibitions process. District Six Museum collection.

15. *Invitation to Public Forum for Displaying the Game* (Cape Town: District Six Museum Foundation, 1996). District Six Museum Collection.

16. *Fields of Play: Football Memories and Forced Removals in Cape Town* (Cape Town: District Six Museum and Basler Afrika Bibliographien, 2010), 16. Exhibition catalog.

17. *Fields of Play: Football Memories and Forced Removals in Cape Town* (Cape Town: District Six Museum and Basler Afrika Bibliographien, 2010). Exhibition catalog.

18. *Sports Memory Project, Cape Flats Tourism Development Framework*, District Six Museum and Cape Town Routes Unlimited for the Department of Economic Development and Tourism, Western Cape, August 2007.

19. *Sports Memory Project.*

20. For another reflection on *Fields of Play* see Ciraj Rassool and Virgil Slade, "'Fields of Play:' The District Six Museum and the history of football in Cape Town," in *Global Perspectives on Football in Africa: Visualising the Game*, eds. Susann Baller, Giorgio Miescher and Ciraj Rassool (London: Routledge, 2013), 50–68.

21. Janet Marstine, "Museologically Speaking: An Interview with Fred Wilson," in *Museums, Equality and Social Justice*, eds. Richard Sandell and Eithne Nightingale (New York: Routledge, 2012), 38–44. Wilson's curatorial and artistic practice challenges the collecting and display histories of traditional museum spaces.

22. *Sports Memory Project, Report to Provincial Government Western Cape, Department of Economic Development and Tourism*, District Six Museum, Second Quarterly Report, 31 October 2007, 4–6.

23. Henry David Thoreau, *The Journal of Henry David Thoreau*, Volume VIII, November 1, 1855–August15, 1856, ed. Bradford Torrey and Francis H. Allen (Salt Lake City: Gibbs M. Smith, Inc., Peregrine Smith Books, 1984), page 270.

24. *The Art of Baseball*, interview with Doris Kearns Goodwin, film, Concord Museum, 2015.

25. See partial object list at the end of the essay.

26. Chris Bergeron, "Concord's Museum Exhibit Examines Baseball's Universal Appeal," *Metrowest Daily News*, May 31, 2015.

27. "In his documentary, *Baseball*, Ken Burns reminded us that the game is "a repository of age-old American verities, of standards against which we continually measure ourselves, and yet at the same time a mirror of the present moment in our modern culture.""

28. Glenn Eames as quoted in: Lisa Lynn, "A Magnificent Obsession," *Vermont Sports* (August 2016): 19.

29. The Fat Bike was originally made with oversized tires for traversing sandy beaches and eventually gained popularity as a commuter bike for both off and on road travel.

30. The sculpture remained on display in the Sheldon's outdoor garden after the exhibit ended.

31. Interviews between Marcus Monenerkit and Kathryn Leann Harris, June 1, 2021, and September 23, 2021.

32. Jose Ortega y Gasset, *The Modern Theme* (New York: Harper, 1961), 82–85; Andrew Light and Jonathan M. Smith, *The Aesthetics of Everyday Life* (New York: Columbia University Press, 2005); S. K. Wertz, "A Response to Best on Sports," *Journal of Aesthetic Education* 18, no. 4 (1984): 105–108.

33. Monty Roessel, *Kinaaldá : A Navajo Girl Grows Up* (Minneapolis: Lerner Publications, 1993); Bazhnibah, "Kinaaldá: Coming of Age in Traditional Diné Ceremony," *Navajo Times*, July 2, 2022, accessed January 31, 2022, https://navajotimes.com/opinion/essay/kinaalda -coming-of-age-in-traditional-dine-ceremony/.

34. "American Indian Stereotypes in Sports," C-SPAN, January 30, 2015, accessed January 31, 2022, https://www.c-span.org/video/?323984-1/american-indian-stereotypes-sports.

35. Interviews, Monenerkit and Harris.

36. Scott L Pratt, *Native Pragmatism: Rethinking the Roots of American Philosophy* (Bloomington: Indiana University Press, 2002).

37. Interviews, Monenerkit and Harris; See also: John Dewey, *The Public and Its Problems* (Chicago: Swallow Press, 1954); Maxine Greene, *Releasing the Imagination Essays on Education, the Arts, and Social Change* (San Francisco: Jossey-Bass, 1995).

38. Paige Ingram, "Deford Reflects on 45 Years of Sports Journalism," *The Media School Report*, April 12, 2007, accessed January 31, 2022, https://mediaschool.indiana.edu/news -events/news/item.html?n=deford-reflects-on-45-years-of-sports-journalism/.

Chapter Six

Empowering with Knowledge

Interpreting Sports through Education

Amanda McAllen

Museums and historic sites are increasingly creating education programs based on sports content; however, they often are doing so with minimal scholarship regarding best practices on integrating sports history and museum education techniques. As museum education consultant Justine Reilly writes, "Even within texts that discuss museum learning . . . the author failed to find even one example of a case study or a reference which discussed the topic of sport in museums."[1] This chapter explores how developments in museum education can guide educators who seek to produce a sports exhibit or program at any history organization. These programs may include school and teacher programs, online platforms, outreach events in communities, or any other program that uses sports content to engage with learners. The themes and methods in this chapter will illuminate unique opportunities for sports museum educators and will show how history organizations can leverage the growing importance of science, technology, engineering, and mathematics (STEM) education and twenty-first-century skills to create successful education programs based on sports content.[2]

Key Interpretive Concepts:

1. *Create Accessible Programming for a Diverse Group of Learners:* Sports content can engage new audiences who would not otherwise visit a sports museum and can add depth and interest that facilitates an enriched learning experience in diverse ways.
2. *Explore Interdisciplinary Subjects:* For many students and visitors, sports can be a compelling hook to build interest in historical or cultural topics, which museums can offer through various educational disciplines.
3. *Apply Museum Education Best Practices:* New modes of thought in museum education can diversify the approaches museums use to engage their audiences in sports topics.

Implementing Sports Education Programs

Creating a substantive sports history educational program at museums and historic sites, even when daunting, is a worthy endeavor that any institution can achieve with concentrated effort. A study of the current landscape reveals a range of educational models, forms, and standards. Some institutions purposefully connect sports history to school curricula and aim to meet specific educational objectives, while others produce programs without formal educational goals.[3] Many sports museums function without trained museum education staff, which can impact their programming standards. Non-sports-related museum and historic site staff often lack subject-matter expertise, and thus avoid generating associated educational programming. The Western Pennsylvania Sports Museum, which functions as a museum within a museum at the Senator John Heinz History Center, offers a useful example of a history museum staff that successfully engages sports content in their program offerings. Educators at the Heinz History Center are not necessarily sports experts (nor, in some cases, even sports fans), yet they effectively use sports to illuminate a range of historical topics. Upon cross-referencing the sports museum's content with school curriculum standards and teacher interests, the museum's educators discovered impactful ways to develop sports programming around a variety of topics for a range of learners.

Instead of shying away, the Western Pennsylvania Sports Museum's educators embraced sports stories in the exhibits to create new activities and explore additional programming topics, a replicable model for any institution seeking to install a sports exhibit. One educational program illuminates the experiences of immigrants who brought their sporting traditions to Western Pennsylvania. Another pairs an investigation of paintings showing African American migrants leaving the South and arriving in Pittsburgh with the story of Josh Gibson, a Negro League baseball player whose family came to Pittsburgh as part of the Great Migration. In a program for early learners, young students can use the museum's interactive stations to learn about popular local pastimes like bocce. By thinking creatively about sports content and applying emerging museum education techniques to these new programs, museum educators successfully used history-based programs to engage learners in new ways. Educators at any type of public history institution can implement similar methods to take advantage of the unique opportunities that sports topic explorations reveal: creating widely accessible programming, using sports as a "hook" for other topics, and integrating museum education best practice to better engage audiences.

Create Accessible Programming in Diverse Ways

Museum educators strive to create programming that develops skills, connects to lived experiences, engages audiences in various ways, and provides memorable museum experiences for all learners at the same time. Teaching through a sports lens is an excellent way to engage social and emotional learning, connect fans to content through bonding experiences and technology, engage new audiences, and promote health and well-being. These are just a few of the many ways that sports history can be the conduit for accessible educational museum programming.

Focusing on Social and Emotional Learning

Educators can work with sports content to facilitate museum experiences that allow students to participate in shared learning. Inherent in the museum visit, sports focused and otherwise, lays an opportunity to connect and learn through emotional interaction that is difficult to quantify and does not always fulfill a specific educational goal, but can be especially impactful for visitors. Sports is an ideal entry point for this kind of "meaning-making," which Lynn Dierking, professor in Free-Choice STEM Learning at Oregon State University, writes is one of the main reasons people visit museums, "to wonder, consider, question, and/or to discover something about themselves, their companions and their place in the cosmos."[4] Much of the existing sports museum literature engages in a critical debate about the practice of glorifying "golden ages" in sports and the "nostalgia market" upon which these museums capitalize.[5] Sports fans' experiences of the highs and lows, camaraderie, competition, and resilience contribute to their social-emotional learning. Nostalgia can be an effective tool for creating excitement and providing glimpses into the sporting past that draws people together. As sports historian Wray Vamplew points out, "sports museums are the best places to replicate the performance, drama, romance, passion, and emotion of sport."[6] While viewing a video of a World Series–winning home run accompanied by the relevant bat, ball, and jersey, visitors can emotionally engage in a way that fosters meaning making as well as collective learning.

Sports history is an effective means for implementing a key social-emotional learning museum educational practice: providing opportunities for learners to "bridge" and "bond" while in the museum. In *The Manual of Museum Learning*, Ngaire Blankenberg, director of the Smithsonian's National Museum of African Art, highlights the ways museums can guide learners to strengthen existing commonalities (bond) and/or come together on the common ground despite their differences (bridge).[7] These are forms of social-emotional learning, which the formal education field recognizes as essential to the development of students beyond their academic learning. Museums, Dierking and John Falk, executive director of the Institute for Learning Innovation and Sea Grant Professor Emeritus of Free-Choice Learning at Oregon State University, point out, "support outcomes such as social learning and bonding, [and] increased self-awareness and self-confidence"; a key value for all sports-related museum work.[8] Visitors can bond over their shared love of certain sports, teams, players, or experiences, and if done well, nonfan visitors will also have opportunities to engage in the content. In the Western Pennsylvania Sports Museum, one exhibit includes feedback cards with these questions: "What does sports mean to you?" and "What impact do sports have on your life?" Responses often reflect the deep sporting heritage of the local area and include comments about how sports cross barriers like race, religion, and country to bring people together. By inviting visitors to respond to the exhibit and including an option for non-sports fans to share other activities that can connect people and cross boundaries, similarly to sports, educators can provide a space for their audience to find "bridges" between themselves and their sports-loving peers or family members.

Going Beyond the Museum Walls

Another way museums can apply these models is to include the surrounding community and visitors in the exhibit process. The FC Bayern World Experience in Munich, Germany, facilitated a fan bonding experience when they solicited artifacts to fill gaps in their collection and archive. While more of a curating activity, it allowed fans to learn about the museum and its mission while contributing their own objects and stories to the historical record of their team. In the program *Boston vs. Bullies*, the Sports Museum at TD Garden impacts student lives by using famous athletes to talk about bullying in schools. The program encourages students to learn more about bullying and create a welcoming environment for all students at their school. The Sports Museum leveraged their access to famous athletes to build an audience. Program facilitators visit schools with athletes to deliver the content. The online curriculum breaks down the information for teachers and provides videos to highlight key information. The whole program is delivered as an outreach activity, allowing the museum to activate the athletes as educators and providing an opportunity to deliver important educational programming beyond the museum walls.[9]

Museums can also leverage technology to engage with audiences who are unable to visit. *La Vida Baseball* is an online platform that collects and celebrates stories of Latino people and baseball—both historic and contemporary.[10] It is a partnership between TeamWorks Media and the National Baseball Hall of Fame and Museum, with the goal of bringing awareness of Latino baseball beyond the walls of the Hall of Fame in Cooperstown, New York. Online platforms like this can highlight the work of the museum through articles that are easily shared on social media among enthusiasts.

By combining these two methods, the National Museum of the American Indian at the Smithsonian Institute influenced societal change with opportunities for engagement beyond the museum walls. Kevin Gover, the then-director of the NMAI, engaged the local and wider communities in conversations at two public symposia, held in 2013 and 2018. By utilizing public programming and technology, the NMAI built interest in the content well beyond the physical museum. Public debate ensued after both events, informing the national discussion and course correcting misinterpretations of Native mascot origins. The Smithsonian broadcasted the 2018 event on YouTube, where it remains for viewing. These methods build interest in content well beyond the physical museum, generating expanded in-person discussions and providing virtual visitors opportunities to bridge and bond online.[11]

Engaging New Audiences

Museums can attract and educate a variety of new audiences by using sports as a historical lens. Teachers know that one of the best ways to pique the interest of their students is to begin a new topic with an exciting hook. For many, sports offer that hook. As Reilly states, sports content "allows museums to explore heritage through the lens of a subject area that many non-traditional audiences are comfortable with."[12] History organizations, therefore, have opportunities to welcome new audiences, which may include groups such as sports fans who do not usually visit museums, non-sports fans who are not typically interested in sports content, and families who enjoy being active together.

By including topics that relate to people who may not usually visit museums, curators and educators can help people feel that museums are for them. Sporting collections often include high-profile memorabilia that intrigues and interests visitors. Sports collections often contain objects that intimately connect the public to everyday passions. The *Innoskate* project of the Smithsonian's Lemelson Center for the Study of Invention and Innovation drew a new audience—skateboarders—to the institution through programming that related museum collections to historical skateboarding culture and innovations. Staff went to the skateboarding community and talked with iconic skateboarders about how the Smithsonian's innovation and invention initiatives connected with their innovations in skateboarding. While some skateboarders were initially skeptical of the outreach, they came to see how their creativity and innovations were worthy of being included and recognized by the Smithsonian. The resulting public program drew skateboarders to the museum, many for the first time, and created moments of meaning-making for both the skateboarders and the museum program staff.[13]

It is especially important that sports museums consider how their exhibits can better appeal to people who are not sports fans. To appeal to a broader audience, look to connect sports content to broader historical events, technological advancements, engineering innovations, or art and design. These links demonstrate a museum's diversity of thought and intention to use their collection and interpretation to generate relevant content for all potential visitors—not just sports fans. As educator and consultant Jennifer Shepherd suggests in her piece about interpretation and informal learning, we must find ways to tell more than one story about an object, event, or person "so that people can discover the story that means the most to them, and begin to understand why that story makes the most sense to them."[14] Sports stories can illuminate different time periods and events for museum visitors in ways that connect closely with their lived experiences.

Impacting Audience Health

Due to the athletic nature of their content and collections, sports museums are well placed to use sports education programs, exhibits, and activities to illustrate the positive impact of physical health and fitness.[15] These fit well with current research and scholarship on understanding museums' community-focused roles and measuring the impact museum programs have on audiences. For example, the increase in the obesity rate and prevalence of health conditions such as type 2 diabetes speak to an increasing need for health and fitness education programs.[16] Sports museums and museums that feature sports content can impact physical health by focusing on improving the health literacy of visitors.

Interactive sports exhibits can incorporate many of the techniques mentioned in this chapter while also linking content to sports medicine, public health, and nutrition. At the Children's Museum of Indianapolis, the new Riley Children's Health *Sports Legends Experience* encourages fitness and healthy eating as a response to community health issues. Chief Executive Officer Jeffrey Patchen stated that the goal was "to create an outdoor and indoor experience to promote an active lifestyle in an immersive experience that would bring families together . . . and to provide educational programs that build character, instill life-enhancing values and promote healthy choices through sports."[17] The museum accomplished this by creating numerous sports-featured exhibits that included artifacts from local sporting figures and interactive installations on which visitors can practice physical activity and learn about healthy choices.

Such efforts are often inspired by public health initiatives like former First Lady Michelle Obama's *Let's Move* program. The program's toolkit highlights museums as having "the ability to educate and inform to spur action in the areas of health, wellness, nutrition, and physical activity." Often focusing on health literacy and nutrition, some have incorporated sports content into programs to encourage physical fitness. At the Children's Museum of Manhattan, the *EatSleepPlay: Building Health Everyday* exhibit and anti-childhood obesity initiative aimed at urban, low-income communities, includes a curriculum for education providers to use alongside a visit to the exhibit or as a standalone program in classrooms.[18] Museums could adapt this model by designing education programs that encourage health and fitness beyond the walls of the institution. In addition to creating resources, they can provide outreach programs in partnership with schools and community sports facilities.

Sports as a Lens for Interdisciplinary Learning

Some of the best education programs find ways to use interest-driven learning by incorporating other disciplines and thinking creatively about the impact of sports across these disciplines. Interest-driven learning, also known as intrinsic motivation, is perhaps the most valuable way to use sports content in museums.[19] Interest-driven learning is an approach that structures content around a subject or topic about which learners are already interested.[20] For students who play or watch sports, learning about history, STEM subjects, or literacy may come easier if teachers present it through the sports lens. As Andrea Sachdeva, senior project manager of Project Zero at Harvard Graduate School of Education, writes, museums should "think of the various entry points and 'lenses' that will help visitors make connections between your collections and their own interests and experiences."[21] This connection to their own lives is a key step in meaning making for students and visitors.

Sports museums and exhibits can be exciting places for students to connect sports to wider topics. As visitors enter the permanent sports exhibit in the National Museum of African American History and Culture, they see a statue of Tommie Smith and John Carlos raising their fists in the Black Power salute on the medal stand at the 1968 Olympics. As Marc Tracy writes in the *New York Times*, the statue signifies the "marriage of athletics and social justice" that many museums highlight in their collections. The statue tells us more about the history of the Civil Rights Movement than it does about the 1968 Olympics. It is but one example of using sports as a lens through which to view other topics.[22]

Museums focused specifically on one sport or one team may find it daunting to intersect with other disciplines. However, the idea should provide a welcome opportunity to engage experts and educators in other fields who can add to staff knowledge and provide advice on techniques and best practice.[23] Sports museums can look to art galleries, science centers, children's museums, community sports organizations, professional leagues and teams, and local youth groups for help in understanding the wider story of the importance of sports. Together, these groups can create relevant and impactful programming that spans many disciplines.

Topical Interdisciplinary Sports Education Examples:

Art: The Olympic Museum in Lausanne, Switzerland, offered a program about sports photography to accompany the *Who Shot Sports: A Photographic History, 1843 to the Present* exhibit. Online resources for teachers provided activities that helped students build a vocabulary about the history of photography, explore the main elements of creating photographs, and trace the history of photography as it relates to the Olympic games.[24] The activities encouraged students to look creatively at an art form that many people consume when reading about sports online or in magazines but rarely explore in any depth.

Social Studies: The Western Pennsylvania Sports Museum uses its Negro League baseball collections to facilitate programs that explore the stories of the Great Migration, the Jim Crow South, and discrimination against African Americans in the city of Pittsburgh. The museum also ties the concept of sportsmanship to the central tenets of civic engagement. Local high-school students compete in a digital game to learn about local sports figures that acted as change agents in their community. This game incorporates examples ranging from professional athletes like Roberto Clemente to local youth athletic organizers at the YMCA and allows educators to layer curriculum-specific topics onto existing exhibit content.

Literacy: The International Tennis Hall of Fame offers a literacy program that uses different types of articles found in newspapers as a teaching tool. The museum carefully differentiates the online lesson plans by grade level and Common Core literacy standards. The program provides examples of source material for writing a feature article on a tennis player, such as career statistics and facts, as well as examples of tennis journalist and television commentator Bud Collins's writing. Students use the information to write a feature article inspired by Collins's style. Teachers can use these lesson plans to support a museum visit, extend the visit back into the classroom, or as a standalone classroom resource linking literacy to sports. For museum educators, the formal education field can provide inspiration for the latter concept. For example, museum educators can incorporate sources like news reports that highlight inequalities in sports to foster discussion about the exhibit and program content.[25]

STEM: STEM education is increasingly important for students and educators. As internationally known museum education leader Mariruth Leftwich writes in the *Journal of Museum Education,* "the importance of STEM education cannot be understated . . . and if history museums are to meet the needs of twenty-first-century education, it will be key to increase integration of STEM skills and concepts."[26] This is especially true of sports content. Museum educators can easily integrate the physics of sports, an athlete's health and nutrition requirements, the statistics documenting sporting success, and even engineering involved in sports equipment. In fact, most sports history-related museum programs and activities tend to relate to STEM. Given

STEM's importance in today's educational environment, sports content is a great asset to the museum field. Some examples of STEM in action include:

- **Science:** Science centers often use sports content to teach their audiences about the human body, nutrition, and the physics of sports. There are many examples of this, including the *Sportsology* exhibit at the Science Museum of Minnesota and the *Highmark SportsWorks* exhibit at the Carnegie Science Center in Pittsburgh. While these exhibits are usually well-funded and feature high-cost interactives and installations, museums with smaller budgets can easily replicate the main ideas of these exhibits. For instance, a museum that features basketball content may not be able to install full basketball courts, but they can build smaller-scale educational activities experimenting with reaction times, demonstrating ball trajectory, or exploring athlete nutrition.
- **Technology:** Museum professionals continue to debate the use of technology in museums, but technology is an excellent way to showcase the interplay between sports and STEM. Technology has led to a number of changes in sports, from replay cameras leading to more accurate refereeing, to developments in clothing allowing athletes to reach new levels of success. Students and visitors could explore these changes by looking at historic photographs or videos of sports to notice what technological developments they can see over time. An exhibit or object-handling collection to accompany the activity could provide examples of historic sports equipment and clothing for visitors to touch, combining an interactive continuity and lesson about change with information that shows how technology has impacted sports.
- **Engineering:** Innovation and design thinking play important roles in professional sports and are integral to connecting sports to STEM learning. Programs relating to engineering and design thinking can teach problem-solving skills and often connect to historical examples of innovation and invention in museums. The San Francisco 49ers Museum offers a wide-ranging program "where students engage in finding real solutions to real-world problems"—the hallmark of STEM education.[27] In one program, students explore how principles of design thinking are reflected in football, from the design of equipment to the stadium that contains the museum.
- **Math:** The Virginia Sports Hall of Fame and Museum school education activities include *Math Academy* programs, in which students apply math skills they have learned in the classroom to sports. In these programs, students investigate topics such as the role of fractions in basketball and the importance of angles in football. The programs are adapted for different age-groups and are offered primarily as outreach programs. An example of a non-sports museum comes from the *Hoop Curves* exhibit at the National Museum of Mathematics, where visitors are invited to shoot a basketball while the height, angle, and velocity are recorded.[28] After the computer analyzes the mathematics behind their shot and suggests ways to improve, visitors can use a robotic ball launcher to perfect their free-throw.

Museums can also combine sports history with systems thinking, a STEM concept whereby students learn how parts of the whole work together to produce outcomes in complex systems. Students can explore this STEM element by thinking about sports as a complex system with parts that include players, equipment, playing area, and rules or regulations. What happens when one of the rules, the area of play, or the equipment of a sport is removed or altered? How does the rest of the system change? What is the impact on the players and spectators? What if we add additional rules, equipment, or players? Another sports system to consider is business and economics. How would professional baseball change if a salary cap were implemented? What would happen if the NFL draft were conducted differently? The Institute of Play's Systems Thinking Design Pack provides advice on the use of systems thinking with students.[29] Educators can incorporate various skills such as collaboration, respectfully working in teams with diverse people, and practicing flexibility and adaptability. All these skills can be combined with sporting principles and implemented into sports museum education programs.

Apply Museum Education Best Practices to Sports Programs

As the field of museum education has grown and developed, the focus has shifted toward not only engaging audiences but also challenging them. While using any of these options, museum educators must remember museum director Brad King's admonition that "the essential museum learning experience is the change in our feelings, interests, attitudes, or appreciation of the subject matter due to the museum display."[30] To create that change for visitors, educators must make programs that focus on the learners and find ways to engage their many interests.

Focus on the Audience(s) and Give Them Space

Sports museums can successfully engage visitors with hands-on sports activities, multimedia displays, and facilitator-led learning experiences that include museum artifacts. Researchers such as Falk and Dierking have influenced exhibit designers and educators to include multiple learning modalities, interpretations, and experiences to better engage the multiple interests of their visitors. These activities allow learners to engage more directly with collections, an important part of object-based learning and a key goal of museum education.[31]

Sports museum designers and educators should also integrate Universal Design wherever possible by including "multisensory, multimodal experiences . . . [that] can help enhance the museum visit so that visitors of varied ages and abilities can fully participate in the experience and have fun doing so."[32] This more interactive and participatory style encourages all learners to feel welcome and valued in museums. At the Boston Children's Museum's *Kid Power* exhibit, staff did not include professional athletes or competitive sports because they understood that not all children feel that they can compete in sports. This decision ensured that children who visit *Kid Power* can leave feeling "that no matter who you are, there is a way for you to enjoy physical activity."[33] This can be difficult in sports museums that invite visitors to play sports and watch videos of sporting events. Instead of assuming a certain level of physical ability and knowledge and trying to convey more content, educators can think of key questions they would like learners to discuss or consider on their visit, such as a question about how sports can bring people together in a positive way.[34]

Educational programs should allow time for students to look around the gallery on their own and self-select information or displays with which to engage.[35] Blankenberg's *Learning for Change* framework highlights the importance of supporting intrinsic motivation in school children, and states that "finding ways to enable choice—the hallmark of museum learning—is key for school programming."[36] This does not just reflect on museum learning, it is also a hallmark of STEM education, where children are encouraged to experiment and investigate on their own and in their own way. A simple way to integrate this for school groups is to make space in a field trip visit for self-guided time or allow a short time within the program for students to look around an exhibit.

Go Beyond Statistics and Trivia, and Focus on the Lesser Known

Tour guides and educators often tend to rely on statistics and trivia to engage audiences. While this may engage some sports fans, those who often demonstrate their fandom by remembering statistics and trivia, it leads to low levels of engagement and can alienate visitors who do not connect with the finer details of sports. Museums have the potential to offer experiences that teach visitors to look beyond a simple recitation of facts. Facilitators can bring in multiple disciplines and approaches, including techniques such as interactive activities and open discussions, to better engage their audiences. Such is the case at the Smithsonian Institute's National Museum of African American History and Culture, whose curator Damion Thomas rarely presented sports statistics. Instead, he highlighted the role of sports in the African American fight for equality.[37] It is important for sports museum educators to remember that for most visitors, it is the stories about the people and places that resonate, not the finer details of specific sporting events.

If you are unsure which topics to address, consider conducting audience research. The Sports Legends Museum in Baltimore, Maryland hired an outside firm to determine the most impactful museum programming for their visitors. "In addition to the psychographic segmentation of current visitors, the audience research illuminated what visitors most valued about Sports Legends Museum."[38] With this core information, museum staff could steer their programming strategy toward topics and methods that evoked the most compelling values, such as "sportsmanship and the player's character."[39] Knowing and understanding your audience's interests can provide a clear direction for content that is engaging and educational for your particular audience.

Focusing on lesser-known sports figures can bring new knowledge to the general visitors as well as the sports fan. For example, Pittsburgh is a sports city where local teams draw the community together like little else can. The Western Pennsylvania Sports Museum could simply be a celebratory museum, where visitors come to revel in the glory of local sports triumph. However, it also celebrates lesser-known sports and athletes who may have simply organized a local softball team, but truly played an important role in community cohesion. In one school program, educators highlight the story of James Dorsey, whose work with building organizations for youth athletics in Pittsburgh's Hill District instigated positive change. Throughout his career, "Dorsey developed a unique perspective of using athletics not only to improve the personal health of people but to extend the benefits of full American citizenship at a time when African Americans had limited civil rights in Pittsburgh and elsewhere."[40] Relaying this lesson in a museum space may resonate with children who play sports that are organized by people like Dorsey, and his story can inspire students to more fully participate in their communities, even if that manifests by simply asking other neighborhood kids to play a game of basketball.

Lean into Difficult Topics

Celebrating sporting achievements has its place in sports exhibits, but museums should not shy away from stories that criticize or illuminate problems in the sporting community or greater society. As museums increase and adapt their community role, they need not avoid difficult conversations. To remain relevant, educational modalities must "accommodate the transformations in history and heritage that are taking place within society."[41] Sports museums can and should be places where past and present inequalities are discussed with students and adults alike. Students can learn important lessons about critical thinking, character development, and continuity. Adult visitors can have the opportunity to expand their understanding of a favorite sport, team, or player.

Holding discussions with visitors on difficult topics in sports begins with informing and equipping staff. Educators should be well-versed in the issues that most impact their local, regional, and national audiences. Some of these topics include inequality, athletes' safety, and the use of performance-enhancing drugs in competition. Educators should be trained in how to facilitate dialogues so visitors feel safe to share their voices, opinions, and viewpoints about these topics. Groups like the International Coalition of Sites of Conscience train staff in leading dialogues with visitors.[42] These conversations can lead to bonding and bridging among visitors and can bring new perspectives into the work of museum educators.

Conclusion

While museum educators specialize in creating opportunities for visitors to engage with museum collections and each other, it must be recognized that this work is not just for museum education departments. Museums are places of learning, and all interpretive staff are, in a sense, educators. By working closely with curators, exhibit designers, archivists, collection specialists, and museum educators can achieve greater success and better engagement with the museum's audiences. With such a great opportunity to apply museum education best practice, welcome new audiences, and explore many subjects through the lens of sports, any museum working with sports content is well placed to drive meaningful engagement with visitors.

Replicable Practices for Education in Sports Museums

- **Break a sport into its component parts**: Create an exhibit or activities that explore each part. What do baseball players have to think about when at bat? What types of bats do certain players choose to use and why? How is pitching affected by the weather? What strategy is involved for the catcher or the outfielders?

- **Host a day of vintage sporting**: Let visitors participate in a sport by playing under early rules and with early equipment. This can also be built into an annual flagship program with specified teams and visitors as spectators.
- **Create an immigration program for school students**: Use sports to explore historical and current immigration. What sports did people bring to this country from elsewhere? What sports did people come to love once they arrived in their new country? What is the value of continuing sports traditions for immigrant groups?
- **Create a family program around health:** Offer sports activities and healthy eating demonstrations to raise visitors' awareness of healthy living. Invite local athletes to attend and interact with their fans or ask student athletes to volunteer to demonstrate parts of their sports.
- **Host a sports history program for local student athletes and their families**: Couple this with the display of a newly acquired artifact or the opening of a new exhibit to build local interest.
- **Connect to STEM curricula through technology:** Create an exhibit that explores technological changes in sports equipment. Offer facilitated activities in the exhibit as a key element of a school field trip package.

CASE STUDY

Boston vs. Bullying: Prevention through Programming

Kathryn Leann Harris

In 2012, the Sports Museum in Boston created its anti-bullying program, Boston vs. Bullies. The program developed in response to a bullying incident involving the son of director Rusty Sullivan. When he asked his son what happened, the answer struck a nerve. Sullivan's son was a bewildered bystander. He had witnessed the incident but was unsure of how to respond. Sullivan sensed an opportunity to utilize the lens of sports and create a museum curriculum addressing the bullying epidemic. The result was a program that successfully carried an anti-bullying message built on contemporary research, delivered by high-profile area athletes, to local school systems. Boston vs. Bullies quickly rose in popularity with area schools, reaching more than 85,000 elementary and middle school students in its first seven years. The program has impacted and influenced a wide audience due to its relevance in promoting the health of the community, ease of access and use, and a solid foundation of empathetic communication.

Sullivan and his staff immediately recognized the overlap of sporting culture and the national childhood bullying epidemic. Sports survive on an atmosphere of competition that can, and often does, involve abuses of power among players, fans, referees, administrators, and team owners. Athletic organizations attempt to ameliorate the effects of this with codes of conduct, ethical standards, and fair-play rules. Yet, bullying persists and, through participating in sports and rooting for a particular team, often becomes a learned behavior for the impressionable minds of the youngest of fans. The bullying incident highlighted a more serious community need, one Sullivan and his staff felt confident in addressing.

Tackling bullying was ideal for The Sports Museum. New England sports fans tout Boston, their largest metropolis, as the "City of Champions" for its storied tradition of sporting success. To date, the city's sports teams have won more professional championships than any other city in the nation except New York. Of more recent vintage, the Bruins (hockey), Red Sox (baseball), Patriots (football), and Celtics (basketball) have earned twelve championships in the last eighteen years. Yet recently, the *Boston Globe* commented on the downside of these successes—the culture surrounding these triumphs can be somewhat brutal. Fans can be quite ruthless toward players, coaches, rivals, and each other. "There is a history," the *Globe* wrote, "written inside the sports arenas where Boston's hypercompetitive fans celebrate their heroes and vilify their losers, sometimes in intensely personal ways."[43] This attitude is reflected in daily life throughout the region, for which "winning" is a cultural ideal. A "win at all costs" environment is fertile ground for breeding a society in which bullying is acceptable behavior.

Together with bullying prevention consultant Kim Storey, The Sports Museum crafted a program that used sports-related phrases and language to educate children about bullying thinking and behavior. The curriculum encouraged the kids to consider a "3- Step Game Plan" for how they would handle a bullying incident and to create their own "Mantra," explaining that this is a strategy often used by athletes to remain calm and focused during a stressful time. The material communicated a healthy way to handle a strong or intense emotional situation: "be assertive, not submissive or aggressive." Both the teachers' and students' books were filled with sports

Figure 6.1.   Ed Donnelly faciliates a role-playing activity as part of the Sports Museum of New England's Boston vs. Bullies program. *Source:* **Sports Museum of New England.**

imagery including the famous athletes featured in the video, local mascots, and kids playing various sports. The soft content offered a relatable message and powerful counterbalance to conflicting messages that are sometimes part of sporting environments and experiences.[44]

Learning to effectively convey an anti-bullying message was vital to the program's success. Athletes impact children. Their uniforms carry tremendous cultural power and kids often view athletes as role models. Given the connection between bullying and the region's fan bases, the museum sought high-profile regional athletes to deliver the primary messages of Boston vs. Bullies. Nine highly recognizable New England professional athletes participated in the program: Mookie Betts of the Boston Red Sox, Martin Bowes of the Boston Cannons, Patrick Chung of the New England Patriots, Andrew Farrell from the New England Revolution, Torey Krug of the Boston Bruins, Kristie Mewis of the Boston Breakers, Olympic Gold Medalist Aly Raisman, Cydney Ross of the B.A.A High-Performance Track Team, and Terry Rozier of the Boston Celtics.[45] The museum banked on star power and it reaped them great dividends. Local children learned strategies to defuse bullying from the very source in which it is often bred and perpetuated: sports. It is a powerful antidote to the bullying epidemic.

Sullivan learned a lot from Storey about the bystander—namely that bystanders consistently embody a predictable and impactful role. Bullying is an abuse of power and the person being bullied has very little power in the situation. The bystander, however, is in the best position to see what the other two are not able to see and illuminate the bully's abuse of power. Far from being powerless, the bystander has the most power in a bullying situation. Boston vs. Bullies addressed this quite effectively, providing a newfound tool to empower bystanders, like Sullivan's son, to defuse a contentious situation when they witness one.[46]

Boston vs. Bullies offers an innovative and replicable approach that museums can use to address the national bullying epidemic—a very real and present issue that directly affects every child in a school. Program content addresses this very complex topic in a way that is digestible and non-alienating. While the topic is multifaceted, the activities are intentionally simple. Each lesson includes handouts with a few direct points, easy for students to grasp. Group exercises and games that allow kids to embody or visualize bullying incidents and ideal responses support these lessons. The professional athletes host video lessons, providing messages in a format that is both exciting and understandable for students. The Facilitator's Guide equips teachers with reflective questions for the groups to consider after each video clip.[47]

Storey's research also helped the Sports Museum craft a supplementary piece that proved invaluable. The most vulnerable members of society are often the most highly targeted for bullying. In the case of schools, students with disabilities are among a bully's most frequent victims (this is especially true for those are on the autism spectrum). In response, the museum drafted the facilitator's guide supplement, *Including Kids with Disabilities in Bullying Prevention*. The guide offers strategies for helping students reduce bullying against disabled students and ways teachers can adapt the activities to include those disabled students in the training.[48]

An empathetic approach to sports and museum education is no doubt what makes the program impactful. In fact, Sullivan has since come to realize that a more appropriate name for the program is Boston vs. *Bullying* instead of *Bullies*, since the issue is not as much about bullies as people as it is about bullying behavior. This stands as a demarcation of the museum's evolving and sensitive understanding of this material. Boston vs. Bullies explains how bullies—just like all children— grapple with their own emotional issues. Bullies are hurting as well, and the program teaches students the importance of not villainizing the bully. Storey and museum staff crafted language teaching students to better understand the emotionally painful plight of the bully, as well as to demonstrate how the person being bullied most benefits from learning to be assertive rather than fighting back or otherwise being submissive to the abuse. Children learn how to approach situations with empathy instead of words or actions that evoke blame, shame, or guilt. By focusing on behavior as the "problem" instead of the person, children become equipped with emotional tools to defuse abuse, support one another, and stop the perpetuation of a cyclical and societal behavioral pattern.

With direct access to the area's highest-profile professional sports figures, the museum capitalized on star power to appeal to the region's youngest and growing fans. Boston vs. Bullies addressed well the impact and effects of bullying. And research supports its success. A Boston University evaluation of the program stated it was generally helpful, made things better, and that students reported less bullying in their classroom after participating in Boston vs. Bullies. The report affirmed that the percentage of students who reported peer victimization decreased significantly and that the adults in the school were more responsive to bullying reports from pre- to post-test.[49]

Most schools continue teaching the program well after the initial visit from the Sports Museum facilitator. This is especially true for schools that subscribe to the museum's direct delivery service (where a museum staff member goes directly to the school to provide program facilitation to the teachers). Education Director Michelle Gormley presumes an unknown percentage of schools offer the program entirely on their own without ever communicating with the museum again.[50] Funding allows the Sports Museum to offer all of the materials and services at no charge and provide links to each of the resources on their website also at no charge, making it easy to access and use.[51] Thus, the museum has created an important program with documented impact, a replicable program that schools can repeat annually with or without the aid of museum staff, and one that uses the museum's sports-related mission to have a documented impact on an issue that impacts both sports and people's everyday lives.

Thus, Sullivan's passion project has become an exemplar of interpreting sports in impactful ways. To date, more than 85,000 children have completed the curriculum. The societal import of the program's message and the very personal impact that the area's children experience has inspired close to $1.5 million in grant funding as well as a robust individual and corporate donation program.[52] Boston vs. Bullies has grown into the Sports Museum's showcase program. "It is easy to turn your back on an artifact. It is harder to turn your back on a kid," Sullivan noted.[53] This is the message that inspires both the community and the children who, through Boston vs Bullies, are learning to embody what it means to stand up for one another.

CASE STUDY

Innoskate: Museum Education Meets Sports & Invention

Jeffery L. Brodie

The Smithsonian's Lemelson Center for the Study of Invention and Innovation was established at the National Museum of American History in 1995 to engage, educate, and empower the public to participate in a world driven by technological, economic, and social change. Through scholarship and exhibitions, the Spark! Lab hands-on invention workshop, and major public programs and festivals, the Center documents, analyzes, and shares insights on inventors and their work, uses the lens of history to develop new perspectives on innovation, and inspires the next generation of creative and inventive thinkers. The Lemelson Center prides itself on embodying the innovative culture it studies, embracing unexpected topics for exploration, and seeking innovative ways to share new ideas with the public through collaborative enterprises. Therefore, when asked by a Smithsonian colleague if the Lemelson Center had ever considered exploring invention through the history of skateboarding, I answered, "No, but maybe we should." The result was a groundbreaking education program, *Innoskate*—a joint collaboration between leaders of the skate community and the Smithsonian that attracted new audiences to local museums around the country to explore connections between history, technology, invention, and culture through the unexpected launching point of skateboarding.

The Lemelson Center believed wholeheartedly that exploring the intersection of skateboarding and invention presented an exciting pathway to engage new audiences in Science, Technology, Engineering, Arts, Mathematics (STEAM) content and challenge traditional stereotypes of inventors: who they are, what they look like, and where invention takes place. Accomplishing these goals required a new and innovative form of public programming—something as dynamic as skateboarding itself. Working closely with leaders from the skateboarding community, ideas quickly coalesced around the creation of a large festival that would spark the imaginations of young people through demonstrations and discussions with legendary skaters and inventors, hands-on invention and STEAM-related activities, community-based art projects, learn-to-skate clinics, acquisition of skate objects for the national collections, and of course, a best-trick contest.

The inaugural *Innoskate* festival took place on June 21–22, 2013 at the Smithsonian's National Museum of American History in Washington, D.C. With the Washington Monument serving as a dramatic backdrop, *Innoskate* brought the skate community together with the larger, broader public in celebration of skate boarding's history and inventive culture. Skateboard designer and inventor Paul Schmitt explored the history of the skateboard from the 1950s to the present and demonstrated the importance of new designs and technologies such as polyurethane wheels, the kicktail, and grip tape to enable skaters to push the boundaries of their sport. He did this by challenging professional skateboarders Chris Haslam and Kyle Berard to attempt modern tricks on older, wider, and heavier boards from earlier eras that were flat (no nose or tail) with outmoded technologies such as clay wheels. Despite their skill, the professional skateboarders experienced "epic fails" when attempting to land modern tricks using these boards. Designers Cindy Whitehead and Shawn Carboy and professional skater Brian Anderson discussed the influence that skate clothing and footwear innovations had on mainstream fashion and culture. Champion skaters Tony Hawk and Rodney Mullen provided insight into their own creative processes for inventing new tricks to break through existing boundaries. Hawk and Mullen observed that risk-taking and resilience in the face of failure were the key factors that enabled them, respectively, to be the first to land a 900-degree spin on a vert ramp and invent almost every trick, including the Flatground Ollie, that now defines street skating throughout the world. A concluding panel explored the history of skateboarding and provided thoughts on innovations that would take skate culture into the future. Additional films, the display of skate objects and archival materials, and hands-on invention activities added depth and texture to the program.

The success of the initial *Innoskate* event inspired the Lemelson Center and the skate community to expand the program and bring the model to local communities across the country. This included new *Innoskate* festivals at the Polk Museum of Art in Lakeland, Florida (2014), the Museum of History and Industry in Seattle, Washington (2014), ESPN's X Games in Austin, Texas (2015), the Children's Museum of the Upstate in Greenville, South Carolina (2015), and the Massachusetts Institute of Technology (MIT) in Cambridge, Massachusetts with the Lemelson-MIT Program (2016). In 2019, the Lemelson Center created the first international *Innoskate* festival with Here East and the University College London's Bartlett School of Architecture in London, England (2019). While each *Innoskate* event is similar in

Figure 6.2.   Professional skater Chris Haslam attempts to perform modern tricks on a 1970s-era skateboard at Innoskate 2013 at the Smithsonian's National Museum of American History. *Source*: **Photo courtesy of Lemelson Center, National Museum of American History, Tyrone Clemons.**

form, structure, content, themes, and activities, the individual festivals reflect the interests of the host museum and its local skateboarding community.

Innoskate: An Educational Model

As an educational model for public engagement, *Innoskate's* most innovative feature is the strong collaboration—the genuine sharing of authority and decision-making—among the Lemelson Center, leaders of the skate community, and the local host museum or institution to create each *Innoskate* festival. Together, we form cohesive project teams that share collective responsibility for developing all aspects of the *Innoskate* programs at all venues, including participant selection, panel discussion themes, public relations, marketing, event schedules, budgets, and fundraising. Collectively, the teams ensure that *Innoskate* presents the interplay between history, invention, and skateboarding culture in an authentic way that skateboarders respect and that help them feel welcomed at the museum. Throughout, the collaborative remains open to learning from each other and appreciating each other's strengths and experiences. As Josh Friedberg, *Innoskate* codirector and CEO of USA Skateboarding, observed:

> on paper, Ph.D. historians and skateboarders do not seem like the exact right mix, but what we found is that with genuine mutual interest and respect for the abilities from both sides of the fence, that it became one of the most fun collaborations that we've worked on. If you believe that the person or group you're partnering with has your best interests in mind and you have their best interests in mind, you can overcome any of those challenges.[54]

In the end, the teams faced and resolved the challenges, disagreements, questions, and discussions that arose from working with disparate groups.

This mutual respect and cooperation underpin every aspect of the *Innoskate* program and provides the essential foundation for achieving three major *Innoskate* goals. First, *Innoskate* encourages new and diverse audiences to join with the broader public to appreciate their own inherent capacity for inventive thinking. Second, *Innoskate* demonstrates the power of using unconventional topics (like sports and skateboarding) as an interdisciplinary focal point to connect disparate subject matter such as history, invention, and innovation, with art, creativity, and culture. And finally, *Innoskate* transforms ordinary spaces into dynamic centers for sharing knowledge and exchanging ideas among diverse groups of people.

In contrast to common misperceptions and stereotypes, *Innoskate* embraces skateboarding as a vibrant part of the American historical landscape and highlights skateboarders as creative inventors and innovators who make substantial contributions to society. This was critical to attract both the skate community to the museum and to open a dialogue between skateboarders and the broader public. As Friedberg noted, "Looking at skateboarding from the invention and innovation angle immediately eliminated the common mainstream cultural misconceptions of skateboarding being an activity only for kids, misfits, or outcasts." Once this veneer was removed, Friedberg stated, "It was thrilling to be able to share what drives skateboarders with a broader public that was intellectually curious about the value skateboarding brings to its participants and the world as a whole."[55] The Smithsonian's commitment to breaking through stereotypes and focusing on the authentic aspects of skate culture built mutual trust and respect that was foundational to the success of the program. Once mutual trust was established the team could focus efforts on how to best share skateboarding history and culture with wider audiences.

Skaters themselves expressed their appreciation for the ways the museum welcomed them with open arms. Skateboarding legend Tony Hawk remarked how skateboarding "has come a long way in terms of legitimacy" and skating in front of the National Museum of American History "validates a lot of effort and a lot of struggles."[56] The significance was not lost on skateboard icon Cindy Whitehead who first thought her invitation to present at the Smithsonian "was a joke" but acknowledged the offer was "the biggest thing that could happen to skateboarding."[57] Perhaps most succinct is the unknown skater who proclaimed with a mixed sense of surprise and appreciation, "DUDE . . . I . . . am . . . in . . . a museum!"[58]

Innoskate also facilitates a dialogue and interactions between more "traditional" museum visitors and the skateboarding community. For Polk Museum of Art director Claire Orologas, the event "provided an environment in which everyone felt welcome and validated by their museum and by their city [attracting a] new and extremely diverse community together—diverse in every way."[59] In Greenville, South Carolina, skateboarding is heavily restricted in public places, and skateboarders are generally regarded with trepidation. But as Nancy Halverson, (former) executive director of The Children's Museum of the Upstate observed, *Innoskate*, "not only brought new audiences into the museum, but created a dialogue between the skateboarders and community leaders about the incredibly constructive aspects of skate culture and how we might better integrate skating in our city."[60] *Innoskate* programs validate local museums as centers of civic discourse and as places that bring disparate parts of the community together in dialogue and shared exploration.

Innoskate also reveals the power of using an unexpected topic, such as skateboarding and culture, to connect diverse subject matter and avenues of inquiry. The constant desire to perform bigger and better tricks continually stimulates new designs and technological advancements in the skating community. Thus, each *Innoskate* program includes a session that explored the relationship between skateboard inventors and the skaters who use that technology. From that launching point, additional discussions between skaters, inventors, engineers, scientists, artists, musicians, and community leaders reveal the creative commonalities among seemingly unrelated disciplines. In Cambridge, conversations between MIT cognitive scientists and skaters explained how the brain learns new skate tricks and how it uses these blocks of information to make innovative leaps. In Seattle, Native American artists talked with skateboarders to explore intersections of creativity and expressions of personal identity. During the Lakeland event, *Innoskate* participants learned how Florida skate pioneers shaped the larger history of skateboarding worldwide. Later, skaters and artists joined together in conversation to explore the common traits of their shared creative processes. In Greenville, community leaders and skaters from Afghanistan and Cuba discussed skateboarding as an international incubator for innovation and explained how smaller American communities like Greenville are connected to the global society. As a whole, the participants remained enthralled with the *Innsokate* panel discussions because they provided the skate audience with an accessible starting point, a love and passion for skateboarding, from which they could become engaged in a wide array of STEAM subjects.

Finally, *Innsokate* illustrates the power and potential for engaging audiences by transforming ordinary spaces into dynamic places of shared learning. Though some *Innoskate* elements take place inside the museums, intentionally, most of the program—skating, panel sessions, demonstrations, art, and DIY projects—are located outside the building on the museum grounds or at a local skate park. Instead of a traditional stage or podium, the skate ramp or skate park becomes the central meeting point for idea sharing thereby shifting the locus of cultural authority and knowledge. More importantly, *Innoskate* features skaters as subject matter experts and as equals with historians, scientists, engineers, and artists, who all share their specific areas of knowledge. *Innoskate* offers an educational programming model for engaging marginalized audiences. Through this model, cultural authority is relocated from the classroom or lecture hall to the field, court, or skatepark where participants learn directly from the leaders of their own community.

Despite its successes, *Innoskate* battles two interrelated challenges common to many informal learning initiatives: sustaining audience interest and funding. Museums, including the Smithsonian, found it difficult to sustain long-term audience engagement with the skate community after the initial festival. In particular, *Innoskate's* digital presence, which museums often utilized to keep visitors engaged with new content following a major event, was quite limited. As a result, staff struggled to build sustained national awareness of the program and its educational messages. Consistently, the project team also encountered a significant hurdle when attempting to secure funding to elevate *Innoskate* into a truly national outreach initiative. While *Innoskate* events attract large, new audiences to the host museums, the festivals are complex undertakings that require a significant investment of staff and financial resources to plan and execute. *Innoskate* was fortunate (and grateful) to secure funding for each individual event from corporations such as Nike and Vans. However, skateboarding is a very competitive marketplace, and many skate companies are reluctant to join to provide the larger funding necessary for implementing a national *Innoskate* education program that could be shared throughout the country. In part, support for cultural or educational events (as opposed to athletic contests) was a fairly new concept to major companies in the skate industry and thus, not part of their traditional business and marketing models. Further experience and education are required to demonstrate the marketing value for supporting *Innoskate*.

The Smithsonian is currently positioned to extend the reach of *Innoskate* to a global, Olympic stage. In 2020, skateboarding made its debut as an Olympic sport in Tokyo. For the International Olympic Committee, the inclusion of skateboarding reflects a growing recognition that they must find innovative ways to attract new audiences to the Games. For skateboarding, this presents an unprecedented opportunity to repeatedly introduce their sport to a worldwide television audience upwards of five billion viewers—most of whom are completely unfamiliar with skateboarding and skate culture. Many in the skateboard community are apprehensive about the potential impact of the Olympic Games on traditional skate culture. Will skateboarding become too mainstream or exploited for its commercial value? Will new audiences truly understand the deeper cultural elements of skateboarding that make it distinct and special, or will they view skateboarding "only" as a sport? Skateboarding's entrance to the Olympic Games overlaps with the International Olympic Committee's new commitment to educate the public about the culture and history of sports at the Games as a critical complement to the athletic competitions.

Innoskate has proven to be a revolutionary, inventive, and innovative museum education endeavor. Powerfully inclusive and notably replicable, the exhibit offers a deeply impactful experience that reaches a broad audience. By giving the skate community a large voice in what the programs features and who presents information at the events, the *Innoskate* team achieves a level of authenticity and respect that attracts new audiences and makes them feel welcome at the museum. Success is based on mutual trust between the Smithsonian's Lemelson Center and the skate community and the willingness to engage openly and fearlessly with one another during the planning process. The planning group must always be focused on two interrelated outcomes: to present the history and culture of skateboarding to the public in an authentic manner and to ensure that the broader public sees the connections between skateboarding—its creativity, its innovation, its musical and artistic spirit, its technology—as an integral part of everyday life. Undoubtedly, there will be obstacles, challenges, missteps, and failures along the way. But, as all skaters and all inventors appreciate, resilience and the ability to get up after you have fallen are part of the process and critical to ultimate success.

CASE STUDY

Know Thy Sports Fan: Lessons from Audience Research

Amanda Krantz and Dean Krimmel

In May 2005, Sports Legends Museum at Camden Yards opened in the historic Camden Station, immediately adjacent to the Oriole Park at Camden Yards in Baltimore, Maryland. The (now-closed) museum, an expansion of the Babe Ruth Birthplace Museum, celebrated Maryland sports with an emphasis on Baltimore's professional teams. Sports Legends included galleries devoted to the Baltimore Orioles (Major League Baseball), Baltimore Colts and Ravens (National Football League), Blast (indoor soccer), Black Sox and Elite Giants (Negro League baseball), Maryland's Olympians, state sports hall of fame members, university athletes, and the Preakness. The museum opened to much fanfare but failed to reach attendance goals in its first two years of operation. Management needed to address this problem quickly so the newly established museum would be a financially stable, impactful organization. Thus, in 2008, under a consulting project coordinator, the museum conducted audience research to address questions about

Figure 6.3.   Sports Legends Museum at Camden Yards, Baltimore, occupied the former Baltimore & Ohio Railroad's Camden Station from 2005 to 2015. *Source*: Photography by Dean Krimmel, 2009.

visitors and non-visitors.[61] The research process revealed useful information that informed museum education recommendations, a practice that any sports museum or museum looking to include a sports exhibit can implement.

Audience Research Design and Results

Audience research at museums provides an invaluable resource for improving the visitor experience. Without visitors, museums and historic sites would cease to exist. Thus, to sustain history-related institutions, we must improve our understanding of visitors by understanding who they are, why they come, and what they value. A myriad of methods can uncover answers to these questions from those who attend, and those who do not attend, a certain museum or exhibition. Audience research projects can be as daunting as they are revealing and must be focused to be successful.

The research teams used a two-pronged approach for the Sports Legends Museum: conducting focus groups with local Baltimore residents and surveying walk-in visitors. Two research firms, Maroon PR and Randi Korn & Associates (RK&A) each worked with one side of the research focus. MaroonPR, a local communications and branding firm, conducted four focus groups with Baltimore residents to better understand perceptions of the museum, the museum decision process, visitor satisfaction, and barriers to visitation.[62] People who had visited the museum previously comprised two of the groups. The other two groups included those who had not visited. The firm revealed that the Sports Legends Museum brand was "fuzzy." Many people in both groups were unsure of what to expect from their visit. Baltimore-area residents also perceived issues with parking (both its cost and availability) and admission cost as the major barrier to visitation, particularly among younger locals. RK&A sought to understand the walk-in visitor perspective.[63] RK&A administered standardized surveys onsite to 319 adult visitors exiting the museum as well as conducted thirty-four in-depth exit interviews with individuals and multi-generational groups about their experiences at the museum. The research showed that adult, walk-in visitors to the museum were predominantly men visiting from outside the state of Maryland with a median age of forty years old.

The research produced results that both validated and surprised staff's presumptions about their visiting base. In some ways, the research confirmed the museum's assumptions about the homogeneity of the audience, particularly the middle-aged male demographic. However, the research also found that the type of sports fan that came to the museum varied. For instance, while the museum assumed they largely attract emotional, die-hard sports fans, there was much more nuance in visitors than expected. A statistical procedure identified visitor segments based on the way they rated several sports statements.[64] Just over 50 percent fell into one of two highly engaged sports audiences: active enthusiasts and TV enthusiasts (figure 1: dark-colored portions of the pie chart). Both groups said sports bring great meaning to their lives. Researchers categorized Active Enthusiasts by their preference to go to sporting events versus watching them on TV and playing sports. TV enthusiasts, on the other hand, preferred to watch their team(s) on television and were less likely to actively participate in sports. By contrast, nearly 50 percent of the polled audience cited a relatively low engagement with sports (figure 1: light-colored portions of the pie chart). Visitors in this third segment, middle-road fans, were more likely to pay attention to sports, but were not as die-hard fans as the Active and/or TV enthusiasts.[65] A small contingency of visitors fell into a category called indifferent companions. This category reflected those who visited the Sports Legends Museum because a companion wanted to; they themselves do not have an affinity for sports.

In addition to the psychographic segmentation of current visitors, the audience research illuminated what visitors most valued about Sports Legends Museum. Most notably, the exhibits evoke a feeling of pride as a sports fan—regardless of whether the visitors were fans of the specific teams represented.[66] This was due in part to exhibited stories of sportsmanship and players' character. Frequently referenced in interviews were Babe Ruth's work with children and Baltimore Orioles' shortstop Cal Ripken Jr.'s. 2,131 consecutive game streak exemplifying his dedication to baseball. In addition to stories of sportsmanship, objects were also a catalyst for nostalgic feelings, which led visitors to share stories and recollections within their visiting group. These results indicated that Sports Legend Museum created powerful displays with which all types of visitors could connect.[67]

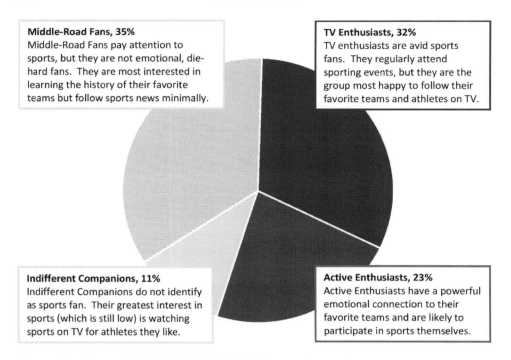

Middle-Road Fans, 35%
Middle-Road Fans pay attention to sports, but they are not emotional, die-hard fans. They are most interested in learning the history of their favorite teams but follow sports news minimally.

TV Enthusiasts, 32%
TV enthusiasts are avid sports fans. They regularly attend sporting events, but they are the group most happy to follow their favorite teams and athletes on TV.

Indifferent Companions, 11%
Indifferent Companions do not identify as sports fan. Their greatest interest in sports (which is still low) is watching sports on TV for athletes they like.

Active Enthusiasts, 23%
Active Enthusiasts have a powerful emotional connection to their favorite teams and are likely to participate in sports themselves.

Figure 6.4. Figure 1. SPORTS LEGENDS WALK-IN VISITOR AUDIENCE SEGMENTATION
Source: **Amanda Krantz.**

Audience Research Implications

After reviewing the audience research results, we, the two authors of this essay, drafted and presented methodological recommendations to the Sports Legends Museum. We took each major point of the research data and assigned to it an applicable museum education and/or marketing methods. Our goal was to help Sports Legends Museum connect to its target audience in a meaningful way that increased traffic to the museum and discussion in the exhibit space. The models listed below are a few examples from our recommended findings. These concepts can help other sports museums or institutions considering sports-related exhibitions or programs.

- **Boy's Night Out**: Embrace the museum's core audience, men over forty years old, by offering a "Boys' Night Out" experience. Forge partnerships with sports bars and cohost special event happy hours, trivia nights, and contests. Research other activities "the boys" do together when they go out that connect to camaraderie, competition, and fun.
- **Home Away from Home***:* Make the Sports Legends Museum feel like a welcoming "home away from home" to appeal to tourists who comprise 90 percent of museum attendance and only visit one time. Focus on hospitality and frontline training to become known as a museum that embraces traveling fans. Leverage the strong seasonal draw by creating flexible admission prices and seasonal passes as

well as working with out-of-town tour companies. Build a "word of mouth" reputation and turn visitors into ambassadors for the institution.

- **Share Your Stories***:* Create opportunities for visitors to share their stories, memories, and sports knowledge to evoke strong emotions and capitalize on the pride many visitors feel as sports fans. Deepen the museum experience by inviting interaction among visitors—facilitated, but not controlled, by museum staff—reminding them that you do not need to be a fanatic to love the Sports Legends Museum or enjoy sports-history content at a museum.
- **Friendliest Museum in Town***:* Devote considerable resources to customer service training and rewards because visitors deeply appreciate the museum's floor staff and face-to-face interaction. Give frontline volunteers and paid staff more authority and responsibility, helping them build a reputation as the friendliest, most responsive staff in town.
- **Go Social***:* Focus marketing and advertising efforts on aggressive, social-media-driven communications that attract younger residents who are event, promotion, and discount driven and often make spur-of-the-moment plans. Make the Sports Legends Museum programming nimble, flexible, and experimental, refining what works and dropping what does not work.

Conclusion

Sports museums and museums with sporting collections can develop their own audience research or evaluation program and should do so thoughtfully. Begin research with the end in mind. Figure out what you want to know and how you will use the information. A focused plan developed from the beginning will prevent a process of drowning in findings. Focus the research on a desired outcome or improvement, not on the many obstacles that stand in the way. Research is most effective when it becomes a mindset, not a luxury. The process of conducting and analyzing research injects critical thinking and purpose-driven planning into every part of your organization.

After conducting research, it is important for museum staff to talk about the most crucial findings and which findings should be addressed. Act quickly on one of your findings. Small successes build confidence and quiet naysayers. It also helps your organization work toward the mindset that comes from research and evaluation. History and museum professionals can use the research process and findings to create sports educational programming that is compelling, capitalizes on the particular interest of the institution's visitors, and works to attract new visitors, even non-sports fans or lesser-reached demographics in certain cases.[68]

Acknowledgments

The Sports Legends Museum at Camden Yards audience research project was funded by a Museum Enhancement Challenge Grant from the Maryland Historical Trust's Museum Assistance Programs.

NOTES

1. Justine Reilly, "Sport, Museums and Cultural Policy, Volume 1 of 2," (PhD diss., University of Central Lancashire, 2014), 60, http://clok.uclan.ac.uk/11324/1/Reilly%20 Final%20e- Thesis%20%28Master%20Copy%29%20Vol%201.pdf.

2. Ceylan Sen, Zeynep Sonay Ay, and Seyit Ahmet Kiray, *Research Highlights in STEM Education Stem Skills in the 21st Century Education*, ISRES Publishing, 2018, https://www .researchgate.net/profile/Ceylan-Sen-2/publication/332574347_STEM_SKILLS_in_the_21 _ST_CENTURY_EDUCATION/links/5cbef5844585156cd7ab8a4d/STEM-SKILLS-in-the -21-ST-CENTURY-EDUCATION.pdf.

3. Murray G. Phillips, ed., *Representing the Sporting Past in Museums and Halls of Fame* (New York: Routledge, 2013), 10.

4. John H. Falk and Lynn D. Dierking, *The Museum Experience Revisited* (Walnut Creek, CA: Left Coast Press, 2013), 300.

5. Wray Vamplew, "Facts and Artifacts: Sports Historians and Sports Museums," *Journal of Sport History* 25, no. 2 (1998): 270.

6. Vamplew, "Facts and Artifacts," 279.

7. Ngaire Blankenberg, "Learning for Change," in *The Manual of Museum Learning*, ed. Brad King and Barry Lord (Lanham, MD: Rowman & Littlefield, 2016).

8. John H. Falk and Lynn D. Dierking, *Learning from Museums*, 2nd ed. (Lanham, MD: Rowman & Littlefield, 2018), 175.

9. Kathryn Leann Harris, "Boston vs. Bullying: Prevention through Programming," in *Interpreting Sports at Museums and Historic Sites*, Kathryn Leann Harris and Douglas Stark, eds. (Lanham, MD: Rowman & Littlefield, 2023), 194–198.

10. "La Vida Baseball," La Vida Baseball, accessed April 16, 2019, https://www .lavidabaseball.com/.

11. Kathryn Leann Harris, "Challenging Branded Appropriation by Uncovering Native Mascot Origins," in *Interpreting Sports at Museums and Historic Sites*, Harris and Stark, eds., 137–143.

12. Reilly, "Sport, Museums and Cultural Policy," 241.

13. Jeffery L. Brodie, "Innoskate: Museum Education Meets Sports & Invention," in *Interpreting Sports at Museums and Historic Sites*, Harris and Stark, eds., 198–203.

14. Jennifer Shepherd, "Planning for Informal Learning: Understanding and Simplifying the Interpretive Process," in *The Manual of Museum Learning*, eds. Brad King and Barry Lord (Lanham, MD: Rowman & Littlefield, 2016), 19.

15. American Alliance of Museums, "Museums On Call: How Museums are Addressing Health Issues" (2013), https://www.aam-us.org/wp-content/uploads/2018/01 /museums-on-call.pdf.

16. Brooke DiGiovanni Evans, Heather Serrill Johnson, and Carole Krucoff, "Health and Wellness in Our Communities: The Impact of Museums," *Journal of Museum Education* 41, no. 2 (2016): 77–81.

17. Dan McGowan, " Sports Legends Experience to Debut," *Inside Indiana Business*, March 15, 2018, http://www.insideindianabusiness.com/story/37736686 /sports-legends-experience-to-debut.

18. "EatSleepPlay: A CMOM Health Initiative," Children's Museum of Manhattan, accessed April 12, 2019, http://cmom.org/outreach/health-outreach/.

19. K. Ann Renninger and Suzanne Hidi's 2017 book, *The Power of Interest for Motivation and Engagement*, deeply explores the benefits of interest-driven learning.

20. Blankenberg, "Learning for Change," 35.

21. Andrea Sachdeva, "Cultural Exhibition: A Museum Model for Cultural Works-in-Progress," in *Manual of Museum Learning,* ed. Brad King and Barry Lord (Lanham, Maryland: Rowman & Littlefield, 2016), 209.

22. Marc Tracy, "African-American Museum Wins New Fans: Athletes," *The New York Times,* May 24, 2017, https://www.nytimes.com/2017/05/24/sports/national-museum-african -american-history-culture-nba-athletes.html.

23. Sachdeva, "Cultural Exhibition," 209.

24. "Who Shot Sports Visit Guide," The Olympic Museum, accessed April 12, 2019, https://stillmed.olympic.org/media/Document%20Library/Museum/Visit/TOM-Schools /Teaching- Resources/2017/Who-Shot-Sports/Who-Shot-Sports-Visit-Guide-EN.pdf.

25. Luke Rodesiler, "Sports-based Text Sets: Fostering Critical Literacy at the Intersections of Sport and Society," *The Clearing House: A Journal of Educational Strategies, Issues and Ideas* 90, no. 2: 35–40, https://doi.org/10.1080/00098655.2016.1255514.

26. Mariruth Leftwich, "New Intersections for History," *Journal of Museum Education* 41, no. 3 (2016): 149.

27. "Grades K-8 Standards-Aligned Education Programs: Creating Moments of Inspiration," The 49ers Museum, accessed April 12, 2019, http://www.levisstadium.com/wp-content /uploads/2017/05/17MUS_ED- PROGRAM_GUIDE-2.pdf.

28. Helene Stapinski, "Don't Foul the Robot (It Doesn't Miss Free Throws)," *The New York Times,* May 18, 2017, https://www.nytimes.com/2017/05/18/nyregion/free-throw-shooting-robot.html.

29. "Design Pack: Systems Thinking," The Institute of Play, accessed April 12, 2019, https://cdn-educators.brainpop.com/wp-content/uploads/2014/07/IOP_QDesignPack _SystemsThinking_1.0.pdf.

30. Brad King and Barry Lord, ed., *Manual of Museum Learning* (Lanham, MD: Rowman & Littlefield, 2015), 4.

31. Sascha Priewe, "Use of Collections in Museum Learning," in *Manual of Museum Learning,* ed. Brad King and Barry Lord (Lanham, MD: Rowman & Littlefield, 2016), 194.

32. Falk and Dierking, *The Museum Experience Revisited,* 129.

33. Emily Kuross, "Kid Power," in *Healthy Kids, Healthy Museums,* ed. Mary Maher (Arlington, VA: Association of Children's Museums, 2010), 3, accessed April 12, 2019, http:// childrensmuseums.org/images/Library/HealthyKids- HealthyMuseums.pdf; Katie Stringer's article "Access for Museum Learning," in *The Manual of Museum Learning* (181-188) provides a succinct description of Universal Design and a short list of best practices for museums to follow regarding access.

34. Sachdeva, "Cultural Exhibition," 208.

35. Falk and Dierking write extensively on this in *Learning from Museums.*

36. Blankenberg, "Learning for Change," 34.

37. Tracy, "African-American Museum."

38. Amanda Krantz and Dean Kimmel, "Know Thy Sports Fan: Lessons from Audience Research at Sports Legends Museum," in *Interpreting Sports at Museums and Historic Sites,* Harris and Stark, eds., 205, 203–208.

39. Krantz and Kimmel, "Know Thy," 206.

40. Samuel Black, "James A. Dorsey and the Support of Black Sport in Pittsburgh," *Western Pennsylvania Sports History* 87, no. 4 (Winter 2004): 45.

41. Leftwich, "New Intersections for History," 150.

42. The National Museum of the American Indian's online resource, "Americans: A Dialogue Toolkit for Educators," is based on methodology used by International Coalition of Sites of Conscience members, and elements of the resource could be adapted to suit sports

content. See https://americanindian.si.edu/sites/1/les/pdf/education/NMAI-Americans-dialogue
-toolkit.pdf.

43. Spotlight Team, "A Bigot in the Stands and Other Stories," *Boston Globe*, December
14, 2017.

44. Michelle Gormley and Kim Storey, *Boston vs Bullies Facilitator's Guide*, 2nd ed. (Boston: The Sports Museum, 2016).

45. At the time of publication, these players were no longer with their respective teams: Martin Bowes of the Boston Cannons, Mookie Betts of the Boston Red Sox, Cydney Ross of the B.A.A High-Performance Track Team, and Terry Rozier of the Boston Celtics.

46. Kim Storey Education Designs website, accessed September 10, 2020, http://kimstorey.com.

47. Gormley and Storey, *Boston vs Bullies Facilitator's Guide*; Michelle Gormley and Kim Storey, *Boston vs Bullies Choose Your Play: Video Modeling Guide* (Boston: The Sports Museum, 2016).

48. Michelle Gormley and Kim Storey, *Boston vs Bullies Facilitator's Guide Supplement: Including Kids with Disabilities in Bullying Prevention*, 2nd ed. (Boston: The Sports Museum, 2016).

49. Jennifer Greif Green, Melissa Holt, Rachel Oblath, and Ellery Robinson, *Boston vs Bullies Evaluation Report* (Boston: Boston University, June 2018).

50. Supporting information throughout from interviews by the author with The Sport Museum Director Rusty Sullivan and Education Director Michelle Gormley, October 2019.

51. The Sports Museum Boston vs. Bullies website accessed September 10, 2020, https://sportsmuseum.org/program/boston-vs-bullies/.

52. Interviews by the author with The Sport Museum Director Rusty Sullivan and Education Director Michelle Gormley, October 2019.

53. Interviews by the author with The Sport Museum Director Rusty Sullivan and Education Director Michelle Gormley, October 2019.

54. Jeffery L. Brodie, "Dude! I'm in a Museum!," text presentation, American Alliance of Museums National Meeting, Seattle, WA, May 19, 2014, https://invention.si.edu/node/13224/p/477-other-innoskate-programs.

55. Joshua Friedberg, interview with author, Washington, D.C., May 18, 2017.

56. "*Skate History on Display at the Smithsonian*," ESPN Video, June 24, 2013, https://invention.si.edu/node/13224/p/469-2013- washington-dc.

57. "*Skate History on Display.*"

58. Exclamation of unidentified skateboarder at Innoskate 2013 overheard by author, National Museum of American History, June 21, 2013.

59. Claire Orologas. Interview by author, digital recording, Lakeland, Florida, June 21, 2014.

60. Nancy Halverson. Interview by author, digital recording, Washington, D.C., June 21, 2019.

61. Because of issues related to leasing Camden Station from the Maryland Stadium Authority (rather than attendance), Sports Legends Museum at Camden Yards closed in 2015. The collections were returned to the Babe Ruth Birthplace Museum, and the organization began seeking a new location. As such, the museum staff was unable to implement changes based on the audience research findings.

62. Maroon PR and FieldVision, "Sports Legends Museum Focus Group Report," unpublished manuscript, 2008.

63. Randi Korn & Associates, "Audience Research: Sports Legends Museum at the Camden Yards Visitor Survey 2008," unpublished manuscript, 2008.

64. Visitors were asked to rate ten statements on a scale from 1, "Does not describe me," to 7, "Describes me very well." Statements include, "I regularly participate in sports," "I regularly attend sporting events," "I watch sports to see the athletes I like," and "When my team is losing, I usually feel bad."

65. While a direct correlation cannot be made, these people matched the concept of "fair-weather fans," those who only pay attention to a team or sports when things are going well.

66. Of the visitors who responded to the survey, 75 percent lived outside Maryland, 20 percent lived in Maryland, and 5 percent lived outside the United States. Visitors from outside the state were more likely to be attending an Orioles game on the day of their visit to the museum than those visitors who reside in state.

67. Furthermore, these results are encouraging for all sports museums and hall of fames as it suggests that, if compelling stories are told and objects selected, the museum can be relatable to visitors regardless of the visitors' specific allegiance (or lack of allegiance) to team, sport, or athlete.

68. For further exploration explore these sources: Maroon PR and FieldVision. "Sports Legends Museum Focus Group Report." Unpublished manuscript. Baltimore, MD, The Sports Legends Museum at Camden Yards, 2008; Randi Korn & Associates. "Audience Research: Sports Legends Museum at Camden Yards Visitor Survey 2008." Unpublished manuscript. Baltimore, MD, Sports Legends Museum at Camden Yards, 2008.

Conclusion

Kathryn Leann Harris and Douglas Stark

As we have seen in the preceding chapters, sports interpretation for exhibition and programmatic purposes has made great strides in the past twenty-five years. Museums (sports related and otherwise) are expanding their interpretive models beyond great moments and individual accomplishments, positioning these achievements within a wider historical context. These new visitor experiences bring insight into the overall impact of sports on society and a more holistic understanding of our culture. Achieving that understanding and greater appreciation is best accomplished by fully incorporating sports into your institution's interpretive planning process. An open dialogue with staff, visitors, and key stakeholders will illuminate the benefits of sports to broaden your audience and impact.

Crafting Your Game Plan

In sports, game plans are often used to guide strategy for approaching a competition. Consider this compilation as a starting point for your playbook. Refer back to the chapter "Starting Line" to construct a supportive framework for your content. Consider your institutional values, primary objectives, and targeted audience. Remember, you do not have to cover every topic to be inclusive. A narrowed focused topic that allows for diversity and a balanced sense of humanity will deliver as authentic, relevant, and supportive of the greater good. Survey thematic and methodological options from the exploratory essays. Then, choose your own adventure! Combine these suggestions on your own, and chart new pathways for expanding and deepening the future of sports interpretation. What direction will you take? We can't wait to see what you create!

In that spirit, below is a summary of building blocks museums can take to develop an in-depth dialogue when interpreting sports and sports-related content:

- **Research:** Building a comprehensive research foundation will provide a stepping-off point to explore a full range of engaging topics.
- **Difficult topics:** Approaching complex issues in a thoughtful manner and providing your audience the opportunity to engage with sports history as it intersects with other

aspects of social, cultural, and/or political history expands your institution's ability to provide relevance to a more socially engaged audience.

- **Framing interpretation:** Move beyond the celebratory and view sports through other frames, asking essential questions about people, society, and the human condition.
- **Inclusion:** Present stories that represent broad cross sections of people in sports—diverse along lines of age, class, gender, ethnicity/race, geographic region, culture, religion, sexual orientation—avoid siloing this under "difficult topics" and thus implying that diversity is always difficult. The universality of sporting interests is part of its strength.
- **Audience:** Understanding your audience, and how to engage and expand it, is instrumental as you incorporate new topics into your interpretation. Consider the different agendas that visitors, fans, participants, sponsors, and stakeholders bring to build a more well-rounded presentation of sports history
- **Programming:** Educating through the lens of athletics opens up the possibilities of whom you target (and ultimately reach) with your interpretation.

Sports offer a unique way to connect people and bring them together. Moving beyond a focus on winning, statistics, and images of victory, and including stories of how sports relate to everyday people, creates a more nuanced and comprehensive understanding of not only sports, but of society as well. Your interpretation will bring stories of triumph, determination, perseverance, agony, grace under pressure, and success and failure to your visitors, thus creating a layered understanding of history. It will provide your visitors and stakeholders with a more deeply developed appreciation of our society and shared cultural history. Sports offer an opportunity to view the surrounding world through the lens of competition, community building, and social interaction. Educating through the lens of sports provides opportunities to discuss a wide range of issues and topics that are both relevant and contemporary. That will ultimately lead to a more holistic understanding of sports and its impact on society. And that is the goal!

It's your turn to choose. How will you utilize this volume? What game plan will you devise and implement? How will your institution become poised to engage in an important, ongoing cultural discussion about sports characterized by interest, intrigue, depth, and societal impact?

Afterword

Kenneth Cohen

Congratulations! After reading the preceding chapters, you're all set to deepen your interpretation of sports and use it to build engagement with diverse visitors and communities. You now know that sports' popularity makes it a relatable tool for crafting relevant dialogue about the past, how it has shaped the present, and how it might inform the future.

But beyond budding community relationships and more impactful exhibits and programming, it's important to conclude this volume by thinking about the broader goals of the work it recommends. What effects should we, as a field, work to realize through an enriched deployment of sport in historical and heritage settings?

As a historian of sports who has worked at and with a range of museums, sites, and parks over the past twenty-five years, I suggest that we train our sights on one overarching issue—one that we can each address through our unique expertise and organizational settings, but that our cumulative efforts can shape to benefit not only our institutions and communities but the nation. Perhaps the most capacious and meaningful place to begin is to explore and explode the notion that sport should "not be political."

A Short History of Sport and Politics in the United States

For over a century, commentaries on the appropriateness of political expression in sports have ballooned whenever athletes have pursued activism in the sporting arena. Most histories of this discourse begin with the 1968 Olympic protest by track medalists Tommie Smith and John Carlos, but the pattern predates them. It has risen to unprecedented frequency since Colin Kaepernick first kneeled for the national anthem in 2016. In a lengthier piece, I could offer hundreds of citations. For a sense of range, though, consider an article in the *New Yorker*, which in 2018 asked, "Should We Keep Politics out of Sports?" In 2020, *Forbes* ran a survey that found that "sports is an escape" for most fans, and entitled its summary "A Case to Separate Sports and Politics." Perhaps the most egregious example offensively was conservative commentator Laura Ingraham's 2018 command to LeBron James: "Shut up and dribble," after he spoke out against racism and criticized then-sitting President Donald J. Trump. James responded with what has become a brand as much as a mantra, "More Than an Athlete," echoing boxer/activist Muhammad Ali's famous retort when the press asked him about his conversion to Islam in 1964: "I don't have to be what you want me to be."[1]

The fact that this debate exists offers an opportunity to historicize sports' place at the heart of American life—because the debate hasn't always existed. For the nation's first century, the politicization of sports was so widely accepted that nobody questioned it. Back then, the country's largest spectator sport was horse racing, and horses were named for candidates and policies to mobilize support for them. Races featured horses named "Anti-Democrat" and "Little Democrat," for instance. At the Spring 1832 meet in Richmond, VA, a horse named "Andrew Jackson" won and the horse "Nullifier"—named for the effort to nullify then-President Jackson's import taxes—lost.[2] Such explicit partisan rallying through sports is completely beyond the pale today. It would be akin to having NFL franchises named the Indianapolis Tax Cutters and the Los Angeles Liberals. Boxers were also promoted by partisan political factions, and candidates frequently campaigned on their sporting prowess.

Roughly twenty percent of all surviving political cartoons published between 1820 and 1860 reflect this commonplace association of sports and politics by picturing politicians competing in games or sports of some kind. Perhaps unsurprisingly, then, this is the era when Americans began describing elections as "races" or "fights," in contrast to the inherited English phrasing of "standing" for office.[3] As meritocratic competitions, sports became a popular metaphor for how the

Figure 7.1. In this emblematic political cartoon depicting an election as sport, the faces of candidates in the 1836 presidential race are plastered onto horses heads, with jockeys representing the forces supporting their candidacy. So, a salt-of-the-earth backwoodsman aboard William Henry Harrison testifies to the print's support for him, while an aging Andrew Jackson drives Martin Van Buren. *Source:* Political Race Course—Union Track—Fall Races 1836," Edward Williams Clay (New York, 1836), lithograph on paper. Courtesy Library of Congress.

country's politics should function. Candidates were increasingly expected to campaign for themselves, chasing (if not literally racing for) votes. They and their backers used sports to help them do that, mobilizing voters by communicating their policies and claiming their fitness for office through sporting metaphors and actual sporting events.

In practice, who could participate in "the Manly Sport of Politics," and how, was constrained both by white men unifying across class lines to define themselves as the only people qualified to play, and by wealthy Americans' successfully misleading portrayal of the country's economy as a level playing field on which the best men won and therefore deserved the most power. Even transcendentalists like Ralph Waldo Emerson thought "commerce is a game of skill, which every man cannot play, which few men can play well." Because "the game requires coolness, right reasoning, promptness, and patience," he wrote, "There is always a reason, in the man, for his good or bad fortune." The importance of sport as a model for American capitalism and democracy is hard to overstate. Its alluring promise of fairness obscured systemic racism, sexism, and classism. The result legitimized political and economic inequality as the just desserts of allegedly inferior losers, even as politicians and parties used the popularity of sports to advertise and claim connections to the broad swathe of Americans who enjoyed sporting events.[4]

Widespread critiques of putting sport in the service of politics only began to surface in the late nineteenth century. Not coincidentally, this sea change surfaced as the Gilded Age's burgeoning commercial sporting sector attracted immigrants and African Americans, whose freedom, success, and prominence threatened existing racial hierarchies. Concerned white commentators suddenly started to wonder about the value of politicizing sport when "the praise that was bestowed upon the colored jockeys for their skill was accepted as a compliment to the entire race, and the porter that made up your berth took his share of it and assumed a perkiness that got on your nerves."[5] These early examples from white critics contain a sense of alarm, such as when they complain that Black champions "strut about the lawns to pre-empt the good seats in the grand stand or go about the resorts of white men flaunting loud stripes and checks and the fifteenth amendment."[6] In other words, once sports' political and social influence might empower people other than the white men who had constructed it, then white men clamored to depoliticize sport. A wave of reform soon followed in the 1890s. Election gambling was more vigorously prosecuted, voting sites were required to be distanced from bars, and voting itself was transformed into a private act that required literacy. Some of these reforms may have had salutary effects, but they also triggered a drop from high voter turnout rates that have never been seen again. And that was certainly the goal, as demonstrated by reform advocates opposed to what they called a growing "democracy complex."[7]

Yet, the depoliticization of sport never actually happened. White men attacked Black communities after boxer Jack Johnson defeated the "Great White Hope" Jim Jeffries in 1910 because they still felt an African American champion threatened their power. Segregated sport both reified and reflected Jim Crow policies. Jackie Robinson and Billie Jean King have been mentioned several times in this volume, and their work on and off the field of play challenged policies rooted in racism and sexism. Even the national anthem began to be played regularly at baseball games during the 1918 World Series, in the midst of World War I and a day after the bombing of a federal building in the host city of Chicago. Patriotism is an expression of nationalism and inherently a

political statement of allegiance to a state. Of course, critics of politicized sport don't
recognize that. Nor do they always see that their calls for depoliticizing sport function
to preserve a political order. Part of the problem is that they only classify calls for
change as "political." In fact, a range of political expression is so woven into sport that
the question is not whether sport and politics can be separated. It's how to help people
acknowledge and engage with their inseparability.

Why the History of Politicized Sport Matters

If we committed our collective professional and institutional capacity to sharing
evidence-based histories that illuminate this contextualized and historicized narrative
about the relationship between politics and sport, multiple significant benefits would
be in the offing.

First, openly exposing and discussing this history would provide support for en-
acting strategies recommended throughout this book. Pointing to the nation's long
history of the politicized sport would anchor this volume's recommended shift away
from "sport as nostalgia" in proof that such a shift really just professes what sport in
the United States was originally understood to be, and has always been, despite more
recent claims to the contrary. Institutional leaders and funders who resist change by
telling you that it will scare off visitors (and be prepared for that gut reaction!) may
require a different kind of evidence, but there's plenty of that, too. Recent surveys by
leading museums, and even AASLH itself, make clear that firm majorities of potential
visitors to historic sites believe museums should "step up" and be a space for "civil
discourse and greater understanding," believe the field should help people "develop
critical thinking skills" and can help with "learning about the past and making conscious decisions to behave differently in the future" as well as encourage "a shared
understanding of the past" that "creates a sense of belonging to a community and to society" more broadly. Taken together, these visitor studies, the popularity of sport, and the
historical relationship between sport and politics provide strong evidentiary support for
more institutions to view sport as a tool for critically engaging diverse communities,
fostering cross-cultural dialogue, and addressing difficult history.[8]

Second, addressing the long history of sport's politicization in the United States
places sport at the center of the story of American democracy. Too often, in scholarship and museum interpretation alike, sport appears either as an "escape" from life
that has little bearing on it, or at the margins as a mere "reflection" of economic,
political, and sociocultural trends. But the evidence of sport's centrality to defining
and defying the boundaries of political participation invites consideration of its power
to shape the nation and its use by diverse communities to make political statements
regardless of their formal membership in the electorate. Exploring the substantive
issues and debates that historical examples of politicized sport have addressed
displaces the debate over the politicization of sport with a focus on its effects that
presumes its legitimacy. Imagine partnering with local youth sports organizations,
asking kids what policies they would advocate through their participation. Or reach
out to local professional athletes whose community work connects with your interpretive plan. Such programming would build on content referencing sport's

political history to both legitimize athlete activism today and put sporting collections at the center of communities' and the nation's history. This approach encourages civic engagement by rooting it in a tradition of advocacy that ends up at the ballot box only after originating in somewhere outside of petitions and legislative assemblies. Indeed, the advice presented in this book need not be applied to programming exclusively tied to sport, but might just as beneficially situate sport alongside various local or national examples of parental, artistic, labor, and religious activism, because sport is just one of many arenas of life that have fomented political movements. If designed following the advice presented in preceding chapters, any of these strategies can foster exactly the kind of evidence-based dialogue from multiple perspectives that publics are asking for, and which is sorely needed in a deeply divisive political environment that threatens the very future of democracy. Given the centrality of sports to the nation's political history, and their popularity across the ideological spectrum, it is no exaggeration to suggest that any path toward a more inclusive, equitable, and sustainable democracy will only reach its destination if sport is consciously deployed in blazing and paving it.

If the goal is not just to show how sports are central to local and national history, but to engage with examples of this fact to help build a more vibrant and resilient democracy, some benefits will accrue from the process behind—not solely the products resulting from—the pursuit of these goals. At the very least, a shared goal presents the opportunity to develop a stronger sense of community among ourselves as practitioners. Every scholar and every museum and site can tell complicated human stories about the power of sport to express identity and make a political statement. But we'll do it more powerfully if we work together. Collaboration should take several forms. On a macro level, we should forge stronger connections between trade associations that can help generate momentum for this work, through joint conference panels, workshops, and white papers linking the International Sports Heritage Association (ISHA) with AASLH and the American Alliance of Museums (AAM). Whether or not such cooperation leads to more Halls of Fame seeking AAM accreditation or more local museums with sporting collections joining ISHA, it could facilitate loans and lead to major research, digitization, and exhibition or programming grants capable of magnifying our work and amplifying its reach.

Such nationwide orchestration should not preclude local partnerships, though. Revealing sport's impact requires research, and increasingly, museums are turning toward research collaborations with community organizations and university faculty and students, in order to dig beneath myths and bring new stories to light. Certainly, any effort to demonstrate the normativity of politicized sport will benefit from sharing examples of people who were not famous doing it. After all, many museums not devoted to sport nevertheless operate more or less as Halls of Fame, enshrining prominent individuals at the expense of a more diverse and relatable cast of characters. Fortunately, community members and local archives are antidotes to this syndrome. Consulting them for overlooked stories, of failure as well as success, and empowering community members to actually shape your end product, will ground it in an approachable authenticity that visitors say has greater influence. And that's our goal. By working together in a kind of national league that helps stimulate the assembly of neighborhood teams, each contributing new evidence-based examples of sport's political punch, we can use sport's popularity to attract visitors and engage them in dialogue on a range of issues—aiming to do nothing less than realize and sustain the dream of an inclusive and fair democracy that sport itself helped promote, and for which so many athletes have been criticized while trying to attain.

NOTES

1. Hua Hsu, "Should We Keep Politics Out of Sports?" *New Yorker* (September 24, 2018); Kirk Wakefield, "Escape From 2020: A Case to Separate Sports and Politics for More Fans and Higher Ratings," *Forbes* (August 28, 2020), https://www.forbes.com/sites/kirkwakefield/2020/08/28/escape-from-2020—a-case-to-separate-sports-and-politics-for-more-fans-and-higher-ratings/?sh=6415c43076ad; Thomas Hauser, *Muhammad Ali: His Life and Times* (New York, 1991), 81.

2. Kenneth Cohen, *They Will Have Their Game: Sporting Culture and the Making of the Early American Republic* (Ithaca, NY: Cornell University Press, 2017), 158.

3. Kenneth Cohen, "'Sport for Grown Children: American Political Cartoons, 1790–1850," *International Journal of the History of Sport* (May–June 2011): 1–18; Cohen, "The Manly Sport of American Politics, or, How We Came To Call Elections 'Races,'" *Commonplace* (April 2012), http://commonplace.online/article/manly-sport-american-politics/.

4. Ralph Waldo Emerson, "The Conduct of Life" [1860], in Brooks Atkinson, ed., *The Essential Writings of Ralph Waldo Emerson* (New York: Modern Library, 2000), 628–29.

5. Harry Keough, "Horse World," *Lexington Leader,* January 14, 1902.

6. Newspaper commentaries published in Katherine C. Mooney, *Race Horse Men: How Slavery and Freedom Were Made at the Racetrack* (Cambridge, MA: Harvard University Press, 2014), 224.

7. Michael McGerr, *The Decline of Popular Politics: The North, 1865–1928* (New York: Oxford University Press, 1986), 203–6.

8. Norman Burns, "Curiosity About History is Growing Across Generations, a New Survey Finds," *AAM Blog* (February 3, 2020), https://www.aam-us.org/2020/02/03/curiosity-about-history-is-growing-across-generations-a-new-survey-finds/; FrameWorks Institute and AASLH, "Communicating About History: Challenges, Opportunities, and Emerging Recommendations" (August 6, 2020), https://www.frameworksinstitute.org/publication/communicating-about-history-challenges-opportunities-and-emerging-recommendations/.

Recommended Resources

Below is a list of recommended scholarly and practitioner sources, resources, and organizations that inform the practice of public history as it pertains to the interpretation of sports history in museums and historic sites. By no means it is comprehensive or exhaustive; with more than six hundred sports museums and archives in the United States alone, the potential list is too long to list here. For a list of repositories, you may wish to consult Victor J. Danilov's *Sports Museums and Halls of Fame Worldwide*. For additional guidance, see also the notes at the end of each essay.

Articles

Alegi, Peter. "Offside: Kick Ignorance Out, Football Unites & Racism Divides, an Exhibit Review." *The Public Historian* 33, no. 3 (June 2011), 154–57.

Allen, Michael Patrick and Nicholas Parsons. "The Institutionalization of Fame: Achievement, Recognition, and Cultural Consecration in Baseball." *American Sociological Review* 71, no. 5 (October 2006), 808–25.

Canevacci, M. "The Anthropological Interpretation of Sport: A Task for Museums." *Museum International* 170, no. 2 (Fall 1991), 74–76.

Danilov, Victor. "Halls of Fame: An American Phenomenon." *Curator* 29, no. 4 (December 1986), 245–68.

Dodd, Mike. "Sports Museums Struggle to Draw Fans, Turn Profit." *USA Today,* November 1, 2011.

Faragher, John Mack. "National Cowboy Hall of Fame Thundering Hooves." *Journal of American History* 81, no. 1 (June 1994), 215–20.

Gems, Gerald R. and Gertrud Pfister. "Sports Museum of America." *Journal of Sport History* 25, no. 3 (Fall 2008), 517–19.

Gibson, Heather J. "Active Sport Tourism: Who Participates?" *Leisure Studies* 17, no. 2 (1998), 155–70.

Hardy, Stephen, John Loy and Douglas Booth. "The Material Culture of Sport: Toward a Typology." *Journal of Sport History* 36, no. 1 (Spring 2009), 129–52.

Howard, Josh. "On Sports, Public History, and Public Sports History." *Journal of Sport History* 45, no. 1 (Spring 2018), 24–40.

Jarzombek, Mark. "The (Trans) Formations of Fame." *Perspecta* 37 (2005), 10–17.

Kidd, Bruce and B. Zeman. "The Public History of Sports: A Critical Look at Sports Halls of Fame." *North American Society for Sports History Proceedings* (1994), 17–19.

Knott, Rick and C. Keith Harrison. "The College Football Hall of Fame Review." *Journal of Sport History* 25, no. 1 (Spring 1998), 152–56.

Moore, Kevin. "Sport History, Public History, and Popular Culture: A Growing Engagement." *Journal of Sport History* 4, no. 1 (Spring 2013), 401–17.

Pecknold, Diane. "Treasures Untold: Unique Collections from Devoted Fans." *Journal of American History* 90, no. 1 (June 2003), 193–95.

Redmond, Gerald. "A Plethora of Shrines: Sport in the Museum and Hall of Fame." *Quest* 19, no. 1 (1973), 41–48.

Ritchhart, Ron. "Cultivating a Culture of Thinking in Museums." *Journal of Museum Education* 32, no. 2 (Summer 2007), 137–54.

Schreiber, James, Andrew Pekarik, Nadine Hanemann, Zahava Doering, and Ah-Jin Lee. "Understanding Visitor Engagement and Behaviors." *Journal of Educational Research* 106, no. 6 (September 2013), 462–68.

Skramstad, Harold. "An Agenda for American Museums in the Twenty-First Century." *Daedalus* 128, no. 3 (Summer 1999), 109–28.

Snyder, Eldon E. "Sociology of Nostalgia: Sport Halls of Fame and Museums in America."*Sociology of Sport* 8, no. 3 (January 1991), 228–38.

Thilgen, Dean R. "Proprietors of the Bat and Ball: Interpreting the National Past Time and its Predecessor Games." *History News* 60, no. 3 (2005).

Triet, M. A. "Sports Museum Is Also a Business." *Museum International* 170, no. 2 (1991), 82–85.

Vamplew, Wray. "Facts and Artefacts: Sports Historians and Sports Museums." *Journal of Sport History* 25, no. 2 (1998): 268–82.

Books

AASLH. *Interpreting* Series (Lanham, MD: Rowman & Littlefield).

Adair, Bill, Benjamin Filene, and Laura Koloski, eds. *Letting Go? Sharing Historical Authority in a User-Generated World* (New York: Routledge, 2011).

Anderson, Gail, ed. *Reinventing the Museum: Historical and Contemporary Perspectives on the Paradigm Shift* (Lanham, MD: Rowman & Littlefield, 2004).

Bodnar, John. *Remaking America: Public Memory, Commemoration, and Patriotism in the Twentieth Century* (Princeton: Princeton University Press, 1993).

Danilov, Victor J. *Sports Museums and Halls of Fame Worldwide* (Jefferson, North Carolina and London: McFarland and Company, Inc., 2005).

Dunning, Eric. *Sport: Reading from a Sociological Perspective* (Toronto: University of Toronto, 1972).

Engelhardt, Tom. *The End of Victory Culture* (Amherst: University of Massachusetts Press, 2007).

Falk, J. H. *Identity and Museum Visitor Experience* (Walnut Creek, California: Left Coast Press, 2009).

Gammon, Sean and Gregory Ramshw, eds. *Heritage, Sport, and Tourism: Sporting Pasts—Tourist Futures* (New York: Routledge, 2007).

Gillis, John R., ed. *Commemorations: The Politics of National Identity* (Princeton: Princeton University Press, 1994).

Glassberg, David. *Sense of History: The Place of the Past in American Life* (Amherst: University of Massachusetts Press, 2001).

Hill, Jeffrey, Kevin Moore, and Jason Wood. *Sport, History, and Heritage: An Investigation into the Public Representation of Sport* (New York: Cambridge, 2012).

Howe, Barbara J. and Emory L. Kemp. *Public History: An Introduction* (Malabar, Florida: Robert E. Kreiger Publishing Company, 1986).

Kammen, Michael. *Mystic Chords of Memory* (New York: Vintage Books, 1991).

King, Richard C. and Charles Fruehling Springwood. *Beyond the Cheers: Race as Spectacle in College Sport* (Albany: State University of New York Press, 2001).

Levin, Amy K. *Defining Memory: Local Museums and the Construction of History in America's Changing Communities* (Lanham, MD: Rowman & Littlefield, 2007).

Levitt, Peggy. *Artifacts and Allegiances: How Museums Put the Nation and the World on Display* (Oakland: University of California Press, 2015).

Linenthal, Edward T. *Preserving Memory: The Struggle to Create America's Holocaust Museum* (New York: Viking Penguin, 1995).

Linenthal, Edward T. and Tom Englehardt, ed. *History Wars: The* Enola Gay *and Other Battles for the American Past* (New York: Holt, 1996).

Markovits, Andrei S. and Lars Rensman. *Gaming the World: How Sports are Reshaping Global Politics and Culture* (Princeton: Princeton University Press, 2010).

Moore, Kevin, John Hughson, and Christian Wacker, eds. *Sports in Museums* (London: Routledge, 2022).

Phillips, Murray G. *Representing the Sporting Past in Museums and Halls of Fame* (Abingdon: Routledge, 2012).

Phillips, Murray G. *Deconstructing Sports History: A Postmodern Analysis* (New York: State University of New York Press, 2006).

Putney, Clifford. *Muscular Christianity: Manhood and Sorts in Protestant America* (Chicago: University of Illinois Press, 1996).

Sevoenko, Liz with Liam Mahoney, ed. *The Power of Place: How Historic Sites Can Engage Citizens in Human Rights Issues* (Minneapolis: The Center for Victims of Torture, 2004).

Simon, Nina. *The Participatory Museum* (Santa Cruz: Museum 2.0, 2010).

Watson, Sheila. *Museums and Their Communities* (New York: Routledge, 2007).

Journal Publications

Curator: The Museum
International Journal of the History of Sport
Journal of Heritage Tourism
Journal History News
Journal of Museum Education

Journal of Sport History Museums Journal
The Public Historian
Sociology of Sport Journal

Organizations

American Alliance of Museums (AAM)
American Association for State and Local History (AASLH)
American Historical Association (AHA)
International Coalition of Sites of Conscience (ICSoC)
International Federation of Public Historians (IFPH)
International Sports Heritage Association (ISHA)
International Sports Museums Association (ISMA)
LA84 Foundation
National Council of Public History (NCPH)
New England Museum Association (NEMA)
Organization of American Historians (OAH)

Index

Page references for figures are italicized.

About the Editors and Contributors

ABOUT THE EDITORS

Kathryn Leann Harris is a writer, public historian, and mindset coach who emphasizes the value of embracing a balanced view of humanity to foster a socially just world. She examines the influence of commemoration practices, specializing in public exhibitions and discourse relating to sports, war, politics, and culture. In compiling this book, she draws upon fifteen years of field research in sports interpretation. Kathryn received a BA in History and English from the University of Mississippi and an MA in History and Public History from the University of Massachusetts, Boston. Professional experience includes positions at the Alabama Sports Hall of Fame, International Tennis Hall of Fame, Boston's Old North Church, Tsongas Industrial History Center, and adidas History Management Department in Nuremberg, Germany. She is a member of the international running community as a three time Boston Marathoner.

Douglas Stark focuses on making history more engaging, relevant, and accessible to a diverse audience. His experience includes strategic planning, fiscal management, project management, facility development, historic preservation, collections care, content and exhibition development, branding and messaging, product development, programming and outreach, and audience engagement. He served as museum director at the International Tennis Hall of Fame in Newport, Rhode Island for thirteen years. He also worked at the Naismith Memorial Basketball Hall of Fame and the U.S. Golf Association. He is the 2016 recipient of the International Sports Heritage Association's W. R. "Bill" Schroeder Distinguished Service Award. He is the past president of the New England Museum Association (NEMA) and received a NEMA Excellence Award in 2021. Douglas is a graduate of Brandeis University where he received his BA in American history with a minor in the History of Art. He pursued graduate studies at New York University, where he earned an MA in American history with dual certification in Museum Studies and Archival Management, Historical Society Administration, and Historical Editing. He holds an MBA with a concentration in nonprofit management from the University of Massachusetts at Amherst. He is also the author of five books on basketball.

For correspondence with the editors visit www.interpretingsports.com.

ABOUT THE CONTRIBUTORS

Jeffrey L. Brodie, PhD, is a historian and deputy director of the Smithsonian's Lemelson Center for the Study of Invention and Innovation, where he is responsible for operations, programming, and strategic planning. In addition to leading *Innoskate,* Jeff heads the Center's exploration and impact of invention and technology in sports.

William F. Brooks Jr., a graduate in history from Kenyon College and a former amateur endurance athlete, now lives in the Champlain Valley of Vermont where he bicycles and kayaks for health and enjoyment. Following a twenty-five-year banking career in Maryland, he earned a graduate degree in American Folk Art Studies from New York University and served as the executive director of the Henry Sheldon Museum of Vermont History in Middlebury, Vermont from 2012 to 2021. He has studied and written articles on American folk carver Henry Leach (1809–1885), Italian folk carver Eliodoro Patete (1874–1953), and Italian American folk carver Aldobrando Piacenza (1888–1976) traveling twice to Italy to view surviving carvings and to interview relatives.

Sarah E. Calise is a public historian and archivist working in Tennessee. Their research and writing focus on civil rights, gender and sexuality, social movements in the United States, and how personal histories are inherently political. They are publicly out as queer, nonbinary, and disabled, and often combine their activism with their archival work through intentional historical documentation of marginalized communities in the Middle Tennessee region. They also founded Nashville Queer History, a website and Instagram page that shares the city's LGBTQ past through archival research and oral history interviews.

Kenneth Cohen is an associate professor of history and director of the Museum Studies Program at the University of Delaware. He has interpreted the past through sport at historic houses from Massachusetts to North Carolina and Texas, as well as at the Smithsonian's National Museum of American History and Le Musée des Civilizations in Abidjan, Côte d'Ivoire. His first book, *They Will Have Their Game: Sporting Culture and the Making of the Early American Republic* (Cornell: 2017) won the James Broussard Prize for the best first book on American history between the Revolution and Civil War.

Nikki Diller serves as the registrar and acting curator at the LBJ Presidential Library. She has participated in a series of the library's special exhibitions, including the main curation, *Deep in the Vaults of Texas: A Campus Collaboration,* and *Get in the Game:*

The Fight for Equality in American Sports. Previously, Diller served as the curator for the Galveston County Museum and exhibition coordinator for Humanities Texas. She has a bachelor of arts degree in United States history from Texas A&M University-Corpus Christi and a Master of Arts degree in art history from Tulane University.

Jenny Ellison is curator of sport and leisure at the Canadian Museum of History. She holds a PhD in history from York University in Toronto.

Shi Evans is a researcher and project assistant at the Smithsonian National Museum of African American History and Culture. She earned a master of public administration degree. She is also the author of *Whiskey Road*.

Kristin L. Gallas is a graduate of the University of Vermont (BS in Education) and George Washington University (MAT in Museum Education). Kristin has worked in museums for over twenty-five years, including the Montana Historical Society, the USS Constitution Museum, and currently the Tsongas Industrial History Center. She is the author of *Interpreting Slavery with Children and Teens* (Rowman & Littlefield, 2021) and coeditor, with James DeWolf Perry, of *Interpreting Slavery at Museums and Historic Sites* (Rowman & Littlefield, 2015). Kristin coaches figure skating at the Massachusetts Institute of Technology and worked two summers in minor league baseball for the Vermont Expos.

Carol L. Haines was a longtime staff member of the Concord Museum until her retirement in 2022. With a BFA in photography and a masters in Library and Information Science, she served as director of Public Relations and, since 2013, as manager of Exhibitions and Design. Involved in bringing to life seventy-five special exhibitions over the course of forty years, she has also overseen the production and design of three exhibition catalogs and seven online exhibitions. Her last project before retirement was working with a team of curators, educators, scholars, designers, media specialists, and fabricators to redesign and reinstall all sixteen permanent galleries at the Concord Museum.

Terence Healy is a founding principal of HealyKohler Design. He creates a dynamic multilayered visitor experience that integrates collections, immersive environments, media and interactive activities, and interpretive graphics. He has created museum experiences for the International Tennis Hall of Fame and Museum, the National Soccer Hall of Fame, and various State Sports Halls of Fames and Museums. Terence has received the prestigious National Endowment for the Arts Presidential Award, the American Alliance of Museums MUSE Gold Award for Innovation, and other recognition awards from the American Institute of Graphic Artist.

Chrischené Julius is a history and museum studies graduate and has worked at the District Six Museum since 2003. She currently heads the Collections, Research and Documentation Department and has been involved in several exhibition and research projects, with a focus on oral history research and the way this methodology has evolved as part of museum practice.

Justine Kaempfer has been with the Green Bay Packers since 2016, currently serving as the Hall of Fame Programs Assistant. Originally from Milwaukee, Justine completed her undergraduate in Anthropology from the University of Wisconsin-Milwaukee and attended Penn State in the History and Philosophy of Sport Program.

Bruce Kidd writes and teaches about Canadian and Olympic sports history as Professor Emeritus, Sport and Public History in the Kinesiology and Physical Education department at the University of Toronto. He is also chair of the selection committee for Canada's sports hall of fame. His most recent book (coedited with Cesar Torres) is *Historicizing the Pan American Games* (Routledge 2017).

Amanda Krantz is the director of Research & Practice at Kera Collective (formerly Randi Korn & Associates/RK&A), a planning, evaluation, and research firm that supports museums and other informal learning institutions. Amanda served as a data analyst for the audience research study conducted by RK&A for the Sports Legends Museum at Camden Yards.

Dean Krimmel is a museum consultant specializing in interpretive planning and exhibition development. As project coordinator for the $5.5 million, 22,000-square-foot Sports Legends Museum at Camden Yards (2003–2005), Dean managed the content development and design process; secured major loans from sports collectors; curated galleries; managed and edited outside writers; managed the fabrication RFP process; and installed exhibitions.

Nicole F. Markham has served as curator of Collections at the International Tennis Hall of Fame since 2001, where she is responsible for the day-to-day development, research, care, and management of the museum's permanent collection. Nicole also works on the development, maintenance, and installation of all exhibitions within the museum. Prior to her tenure at the ITHF, Nicole worked at the UPENN Museum of Archaeology and Anthropology, the Bata Shoe Museum, the Ontario Workers Arts & Heritage Centre, the Ontario Heritage Foundation's Ashbridge Estate, and Cultural Resource Specialists. She also serves as a consultant and guest curator for the Joseph N. Goff House Foundation in her hometown of East Hampton, Connecticut.

Elizabeth L. Maurer is the former director of the Program for National Women's History Museum in Alexandria, Virginia, the mother of a soccer-playing girl, and a former Miss Majorette of Michigan. She is currently the Curator of Education for a federal museum in Arlington, Virginia.

Amanda McAllen is the former School and Teacher Programs Coordinator at the Senator John Heinz History Center in Pittsburgh, where she was responsible for creating education programs that connect museum collections to topics such as history, civics, and STEM. She holds a master's degree in history from the University of Southampton, and previously worked as an educator in history and art museums in the United Kingdom. Amanda is passionate about helping students to find relevance in museum collections through exciting and multidisciplinary education programs.

Marcus Monenerkit, a member of the Comanche Nation, is currently director of Community Engagement at the Heard Museum, Phoenix, Arizona. His work focuses on producing cultural art workshops in regional Indian communities, documenting the process of the transference of cultural art knowledge where permissible, and sharing that documentation with the broader American public through special films and lectures. Monenerkit has a firm belief that art works for a greater public benefit, creating expressive patterns of communication between individuals, communities, and beyond. He believes art provides a vital link in a tripartite model of human development, establishing lessons for increasing the capacity of human, social, and economic capital.

Kevin Moore is a museum director, author, and an academic in museum studies and social and cultural history. In 1997, Kevin took the opportunity to become the first director (CEO) of the project to set up the National Football Museum in Preston, England. The permanent home of the FIFA Collection, this £15 million museum opened in 2001 and attracted over 100,000 visitors each year. Since 2020, he has been the deputy director, Curatorial Affairs at Qatar Olympic and Sports Museum, Qatar Museums.

Erin Narloch is the founder/consultant of PastForward, Head of NFTs for tech startup Enwoven, and member of the Design Everywhere Museum Council. She consults on marketing, brand storytelling, and knowledge management. She brings two decades of experience in art, design, and cultural institutions, where she held roles in education, curatorial practice, and leadership. More recently she has worked in the adidas archive at their world headquarters in Germany, focusing on the emotive power of sports-related storytelling, and developed and led the professionalization of Reebok's global brand archive in Boston. Erin holds a BS in Art with a concentration in Art History from the University of Wisconsin-Madison and an MA in Museum Studies from Johns Hopkins University.

Murray G. Phillips is a professor of Sport History in the School of Human Movement and Nutrition Sciences at the University of Queensland. He is the president of the North American Society for Sport History, former president of the Australian Society for Sport History, and former Editor of the Journal of Sport History. His books include Representing the Sporting Past in Museums and Halls of Fame (London: Routledge, 2012).

Jason Rose received his PhD in Philosophy and Literature from Purdue University in West Lafayette, Indiana. He received a bachelor of arts in Creative Writing and a master of arts in Philosophy from Louisiana State University in Baton Rouge, Louisiana. His studies focus on the intersection of Continental Philosophy, particularly the works of Friedrich Nietzsche and Gilles Deleuze, and Cultural Studies, particularly in the fields of Literary Theory and Game Studies. His dissertation was a philosophical treatise on the nature and origin of the phenomenon of play, the study of which has received a surge of interest in the past few decades from scholars across a wide variety of disciplines.

Julia Rose is the director/curator of Homewood Museum at Johns Hopkins University in Baltimore, MD. Previously, she was the director of the West Baton Rouge Museum, in Louisiana. Her primary research interests focus on interpreting difficult histories. Rose served eight years on the executive committee for the Council for the American Association for State and Local History. She received a PhD from Louisiana State University, a master of arts in Teaching in Museum Education from the George Washington University, and a BA in Fine Art and Education from the State University of New York at Albany. She is the author of *Interpreting Difficult History at Museums and Historic Sites* (Rowman & Littlefield, 2016).

Elizabeth Semmelhack is the senior curator of the Bata Shoe Museum. Her work focuses on the construction of gender in relation to dress, with a particular interest in the history of footwear. She has curated over thirty exhibitions and has written many articles, chapters, and books including *Shoes: The Meaning of Style* (Reaktion Books, 2017) and *Out of the Box: The Rise of Sneaker Culture* (Rizzoli, 2015)

Daniel J. Simone was awarded his BA in Sociology from Rowan University in 1995. He earned his MA in History at North Dakota State University in 2003 and PhD in American History at the University of Florida in 2009, with specializations in environmental, oral, public, and sport History. He taught at Middlesex Community College from 2010 to 2014 and at Monmouth University from 2011 to 2015. Dr. Simone served as curator at the NASCAR Hall of Fame from 2016–2021.

Damion Thomas is the supervisory museum curator of sports at the Smithsonian National Museum of African American History and Culture. He earned his BA, MA, and PhD at UCLA. He is the author of *Globetrotting: African American Athletes and Cold War Politics*.

Annemarie de Wildt is a historian and curator at the Amsterdam Museum. She has (co)curated many exhibitions, with a variety of objects, often a mix of "high" and "low" culture and with a strong input of human stories and a focus on difficult and uneasy subjects. She has presented and written about city museums, practices and dilemmas of curating and (contemporary) collecting, prostitution, Amsterdam's connection to slavery as well as protest movements.

Dan Yaeger was named as an executive director of NEMA in April 2010. His passion is to strengthen capacity in museums and build skills in the leaders that serve them. Dan has a twenty-year history with museums, most recently as the director of the Charles River Museum of Industry & Innovation in Waltham, Massachusetts. He has developed communications programs for the Museum of Fine Arts/Boston, Peabody Essex Museum, Cleveland Museum of Art, Portland Museum of Art, Currier Museum of Art, Old Sturbridge Village, John F. Kennedy Library, and Plimoth Plantation among others. He has been an adjunct professor, guest lecturer, advisor, and fellow at Tufts, Harvard, Brown, and Bentley universities and Lasell College. Dan holds a BA from Gettysburg College and received his master's degree from Harvard University.

Krissy Zegers served as the Green Bay Packers Hall of Fame and Stadium Tours manager from 2005 to 2020. Originally from Green Bay, Krissy has worked in sports for over fifteen years in various capacities. She completed her undergraduate degree at the University of Wisconsin–La Crosse in Exercise Science with an emphasis in sports management and her master's degree from West Virginia University in sport.